MAKING GLOBALIZATION
WORK FOR WOMEN

SUNY Series, Praxis: Theory in Action

Nancy A. Naples, editor

MAKING GLOBALIZATION

WORK FOR WOMEN

*The Role of Social Rights and
Trade Union Leadership*

EDITED BY

VALENTINE M. MOGHADAM
SUZANNE FRANZWAY
MARY MARGARET FONOW

*For Medea,
In solidarity and with
hope for a better future,
Val Moghadam
Boston
Oct.
2014*

STATE UNIVERSITY OF NEW YORK PRESS

Published by
STATE UNIVERSITY OF NEW YORK PRESS, ALBANY

© 2011 State University of New York

For information, contact
State University of New York Press, Albany, NY
www.sunypress.edu

Production, Laurie Searl
Marketing, Fran Keneston

Library of Congress Cataloging-in-Publication Data

Making globalization work for women : the role of social rights and trade union leadership /
edited by Valentine M. Moghadam, Suzanne Franzway, and Mary Margaret Fonow.
    p. cm. — (SUNY series, praxis: theory in action)
Includes bibliographical references and index.
ISBN 978-1-4384-3960-0 (pbk. : alk. paper)
ISBN 978-1-4384-3961-7 (hardcover : alk. paper)
    1. Women's rights.   2. Women in the labor movement.   3. Globalization.   4. Feminism.
I. Moghadam, Valentine M., 1952–   II. Franzway, Suzanne.   III. Fonow, Mary Margaret, 1949–

HQ1236.M3427 2011
331.87082—dc22   2011007664

10 9 8 7 6 5 4 3 2 1

CONTENTS

PART II
REPORTS FROM THE FIELD:
TRADE UNION AND MULTILATERAL PERSPECTIVES

PART III
WHERE NEXT FOR FEMINISM AND THE LABOR MOVEMENT?

FIGURES AND TABLES

FIGURES

TABLES

PREFACE AND ACKNOWLEDGMENTS

This book originates in the common interests of the three editors, and a shared concern that academic and policy discussions of women's economic participation and rights under conditions of globalization needed to be revived. Val Moghadam, Mary Margaret Fonow, and Suzanne Franzway met for a panel discussion in 2004, and discussed the importance of dialogues between feminist academics and feminist trade unionists around women's work conditions, labor legislation, the strengthening of social and economic rights, and the role of female trade union leaders in advocacy for women's economic citizenship. In 2006 we met again in Nantes, France, where Val Moghadam organized a workshop on women, social rights, and trade union leadership co-organized by UNESCO and the French trade union Confédération Française des Travailleurs Chrétiens (CFTC). By that time we were involved in an international research and policy network that Val formed while working for UNESCO; all but three of the papers in this volume were commissioned at that time.

We are grateful to all the contributors for their thoughtful and engaged chapters, which address critical issues, provide sophisticated analyses, and offer important recommendations. We also extend our thanks to Larin McLaughlin, senior editor at SUNY Press, who was supportive of the book project from the outset. Val would like to thank Alice de Roffignac, her intern at UNESCO, who did background research on trade unions and international labor legislation and put Val in contact with the CFTC when the Nantes workshop was being conceived. (It was a source of pride to Val that Alice obtained a job with the CFTC after her internship.) A special thank you is reserved for Megan Kee, who was a dean's scholar at Purdue University assigned to work with Val during the spring 2009 semester. She became an indispensable research and editing assistant and continued working with Val on the book project long after her assignment officially came to an end. Mary Margaret would especially like to thank her incredibly talented research assistants at Arizona State University, Corie Hardy, Debjani Chakravarty, and Eva Lester. She also is grateful for the research support she received from Linda Lederman, dean of social sciences at Arizona State University and from her assistant Jane Little. Suzanne would like to thank her colleagues at the Research Centre for Gender Studies at the University of South Australia, her research assistant Valerie Adams, and union feminists and scholars, Kathie Muir (University of Adelaide) Sandra Dann (Working Women's Centre), and Janet Giles (SAUnions).

GLOSSARY OF ACRONYMS AND TERMS

AFTURD	l'Association des Femmes Tunisiennes pour le Recherche et Développement
AMMAR	Asociación de Meretrices de la Argentina [Argentine Association of Prostitutes]
ANC	African National Congress (South Africa)
ATE	Association of State Workers (Argentina)
ATFD	l'Association Tunisienne des Femmes Démocrates, also referred to as the *Femmes Démocrates*
CAWTAR	Center for Arab Women Training and Research
CDWU	Coalition of Domestic Workers Unions (Hong Kong)
CEC	Central Executive Committee of COSATU
CEDAW	Convention on the Elimination of all Forms of Discrimination against Women (United Nations)
centres d'écoutes	Lit., listening centers; North African counseling centers or shelters for women
CEPAL (also ECLAC)	Comisión Económica para América Latina y el Caribe (United Nations Economic Commission for Latin America and the Caribbean)
CFTC	Conféderation française des travailleurs Chrétiens
CGT	General Confederation of Workers (Argentina)
COSATU	Congress of South African Trade Unions
CTA	The Congress of Argentine Workers
DENOSA	Democratic Nursing Organisation of South Africa
dunams	Unit of area used by Palestinians in Israel (1,000 square meters or 10,764 sq ft)
ENDA	Environment and Development Action in the Third World (an international NGO)

EPZ	Export Processing Zone
ETUC	European Trade Union Confederation
GEM	Gender Empowerment Measure (used in UNDP's *Human Development Report*)
goyo kumiai	A Japanese term (with a negative connotation) for unionism- literally, a union at his majesty's (or management's) service.
GUF	Global Union Federation
HDR	*Human Development Report* (UNDP)
ICESCR	International Covenant on Social, Economic, and Cultural Rights (UN)
ICFTU	International Confederation of Free Trade Unions
IGTN	International Gender and Trade Network
ILO	International Labour Organization (UN agency)
IMF	International Metalworkers Federation
IOM	International Organization for Migration
ITUC	International Trade Union Confederation (formerly ICFTU)
KAD	Women Workers' Union in Denmark (*Kvindeligt Arbejderforbund i Danmark*)
khul	A form of divorce a wife can seek without her husband's consent (Egypt)
Knesset	The legislative branch of the Israeli government
KWTU	Korean Women's Trade Union
KWWAU	Korean Working Women's Association United
LWU	Lao Women's Union
Mahr	In Islamic law, the monetary value a husband owes his wife; determined prior to marriage; typically payable in full upon divorce.
MDG	Millennium Development Goals (United Nations)
MENA	Middle East and North Africa
MSN	Maquila Solidarity Network <http://en.maquilasolidarity.org/about>

MTA	Movimiento de los Trabajadores Argentinos (Movement of Argentinean Workers)
mudawanna	Family code of Morocco
NATO	North Atlantic Treaty Organization.
NEHAWU	South African Health and Public Servants' Union
NGO	Non-governmental Organization
NIS	New Israeli Shekel (currency in Israel)
NTAE	Non-Traditional Agricultural Export (Ecuador)
NUMSA	South African Metal Workers' Union
NUT	National Union of Teachers (United Kingdom)
OECD	Organization for Economic Co-operation and Development
PDR	Lao People's Democratic Republic
piqueteros	picketers (Argentina)
PSI	Public Services International
RMSM	Red De Mujeres Sindicalistas de Mexico, or Network of Union Women of Mexico
SADTU	South African Teachers' Union
SAMWU	South African Municipal Workers' Union
SEWA	Self-Employed Women's Association (India)
STDs	Sexually Transmitted Diseases
TUAC	Trade Union Advisory Committee (United Nations)
TUC	Trades Union Congress (United Kingdom)
UGTA	Union générale des travailleurs Algériens (General Union of Algerian Workers)
UGTT	Union générale des travailleurs Tunisiens (General Union of Tunisian Workers)
ujrat-ul-methl	In the Islamic Republic of Iran, the monetary value of the domestic work a woman has performed for her husband over the years
UNDP	United Nations Development Program

UNESCO	United Nations Education, Scientific, and Cultural Organization
UTAP	Tunisian Union of Agriculture and Fisheries
UTICA	Tunisian Union for Industry, Commerce and Handicrafts
WAC	Workers Advice Center (Israel)
WEDO	Women's Environment and Development Organization
WICEJ	Women's International Coalition for Economic Justice
WIDE	Women in Development Europe
WTUL	Women's Trade Union League (Britain)
WTO	World Trade Organization

ONE

INTRODUCTION AND OVERVIEW

Globalization and Women's Social Rights

Mary Margaret Fonow, Suzanne Franzway,
and Valentine M. Moghadam

The worldwide financial crisis has sparked a renewed interest in the complexities and contradictions of the neoliberal model of globalization, while growing unemployment and other hardships faced by working people raise questions about the viability of the global economy. The past three decades have seen the increasing involvement of women in the global economy, but there also has been a steady erosion of labor rights. This volume seeks to bring the notions of *social rights* and *economic citizenship* to the center of academic, policy, and political discussions, with a focus on the social and economic rights of women and the role that trade unions can play in their advancement.

Globalization, fortunately, is not a static force acting on people; it also has produced new social movements, transnational advocacy networks, and dynamic new forms of activism around the world. Labor unions, as well as a growing number of nongovernmental or civil society organizations, including numerous women's groups and transnational feminist networks, have criticized the economic policies and the international institutions that are behind the erosion of seconomic conditions and social rights. They are calling for a rights-based approach to development and growth, which would include social clauses guaranteeing that trade agreements will not undermine the rights of workers, women, or the environment.

1

DEFINING SOCIAL RIGHTS AND ECONOMIC CITIZENSHIP

The framework for the definition and application of the rights of citizen-ship in a national context was elaborated by the late British sociologist T.H. Marshall (1964), who elucidated the origins and historical evolution of the civil, political, and social rights of citizens. Marshall explained that civil rights emerged and were codified in the 18th century (with its demo-cratic revolutions); that the 19th century saw the extension of political rights (at least for the male population); and that the 20th century saw the adoption of social rights with the rise of politicized labor movements and the welfare state. Civil rights were rights over the body, including the right to move freely and to seek work at an occupation of one's choice. Political rights pertained to independent organizing and participation in electoral processes. Social rights were those connected to education, train-ing, a decent standard of living, and good work conditions. There are gaps in the framework, even for the history of the industrialized countries that Marshall described. Black men in America, for example, were unable to exercise their civil or political rights in Southern states until well into the second half of the 20th century. Women did not receive many of the civil and political rights—notably the rights pertaining to residence, choice of occupation, nationality, and the vote—until the early 20th century (e.g., England and the United States) or even the mid-20th century (France and Switzerland). What is more, feminists have identified reproductive rights and choice as a key civil right for women, and these were not codified until well into the second half of the 20th century (Lister, 1997; Misra & King, 2005; Moghadam, 2006). Other scholars have noted that the development of the welfare state—and therefore of the social rights of citizens, or their economic citizenship—varies across liberal capitalist democracies (e.g., the United States and Switzerland), social democracies (the Nordic countries), and corporate social democracies (most of continental Europe). Social rights refer to the gains made by labor movements in the early part of the 20th century and their codification in the labor laws and social policies of welfare states, particularly around health, education, vocational training, and social insurance. Social rights and economic citizenship are most advanced in the Nordic countries (Esping-Anderson, 1990; Janoski, 1998). A summary of civil, political, and social rights of citizenship as per Marshall, with some minor adjustments, is presented in Table 1.1.

During the Cold War, civil and political rights tended to be empha-sized by the United States and its capitalist allies, whereas the rights of citi-zens to full social and economic rights (including the rights of ethnic groups and nationalities) were stressed by the Soviet Union and its socialist allies. This was so despite the references to civil, political, *and* social rights in the

Table 1.1. Summary of Civil, Political, and Social Rights of Citizenship

Civil Rights	Political Rights	Social Rights
Right to contract	Right to vote	Health services
Equal treatment under the law	Right to run & hold office	Family allowances
Freedom of expression	To form or join a political party or trade union	Primary and secondary education
Freedom of religion	To engage in fund-raising	Higher education
Right to privacy	Nationality rights	Vocational education
Control over one's body	Refugee and contract worker rights	Social insurance
Choice of residence	Minority rights	Compensatory rights
Choice of occupation	Dissident rights	

Source: Moghadam (2003), adopted from Janoski (1998) and Marshall (1964).

1948 Universal Declaration of Human Rights. The United Nations, therefore, agreed on two new covenants, both issued in 1966: The International Covenant on Civil and Political Rights (ICCPR), and the International Covenant on Social, Economic, and Cultural Rights (ICESCR). The latter remains the central framework for social and economic rights as these are known internationally. The ICESCR prescribes the right of people to a freely chosen job; equitable and equal wages for work of equal value; dignified working conditions for workers and their families; professional training; equal opportunities for promotion; protection for families, especially for children; maternity protection; protection of boys, girls, and teenagers against economic exploitation. These are consistent with the standards and norms promoted by the International Labor Organization (ILO). Throughout the 20th century, the ILO—through its tripartite arrangement of meetings and agreements among governments, employers, and trade unions—issued a large number of conventions, declarations, and recommendations pertaining to the rights of workers. Not all have been adopted by states, and even where they have been adopted the norms or policies are not always enforced. States have, however, agreed on four core labor standards represented by eight conventions, which call for freedom of association and the prohibition of child labor, forced labor, and discrimination in employment.[1] Important as the core labor standards are, they represent but a segment of the broader array of social and economic rights that citizens should enjoy.

As understood today by academics, trade unionists, and feminist activists, "social and economic rights" generally include decent work and decent wages, independent unions and other associations, worker education and the capacity to move up the occupational ladder, social security, the absence of ethnic or gender discrimination, a healthy work environment free of sexual harassment, and work–family balance. We would add that in the 21st century, rights for migrant workers, Lesbian, Gay, Bisexual and Transgender workers, inclusion of domestic workers in the provisions of labor law, workplace democracy, and recognition of the value of the care economy also should be understood as social and economic rights.[2] What is more, the era of globalization calls for global social policy, such as recent calls for a "global social floor" to end poverty and provide social protection for all (van Ginneken, 2009).

There is no single instrument spelling out the social and economic rights of women, although such rights are referred to in the 1979 UN Convention on the Elimination of All Forms of Discrimination Against Women, the 1995 Beijing Platform for Action, the *Charter of Women Workers Rights* of the International Confederation of Free Trade Unions (ICFTU),[3] and the ILO conventions pertaining to maternity protection, nondiscrimination, and equal remuneration.[4] We note, too, that women's social and economic rights—including labor rights—are typically inscribed in national labor laws and in some constitutions. Across the globe, the content of such laws, and the social rights that citizens enjoy, vary. In many countries, women workers enjoy rights to paid maternity leave, crèches at the workplace with nursing breaks to feed their babies, subsidized child-care facilities in the community, and retirement that is several years earlier than that of men. (The latter is to compensate for their double duty as workers and mothers.) Women also may be the beneficiaries of laws against discrimination in employment and pay, and against sexual harassment.

Therefore, there are good reasons why special attention should be devoted to women's economic participation and rights. First, the current era of neoliberal globalization is characterized by the feminization of labor; the feminization of poverty; the huge numbers of migrant women working as nannies or domestics; the growth in the trafficking of women; and women's continued responsibility for child care, housework, and elder care. Second, the work that women do spans both the productive and reproductive spheres, or the market economy and the care economy. Third, the vulnerabilities inherent in global capitalism affect women disproportionately, whether in their productive or reproductive roles.

Implications of Globalization for Women's Social Rights and
Economic Citizenship

Economic globalization and its correlate, trade liberalization, offer women opportunities for employment and entrepreneurship, but there are risks and social costs as well. There is little consensus among researchers about the short- and long-term impacts of liberalization. In the mid-1990s, development economist Paul Streeten (1997) delineated the costs and benefits of globalization. His "balance sheet" is reproduced in Table 1.2, and it is remarkable for its prescient insights. The UN Development Agency's Human Development Office subsequently produced a report on globalization that presented it as "janus-faced," that is, capable of creating both winners and losers (UNDP, 1999).

One may question whether Streeten was correct in suggesting that economic globalization would be a uniformly negative experience for women. Women with higher education, mobility, and cross-cultural skills have been able to benefit from the employment opportunities of economic globalization and the imperatives of the "knowledge economy." And certain segments of the female population across the globe have been able to take advantage of privatization and the encouragement of small business development to

Table 1.2. Balance Sheet of Globalization

Good for:	Bad for:
Japan, Europe, North America	Many developing countries
East and Southeast Asia	Africa and Latin America
Output	Employment
People with assets	People without assets
Profits	Wages
People with high skills	People with few skills
The educated	The uneducated
Professional, managerial, and technical people	Workers
Flexible adjusters	Rigid adjusters
Creditors	Debtors
Those independent of public services	Those dependent on public services
Large firms	Small firms
Men	Women, children
The strong, risk takers	The weak and vulnerable
Global markets	Local communities
Sellers of technically sophisticated products	Sellers of primary and standard manufactured products
Global culture	Local cultures
Global peace	Local troubles (Russia, Mexico, Turkey, former Yugoslavia)

Source: Streeten (1997).

obtain credits and loans to start their own businesses. Nonetheless, the environment in which even middle-class women work—that is, the environment of neoliberal economic globalization—is neither women-friendly nor conducive to social and economic rights. Many critics feel that the current neoliberal trade agenda does little to advance economies, let alone social groups such as workers and women. Activists in the global justice movement—including transnational feminist networks such as the Women's International Coalition for Economic Justice (WICEJ), the International Gender and Trade Network (IGTN), Women in Development Europe (WIDE) and the Women's Environment and Development Organization (WEDO)—argue that the new trade agenda benefits the big corporations and rich countries, squeezing out small producers and wage earners (see Moghadam 2005). Even policymakers who are committed to a liberalized trade regime disagree on trade rules and their implications for different countries and different sectors of their economies. To satisfy their own populations, including powerful unions, the countries of the North continue to protect certain of their products or enter into bilateral trade agreements with specific terms. The countries of the South are determined to enter the rich country markets, but to do so they must open up their own markets to competition. The evidence on the impact of trade liberalization thus far is mixed for developing countries, according to economist Lance Taylor. His long-term study of 14 countries undergoing liberalization found mixed results, with four countries in his study reporting increased "informality" of employment. Given the evidence, Taylor (2004) expresses "amazement at the continued insistence on the part of proponents of orthodox neoclassical theory, whereby increased integration of world commodity and capital markets is conducive to growth and is expected to be welfare-improving" (p. 29). His skepticism was entirely warranted, for the global financial crisis and economic recession of 2008–2009 put into sharp relief the deficits of a global financial and trading system that resulted in stock market collapses and the rising cost of food and fuel in developing countries.

China—currently the world's factory—usually is cited as an example of a successfully liberalized economy that has benefited enormously from massive amounts of foreign direct investment. Certainly it has enormous reserves of educated workers ready to serve in the countless factories that have been set up to produce and export goods. India—with its huge reserves of educated, English-speaking middle-class workers—has become a major site of offshore services (teleservices) by credit card companies, airlines, banks, and other service providers. In both countries, however, although some workers and some producers have clearly benefited from liberalization, poverty and inequalities remain massive. The Chinese workforce experiences significant exploitation and extremely hazardous work conditions. Both economies have seen growth and wage increases, but social exclusion and relative poverty have grown, too, and there are many concerns about environmental degradation (UNDP, 2005). Not surprising is the recent upsurge in Chinese labor activism (Chen, 2006; Lee, 2007; Ngai, 2005).

Much research on free-trade agreements (FTAs) indicates that they often stimulate new jobs that are without benefits or stability, encourage urban development without environmental regulations, and hurt women workers and the poor (WIDE, 2007). As transnational corporations expand their operations, low-wage workers may initially enjoy more choices in employment, but ultimately they find fewer opportunities as traditional income sources and local businesses give way to a small set of transnational investments. Meanwhile, women generally continue to receive lower wages than men for the same work, and a low-wage female labor force often becomes the preferred employee (Henrici, 2005; WIDE, 1998). Compounding that vulnerability, women in low-income or irregular employment, or women who lack substantial financial assets or have no say in trade unions play no role in responding to, much less shaping, any FTA. The combination of flexible labor markets, trade agreements under neoliberal conditions, and traditional gender ideology works to the disadvantage of most women in the labor force. What is more, the global economic crisis of 2008–2009 exacerbated unemployment and threatened to sideline labor rights or social and economic rights even further.

A counterweight to this state of affairs would appear to lie with social movements and civil society organizations, notably trade unions and women's organizations. Unions have protested the negative effects of economic globalization, and many of the more progressive ones have engaged in efforts to enhance women workers' social/economic rights through movement activism and the adoption or enforcement of pro-worker legislation. Women have made impressive inroads into trade union decision making in a number of countries and regions around the world (e.g., Latin America, the Caribbean, the Philippines, Australia, Canada, Scandinavia) and they have the support of global union federations as well as national-level peak bodies. In general, reflecting a still sex-segregated labor market, trade unions representing feminized sectors (e.g., health, education, social welfare, and to a certain degree, civil service) tend to have strong female involvement in decision making. The global union federations are setting the standard by instituting mechanisms to ensure the representation of female trade unionists on decision-making bodies. And they are urging trade union affiliates to organize more women workers, elect more women to decision-making positions, and take up issues such as sexual harassment and other issues that enhance the social rights and economic citizenship of working women. (See especially chapters by Olney and Wintour, this volume.)

We propose that the trade union movement, a traditional institution of political activism, provides valuable sites for meaningful challenges to globalization. It is useful on two counts. First, by virtue of its characteristics of solidarity and universality, it has the capacity to challenge the political and cultural economy of globalization, including women's work. Second, trade unions are a potentially important resource for feminist politics because women have made some gains within the trade union movement. In particular, coalitions between trade unions and women's organizations at the national level, along with coalitions between global union federations and transnational feminist networks, could help advance women's social and economic conditions, participation, and rights. It is here, too, at the nexus of the women's movement and the labor movement, that *difficult dialogues* have taken place or could do so, on such issues as sexual and reproductive health and rights, immigration, environmental protection, and social clauses.

This book has two objectives. First, it seeks to examine the role of international law and human rights instruments in the protection and expansion of women's social and economic rights, and how these laws affect legal frameworks, policies, and advocacy campaigns at the national level. Second, it seeks to examine the part played by trade union feminists in (a) bridging the divide between the labor movement and the women's movement, and (b) promoting policies to enhance the working conditions and social/economic rights of women in the labor force. Key questions are:

- Do existing legal frameworks and instruments adequately protect working women? Is there adequate knowledge of these instruments?

- Can social/economic rights be enhanced through a strategy to increase women's participation in trade union decision making? How are trade union feminists addressing the erosion of working women's conditions and rights? What are unions doing to increase women's leadership? What are the obstacles and successes?

- Are feminist organizations and trade unions working together to enhance social and economic rights? Are trade union feminists the bridge between the women's movement and the labor movement?

Through an analysis of economic conditions facing women across countries, an examination of labor codes, social policies, and international rights instruments, and reports on trade union activities with respect to gender and social equality, the book elucidates the gaps in legislation and failures of state policy, the extent of nongovernmental organization (NGO)–trade union collaboration, and the capacity of trade union feminists to influence the culture, priorities, and partnerships of their unions. Conceptually, the book draws on and contributes to social movement and world-systems theories, as well as to gender studies and globalization studies. The chapter authors provide theoretical framing, showing how feminist and labor theorizing conceptualizes labor rights and women's social/economic rights in legislation as well as in labor movement policies, campaigns, and resources. At the same time, the uneven application and enforcement of these measures validate world-system theory's focus on global inequalities and hierarchies across the countries of the core, periphery, and semiperiphery; and suggest the different political opportunities available to activists attempting to build social movement organizations and enhance participation and rights across the world system. We draw on and contribute to the literatures on transnational processes, including international advocacy and transnational feminist politics and practices in an era of globalization.

UNION FEMINISM

Union feminists are playing an important role in challenging the sexual politics of unions and in mobilizing women's participation in transnational campaigns for labor rights and economic justice. Our research suggests that union feminists, with their structural ties to both organized labor and the women's movement, are in a unique position to mobilize within both movements in response to the issues and concerns that rapid economic globalization raises for all workers. Because union renewal depends on developing new ideas and resources for organizing new types of workers and new types of workplaces, it is important for unions to create a central place for the participation of union feminists in their organizations, campaigns, and struggles.[5]

We view union feminism as goal-oriented collective action taken on behalf of the rights of women as a group. Union feminism emerges out of the day-to-day struggles by women for equality, respect, and dignity at home, in the workplace, in their unions, and in society as a whole. Union feminists use discursive tools (such as conference resolutions, policy statements, educational programs, Websites, and newsletters), as well as institutionally sanctioned spaces (including conventions, workshops, labor schools, and committee structures) to fashion a network of resources that can be called into action to mobilize union members and their potential supporters at strategically important moments. This network helps to establish and sustain more permanent structures of organizational participation and a collective identity based on the belief that social and political action taken by a group can make a difference (Fonow, 2004).

As a political environment, globalization has reconfigured the opportunities for politics and the repertoire for collective actions available to social movements (Moghadam, 2005; 2009). For example, emerging new political opportunity structures such as transnational labor advocacy networks provide union women with the opportunity to participate in the ongoing construction of transnational labor solidarity. Networks can serve both as actors in politics and as a way to mobilize and structure the actions of participants. However, the existence of networks in and of themselves does not produce collective action; networks have to be framed by movements as useful circuits for mobilization.

Unions have always been involved in international labor networks, but more recently their networks have become thicker and more diverse. There has been a proliferation of political spaces where the interests of labor overlap with other movements and with advocacy organizations concerned about labor rights and development. Increasingly campaigns for labor rights are organized and funded with nonunion support from churches, foundations, NGOs, and universities. Labor conferences and periodicals focus more on noncontract issues such as worker empowerment, organizing, union democracy, and feminism. Contract issues are being defined in new ways, and many unions are actively engaged in equity bargaining (Kidder, 2000). New players from the nonprofit sector and activists from other social movements are joining with unions as strategic partners in the growing transnational advocacy network for labor rights.

These collaborations help to expand traditional ideas about the roles that unions can play in the movement for global justice. Transnational labor advocacy networks have become mobilizing structures for feminists and labor activists and have opened the way for union feminists to play an active role in shaping the discourses and mobilizing strategies of organized labor. Within these networks union feminists challenge at least two conventional notions. The first challenge is to the class-based solidarity of the labor movement, by acknowledging the differences of gender, race, sexuality, and ethnicity within class. The second challenge is the gender-based solidarity of the women's movement, by recognizing the class and ethnic differences among women. The formation and articulation of gender-specific class-based political demands change the boundaries of those included and excluded in the process of social movement formation, thus creating new types of political claims and new solidarities—what Curtin (1999) labels contingent solidarities. As a tool of analysis, the concept of contingent solidarities provides a framework for identifying how and why women have defined their political interests within particular political fields. This concept "allows for a cross-national analysis of the ways in which class, welfare state, labor markets and cultural discourse have included or excluded women and how women trade unionists themselves have influenced the construction and formulation of claims, strategies and solidarities" (Curtin, 1999, p. 60). In the case of union feminists, these contingent solidarities are mediated through activist and advocacy networks.

Those concerned with the renewal of the labor movement must come to terms with the fundamental way that gender structures neoliberal globalization, labor markets, and FTAs. We argue for feminist analysis of gender because sexual politics is integral to trade unions, globalization, and efforts to challenge the neoliberal agenda. The labor movement already has within its ranks a group that can significantly aid the necessary renewal—union feminists (Ledwith, 2006). Union feminists already active within the network of global union federations are situated to understand the tensions and contradictions between productive and social reproductive spheres, the sexual politics of trade unions, and the importance of building transnational solidarities contingent on an understanding of cultural and social differences among workers (Franzway, 2001).

Union feminists weave together strengths and strategies that emerge from the labor movement and the women's movements. By building and mobilizing transnational networks and alliances between these various movements, union feminists create political spaces for new workers and for a new understanding of workers' issues and concerns that arise out of the rapidly changing impact of globalization on both workplaces and intimate lives.[6] However, for labor to benefit from the work of union feminists they must increase and enhance the participation of women within their ranks. This requires a rethinking of structures and practices that perpetuate male dominance in the labor movement.

BACKGROUND AND ORGANIZATION

This project was initiated in San Francisco in August 2004, during the annual meetings of the American Sociological Association (ASA). Mary Margaret Fonow and Suzanne Franzway presented a paper on women and trade unions at a panel on transnational social movements organized by Val Moghadam. We met after the panel to discuss a collaborative project on women, unions, and economic citizenship. Subsequently, Franzway and Fonow began work on a book manuscript on feminist trade unionism, while Moghadam and a research assistant at UNESCO examined international legal instruments and conducted interviews with trade unionists in France and at the ICFTU and ETUF in Brussels, Belgium. Moghadam organized a roundtable on *Women, Socio-economic Rights and Trade Union Leadership* that took place on July 12, 2006, during the second World Forum on Human Rights, in Nantes, France.[7]

The three co-editors met again, for a panel on feminism and the labor movement at the ASA conference in August 2006; the papers in this book by Linda Briskin and Jennifer Curtin were initially conceived as papers for that panel. In July 2008, Moghadam presented her research on globalization and women's social rights in the Maghreb, at a conference in Cairo, Egypt, organized by the Friedrich Ebert Stiftung (Conference on *Labor, Economic Crisis and the Future of Social Policy in the Arab* Countries). In September 2008, Fonow and Franzway participated in the *Labouring Feminism 2* conference in Stockholm, Sweden where they presented their research on queer labor organizing; this is work that grew out of Fonow's participation in the conference, *Toward a Vision of Sexual and Economic Justice*, held at Barnard College, in the United States, in 2007.[8] And in July 2010, the research network and book project were discussed at the World Congress of Sociology, in Gothenburg, Sweden.

We bring together here the work of feminist scholars, labor activists, and women leaders from labor unions to discuss women's activism and leadership for social and economic rights across a wide range of occupations, unions, and labor market sectors. The case studies here represent a variety of regions throughout the world including Asia, Europe, North America, South America, Middle East, Africa, and Australia. Illustrations and examples are drawn from Algeria, Morocco, Tunisia, Egypt, South Africa, Argentina, France, Ecuador, Ukraine, Laos, New Zealand, Israel, Japan, Canada, Australia, Britain, and the United States.

The authors in Part I—Women, Work, and Social/Economic Rights Across the Globe—provide frameworks and empirical findings for understanding how globalization has affected women's opportunities to find decent work and how globalization provides a context for understanding women's collective action and claims and for economic citizenship and social rights. Each explores the contradictions of globalization and the gaps between equity/labor laws and policies and the reality of women's economic lives on the ground. Each chapter emphasizes different paths to economic citizenship for women but also focuses on how social movements and activists with similar goals are coming together in the struggle for women's economic and social rights.

In the first chapter, "Toward Economic Citizenship: The Middle East and North Africa," Valentine M. Moghadam draws attention to the limitations of women's economic citizenship in countries of the Middle East and North Africa (MENA), which emanate from both neoliberal globalization and Muslim Family Law. In particular, she shows how the absence of a key civil right—women's right to mobility and to an occupation of their choice—constrains women's economic citizenship and reinforces economic dependence on male kin. Examining the paradoxes of globalization, she uncovers the opportunities that globalization presents for women's collective action and documents how women's rights organizations in the MENA countries are making claims for social rights with varying levels of success.

In "Promoting the Social Rights of Working Women: The Case of Palestinian Women in Israel," Michal Schwartz continues the analysis of women's social and economic rights in the Middle East, with a focus on Arab women citizens of Israel. She argues that their low rate of labor-force participation is an indicator of their low economic and social status and, in turn, helps to reproduce it. She provides a comparative analysis of the status of Jewish and Palestinian women and demonstrates the wide gap between them on most every indicator of progress—a gap she attributes to institutional forms of discrimination against Palestinians. For Schwartz, the right to work outside the home and to organize and unionize is vitally important in the struggle for equality between the two ethnic groups as well as between the sexes. Her case study describes how the Workers' Advice Center—in the absence of effective organizing by Israel's main union, the Histadrut—advocates for Palestinian women employed in agriculture, a sector where they face stiff competition from imported workers.

In "Tunisia: Women's Economic Citizenship and Trade Union Participation," Hafidha Chékir and Khédija Arfaoui explore the contradictions and loopholes in the human rights conventions and labor laws as they apply to women in Tunisia, and point to the limitations of trade union action with respect to working women. Notwithstanding the importance of legislation passed in 2004 against sexual harassment—a key element in women's economic citizenship in Tunisia as elsewhere—women find it difficult to bring forth charges of workplace harassment for fear of job loss. And although the government of Tunisia officially championed women's rights, its adoption of the neoliberal model undermined gender and social equity alike. This reality helped motivate the protests of early 2011, which led to the government's collapse. Chékir and Arfaoui explore the gap between equity law and reality on the ground and explore the obstacles that will need to be removed before women play a role in union decision making.

Next, in the chapter by Graciela Di Marco, "Gendered Economic Rights and Trade Unionism: The Case of Argentina," attention is drawn to the struggle for social rights within the context of a history of political repression, the rise of neoliberalism and the emergence of new types of social movements. In one of her case studies Di Marco focuses on the role of women in the Congress of Argentine Workers (CTA), a new type of social movement organization founded on the principles of direct membership, participatory democracy, and political autonomy. In 2000, the CTA created a Secretariat for Gender Equality with female quotas for executive leadership and outreach to feminist organizations that has resulted in adoption of more radical feminist goals. Di Marco contends that the struggle to protect and fulfill women's economic and social rights will need the cooperation of many political actors, including trade unions, social movements, and women's movements.

In the final chapter in the section, "Can a Focus on Survival and Health as Social/Economic Rights Help Some of the World's Most Imperiled Women in a Globalized World? Cases from Ecuador, Ukraine, and Laos," Rae Lesser Blumberg and Andres Salazar-Paredes focus on the struggles for social rights and economic justice for women in Ecuador, Ukraine, and Laos. Each case presents a different set of challenges and different opportunities for activism. They confront head on the major paradox of globalization; is the income provided by precarious work worth the risk to health, safety, and survival? To answer that question they turn to the experiences of women in Ecuador who work in the nontraditional agriculture sector of export flowers and broccoli, to women in Laos who work as bar hostesses, and to women in the Ukraine who are compelled to migrate abroad to find work and who may become trapped in sexual slavery. To counter the ill effects, they recommend unionization, exporting more to countries with higher health and safety standards for their products (green label), leveraging various ILO conventions and standards, criminalizing the traffic in people but professionalizing jobs that service the tourist industry, supporting NGOs that work to reintegrate women who were forced into the sex trade back into society, and protecting workers' health from pesticides and from sexually transmitted diseases.

Part II—Reports From the Field: Trade Union and Multilateral Perspectives—offers trade union and multilateral perspectives that were initially presented at the second World Forum on Human Rights held in Nantes, France in 2006. Each report examines the status of women and equity mechanisms within federated labor organizations designed to provide national labor unions the opportunity to connect with multilateral agencies that represent the interests of workers across national boundaries. Nora Wintour of Public Services International (PSI) and Jo Morris of Britain's Trade Union Congress (TUC) noted that women were now 40% to 50% of union workers but still had a way to go before becoming at least 30% of the decision makers and leaders in the trade unions. The women's committees of each federation are networked through the coordinating activities of the International Trade Union Confederation (ITUC), which in 2003 initiated a major campaign to increase significantly women's membership in unions worldwide and their representation and participation in union programs, activities, and decision-making structures.

The ILO is the oldest of the UN agencies and a tripartite organization bringing together governments, employers, and trade unions. For some years, the ILO has been encouraging increased female participation within the delegations who meet annually in Geneva. Between 2000 and 2006, according to Shauna Olney in "The ILO, Gender Equality, and Trade Unions," there was a slight increase in the number of government and employer female participants—from 26% to 30.5% for governments, and from 15% to 19.7% for employers. However, the number of female participants from workers' organizations decreased during the same period—from 19.5% to 17.2%. Clearly, the trade unions, especially those from the developing world, need to be more gender aware and inclusive.

PSI represents unions and workers in the fields of health, education, and public utilities. In the 1990s, on most decision-making bodies, women made up only 20% to 30% and PSI's senior officers were all male. In 2002, PSI amended its Constitution to allow for gender parity on all decision-making bodies and to elect co-chairs for all committees, one man and one woman. Overnight, as Wintour explains, the proportion of women on the highest decision-making body, the Executive Board, jumped from 22% to 50%. However, the situation in the affiliates had not yet followed this model: Men remained the vast majority (about 85%) of presidents and general secretaries of PSI affiliates.

What about women and decision making in country-level "peak bodies" (union federations)? As a committed trade unionist, Jo Morris defends the historical record of the British labor movement in the struggle for social equality and welfare while also recognizing shortcomings in gender equality and leadership. In Britain's TUC, women's union density is about the same as men's, and women are more likely than men to join unions, but their share of decision-making positions remains disproportionately small. The low number of women represented on the union's main decision-making body, the National Executive Committee (NEC), has been an important issue for those campaigning for equality. Representation has in some cases been improved by the introduction of reserved seats. In most cases, women's representation on the NEC is proportional to the overall female union membership of the TUC-affiliated union.

In the final chapter, "The Role of Unions in the Promotion of Gender Equality in France," trade unionist Pascale Coton provides a brief historical overview of women's participation in French unions and in French labor markets. Coton argues that unions are a reflection of the larger society and as such they recreate, reflect and interrogate gender perspectives within and outside of their structures. Efforts to integrate women into the Confédération Française des Travailleurs Chrétiens (CFTC) have an uneven past with no real improvement occurring until the 1980s when unions experienced a decline in numbers and became aware of the needed to build new structures in order to attract new members. This coincided with a large increase in the number of women entering the workforce and feminists seized this moment as an opportunity to build alliances with labor to promote women's social rights and to advocate for the equality of women within unions. Coton describes a CFTC initiative to improve gender equality and work–family balance, and she points to international resources that can be leveraged in the pursuit of gender justice and social rights.

The book's third and final section asks, Where Next for Feminism and the Labor Movement? Linda Briskin's chapter, "Trade Unions, Collective Agency, and the Struggle for Women's Equality: Expanding the Political Empowerment Measure," argues that trade unions are well situated as vehicles for women's equality, especially in the current global context. The chapter demonstrates that trade unions have the potential to improve work-place conditions and relations at multiple levels and geographies, that is, at local, regional, national, and transnational levels as indicated by a range of quantitative as well as qualitative measures. These include macro indictors such as union density, and institutional indicators such as programs to ensure equality representation; structures of representation such as women's com-mittees and other constituency structures; and the codification of equality in union charters. Briskin poses the question: to what extent is collective bargaining an equality vehicle? As vehicles for the collective agency of women and other marginalized groups, trade unions are central to transna-tional campaigns for social and economic rights.

The argument that union women's organizing has contributed to the recognition of gender politics parallels the argument by Franzway and Fonow in Chapter 14 on the emergence of queer organizing in trade union move-ments. However, unions remain undertheorized and underrated as instru-ments towards these ends. In taking issue with the persistent and often ungrounded views of unions as unreconstructed patriarchal institutions (and echoing the arguments of Jo Morris and Nora Wintour), Briskin shows that union women, and other equality-seeking groups, have had an enormous impact on the practices, policies, and discourse of unions in many Western countries, and to some extent in unions of the South. They also are well situated to promote women's social rights and economic citizenship.

Drawing on her fieldwork conducted in Japan since 2003, Kaye Broadbent in "Women-only Unions and Women Union Leaders in Japan," investigates the possibilities of Japan's women-only unions, and argues for both their necessity and their potential. The chapter traces the 20th-century history of Japanese unions in the context of the Japanese labor market. This reveals the discrimination women face in the workforce and the reluctance of mainstream unions (enterprise unions) to address women's inequality, workplace harassment, or sexism. Broadbent builds on Briskin's analysis of women's organizing and the differences between women-only unions and predominantly female-dominated workers centers such as Domestic Workers

United in the United States. Japanese women-only unions were formed as a strategy aimed at achieving equality by addressing these issues.

These women-only unions differ from mainstream unions not only in terms of their focus on women, but more specifically in their focus on workers outside the boundaries of the large enterprise as well as nonregular workers. The chapter presents a case study of the formation and impact of Japan's largest women-only union, Josei Union. Although the membership is small, the union has won the right to collective bargaining, which has given it more legal power than the nongovernment or nonprofit labor organizations that are on the increase in Japan. It is this legal power that has allowed Josei Union to pursue cases involving discrimination in employment conditions. The union has also managed to establish international networks with external women's organizations and labor movements. Like Briskin, Broadbent underlines the value of democratic organization as essential to achieving social/economic rights for working women, and points to centers and associations for working women as having the potential to work with the trade unions to address women's economic conditions and rights. But she also warns that care is needed since alliances with broad based women's organizations could draw the orientation away from the working class.

Neva Seidman Makgetla's chapter, Women's Leadership in the South African Labor Movement, provides a telling analysis of the kinds of contradictions that women experience in attempting to make trade unions work for women's social/economic rights. South Africa has constitutional and discursive commitments to gender equity, but patriarchal relations continue to subordinate women in the home and at work. Based on her own fieldwork as well as national surveys, Seidman Makgetla analyses the very limited gains that women have made in trade union leadership. In contrast to Briskin and Broadbent, she queries the value of democratic processes since leadership elections do not appear to benefit women. But she goes on to show why this was the case in South African unions.

Although women make up almost half of total union membership in South Africa, they occupy less than one-fourth of the leadership positions, most of which are the low-status positions of deputy president or treasurer. Seidman Makgetla addresses possible factors, starting with the social reality that women have little formal power in the rest of South African society. Black women faced extraordinary levels of unemployment, and if they had a job they generally remained in subordinate positions and low-wage jobs. They were largely excluded from the traditional strongholds of South African unionism in heavy industry and the mines.

Overall, the limiting conditions are familiar to union women and researchers and include responsibility for household labor, occupational segregation in a few industries, and socialization. But Black South African women experienced an additional burden imposed by apartheid policies, and their legacy, which confined them to their homes while the men worked elsewhere. Women's capacity to participate in trade unions is further undermined by indifferent or hostile male union leadership and inadequate union structures. Attempts at self-organizing through women-specific structures were eroded by their weak structural location, lack of resources, and resistance by the male leadership. Seidman Makgetla provides a valuable case study that shows clearly that overcoming resistance by men leaders is an important element in gaining rights for women workers, and that the situation is exacerbated by the weak position of the labor movement in society.

In their chapter, "Demanding Their Rights: LGBT Transnational Labor Activism," Suzanne Franzway and Mary Margaret Fonow extend the ambit of social and economic rights by investigating how labor movement networks are being mobilized for the inclusion of lesbian, gay, bisexual, and transgender (LGBT) workers, and they consider the goals, discourses, strategies, and tactics of queer labor organizing at national and transnational levels. A renewed notion of sexual politics (following the tradition of Kate Millet) provides the basis for an analysis because it incorporates both the sexual and the political. This is an important move toward understanding the dominance of heteronormativity, and the response of queer activism in relation to the labor movement. As recognition of the needs of LGBT workers grow, it becomes clear that this is not a homogenous category, and that persistent political activism is critical if gains are to be made for workers' rights. As with all the chapters in this section, political spaces won by self-organizing have assumed an integral dimension of rights campaigns within trade unions. Franzway and Fonow document historical and current examples of campaigns and strategies that have been developed from the local to transnational levels. They argue that mutual benefits are possible and evident as queer activists and feminists have the potential to revitalize and expand the boundaries of the labor movement by pushing unions to consider new forms of organizing, new types of workers and workplaces, and new agendas.

In the final chapter, "Ne'er the Twain Shall Meet? Reflections on the Future of Feminism and Unionism," Jennifer Curtin reflects on the future possibilities for feminism and unionism, identifying three divisions that continue to have an impact: the historically hostile relationship between feminism and labor; the disciplinary divisions among researchers that sees trade unions and feminism trapped between separate intellectual silos; and finally women's activism within the trade union movement is often forgotten (hence the value of this book). Curtin begins by reviewing the way in which feminist strategies have been articulated in discussions of gender and political theory and explore the difficulties associated with categorizing strategies of inclusion as inherently nontransformative. She identifies how union women have taken up these strategies and through a consideration of their impact demonstrates that analysis benefits feminism as well as union women. Curtin pays particular attention to the question of political space as she terms it, and argues that it is possible to suggest that the activism of labor movement feminism is potentially transformative despite its guiding principle being one of inclusion.

Curtin goes on to examine inclusive strategies with a particular focus on the strategies of separate organizing and women's representation and reflects on how these might be interpreted as potentially transformative. While separate women-only unions have become rare (see Broadbent, Chap. 13, this volume. for an example), Curtin finds that such strategies have contributed to a degree of transformation of internal trade union agenda and a reconfiguring the gendered dimensions of labor market participation. In conclusion, Curtin argues that feminism and unionism have much in common under current conditions of globalization, and that it makes sense to pool resources for the promotion of social rights and economic citizenship.

CONCLUSIONS

Making globalization work for women would appear to be a tall order. Researchers and activists alike have rightly criticized the current model of globalization for the growth of inequalities, unemployment, unfair trade, financial crises, and environmental disasters. Proposals for alternatives abound—from the ILO's decent work agenda to the more wide-ranging proposals for economic democracy and systemic transformations emanating from those within and around the World Social Forum. This book volume is a contribution to the discussions taking place at both national and global levels.

Bringing together trade unionists, academics, and activists committed to gender equality and economic citizenship, this book project has been as much a political endeavor as an intellectual one. The complexities and contradictions of the neoliberal model of capitalist globalization call for conceptual work, political critiques, and policy recommendations, which the contributors to this book provide. In addressing the deficits of globalization, we offer a feminist intervention in the debates currently taking place within trade unions, intergovernmental organizations, and research networks. And by placing social rights and economic citizenship at the center of our analyses and recommendations in order to make globalization work for women, we present an alternative framework to the flawed model of neoliberal capitalism.

NOTES

1. For details on the ILO's labor standards, and for information on its *decent work* campaign, see www.ilo.org.

2. The care economy, or what some call the sphere of reproduction (as distinct from material production) refers to activities associated with the care of individuals, households, and families, whether paid or unpaid. Child care, housework, and elder care typically are carried out by women in the family, migrant workers, or undocumented workers. See, for example, Folbre (2006) and Beneria (2008).

3. The ICFTU was renamed the International Trade Union Confederation (ITUC) following a merger in 2006.

4. A number of cross-national datasets measure women's rights, including political, economic, and social rights. See, for example, the Cingranelli-Richards (CIRI) Human Rights Dataset, which covers 195 countries: http://ciri.binghamton.edu/.

5. There is a robust body of research by feminist scholars that examines the role women and feminists play in the revitalization and democratization of organized labor at the national, regional and transnational level. See Boris and Klein (in press), Broadbent and Ford (2008), Brooks (2007), Chatterjee (2001), Cobble (2007), Colgan and Ledweth (2000), Foley and Baker (2009), Gupta (2008), Latour (2008), Moccio (2009), Seidman (2007), Soonok (2003), and Xin (2008).

6. Fantasia and Voss (2004) argue for a new "labor metaphysic" that addresses organizationally and symbolically the spaces between unions. They believe that union renewal lies in the active cultivation of the spaces between existing unions and between unions and other institutions (communities, churches and religious organizations, civic associations, social movements, etc.) and between the labor movement and those stigmatized groups previously ignored by the labor movement. This is the way for labor to regain some of its former significance in the symbolic vocabulary of society.

7. For a summary description, visit the UNESCO Website: http://portal.unesco.org/shs/en/ev.php-URL_ID=8102&URL_DO=DO_TOPIC&URL_SECTION=201.html and http://portal.unesco.org/shs/en/ev.php-URL_ID=9429&URL_DO=DO_TOPIC&URL_SECTION=201.html

8. http://www.barnard.edu/bcrw/justice/index.htm

REFERENCES

Beneria, L. (2008). The crisis of care, international migration, and public Policy. *Feminist Economics, 14*(3), 1–21.

Boris, E., & Klein, J. (in press). *Caring for America: Home health workers in the shadow of the welfare state.* Oxford: Oxford University Press.

Broadbent, K., & Ford, M. (Eds.). (2008). *Women and labour organizing in Asia: Diversity, autonomy and activism.* London: Routledge.

Brooks, E.C. (2007). *Unraveling the garment industry: Transnational organizing and women's work.* Minneapolis: University of Minnesota Press.

Chatterjee, P. (2001). *A time for tea: Women, labor, and post/colonial politics on an Indian plantation.* Durham, NC: Duke University Press.

Chen, F. (2006). Privatization and its discontents in Chinese factories. *The China Quarterly, 185,* 42–60.

Cobble, S. (Ed.). (2007). *The sex of class: Women transforming American labor.* Ithaca, NY: Cornell University Press.

Colgan, F., & Ledwith, S. (Eds.). (2002). *Gender, diversity and trade unions: International perspectives.* London & New York: Routledge.

Curtin, J. (1999). *Women and trade unions: A comparative perspective.* Aldershot, UK: Ashgate.

Esping-Andersen, G. (1990). *The three worlds of welfare capitalism.* Princeton, NJ: Princeton University Press.

Fantasia, R., & Voss, K. (2004). *Hard work: Remaking the American Labor Movement.* Berkeley: University of California Press.

Folbre, N. (2006). Measuring care: Gender, empowerment, and the care economy. *Journal of Human Development, 7*(2), 183–189.

Foley, J.R., & Baker, P.L. (Eds.). (2009). *Unions, equity, and the path to renewal.* Vancouver: UBC Press.

Fonow, M.M. (2003). *Union women. Forging feminism in the United Steelworkers of America.* Minneapolis: University of Minnesota Press.

Franzway, S. (2001). *Sexual politics and greedy institutions: Union women, commitments and conflicts in public and in private.* Sydney: Pluto Press Australia.

Henrici, J. (2005). *Gender and free trade: Peruvian alternative trade organizations and women's projects.* Retrieved December 12, 2008. http://www.globaljusticecenter.org/papers2005/henrici_eng.htm#_edn3.

Janoski, T. (1998). *Citizenship and civil society: A framework of rights and obligations in liberal, traditional, and social democratic regimes.* Cambridge, MA: Cambridge University Press.

Kidder, T. (2002). Networks in Transnational Labor Organizing. In S. Khagram, J. V. Riker & K. Sikkink (Eds.), *Restructuring world politics: Transnational social movements, networks and norms* (pp. 269–293). Minneapolis: University of Minnestoa Press.

Latour, J. (2008). *Sisters in the brotherhoods: Working women organizing for equality in New York City.* New York: Palgrave/Macmillan.

Ledwith, S. (2006). Feminist praxis in a trade union gender project. *Industrial Relations Journal, 37*(4), 379–399.

Lee, C.K. (2007). *Against the law: Labor protests in China's rustbelt and sunbelt.* Berkeley: University of California Press.

Lister, R. (1997). *Citizenship: Feminist perspectives.* London: Macmillan.

Marshall, T.H. (1964). *Citizenship and social class.* Cambridge, UK: Cambridge University Press.

Misra, J., & King, L. (2005). Gender and state policies. In T. Janoski, R. Alford, A. Hicks, & M. Schwartz (Eds.), *The handbook of political sociology* (pp. 526–545). Cambridge and NY: Cambridge University Press.

Moccio, F.A. (2009). *Live wire: Women and brotherhood in the electrical industry.* Philadelphia: Temple University Press.

Moghadam, V.M. (2003). Engendering citizenship, feminizing civil society: The case of the Middle East and North Africa. *Women & Politics, 25*(1–2), 63–88.

Moghadam, V.M. (2005). *Globalizing women: Transnational feminist networks*. Baltimore, MD: The Johns Hopkins University Press.

Moghadam, V.M. (2006). Maternalist policies vs economic citizenship? Gendered social policy in Iran. In S. Razavi & S. Hassim (Eds.), *Gender and social policy in a global context: Uncovering the gendered structure of "the Social"* (pp. 87–108). Basingstoke and Geneva: Palgrave Macmillan & UNRISD.

Moghadam, V.M. (2009). *Globalization and social movements: Islamism, feminism, and the global justice movement*. Lanham, MD: Rowman & Littlefield.

Monisha Das Gupta, (2008). *Housework, feminism, and labour activism: Lessons from domestic workers in New York*. Signs 33(3), 532–536.

Ngai, P. (2005). *Made in China: Women factory workers in a global workplace*. Durham, NC: Duke University Press.

Seidman, G.W. (2007). *Beyond the boycott: Labor rights, human rights, and transnational activism*. New York: Russell Sage Foundation.

Soonok, C. (2003). *They are not machines: Korean women workers and their fight for Democratic trade unionism in the 1970s*. Bodmin, Cornwall: Ashgate.

Streeten, P. (1997). Globalization and competitiveness: Implications for development thinking and practice? In L Emmerij (Ed.), *Economic and social development into the XXI century* (pp. 107–146). Washington, DC: Inter-American Development Bank.

Taylor, L. (2004). External liberalization in Asia, post-Socialist Europe and Brazil. In E. Lee & M. Vivarelli (Eds.), *Understanding globalization, employment and poverty reduction* (pp. 13–34). New York: Palgrave Macmillan.

UNDP. (1999). *Human Development Report 1999*. New York: Oxford University Press.

UNDP. (2005). *Human Development Report 2005: International cooperation at a crossroads: Aid, trade and security in an unequal world*. New York: Oxford University Press.

Van Ginneken, W. (2009). Social security and the global socio-economic floor: Towards a human rights-based approach. *Global Social Policy*, 9(2), 228–244.

Women in Development Europe (WIDE). (1998, February). *Women's economic and social rights*. Brussels: Author.

Women in Development Europe (WIDE). (2007, November). *EU bilateral and regional free trade agreements: Bringing women to the centre of the debate* (Report of a WIDE public consultation). Brussels: Author. www.wide-network.org.

Xin, T. (2008). Women's labor activism in China. *Signs, 33*(3), 515–518.

Yuki, M. (2008). The women's movement within trade unions in Germany. *Signs, 33*(3), 519–526.

PART I

WOMEN, WORK, AND
SOCIAL/ECONOMIC RIGHTS
ACROSS THE GLOBE

TWO

TOWARD ECONOMIC CITIZENSHIP

The Middle East and North Africa

Valentine M. Moghadam

The era of globalization has seen two parallel but contradictory developments. On the one hand, global economic processes have been accompanied by rising unemployment, growing inequalities, a decline in the capacity of the welfare and developmental state, and the flexibilization of labor. On the other hand, the same economic processes have led to increases in female labor-force participation, with an expansion also of global norms, policies, and networks calling for gender equality and human rights, including social and economic rights for citizens and migrants alike.

Analyses of the emergence and evolution of social rights and economic citizenship are found in historical and sociological studies, notably those by T.H. Marshall (1964) and Alice Kessler-Harris (2001, 2003). Marshall identified "the right to work at an occupation of one's choice" as a key civil right that was won in the course of the transition from feudalism to capitalism and in the early modern period. Women, however, did not begin to enjoy this right until the latter part of the 20th century. As feminist scholars have noted, the sexual division of labor and the private–public divide effectively denied women the citizenship rights accorded to, and in fact defined by, men (Lister 2003; Pateman, 1988; Walby 1994; Yuval-Davis 1997). With respect to social and economic rights, Kessler-Harris (2001) has described how American women fought a long struggle for economic equity, including the right to work at occupations considered off limits to women and the right to equality in social security. This is a struggle that is now taking place in countries of the Middle East and North Africa (MENA).

National policies and international instruments for social rights and economic citizenship gained currency during the post-World War II "golden age of capitalism" and Keynesian economics, the period of Third World state-led development, and the era of socialist development. As stated in Chapter 1, social and economic rights are found in the International Covenant of Economic, Social, and Cultural Rights (ICESCR) and in various conventions and declarations of the International Labour Organization (ILO). For women they also are found in the 1979 Convention on the Elimination of All Forms of Discrimination against Women (CEDAW) and the 1995 Beijing Platform for Action—both of which are important planks in what is known as the global women's rights agenda.[1]

Policies and discourses of economic rights declined with the shifts in the international political economy that took place in the late 20th century. From about 1980 onward, Keynesian or socialistic policies of full employment, strong public sectors, and protection of domestic industries gave way to neoliberal policies of "flexible" labor, privatization, export-led growth, and encouragement of foreign investment. This shift entailed the demise of the welfare or developmental state, the weakening of trade unions, and the curtailment of many social benefits and entitlements. The so-called feminization of labor, which was coined to refer to the growth of the female labor force at a time of deteriorating work conditions, was accompanied by the feminization of poverty. In the global South, public sectors are no longer a source of guaranteed employment for graduates, and the private sector typically does not offer benefits to women workers, such as paid maternity leaves.

This is the context in which critics of economic globalization argue that social rights and economic citizenship have been eroded by privatization, flexible labor markets, and trade liberalization (see, e.g., ESCWA 2008; Kessler-Harris, 2003). In particular, feminist scholar-activists across the globe maintain that any benefits of increased demand for female labor and entrepreneurship have been offset by deteriorating work conditions and wages, pressures on women-owned businesses, continued gender-based discrimination, and weakly enforced or inadequate labor legislation (CAWTAR 2001, 2006; Moghadam 2005a; WIDE 1998, 2007). Civil society organizations such as unions, progressive nongovernmental organizations (NGOs), and women's groups have criticized the economic policies, social relations, and international institutions that are behind the erosion of workplace conditions and economic rights. They are calling for a rights-based approach to development and growth, which would include social clauses in bilateral agreements guaranteeing the protection of workers, women, children, and the environment. In particular, activists in transnational feminist networks are concerned that trade agreements should not lower wages, or undermine women's businesses, or create unemployment. On the contrary, the effects of trade and investment should be consistent with the spirit of international human rights instruments, and should not violate the objectives of the global women's rights agenda.

Broadening T.H. Marshall's conceptualization of social rights, Alice Kessler-Harris (2003) defined *economic citizenship* as

> the right to work at the occupation of one's choice (where work includes child-rearing and household maintenance); to earn wages adequate to the support of self and family; to a non-discriminatory job market; to the education and training that facilitate access to it; to the social benefits necessary to sustain and support labor force participation; and to the social environment required for effective choice, including adequate housing, safe streets, accessible public transport, and universal healthcare. (pp. 158–159)

This chapter follows her definition, emphasizing labor rights, social justice, and women's equality. The right to gainful employment, along with public education, vocational training, fair wages, a healthy workplace, trade union organizing, and social welfare are key elements of economic citizenship and are especially important in the context of democratic transitions in the Middle East and North Africa, where the "Arab spring" of 2011 has been followed by attempts in Egypt, Tunisia, and elsewhere to replace authoritarian rule with democracy and rights-based development. Additional requirements for women's equality and full citizenship are a workplace free of sexual harassment, paid maternity leave, and affordable quality child care. Will such conditions be met? This chapter makes a case for such conditions, examining the longstanding deficits in women's economic citizenship and describing the activities of feminist organizations to enhance women's economic participation and rights.[2]

SOCIAL RIGHTS, ECONOMIC CITIZENSHIP, AND THE CHANGING POLITICAL ECONOMY

In the developing world, the origins and evolution of the civil, political, and social rights of citizenship as elaborated by Marshall did not follow the same pattern or trajectory as in the advanced industrialized countries of the West. Postcolonial state development had its own history and logic; in some cases, social rights were accorded to citizens while civil and political rights were not. Where civil and political rights did exist, they varied greatly between women and men. In the MENA countries, civil and political rights were limited by one-party rule or personalist monarchies or ever-present militaries. The right to form independent trade unions, political parties, or other civil society organizations was largely nonexistent; and women's civil, political, and social rights were limited by law and by tradition (Joseph, 2000; Moghadam, 2003). Nevertheless, a kind of social contract between states and their social bases did exist during the period of development and growth, roughly the 1960s to the 1980s. The regional oil economy and populist regimes allowed for the provision of state-sponsored education and health care, as well as an array of subsidies to citizens (Karshenas & Moghadam, 2006). Those in government employment, whether from the middle or working classes, were beneficiaries of stable jobs and good benefits, while graduates were guaranteed employment in the growing public sector. The regional oil economy and labor-capital flows across countries provided male workers with relatively high wages, while oil revenues enabled governments to pursue capital-intensive industrialization. All of this depressed demand for female labor, although a segment of the female middle class was found in the civil service, employed mainly as teachers and health workers (Moghadam, 1995, 2003).

Challenges to the social contract began to emerge in the late 20th century, first by the structural adjustment policies of the 1980s and 1990s (which led to privatization, the declining quality of many social services, and the erosion of social rights); then by the emergence of feminist movements (which challenged women's secondary citizenship); and subsequently by broad globalization processes (which challenged state authority and encouraged civil society growth). The changes to the social contract were met with resistance in various forms. Worker protests and trade union action in Egypt, Morocco, Tunisia, Turkey, and elsewhere showed fierce opposition to the "structural adjustments" and "labor market reforms" (Hakimian & Moshaver, 2001; Harik & Sullivan, 1992; Pripstein-Posusney, 2006). At the same time, the women's movement began to grow in the region, and demands were raised for greater participation and rights (Moghadam, 1998, 2003). Governments pressed ahead, however, embracing the neoliberal agenda of the globalizers in the West.

Regional experts have examined the weaknesses of the region in meeting the imperatives of globalization and attracting foreign direct investment, or they have highlighted the adverse social effects of the economic restructuring that was completed by the turn of the new century. A consensus among MENA specialists at the turn of the new century was that the region had not been able to cash in on opportunities for investment and trade and was one of the least integrated regions (CAWTAR, 2001; Springborg & Henry, 2001; World Bank, 2003). Reasons included the closed political and economic nature of many of the regimes, along with the continued centrality of oil in the economies and exports of many countries of the region. Despite years of attempted diversification, those countries with substantial

oil reserves (e.g., large countries like Algeria and Iran) had remained dependent on oil exports for foreign exchange earnings. With a few exceptions,
modern manufactured goods and services—not to mention high-tech sectors—had not developed fully for export. According to the World Bank,
large hydrocarbon exports were accompanied by high and increasing product
concentration, loss of export dynamism in non-fuel exports, and little participation in global production sharing (World Bank, 2003). Nonetheless,
and in line with changes elsewhere in the world economy, MENA governments adopted World Bank and International Monetary Fund recommendations for liberalization, de-nationalization, and privatization, and revisions of
labor codes to allow more "flexibility" in labor markets. The social effects
were predictable: By the late 1990s, precarious forms of work were expanding, unemployment rates were extraordinarily high, and inequalities were
growing (El-Ghonemy, 1998; ESCWA, 2008).

The MENA region encountered the age of globalization, and especially the new global trade regime, with some distinct disadvantages. The
region's political volatility and its lack of stable and transparent institutions
made it a risky environment for investment. Despite high unemployment in
the MENA region, high school graduates continued to expect office work,
whereas those with bachelor's degrees typically did not all have the fluency
in another language required for work in international NGOs or the international business sector. (This was not necessarily the case in the Maghreb,
where French as well as Arabic is used in universities.) In particular, the
region lacked the kind of educated female labor force willing to work—or
be exploited—in factories and services that made countries such as China,
Vietnam, Malaysia, and India attractive to foreign investment. Despite state
investments in the education sector over several decades, which had led to
dramatic increases in literacy, educational attainment rates in the MENA
region were relatively low and the quality of schooling was deteriorating. To
be sure, gender gaps in literacy and educational attainment were narrowing
and school enrolments were increasing, but the benefits of this progress
would not be felt for some time. As noted by Karshenas and Moghadam
(2006): "Indeed, it is in the area of education that the handicaps of social
development in the MENA region are most prominent, and where the main
disjuncture between social and economic development is most pronounced"
(p. 10). The authors concluded that both the educational deficits and female
marginalization from paid employment had rendered MENA countries either
vulnerable to the vagaries of economic globalization or too weak to influence its direction.[3]

Quite apart from the effects of conflicts in the MENA region, governments have contributed to economic stagnation through continued policies of privatization and flexibilization in the absence of robust domestic

or foreign investments. This has led to worker protests, strikes, and demonstrations in Egypt and Iran (Beinen, 2008, 2010; Mather, 2010), policy papers calling for alternative development strategies (ESCWA, 2008; UNDP, 2009), and women's movements demanding greater participation and rights. Economic difficulties were behind the nonviolent protests that led to the collapse of governments in Tunisia and Egypt in early 2011.

In the authoritarian countries of the MENA region, unions have not been historically strong or independent, although there have been times in different countries where unions have been vocal and visible. On some occasions, they have valiantly tackled the state's economic policies (e.g., protests against structural adjustments in North Africa in the 1980s), but on the whole they have been largely masculine and masculinist bodies without strong female representation, participation, or influence. In recent years, however, one notices some movement toward collaboration around the agenda of rights-based development involving women's organizations and trade unions in Algeria, Morocco, and Tunisia. And in the Islamic Republic of Iran, widespread grievances over political repression, social restrictions, and economic injustices have led to a confluence of women's, workers', and youth demands for democratic participation and rights.[4] It would appear, therefore, that the contradictions of globalization have fueled collective action in some countries, offering possibilities for the renegotiation of social and gender contracts between the state and civil society groups.

What would a new agenda for women's social and economic rights entail, and not only for the Middle East? A necessary condition for the enjoyment of economic citizenship is the right to work and to earn an income; other requirements are access to productive employment, including decent wages, equal pay for equal work, and social insurance.[5] These are important for men as well as women, but as noted, women also require such social rights as paid maternity leave and quality child-care facilities. Paid paternity leave should be part of the list, too, as it would encourage fathers to take part in child care and elder care, help transform the sexual division of labor, and facilitate work–family balance. Other social/economic rights for working women include vocational training, skills upgrading, opportunities for advancement, and prohibition of discrimination and sexual harassment. Thus:

- the right to gainful employment without the need to obtain a husband or male relative's consent;

- to own, acquire, manage, and retain property brought into marriage and to control one's own income from gainful employment;

- to obtain a passport and travel abroad without permission of husband or male relative's consent;

- the right to equal inheritance;

- to confer citizenship to children or a husband;

- the freedom to choose a residence/domicile;

- to participate in social, cultural, and community activities;

- the right to an education, including adult education and vocational training;

- the right to health care and a healthy work environment;

- equal pay for equal work, and non-discrimination by employer;

- equality in hiring and promotion and in social security;

- the right to be free from sexual harassment in the workplace; and

- paid maternity leave and affordable quality child care.

How do MENA countries fare in the adoption of standards and norms pertaining to the social/economic rights of citizenship? Table 2.1 presents a listing of some of the relevant international legislation, along with the years of ratification, of a number of MENA countries. Of the five countries listed, all but Iran have signed CEDAW, albeit with reservations; only Morocco recently signed the ILO convention on maternity protection. Many of the rights listed here and in the international conventions identified in the table are enjoyed by a relatively small proportion of the female working population, especially in developing countries. (In the United States, not all working people are able to enjoy guaranteed health care and there is no national legislation on paid maternity leave.) Domestic workers, agricultural workers, informal workers, migrant workers, and many workers in the small- and medium-sized business sector are deprived of social rights and protection. In some cases, women factory workers may be fired for becoming pregnant; or their paid maternity leave is extremely limited; or they endure forms of harassment and violence from male colleagues. In other cases, women may not be permitted to work in certain occupations; or they endure degrading treatment as migrant workers; or they receive no formal compensation or recognition as unpaid family workers and care providers. In some cultural contexts, women do not have property rights or have unequal rights to inheritance; and they may be denied adequate credits and loans to start their own businesses. In many developing countries, labor laws are weakly enforced, but especially so for women workers. And in many Muslim-majority countries, an institutional barrier to women's economic citizenship takes the form of Family Law, sometimes known as the personal status code.

Table 2.1. International Conventions on Women's Social/Economic Rights, Year of Ratification, Selected MENA Countries

Convention	Algeria	Morocco	Tunisia	Egypt	Jordan	Iran
Convention on the Elimination of All Forms of Discrimination Against Women (CEDAW), 1979 (with or without reservations)	1996	1993	1985	1981	1992	
Optional Protocol, 1999	1996		1996			
Beijing Declaration and Platform for Action, 1995 (adopted)	Adopted[a]	Adopted[a]	Adopted[a]	Adopted[a]	Adopted[a]	Adopted[a]
International Covenant on Economic, Social and Cultural Rights (ICESCR), 1966	1989[a]	1979	1969	1982	1975	1975
International Covenant on Civil and Political Rights (ICCPR), 1966	1989	1979	1969	1982	1975	1975
International Convention on the Protection of the Rights of Migrant Workers and Their Families, 1990	2005	2003		1993		
UNESCO Convention: Discrimination in education, 1960	1968	1968	1969	1962	1976	1968
ILO Convention 111: Discrimination in employment/occupation, 1958	1969	1963	1959	1960	1963	1964
ILO Convention 100: Equal remuneration for men and women for equal work, 1951	1962	1979	1968	1960	1966	1972
ILO Convention 87 & 98: Freedom of association and right to organize, 1948	1962		1957	1957, 1954	1968	
ILO Convention 182: Worst Forms of Child Labor	2001	2001	2000	2002	2000	2002
ILO Convention 183: Maternity protection, 2000		2011				

[a]Made general and interpretative statements or expressed reservations.

MUSLIM FAMILY LAW AND WOMEN'S ECONOMIC CITIZENSHIP

The extent of social rights enjoyed by citizens is dependent upon a country's wealth and the nature of the state. In the MENA region, social rights, as well as women's rights, have been most extensive in Tunisia. They are least available in Yemen, one of the poorest MENA countries. But even the social rights in the region are in need of reform, as educational systems are under severe strain, and social insurance/protection is not available to all citizens. Moreover, women in some MENA countries lack certain basic rights, including the "right to an occupation of one's choice," a key civil right that is a necessary condition for economic citizenship. The absence of this right is rooted in Islamic law, which privileges men and places women under the protection (or control) of male kin.

As in other parts of the world, MENA women's formal rights of citizenship are based on two pillars: (a) international treaties and norms, and (b) national legislation, including constitutions, family laws, and labor laws. As seen in Table 2.1, governments have signed a number of key international instruments pertaining to women's participation and rights. However, such instruments often are weakly enforced, or they are rendered moot by virtue of their conflict with some national legislation. The UN's CEDAW has been signed by many of the region's governments, but with reservations that pertain to areas of disagreement between Sharia law and CEDAW.[6] In most cases, the disagreements focus on women's roles within the family, including equal access to inheritance.

In many MENA countries (notable exceptions are Iran and Saudi Arabia), the constitution gives women and men alike the right to work, and the labor laws themselves do not discriminate explicitly against women. Indeed, they tend to stipulate that women should receive equal compensation for equal work; they offer maternity leave benefits; and they protect women against job termination in case of marriage and pregnancy. But the benefits granted by the labor laws often are unattainable, because they are weakly enforced and because women frequently lack recourse to justice. What is more, some labor regulations end up indirectly discriminating against women—and in turn their families—through conditions set on nonwage employment benefits. For example, tax- and employment-related benefits to families are channeled only through men. A woman can receive such benefits only if she is officially the head of the household (if she is widowed or proves that her husband is old or incapacitated). This differential treatment effectively reduces a woman's compensation even when she holds the same kind of job as a man (Chamlou, 2007).

Domestic legal frameworks can be inconsistent in MENA countries, with contradictory provisions pertaining to the status of women across constitutions, family laws, labor laws, and social security policies. In Algeria and Egypt, the equality clauses of their constitutions and the labor laws that signify women as workers with certain rights are contradicted by the Sharia-based family laws that place women under the authority of male kin and deny women equal access to family wealth.[7]

Perhaps most disconcertingly, Marshall's "right to work at an occupation of one's choice," a key civil right that Kessler-Harris has defined as central to women's search for equity and economic citizenship—is not present in all countries. For example, in the Islamic Republic of Iran, the labor law specifically states that a woman cannot be a judge, and the constitution stipulates that women's rights are subject to "Islamic criteria." In Saudi Arabia, the legal frameworks do not give women the unqualified right to work, and women do not even have the right to drive. In the Gulf states, migrant women from across Asia are brought in to fill occupations and professions that local women cannot: nannies, nurses, and restaurant and hotel employees. What the laboring classes of Europe and America won in the transition from feudalism to capitalism and in the process of modernity—the right to move, to exchange their labor for a wage, and to freely seek an occupation—has yet to be won by all women in the MENA region.

Muslim Family Law is a social policy intended to regulate family life according to the norms of the Sharia, or Islamic law. It also is a key element of the state's gender policy. Family Law is meant to ensure the rights and responsibilities of family members, especially those of the head of the family; and it aims to guarantee security to the wife in the event of divorce or widowhood. The content of Family Law varies across countries Muslim countries, depending on the particular school of Islamic jurisprudence in place, and depending also on the nature of the state and social structure (Charrad, 2001). Hence, the enormous gulf in the legal status and social rights of women in, for example, Tunisia compared with Saudi Arabia.

In its ideal-typical form, the broad features of Muslim Family Law are the following. The highly formal Islamic marriage contract requires the consent of the wife, and in some countries women may insert stipulations into the contract, such as the condition that she be entitled to a divorce if her husband takes a second wife without her consent (An-Naim, 2002). Marriage, however, remains largely an agreement between two families rather than two individuals with equal rights and obligations. Moreover, marriage gives the husband the right of access to his wife's body, marital rape is not recognized, and a wife is required to obey her husband (Shehadeh, 1998; Welchman, 2004). Obedience is in return for maintenance and for the *mahr*, or dower, provided or promised by the groom to the bride when the marriage is contracted and is stipulated in the marriage contract. Typically, the *mahr* is deferred until divorce or widowhood.

Under Muslim Family Law, children acquire citizenship and religious status through their fathers, not their mothers. Muslim women are not permitted to marry non-Muslim men. Women have the right to own and dispose of property, but they inherit less property than men do. Non-Muslim widows cannot inherit from Muslim husbands. Muslim Family Law—like Sharia law in general, from which it is derived—distinguishes principally between women and men and between Muslims and non-Muslims. Men have more rights than women, and Muslims more than non-Muslims. The principle of patrilineality underlies the provisions of Muslim Family Law that give men legal guardianship over their children and custody in the case of divorce. It also explains why Muslim men may marry non-Muslim women (because they confer their nationality and religion on their children), whereas Muslim women may not marry non-Muslim men. Even so, interfaith marriages are difficult in the Middle East, and usually the non-Muslim wife is the one who converts.

Patrilineality, which confers privileges to male kin, is hardly unique to Islam or Muslim cultures; in the West, modernity, feminist movements, and legal reform have eroded it. Challenges may be observed in MENA, too, but there is much resistance to changing what is believed to be a divinely mandated set of laws and norms. Thus, it remains in force in many countries, even in those countries that have signed international legislation such as CEDAW. The result is that CEDAW is reduced to a mere formality.

The Iranian Nobel laureate Shirin Ebadi—who is a veteran lawyer and served as a judge prior to the Islamic revolution—often has pointed out the injustice and absurdity of a legal system whereby her testimony in court would count only if supplemented by that of one other woman, whereas the testimony of a man, even if illiterate, would stand alone. But Family Law also has implications for women's socioeconomic participation and rights. Together with the region's political economy (oil revenues and the rentier state), Muslim Family Law may be a major contributing factor behind women's relatively low levels of labor force participation, employment, and earned income—thus an obstacle to women's social and economic rights.

Provisions regarding obedience, maintenance, and inheritance presume that wives are economic dependents, thus perpetuating what I have called the "patriarchal gender contract" (Moghadam, 1998). For example, in most MENA countries, women are required to obtain the permission of father, husband, or other male guardian to undertake travel, including business travel. In Iran and Jordan, a husband has the legal right to forbid his wife (or unmarried daughter) to seek employment or continue in a job. Although wives—at least those who are educated and politically aware—may stipulate in their marriage contract the condition that they are allowed to work, many wives make no such stipulations, and courts have been known to side with the husband when the issue is contested (see, e.g., Sonbol, 2003). In this respect, both national (constitutions and labor laws) and international laws (the ICESCR, CEDAW, and the Beijing Platform for Action) are contravened.

The unequal inheritance aspect of Muslim Family Law compromises women's economic independence but is a sensitive issue; it is seen on one level as a divine imperative revealed in the Qur'an and on another level as an important part of the patriarchal gender contract whereby women are provided for by their fathers, husbands, or brothers. Sons inherit twice as much as daughters, but they are also expected to look after their parents in old age. Polygamy is not practiced widely in MENA, but it does occur, along with divorce. A deceased man's inheritance and his pension are divided among his widows, children, and other relatives that he may have been supporting. As a result, many widows receive insignificant pensions. Sonbol (2003) reports that this is recognized to be a problem in Jordan. The situation is exacerbated in a country like Egypt where, as recently as 2000, more than 50% of the female population did not hold an identity card—which is required to apply for a pension or social assistance, to withdraw savings from a bank account, or to sue for land ownership. Hence, "poverty is more often found among unmarried, divorced, widowed and abandoned women than in any other social group" (Loewe, 2000, p. 3). Even though Islamic norms and some laws require that fathers and husbands financially support their daughters and wives, it is also the case that divorced, widowed, or abandoned women without access to jobs or a steady source of income, especially among the low-income social groups, often are left in a state of impoverishment. Indeed, for low-income women, being divorced can mean loss of children and home, and a life of destitution.

Muslim Family Law may be seen not only as a premodern or pre-feminist code for the regulation of family relations, but also as a way of retaining family support systems in the place of a fully functioning welfare state predicated on concepts of citizen contributions and entitlements. The welfare of wives and children remains the responsibility of the father/husband. When a woman seeks a divorce or is divorced, her maintenance comes not in the form of any transfers from the state, and even less in the form of employment-generating policies for women, but in the form of the mahr that is owed to her by her husband, or (in the Islamic Republic of Iran) the ujrat-ul-methl, which is the monetary value of the domestic work she has performed for her husband over the years (Hoodfar, 2000).

Family Law reform has gained urgency because of the aspirations of increasingly educated and employed MENA women who have formed the movements, organizations, and campaigns calling for the reform. The issue is framed in at least three ways. One argument is that existing family laws are in stark contradiction to the international human rights instruments that the MENA governments have signed, as well as to the discourses and objectives of the UN's global women's rights agenda. The "Islamic feminist" frame is that the laws actually contravene the ethical, egalitarian, and emancipatory spirit of Islam. Finally, in a kind of sociological argument, women activists point to Family Law's divergence from the social realities and actual family dynamics, whereby women must seek work to augment the family budget and are increasingly looking after their elderly parents. These arguments are made by women's rights groups throughout the region, but most notably by the North Africa-based Collectif 95 Maghreb-Egalité and by the One Million Signatures Campaign in the Islamic Republic of Iran (Moghadam & Gheytanchi, 2010).[8]

For example, until relatively recently, there were few employment opportunities for working-class women in oil-rich Algeria compared with Morocco, where export-oriented manufacturing work expanded in the 1980s and 1990s and created a demand for female labor. Evidence from unemployment statistics and small surveys, however, suggests a growing pool of job-seeking women in Algeria. In the new century, one effect of high male unemployment and out-migration is that more Algerian women have been seeking jobs to augment household incomes, and they are now seen in nontraditional occupations. In the span of a decade, Algerian women's labor-force participation rate doubled to about 20%. An advocacy manual produced by the Collectif 95 Maghreb-Egalité notes the increasing rates of female employment while also asserting that more women in the region are assuming responsibility for elder care and other family care.[9] Indeed, for the MENA region as a whole, liberalization seems to have triggered an increase in female labor-force participation, in both formal and informal activities. It is this reality that Muslim Family Law ignores.

At present, none of the family laws are gender-egalitarian, although Tunisia's—first promulgated in 1956—comes closest, especially with the amendments of the 1990s. But there has been some progress. Egypt's Family Law now allows women to seek a *khul* divorce, an option not available to them previously, and since 2000 wives no longer require the written permission of their husbands to travel or obtain passports. In 2003–2004, the reform of Morocco's *mudawanna*, among the most conservative in the Muslim world, was the result of a 10-year-long campaign on the part of women's rights organizations, along with a change in government and the support of the king (Sadiqi & Ennaji, 2006).

In her study of "the search for gender equity" in the United States, Kessler-Harris showed how women were seen as economic dependents and tied to family roles until well into the 20th century. Similarly, MENA women's association with family roles remains codified in outdated family laws—which, however, are contested by a growing array of women's organizations.

ADVOCACY AND ACTIVISM FOR SOCIAL RIGHTS

In order to accomplish their goals of full citizenship rights for women—including social rights and economic citizenship—women's groups have engaged in collective action, often in partnership with other civil society groups and with international NGOs and transnational advocacy networks. Collective action has taken the form of public protests; lobbying, advocacy and awareness-raising; and coalition-building with unions, political parties, or human rights organizations. In some instances, as in the case of the Moroccan family law reform, alliances between women's groups and allies within government result in effective policymaking. Activism also takes place transnationally, for example, in the form of the well-known Collectif 95 Maghreb-Egalité, which was formed in the run-up to the Beijing Conference and continues to be active and visible. Members of the Collectif have taken part in activities of the Marche Mondiale des Femmes, a transnational initiative of Québecoise feminists against poverty and violence, and in transnational feminist networks such as the Women's Learning Partnership (Moghadam, 2005a, 2009). Likewise, Iran's One Million Signatures Campaign has drawn heavily on its transnational links via the Internet, especially in a context of growing state repression and the hostility of the authorities toward feminist activism. Such mobilizations are the result of the global diffusion of the UN-sponsored women's rights agenda, coupled with the expansion of a population of educated and employed women in MENA with social, economic, and political concerns.

Efforts to enhance women's social rights and economic citizenship are found throughout the region. In Egypt, a concerted campaign against sexual harassment has been launched by the Egyptian Center for Women's Rights.[10] In Jordan, women's rights lawyer Asma Khader and her organization are advocating for the concept of marital property to be shared and divided in the event of divorce. At present a woman can insert such a stipulation in her marriage contract, but lower-income women in particular are at a disadvantage in this regard. In Turkey, one women's rights group has helped to form a regional cooperatives network to empower rural women. In Morocco, women of the rural Soulaliyates ethnic community won the right to benefit from collective lands. In Bahrain, women's groups have called for a new law eliminating fees for health and education services for non-nationals. Another advocacy campaign pertains to the gender impact of trade; with the end of the Multifibre Agreement, about 3,000 women, mostly from minority groups who had been working in the world factories, lost their livelihoods. In Lebanon, a feminist group has launched an economic rights project, with a focus on the 40 women-led cooperatives in the male-dominated agri-processing sector. (Of the roughly 1,000 cooperatives, only about 40 are women's cooperatives.) By conducting leadership training workshops, the organization helped the women's cooperatives make their own case for support and rights. As explained by Lina Abou-Habib: "They are gaining confidence and assertiveness. Some of the women subsequently ran in the municipal elections or otherwise became involved in them."[11]

In North Africa, women's rights groups have worked with human rights organizations and trade unions to push for reform, raise public awareness, and build institutions. The various *centres d'écoutes*—counseling centers or shelters for women victims of domestic violence or workplace sexual harassment—are products of feminist activism that entail collaboration with other local actors as well as with international donors. The first centre d'écoute was established by Tunisia's Femmes Démocrates a feminist group that also lobbied successfully for an anti-sexual harassment law in 2004. In Algeria, le Centre d'Ecoute et d'Assistance aux Femmes Victimes d'Harcelement Sexuel is housed at the UGTA and financed by the trade union. The center was born following a consciousness-raising campaign of the National Commission of the Women Workers and of human rights groups, and in December 2003 the center's Soumia Salhi also started a hotline for women victims of sexual harassment.[12] The work of the union and the women's commission resulted in the government's adoption of a new policy against sexual harassment. In October 2004, the National Popular Assembly adopted an amendment to article 341 of the Algerian penal code. This amendment, which condemns men guilty of sexual harassment to a prison sentence, was introduced in the penal code at the initiative of the National Commission of Women Workers and the Algerian League of Human Rights. One labor and women's rights activist, Souad Charid, has said that the law against workplace sexual harassment and the establishment of the centre d'écoute was a major victory.[13]

Morocco's labor law now reinforces the principle of nondiscrimination against women, improves maternity rights, and recognizes women's right to unionize. It gives men and women equal rights in the workplace and prohibits discrimination against women in the workplace. In general it grants rights to male and female workers and provides for specific rights for women. The labor law recognizes workplace sexual harassment at work as a serious offence with compensation for the victim by the employer. It is also a criminal offence under Article 503-1 of the revised 2003 Penal Code. Given the high incidence of sexual harassment of women workers publicized by feminist groups in the 1990s (Moghadam, 1998), the new anti-harassment legislation is regarded as an achievement of women's economic citizenship as well as their human dignity. Various articles of the labor law stipulate the following:[14]

- Equality of treatment between women and men.

- Women's rights to sign a contract without the agreement of a male guardian.

- Women's rights to unionize and participate in collective bargaining without discrimination. (Article 9)

- The right to 14 weeks of paid maternity leave. (Article 152)

- Guaranteed employment during maternity leave. (Article 159)

- The right to a 1-hour nursing break for 12 months after childbirth. (Article 160)

- Access to a breastfeeding room in the firm. (Article 162)

- The right to special conditions and protection in night work. (Article 172).

Legal and policy reforms certainly are taking place in the region, but they are occurring in an untoward economic context. In Algeria, for example, unemployment insurance and antidiscrimination legislation have been introduced, along with laws against sexual harassment in the workplace; but irregular forms of labor, low wages, and the absence of a national policy on paid maternity leave serve to undermine women's social rights and economic citizenship. Algeria, Morocco, and Tunisia have signed a number of key ILO conventions, but they have not yet signed Convention 183 on Maternity Protection (see Table 2.1). Other issues that need to be addressed include women's participation and rights in local governance; the rights of women migrants to decent work conditions and wages; the place of agricultural labor, domestic labor, and informal labor in labor law; enforcing laws against child labor; and social security reform for equality of access for women.

CONCLUSIONS

Neoliberal globalization has been accompanied by widening inequalities, rising unemployment, and deteriorating labor conditions. Paradoxically, globalization also has offered opportunities for collective action at both national and transnational levels. It is, therefore, an historical irony that just as neoliberal globalization has undermined the welfare state and the development state, feminist organizations have emerged to call for an extension of women's civil, political, and social/economic rights of citizenship. Working women across the globe are engaged in various forms of collective action to defend and extend their social rights of citizenship, to advance economic participation and rights, to harmonize work life and family life, to gain recognition for reproductive labor, and to take part in economic decision making.

In the MENA region, the era of globalization has seen economic liberalization, Islamization, and demands for women's participation and rights emerging in tandem and often in conflict with each other. As a result, the protection or expansion of women's social/economic rights confronts at least two barriers: aspects of neoliberal globalization and in particular the growth of precarious employment with little or no social protection; and the persistence of a gender ideology that has rendered women marginal in trade unions, government bodies, and other influential societal organizations, as well as subject to restrictions under Family Law (Moghadam, 2005b). Women's collective action, therefore, has centered on the expansion of women's organizations (e.g., feminist networks, cooperatives, businesswomen's associations, various NGOs, and women's policy agencies) that engage in advocacy, lobbying, and coalition-building to enhance women's participation and rights. In many countries, calls for legal and policy reform center on both family law and labor legislation, and to achieve these goals, women's organizations have built coalitions with trade unions and human rights groups, and sometimes with sympathetic government agencies and officials.

On March 8, 2011, ITUC secretary-general Sharan Burrow visited Tunis to help celebrate International Women's Day and to launch a new network of women trade unionists in 8 MENA countries. Such an initiative, with its emphasis on women's trade union leadership, is a promising start for women's economic citizenship, but this chapter's concerns about family law also will need to be addressed. Male privilege in inheritance is anachronistic in the 21st century, given contemporary norms of gender equality as well as the reality of women's labor-force participation and care for family members.[15] Therefore, barriers to women's right to seek gainful employment without permission of a male kin must be removed. National laws and social policies should be more consistent with the international laws and global social policies that governments have formally adopted, and the gaps between formal and substantive rights should be removed. The ICESCR should become a reality, not mere words on paper. Governments should adopt the ILO's convention 183 on maternity protection and make their own national policies more generous in order to encourage women's social participation and ultimately enhance their economic citizenship. In a context of extensive labor migration, governments need to be mindful of the rights of both their citizens working abroad and foreign migrant workers in their own countries.

The current model of neoliberal economic relations is of course a structural barrier to the enhancement of social rights and the realization of economic citizenship. Ultimately, change will come about because governments respond to the demands of social movements and civil society organizations, whether at the national or transnational levels. Partnerships across civil society organizations, and especially between women's rights organizations and trade unions, can create a powerful constituency for the implementation of a rights-based development and social policy agenda.

NOTES

1. Promoted by the UN system, the global women's rights agenda takes the form of conventions and declarations such as the Convention on the Elimination of All Forms of Discrimination against Women (1979); the Beijing Declaration and Platform for Action (1995); the Millennium Declaration and Goal 3 of the 8 Millennium Development Goals (2000); Security Council Resolution 1325 on women, peace and security (2000); and such ILO conventions and recommendations as those on nondiscrimination in employment, equal remuneration for women and men, and maternity leave. For more information on the ILO's Bureau for Gender Equality activities, see www.ilo.org/gender. For the ILO database of international labor standards, see http://www.ilo.org/ilolex/english/convdisp2.htm; http://www.ilo.org/ilolex/english/profileframeE.htm

2. The MENA region includes the Arab countries, Iran, and Turkey. Geographically, Israel is part of the Middle East, but it is designated a part of Europe in intergovernmental organizations. In any event, this chapter is concerned with the Muslim-majority countries of the region, which share the features of authoritarian, rentier states; oil-based economies; relatively low female labor force participation; and Muslim family law.

3. The Gulf states—Qatar and the United Arab Emirates in particular—were exceptions, as they became the most globalized in the region. High levels of immigrant labor; petrodollar investments in construction, retail, banking, education, and tourism; the expansion of Arabic-language media—all were indicators of the Gulf countries' integration in and contribution to globalization processes. Elsewhere, the growth of multinational telecommunications enterprises—such as the Egypt-based Orascom holding group—indicated MENA involvement in globalization. Still, for better or for worse, the region was less integrated in the global economy than were Latin America and East and Southeast Asia.

4. As described by Mather (2010), four working-class organizations—the Syndicate of Vahed Bus Workers, the Haft Tappeh sugar cane grouping, the Electricity and Metal Workers Council in Kermanshah, and the Independent Free Union—published a joint statement declaring support for the Green Protests of June–July 2009 and identifying what they called the minimum demands of the working class: an end to executions, release of imprisoned activists, freedom of the press and media, the right to set up workers' organizations, job security, abolition of all misogynist

legislation, declaration of May 1 as a public holiday, and expulsion from workplaces of state-run organizations. Additionally, Tehran's bus workers issued a call for civil disobedience to protest the continued imprisonment of independent trade unionist Mansour Osanloo. This exemplifies the convergence of social movement and civil society demands in Iran, notably those of feminists and trade unionists.

5. Many scholar-activists, particularly those in and around the Global Justice Movement and the World Social Forum, would argue for workplace democracy as an essential element of economic citizenship and social justice. I concur; ultimately, systemic change is needed, but in the meantime, measures such as those delineated in this chapter not only would remove the structural and institutional barriers to women's economic citizenship, but they also would help bring about broader societal transformations.

6. For an examination of the CEDAW treaty, see http:/www.un.org/womenwatch/daw/cedaw/.

7. Some countries have a separate family code (e.g., North Africa, Lebanon), whereas others include provisions on the family within their civil codes (e.g., Egypt, Iran). In contrast, Saudi Arabia bases its entire legal framework—notably, its constitution, family law, and penal code—on the most conservative and patriarchal interpretation of Sharia law.

8. See Collectif Maghreb Egalité 95 (2005) and the Website of the One Million Signatures Campaign: http://www.change4equality.com/english/

9. Collectif Maghreb Egalité 95 (2005). On Algerian women's conditions, see Slackman (2007).

10. See their newsletters and press releases on www.ecwronline.org.

11. The information above comes from a meeting of the transnational partners of the Women's Learning Partnership, and interviews by the author with individual partners, in Jakarta, Indonesia, April 10–14 2010. See also http://www.learningpartnership.org/en

12. The Collectif 95 Maghreb-Egalité had conducted a survey on violence against women, and its disturbing findings publicized. Algerian President Bouteflika referred to the survey in his International Women's Day address of 2002.

13. See her interview at http://www.categorynet.com/v2/index.php/content/view/4518/400. Retrieved February 12, 2007.

14. http://www.tanmia.ma/IMG/pdf/Brochure_Campagne_1_.pdf. Retrieved February 2007. See also Women's Learning Partnership, "Morocco adopts landmark family law supporting women's equality." Available online at http://www.learning-partnership.org/en/node/587

15. Such enhancements of women's citizenship were stressed at a roundtable on the Arab spring held at UNESCO in Paris on June 21, 2011. Lawyer and Maghreb 95 director Alya Chérif Chammari and professor Latifa Lakhdar, vice-president of the transitional monitoring association l'*Haute instance pour la realisation des objectifs de la revolution, de la réforme politique et de la transition démocratique*, called for not only the defense of existing women's rights in Tunisia but further advancements such as equal inheritance and parity in political decision making. (Author observations and notes.)

REFERENCES

An-Naim, A. (2001). *Muslim Family Law: A sourcebook*. London: Zed Books.

Beinin, J. (2008). Underbelly of Egypt's neoliberal agenda. *Middle East Report On-line*, April 18, 2008, http://www.merip.org/mero/mero.html (accessed December 2008).

Beinin, J. (2010). *The struggle for worker rights in Egypt*. Washington, DC: Solidarity Center.

CAWTAR. (2001). *Globalization and Arab women's economic participation*. Tunis and New York: CAWTAR & UNDP.

CAWTAR. (2006). *Gender impacts of trade liberalization in the MENA region*. Tunis: Author.

CAWTAR & World Bank. (2007). *Women entrepreneurs in MENA: characteristics, contributions and challenges*. Tunis: CAWTAR & IFC.

Chamlou, N. (2007, May). *Gender, development, and the law in the Middle East and North Africa*. Paper presented at the Kelly Day Conference, Rice University, Houston, TX.

Charrad, M. (2001). *States and women's rights: The making of postcolonial Tunisia, Algeria, and Morocco*. Berkeley: University of California Press.

Collectif Maghreb Egalité 95. (2005). *Guide to equality in the family and in the Maghreb*. Bethesda, MD: Women's Learning Partnership for Rights, Development, and Peace.

El-Ghonemy, M.R. (1998). *Affluence and poverty in the Middle East*. London: Routledge.

ESCWA. (2008). *2007–2008 survey for economic and social development in the ESCWA region*. Beirut & New York: United Nations.

Hakimian, H., & Moshaver, Z. (Eds.). (2001). *The state and global change: The political economy of transition in the Middle East and North Africa*. Surrey, UK: Curzon Press.

Harik, I., & Sullivan, D. (Eds.). (1992). *Privatization and liberalization in the Middle East*. Bloomington: Indiana University Press.

Hoodfar, H. (2000). Iranian women at the intersectionality of citizenship and the family code: The perils of "Islamic criteria." In S. Joseph (Ed.), *Gender and citizenship in the Middle East* (pp. 287–312). Syracuse, NY: Syracuse University Press.

Joseph, S. (Ed.). (2000. *Gender and citizenship in the Middle East*. Syracuse, NY: Syracuse University Press.

Karshenas, M., & Moghadam, V.M. (Eds.). (2006). *Social policy in the Middle East: Economic, political, and gender dynamics*. Basingstoke, New York, & Geneva: Palgrave Macmillan & UNRISD.

Kessler-Harris, A. (2001). *In pursuit of equity: Women, men, and the quest for economic citizenship in 20th century America*. New York: Oxford University Press.

Kessler-Harris, A. (2003). In pursuit of economic citizenship. *Social Politics, 10*(2), 157–175.

Lister, R. 1(997). *Citizenship: Feminist perspectives*. London: Macmillan.

Loewe, M. (2000, October). *Social security in Egypt: An analysis and agenda for policy reform*. Background paper presented at the seventh annual conference of the ERF, Amman, Jordan.

Marshall, T.H. (1964). *Citizenship and social class*. Cambridge, UK: Cambridge University Press.

Mather, Y. (2010). Iran: Reform and revolution. *New Politics, 13*(1), www.newpol.org/node/345..

Moghadam, V.M. (1995). A political economy of women's employment in the Arab region. In N. Khoury & V.M. Moghadam (Eds.), *Gender and national development* (pp. 6–34). London: Zed Books.

Moghadam, V.M. (1998). *Women, work, and economic reform in the Middle East and North Africa*. Boulder, CO: Lynne Rienner.

Moghadam, V.M. (2003). *Modernizing women: Gender and social change in the Middle East* (2nd ed.). Boulder, CO: Lynne Rienner.

Moghadam, V.M. (2005a). *Globalizing women: Transnational feminist networks*. Baltimore, MD: The Johns Hopkins University Press.

Moghadam, V.M. (2005b). Women's economic participation in the Middle East: What difference has the neoliberal policy turn made? *Journal of Middle East Women's Studies, 1*(1), 110–146.

Moghadam, V.M. (2006). Maternalist policies vs economic citizenship? Gendered social policy in Iran. In S. Razavi & S. Hassim (Eds.), *Gender and social policy in a global context: Uncovering the gendered structure of "the Social"* (pp. 87–108). Basingstoke & Geneva: Palgrave Macmillan & UNRISD.

Moghadam, V.M.,& Gheytanchi, E. (2010). Political opportunities and strategic choices: Comparing feminist campaigns in Morocco and Iran. *Mobilization, 15*(3), 467–488.

Naples, N., & Desai, M. (Eds.). (2002). *Women's activism and globalization*. London & New York: Routledge.

Pateman, C. (1988). *The sexual contract*. Palo Alto, CA: Stanford University Press.

Pripstein-Posusney, M. (2006). Globalization and labor protection in oil-poor Arab countries: Racing to the bottom? *Global Social Policy, 3*, 267–298.

Sadiqi, F., & Ennaji, M. (2006). Feminist activism and the family law: The gradual feminization of the public sphere in Morocco. *Journal of Middle East Women's Studies, 2*(2), 86–114.

Shehadeh, L. (1998). The legal status of married women in Lebanon. *International Journal of Middle East Studies, 30*(4), 501–519.

Slackman, M. (2007, May 26). A quiet revolution in Algeria: Gains by women. *New York Times*, p. A1.

Sonbol, A. al-A. (2003). *Women of Jordan: Islam, labor and the law*. Syracuse, NY: Syracuse University Press.

Springborg, R., & Henry, C. (2001). *Globalization and the politics of development in the Middle East*. Cambridge: Cambridge University Press.

UNDP. (2009). *Arab Human Development Report 2009: Challenges to human security in the Arab region*. New York: Author. http://hdr.undp.org/en/reports/regionalreports/arabstates/ahdr2009e.pdf.

Walby, S. (1994). Is citizenship gendered? *Sociology, 28*(2), 379–395.

Welchman, L (Ed.). (2004). *Women's rights and Islamic Family Law: Perspectives on reform*. London: Macmillan.

Women in Development Europe (WIDE). (1998). *Women's economic and social rights.* Brussels: Author.

Women in Development Europe (WIDE). (2007). *EU bilateral and regional free trade agreements: Bringing women to the centre of the debate.* (Report of a WIDE public consultation.) Brussels: Author.

World Bank. (2003). *Unlocking the employment potential in the Middle East and North Africa: Toward a new social contract.* Washington DC: Author.

Yuval-Davis, N. (1997). *Gender and nation.* London: Sage.

THREE

PROMOTING THE SOCIAL RIGHTS
OF WORKING WOMEN

The Case of Palestinian Women in Israel

Michal Schwartz

This chapter deals with the situation of Palestinian-Arab women, who are Israeli citizens, from the lower income groups: They are either nonprofessional workers or do not work at all. A class perspective is provided on the situation of Palestinian women in Israel, by examining the overwhelming majority of unskilled manual laborers, housewives, and young women who do not participate in the workforce. The chapter argues that the low participation of Palestinian-Arab women in the workforce (19.1) is the most telling indicator of their low economic, social, and personal status, and in its turn, reproduces it. It is a central reason for the poverty of the Palestinian-Arab population in Israel, and it increases isolationist and regressive trends as well.

Statistics comparing the status of Palestinian and Jewish women demonstrate the gap between Jewish women who live in a Western industrialized society and Palestinian women who live in a poor, undeveloped Third-World society (Mtanes, 2004a). All are citizens of the same country, and yet they exist in worlds apart. In comparison to the low economic participation rate of Palestinian women, almost 56.2% of Jewish Israeli women work (Natan, 2007a). The situation of Palestinian-Arab women in Israel is an extreme expression of the Israeli state policy of deliberate discrimination against the Arab population. Among other things, it prevents the realization of Palestinian women's social rights and economic citizenship.

In Israel, Palestinian women who are Israeli citizens are on the lowest rung of the social ladder. First, they belong to the Palestinian national minority, which the state discriminates against. Second, patriarchal norms and growing religious influence restrict their development and independence. Third, the neoliberal economic policies implemented in Israel during the past two decades have made them even more vulnerable and devoid of social protection.[1]

Some claim that the plight of Palestinian women is an outcome of their Islamic culture. Among those with higher education, however, the majority does work. Some 50% of female residents of mixed Jewish and Arab cities also work. This proves, in our view, that when decent job opportunities exist, Palestinian women do in fact work outside the home. On the other hand, hard, unorganized, and badly paid labor gives them little incentive to leave their homes. In recent years, the deepening poverty of Palestinian families has forced many of the women to seek unorganized work, where they fall prey to the anarchy of the labor market and the greed of subcontractors. Although employed, these women remain dependent and poor.

The entry of Palestinian women into the labor force on an organized basis is a precondition for their becoming a social force and changing traditional attitudes toward them. It also is a precondition for enabling the Palestinian citizens of Israel to climb out of their chronic poverty and achieve equality with Jewish Israelis. The right of Palestinian women to work outside their homes, to organize and unionize is vitally important in the struggle for equality between the two ethnic groups, and equality between the sexes. Without such a basis, attempts to empower these women will be limited and short-lived.

I am the coordinator of the women's commission of the Workers' Advice Center (WAC, known as MA'AN in Arabic), a trade union initiative aiming to defend and organize unorganized workers in Israel, both Arabs and Jews.[2] The main thrust of WAC's gender work is the struggle against poverty and for equal opportunities and full equality between Arab and Jewish women, and between men and women. WAC works with and for the impoverished majority of Palestinian women, who have no profession. This work has three complementary aspects. First, WAC strives to integrate Palestinian-Arab women in organized work, mainly in agriculture, and in trade union activities. Second, it helps develop the women workers' gender consciousness, with a view toward their empowerment. Third, WAC appeals to public opinion and lobbies the government to change its policies regarding the employment of Arab women.

The overall goals of WAC's gender work are to (a) overcome the chronic poverty among Arab families in Israel; (b) promote equal status for women in Arab society and enhance their economic citizenship in Israeli society; and (c) open job opportunities in agriculture for Arab women. As such, WAC strives to integrate Palestinian women into the labor market and to introduce them to the concept of a trade union. WAC also provides them with the classic gender activity of consciousness-raising and empowerment; and it introduces them to public activity in order to defend and advance their rights.

The decision to focus on women who hold manual unskilled jobs with little social prestige presents a challenge and our task as a whole faces major difficulties. First, there is a legacy of discrimination, fully admitted by the government. Moreover, since the late 1980s, the state has adopted neoliberal policies, by which private profit takes precedence over social development. Additionally, patriarchal village society prefers to keep the Arab woman within the confines of her village, where there are no jobs (Schwartz, 2007; Schwartz & Abgharieh-Zahalkha, 2008).

WAC operates within the context of the Israeli–Palestinian conflict and in a society ethnically divided into two basic groups: Jews and Arabs. Our approach is universal. Arabs and Jews work side by side in both organizations, united by a joint vision: to create a society where all humankind has access to equal rights and opportunities, with a particular emphasis on the rights of women and the right to a job—which is a key element of economic citizenship and the basis of social rights.

THE STATUS OF PALESTINIAN WOMEN IN ISRAEL

In September 2008, the Palestinian citizens of Israel numbered 1.12 million, 15.5% of the general population (not including East Jerusalem and the Golan Heights). Almost half are women (Government of Israel, 2008). As of 2001, 87% lived in 107 segregated, undeveloped communities, mainly villages, far from the economic centers of Israel. Only 8% lived in mixed Jewish and Arab cities. The rest (5%) lived in unrecognized villages (Haidar, 2005a). The status of women is differentiated by religion and other factors. Arguably, the worst situation is that of the Palestinian Bedouin women from the south and the residents of unrecognized villages (Muhammad, 2004).

The social status of Palestinians is beset by deep contradictions (Ghanem, 2005). On the one hand, Palestinian citizens of Israel enjoy formal democratic rights, such as the right to vote and form parties. In principle, they are the beneficiaries of the civil and political rights of citizenship. At the same time, Israel regards them suspiciously, as a potential fifth-column and a demographic threat to the Jewish majority. Among other things, this is illustrative of the gap between formal and substantive rights of citizenship, as is seen in the following section.

PALESTINIAN CITIZENS OF ISRAEL—
INSTITUTIONALIZED DISCRIMINATION

Discrimination against Palestinian citizens of Israel affects all aspects of life—the economy, education, housing, health, and legal and civil rights. Aziz Haidar (2005b) cites five expressions of economic discrimination: expropriation of property; nonallocation of funds for the encouragement of economic activities; no development of economic infrastructure; no professional training; and the Palestinians' lack of access to governmental decision making. Palestinians are Israel's poorest citizens. In 2006, their average annual per capita income was $7,700, whereas the average in Israel as a whole was $19,000 (Fares, cited in Nahmias, 2007). The share of the Palestinians in the domestic national product is only 4% of the total (Mtanes, 2004a). After the confiscation of most of their lands, Palestinian local authorities have jurisdiction over only 2.5% of the territory of Israel. No land has been allocated to them for industrial areas, public buildings, and trade centers (Haider, 2005a). This further narrows women's job opportunities because commuting to Jewish workplaces is not an option for most. Their role is confined to reproduction, and as such are marginalized from the sphere of production.

Palestinian women also lag behind in education. They have the highest illiteracy rate—14.7%—compared with 4.5% for Jewish women, and 6.2% for Palestinian men. According to an official 2005 report, fully 9.9% of Palestinian women did not attend school, a figure triple that of Jewish women. Just 32.7% of Palestinian women complied with university entrance requirements, compared with 52.5% of Jewish women, and 7.1% of Palestinian women have received a university education, compared with 19% of Jewish women (Tamir, 2007). Clearly, their social rights of citizenship are severely circumscribed (Working Group, 2005).

Israel's government ministries maintain no offices in Palestinian communities. In 2002, one Palestinian woman worked in the Ministry of Religious Affairs and one in the Ministry of Environment, whereas the Ministry of Industry and Trade employed two. None worked in the other ministries (Boulus, 2003). Whereas the state has created an impressive infrastructure of day-care centers and kindergartens that enables Jewish women to work, it has consistently neglected the Palestinian population, with the excuse that Palestinian women in any case stay at home.

Since the turn of the new century, and as a result of political pressure, the Israeli governments have taken dozens of decisions to develop the Arab community in aspects such as infrastructure, education, and employment. However, a report on the government's policy toward its Arab citizens reveals that the government did not implement most of these decisions, or did so very partially, while the decline in employment and education perpetuated the gaps (Haidar, 2005b). What is more, in May 2006, Israel's High Court of Justice denied an appeal against an amendment to the Citizenship and Entry Law, which denies the right of Israeli citizens who marry Palestinians from the Occupied Territories to reside with their spouses in Israel. Thus, the state denies these couples' rights to a family life. This law demonstrates Israeli democracy's double standard toward its Palestinian citizens, and the ways in which civil rights are limited.

THE PRESERVATION OF THE PATRIARCHAL FAMILY

Despite the modernization processes that the Palestinians in Israel have been undergoing, the patriarchal family (the *Hamula*) is still present, enhanced by both tradition and state policies. One expression of the patriarchal family is intermarriage. Among Palestinian women in Israel, fully 38.9% marry a relative from which 22.3% of them marry a first-degree cousin. In most of these cases, one can assume that the marriage is prearranged. Early marriage is common, and the phenomenon intensifies at times of economic recession; the median age at first marriage is 20.67 years for Palestinian women, compared with 24.8 for Palestinian men (Muhammad, 2004).

Among the Bedouin in southern Israel, polygamy is widespread. According to a 1999 survey, 40% of Palestinian Bedouin women were in a polygamous marriage. Domestic violence is widespread; 50% of married Palestinian women are physically abused at least once a year. So-called "honor killings" occur with some frequency. Women's groups recorded 66 cases of murder between 1992 and 1998. The courts tend to treat violence against family members less seriously (HRA, 2003).

Palestinian women have a higher fertility rate than Jewish women, and Palestinian families are generally larger (averaging 4.9 persons) than Jewish (3.1 persons). Whereas natural growth among Jewish families is 11.7 per 1,000, among the Palestinians it is much higher, varying according to religion: 34.2 for Muslims, 21.4 for Druze, and 18.4 for Christians (Haider 2005a). Differential access to women's education is one reason for these variations in the high fertility rates, but there are other reasons why large families still have such a hold on Palestinian women. One is the segregation in living locations. Unable to live where they please, Palestinian citizens cannot undergo a normal process of urbanization, which plays an important role in loosening the hold of the patriarchal family. They have to confine themselves to their own rural communities. Lacking state-supported infrastructure in the form of housing, a young Palestinian couple has no choice but to build an apartment on the family property, if there is any, often in the form of an additional storey, with little prospect of privacy. At times of unemployment or illness, the extended family replaces the indifferent state by offering shelter and childcare. In this way, discrimination by the state reinforces the patriarchal family. The state has an interest in doing so, because it is relatively easy for it to exercise political control through the head of the extended family (Hasan, 1999).

Officially, Palestinian women are entitled to inherit the family property. However, the family expects them to give their share of the inheritance to their brothers who, in return, monitor their sisters' fate after marriage. The brothers intervene in case of violence and provide them with shelter if they have to flee their homes (Hasan, 1999). Should a woman divorce, she does not have the economic means to rent a flat and live alone with her children, nor do social conventions approve this. Such a woman would become an outcast. Instead, she has to return to her parents, often becoming a burden and a source of shame. Battered women rarely seek refuge in a women's shelter for the same reasons. A woman who lives outside the community cannot be trusted, and contradicts the codes of the family honor.

No secular marriages are permitted in the State of Israel. Marriages are organized by the religious courts, which are male-biased. This perpetuates the separation between Jews, Muslims, and Christians and enhances the power of the patriarchal family. It is also a key limitation to the civil rights of citizens as understood in the framework of international standards and norms.[3]

The political representation of Palestinian women in Israel is negligible. In the entire history of elections to the Knesset (120 members), from 1950 to 2008, only twice was a Palestinian woman elected, both times in Israeli Zionist parties. No Arab party has ever placed a Palestinian woman in a realistic place on its list of Knesset candidates. Only four Palestinian women have ever been elected to local councils. In many cases, women cannot vote for the candidates they want. The larger family decides who will get their votes. In some cases, a senior family member collects their ID cards and votes in their name. Parties seeking the votes of the Palestinians cut deals with the patriarchal head of a clan in each village to secure a certain amount of votes *en bloc*. Although the ballot is secret, women usually are afraid to disobey. Villages are geographically divided by families. If someone does not vote as expected, the anomaly is noticed at once and conclusions may be drawn.

THE ECONOMIC SITUATION OF PALESTINIAN WOMEN:
THE IMPACT OF GLOBALIZATION

From 1985 onward, Israel adopted strict free-market policies in the spirit of globalization (Boxbaum, 2008). This in turn contributed heavily to the poverty of the Palestinian population. In particular, it has adversely affected the social rights and economic citizenship of Palestinian women. The impact of globalization has been seen in at least two areas: structural changes in the nature of the economy and production—the move to high-tech economic activities—and the importation of foreign labor, largely but not exclusively from Asia. The transition to global markets entailed a shift toward technologically intensive industry, finance, and services, whereas labor-intensive factories, where Palestinian women worked, became redundant. Although in 1990 labor-intensive industries employed 110,000 workers—34% of the Palestinian workforce in Israel—by 2002 they employed only 27% (Mtanes, 2004b).

With respect to labor, the closure of the West Bank and Gaza Strip, which became a policy with the implementation of the 1993 Oslo Accords, resulted in the mass import of cheap labor from Asia, eastern Europe, Central America, and Africa. By 2003, some 350,000 migrant workers, who constitute more than 10% of the labor force in Israel, occupied the branches of construction, agriculture, and domestic service. In 2003, migrants made up 27% of the workforce in agriculture, and 7% in domestic service. In agriculture, imported labor caused a 31% decline in the Palestinian workforce. This policy also caused a decline in the wages paid in these sectors (Mtanes, 2004b). In 2008, some 50% of the workforce in agriculture was foreign (Natan, 2008). Imported workers are "shackled." They cannot leave their boss unless they succeed in gaining a special permit, and their entrance papers indicate where they work. If they move to another boss of their free will, they become "runaways." If "caught" they are detained, fined, and deported.

Russian immigration has become a factor in the displacement of Palestinian labor. In the early 1990s, after the collapse of the Soviet Union, Israel encouraged a large wave of immigration from the countries of the former Soviet Union. Some 175,000 immigrants entered the labor force, occupying jobs where traditionally Palestinian women (and men) used to work, in the food and textile industries, as salespersons, receptionists, nurses, and so on (Mtanes, 2004b).

Israel adopted the so-called "flexible labor market" policy, which reduces the power of unions (Adiv, 2006). Subcontractors and personnel companies have become the norm in employment, including the public sector. The vast majority of workers remain nonunionized. The jobs are underpaid and temporary; employees generally do not enjoy social benefits. Israel proportionally has more people working through such firms than any other country in the Western world. Women of both ethnic groups form 65% of the employees of personnel firms (Wartzberger, 2003).

Overall, the globalization process has left the Palestinian citizens of Israel more marginalized than before; socioeconomic gaps have widened, and prospects for closing them are bleak. What is more, social rights and economic citizenship are severely limited when conditions of poverty are pervasive, as seen in the section below.

PALESTINIAN WOMEN AND POVERTY

In 2006, some 50.1% of the Palestinian women were poor in comparison to 14.8% of the Jewish women. Nearly 50% of the Palestinian families were poor in comparison to 16% of the Jewish families (Tamir, 2007). Poverty among the Palestinians is deep, entrenched, and chronic (Mtanes, 2004a). One of the main reasons for poverty in the Palestinian population is the fact that in fully half of the households, only *one* person works, and in 21% of the households *no one* works. Among the Jewish population, by contrast, in almost 50% of the households at least *two* people work (Mtanes, 2004a). Other reasons are the concentration of the Palestinians in traditional low-paying jobs, discrimination in payment for the same jobs, and large families. Because most women are economically dependent, they (and their children) are the first to suffer.

A document commissioned by the Knesset (Israel's parliament) showed that although unemployment among Palestinian women in Israel in 2005 measured 17%, the unemployment rate of Jewish women was 8.5% (Natan, 2007a). According to the same document, 50% of the employed women held part-time jobs. As noted, only 19.1% of all Palestinian women work, compared with 51% of the Jewish women.

The growing unemployment of Palestinian men and women has exacerbated poverty and led to greater competition between Palestinian men and women for the limited job options. Also, in the two main branches of Palestinian female labor—agriculture and textiles—the percentage of Palestinian employees dropped between 1990 and 2002: in agriculture from 4.2% to 1.9%, and in industry from 21.7% to 16.5% (Mtanes, 2004b; Hazan, 2007). When more than 150 textile plants in Palestinian villages closed down in the mid-1990s, the total number of female workers in the textile industry decreased from 45,000 to 22,000 (Nasser & Assaf, 1996).

Women receive low pay. In 2004 the average monthly wage of women was NIS 5,457 ($1,213 US), whereas that of men was NIS 8,459 (approximately $2,443 US). Additionally, child allowances dropped by 40% between 2001 and 2004, unemployment benefits fell by 43%, and welfare allowances by 20%. Taxes were lowered, but women hardly benefit from this because the low wages that most of them earn exempt them from tax. Both Jewish and Arab women pay only 18.5% of governmental revenues from income tax (Swirski, 2006).

Government budget cuts have adversely affected Palestinians. The main reasons for poverty among Palestinians derive from governmental policies. Israeli budgets since 2001 have been detrimental to the poor in general and to women of both ethnic groups in particular. Deep cuts were made in government expenses, mainly in social security funds, as well as in educational, public health, and welfare services. Women are more vulnerable to these cuts because they constitute a high percentage of the staff in these ministries. They also suffer more from cuts in the health services, because they need them more, due to pregnancies, births, and a longer life expectancy (Swirski, 2006). These cuts in government services undermine social rights, especially for low-income, marginalized, and other vulnerable sections of the population.

LABOR LAWS AND THE ROLE OF THE HISTADRUT

Since its founding, the Histadrut has acted as a body with two functions: as a trade union and as a tool for colonizing Palestine. Its composition and characteristics reflect these contradictory functions. In its first years, the Histadrut had a major hand in making Israel a Jewish state. Its role as a trade union was minor. Its central position and economic power gave it absolute dominance over the labor market. Until the 1990s, the Histadrut was the country's only significant factor in the field of labor relations.

Although there is no constitution in Israel, its basic labor laws are quite progressive. Many were written during the state's early years, when socialist norms were still dominant. At that period, the government was the largest employer and the Histadrut the second largest. Labor governments cooperated with the Histadrut, a corporatist trade union, controlled by the same Labor Party. Most of Israel's citizens were members of the Histadrut because of its health service. There were no foreign workers in the country at that time.

The structural changes that Israel has experienced since the 1990s have changed the picture radically. The Histadrut separated itself from its health service. Largely because of this, membership dropped from 1.8 million in 1994 to 500,000 after January 1995, when—by law—health insurance payments became the province of the National Insurance Institute. Many Histadrut unions ceased to exist, because foreign workers replaced local ones. The Histadrut concentrated on the better-paid labor sectors, and this had the result of excluding Palestinians in Israel from the new economic sectors. Led by the Labor Party, the Histadrut accepted the privatization of government companies and the transfer of workers to personnel agencies without union protection. In tandem, the Histadrut began privatizing the factories owned by its Workers' Company, thus becoming a major force in the privatization of Israel's economy. It cooperated both with the closure policy, which had a devastating effect on Palestinian workers, and with the policy of importing cheap labor from afar.

Until the end of the 1980s, there were a few laws dealing specifically with gender equality. They were the Equal Pay Law (Male and Female Employees), which dated from 1964 and was replaced in 1996; the Women's Equal Rights Law of 1951, which does not deal explicitly with labor-related issues; and the Equal Retirement Law–1987, which prohibits employers from forcing early retirement on female workers. The Equal Employment Opportunities Law of 1988 prohibits discrimination in the workplace based on gender, sexual orientation, marital status, parenthood and other criteria. The problem with these laws, as acknowledged in an Israeli Convention on the Elimination of All Forms of Discrimination against Women (CEDAW) Report, has been that "The lack of legislative activity, combined with the fact that the few laws which were enacted failed to provide serious remedies or enforcement tools, resulted in a parallel litigation" (Government of Israel, 1997, pp. 1–2). In 1987 the Minimum Wage Law was enacted. However, neither it nor existing collective labor agreements are applied to migrants or to people working through personnel agencies and subcontractors. Moreover, the minimum wage, which is today NIS 21 (approximately $4 US) per hour, does not enable the earner to live above the poverty line.

Agriculture is the arena where today's Palestinian workers most need the backing of a union. In fact, a collective agreement covering the agricultural and packing branch has existed since 1993, granting workers, including temporary ones, full social benefits. The problem is that this remains on paper. Most female agricultural workers earn about 60% of the legal minimum wage.

PALESTINIAN WOMEN IN ISRAEL'S WORKFORCE

The structure of the Arab female workforce has the shape of an upside-down pyramid: Among the minority with jobs, about 70% are independent professionals, in education, health or social work, whereas most of the remaining 30% are nonprofessionals in industry, agriculture, cleaning, and other services.

Many acknowledge that the low participation of Palestinian women in the labor market plays a critical role in the economic weakness of the Palestinian community. These make up 5.8% of all working women in Israel (Fichtelberg, 2004). In comparison, 62% of working-age Palestinian males had jobs in 2002 (down from 68% in 1992; Mtanes, 2004b). In 2005 the situation changed only a little; 19.1% (79,200) of the working-age Palestinian women participated in the labor force, compared with 56.2% of the Jewish women (Hazan, 2007). In 2008, there were 315,684 Palestinian women of working age (15 to 64 years), but only 19.1% of them (60,295) actually worked, according to official data (Government of Israel, 2008).

Actual female participation in the market economy, however, is higher than the statistics indicate. Some women prefer to deny their employment outside the house for cultural reasons or to avoid paying taxes or to receive welfare benefits. This is especially evident when women work in agriculture, when work is seasonal, or when it bears a stigma, as does cleaning other people's homes. Even so, this discrepancy would account for only a small fraction of the gap between Jewish and Palestinian women (Lewin-Epstein & Semyonov, 1993). In any event, there is no doubt that Palestinian women's contribution to the economy is far below their potential.

The underdeveloped infrastructure in the Palestinian communities and the women's reluctance to commute play an important role in women's low labor-force participation. Among the problems affecting women are the lack of day-care centers for children, insufficient professional training, scarcity of transportation from the Palestinian villages to the cities, compounded by disrespect for the labor laws and super-exploitation (Boulus, 2003). The chronic lack of jobs and the inferior nature of those that are offered, coupled with traditional attitudes, have caused many Palestinian women *not* to regard themselves as part of the labor market at all.

Knowledge of Hebrew also plays an important role. Of those who take part in the labor force, 82% are fluent in Hebrew; of those who don't, only 47% are fluent (Government of Israel, 1997). In a survey published in 1999, 48.3% of Palestinian women claimed that they do not want to work, and 13.5% were indifferent to the question. Only 38% stated a desire to work. They gave various reasons that prevent them, such as children, the opposition of the husband or parents, the lack of jobs, and low pay (Fares, 1999). Again, differential access to education explains this variation in language acquisition. In 2002, when the Israeli economy was in recession, 10,300 Palestinian women reported that they despaired of seeking work. Had they continued to look for jobs, participation would have been 19.9% (Fichtelberg, 2004).

In a 2005 survey by Women against Violence, Palestinian women cited the following considerations as influencing their decision to work: taking care of the children (74.8%), agreement of parents/husband (74.5%), availability of workplaces in their vicinity (58.9%), and the economic situation (56.7%; Hazan, 2007). Another reason for Palestinian women's reluctance to work is that in the lower socioeconomic sectors of their society, single women are considered an integral source of income to the family, and must hand over their salaries in full to the family (Government of Israel, 1997). Many young unmarried women work temporarily in order to finance a brother's academic studies or the construction of a house. Not surprisingly, they regard it as a sort of forced labor and are eager to stop working.

There are noticeable differences in labor-force participation among Christian (36%), Druze (24.2%), and Muslim women (14.8%; Haidar,

2005a). Christian Palestinian women are disproportionately represented in the total population of Arab working women, given that Muslims make up 79% of the Palestinians in Israel, Druze 9%, and Christians 12%. The labor-force participation rates of Palestinian women of the different religious communities correlate with number of children, education, and locality (city or village). Only 4.3% of Palestinian women live in mixed cities. Of these, the percentage of working women in the 18- to 50-year age range reaches almost 50%, which is near that of Jewish women. Among those who live in small and medium villages, the rate for this age range is much lower: 24% (Fichtelberg, 2004).

The labor-force participation of mothers with one to three children doubled in the course of the decade, from 12% in 1990 to 24% in 2002. That figure is still low. It shows that many Palestinian women still drop out of the labor market after the birth of their first child (Fichtelberg, 2004).

WHERE PALESTINIAN WOMEN WORK

From 1990 to 2001, the participation of women with academic degrees in the workforce rose from 3.7% to 11%. However, female semiprofessional and manual laborers dropped during the same years from 33.5% to 19%. There is a sharp decline of participation in agriculture and industry, as opposed to the rise in trade, education, health, and welfare services (Mtanes, 2004b).

Israeli sociologists have identified the presence of ethnic enclaves and their social consequences (Lewin-Epstein & Semyonov, 1993). The difficulty of competing with Jewish workers in the high-tech Hebrew-speaking industries results in a lack of job opportunities, impelling half of the Palestinian employees of both sexes to find work in their own segregated communities. These suffer from a scarcity of jobs. Those that exist are mostly manual and low paying. Exceptions are positions in education, health, and social services in the Palestinian community, where Arabic is the required language, and therefore Jewish women can not compete. Palestinian women occupy these jobs in higher proportions than men do. In recent years, however, this labor market has become saturated. Thus, more than half the working Palestinian women are employed as professionals or semiprofessionals in their own villages. Beyond their enclaves, Palestinians of both sexes supply a disproportionately high number of workers with low-paying, low-status, blue-collar manual jobs.

Palestinian society in Israel has undergone class differentiation, creating a noticeable gap between a small upper- and middle-class and a much larger class of the unemployed and the poor. Women who acquired higher education and work in professional jobs have become part of the Palestinian middle classes; they tend to be less tied to the traditional way of life. Of all Palestinian women, the percentage involved in academic work rose from 3.7% in 1990 to 11% in 2001 (Mtanes, 2004b), and it remained the same in 2005 (Hazan, 2007). More recently, however, because of the growing numbers of women with higher education and the intensifying competition for a limited number of jobs, we are witnessing a decline in this sector as well. Educated women are taking the place of the lesser educated, who have been ousted from the workforce altogether (Mtanes, 2004b). We also have noticed a growing number of Palestinian women who work in independent Palestinian nongovernmental organizations (NGOs). The higher the education of women, the greater their participation in the labor force.

THE PLIGHT OF WOMEN IN AGRICULTURE

Agriculture plays a major role in the employment of Palestinian women. The employment ratio of Palestinian women is significantly enhanced by the proportion of agricultural employment in the community and by job availability (Lewin-Epstein & Semyonov, 1993). Prior to the establishment of Israel, 90% of the Palestinian population lived from agriculture. By 1983, the figure was only 7% (most of these were women). Today only 4% of the land in Israel remains in Palestinian hands (Haider, 2005a; Working Group, 1997). The decline in agriculture, which used to be a central economic branch for the Palestinians, has had a very detrimental impact on Palestinian women.

In agriculture one finds the worst kind of exploitation. The young women are bussed to work collectively by a male responsible for them (the *ra'is*), who often is a family member. He gets the money from the employer and divides it among the workers, skimming some 40% for himself. The women workers are paid NIS 80 to 100 per day ($23-$29 US), although the minimum daily wage is NIS 165 (approximately $55 US). The farm owner does not consider himself responsible for his workers, and often does not give them a wage slip. That means that the workers do not enjoy any social benefits; in cases of injury, for example, they must fend for themselves.

Competition with the cheap foreign workers is impossible, because they labor up to 14 hours a day without social benefits and rarely earn more than NIS 13 ($3.75 US) per hour, whereas the hourly minimum wage is NIS 21 (approximately $6 US). Thus, Palestinian women must either stay out of work or give up their rights (Adiv, 2005).

Addressing such a state of affairs should be the target of campaigns by the major trade union. However, as discussed previously, the Histadrut has been complicit in the adoption and implementation of new economic policies that have either displaced Palestinian workers in Israel or contributed to their marginalization, especially in the case of women. For this reason, WAC, along with several other civil society organizations, has taken on the issue of organizing workers and helping to defend and advance their social and economic rights.

ORGANIZING WORKING WOMEN: THE EXPERIENCE OF WAC

WAC arose as an independent initiative by Jewish and Arab activists who had amassed much experience in the struggle against the occupation of the Palestinian territories and in the fight for equality within Israel. The new situation raised the need to start a trade union movement that would fill the vacuum left by the Histadrut. Given growing unemployment and poverty among Palestinian citizens of Israel, many Palestinian women, including mothers of small children, must work. However, exploitation, low wages, the stigma of menial labor and the temporary, seasonal nature of most jobs keep many Arab housewives from seeking work. We target precisely these invisible women, the thousands who lack professional training, in order to bring them into the work process. Agriculture is a natural choice. It is a vital branch in Israeli economy, which can receive unprofessional women by the thousands.

Although work is a precondition for empowerment, it does not automatically empower women, especially those from the lower class. They need to be organized and unionized. They must go through a personal process with a support group in order to tackle the pressures from the traditional environment and to handle the double burden of work at home and outside. Therefore, WAC offers these women empowerment meetings, trade union education, and public activity.

Since March 2005, WAC has organized hundreds of women in agriculture, with social rights and the legal minimum wage. By helping to change the material conditions of these women, their families and their community, WAC contributes to the struggle against poverty and underdevelopment in a concrete way. It also contributes to the struggle to organize the working class, and change the relationship between the sexes. This huge change in their financial situation and social status can bring about a change in the male society's attitude toward women. It may help create solidarity among all victims of neoliberalism, women and men, Arabs and Jews. It may foster, at last, a healthy dialogue between the Arab and Jewish communities. WAC's specific objectives are to:

- Persuade Israeli farmers to employ Arab women according to legal wage and working conditions.

- Show Arab women that work is available and to strengthen them in standing up to social pressure.

- Encourage Arab women workers to become factors for positive change in the community.

- Persuade the government to change its policy concerning the labor market in agriculture.

- Raise the issue of jobs for Arab women in Israeli public opinion, academic circles, civil society and the media.

- Persuade the farmers to take on a WAC work team.

Our strategy requires painstaking effort, patience, and skill. WAC does not ask that employers stop using the Thai workers they already have. WAC asks only that, rather than import more, they also include local Arab women, organized within WAC. They are reminded that by doing this they will help solve unemployment in the country. Surprisingly, this argument helps. WAC also points out that its work teams include women who speak basic Hebrew, so farmers need not suffer from the language barrier they have with the Thai workers. The farmers are told that WAC can mediate labor problems, and ensure that the teams are suitable for the work. WAC suggests that they don't put all their eggs in one basket and should prepare for the day when the government will stop the mass importation of cheap labor. Where farmers are willing, WAC then negotiates an agreement.

To reach farmers, WAC coordinators visit farms on a daily basis. They use a brochure in Hebrew directed to the farmers, explaining the advantages of working with WAC. Another way to reach farmers is through cooperation with the Ministries of Agriculture and Employment. WAC coordinates with the Ministry's planning branch and with its regional branches. When farmers come asking for workers, the Ministry's regional managers direct them to WAC, while also informing WAC of farms that may be able to take on workers.

To organize women workers, WAC activists visit homemakers, starting with the relatives of male WAC members, to convince them of the advantages of joining WAC and working outside their homes. They also visit women who are employed through subcontractors for less than the minimum wage. Often women who already work through WAC join the visits and relate their own experiences. On this basis WAC proceeds to organize groups of women, at least one of whom is a driver with a car, so they can reach work. Each becomes a member of WAC by paying monthly dues (specifically, NIS 35 or about $10 US). WAC activists make regular visits to the farms that employ WAC members to follow developments and solve problems. In case of major difficulties with the employer, WAC's lawyers provide help.

Once the first groups break the ice, more women ask to join. When dozens of women from the same village receive organized jobs in agriculture, immense interest develops around them. At first, Wafa Tiara, 32, a mother of four, reported that her relatives pitied her and thought that her husband was useless because he allowed her to work. She patiently explained to them the difference between working for a subcontractor who abused her and working through WAC, which guarantees her salary and rights. Wafa's experience led other women in her village to seek similar jobs (Tayara, 2006). Joining WAC opened up new horizons for working women. Women are present at every level of leadership at WAC. "Going out to work was a turning point in my life," said Wafa at the May Day demonstration of 2006. In the winter of that year, WAC decided to launch a workers' party. Five women workers became candidates for the Knesset, taking inspiration from the top candidate, Asma Aghbarieh, who is also a WAC activist.

For its part, WAC has embarked on an educational campaign with workers about the importance of working women. WAC avoids an ideological debate on feminist issues, but presents simple figures that prove how a working mother can give her children more than a full-time homemaker whose refrigerator is empty, and why her work is essential for surmounting the poverty line. Consequently, many WAC male workers are setting an example to others by encouraging their wives to work (Nasser, 2008).

PERSONAL AND COLLECTIVE EMPOWERMENT

WAC expands its offices into social and cultural centers, including a framework of activities for workers' children and an annual summer camp, enrichment courses for high school students and young workers, women's meetings and cultural activities for the whole village population. In order to complement economic with personal empowerment, female members of WAC participate in weekly meetings with professional trainers. The meetings are aimed at strengthening their self-image, enhancing their influence at home and society, creating a support group for them and, ultimately, transforming them into activists and leaders who can draw more women into the circle. Thus, the aim of empowerment is twofold: to strengthen each woman as an individual and, at the same time, to create collective awareness and loyalty to the group of co-workers and to WAC.

Personal support is important because of the traditional view that a woman who works outside her home (especially in exhausting manual labor) will neglect her duty toward her family. Palestinian women are aware of their low status in society. Although they compare their situation with that of Jewish women, they are attached to their traditions. These are some of the dilemmas that arise at the empowerment meetings (Schwartz, 2007).

The empowerment sessions also invite women to look critically at existing social attitudes and at the patterns of behavior imposed on women, with an eye to alternatives. The sessions seek to develop communication skills while women discuss the changes that have taken place in Palestinian-Arab society in Israel, including relations within the family. And there are monthly events. Women who regularly participate in the empowerment meetings invite a wider circle of women in their village to public lectures on a variety of issues, such as health and child care, or on labor-related issues.

When problems arise within a group or with the employer, the recruiting coordinators invite the group to a meeting at the WAC Center to air complaints. Here they further educate the co-workers on the issue of solidarity. Experience shows that these meeting are very effective, strengthening the bond between WAC and its members. Workers who demonstrate a sense of responsibility become candidates for the trade unionist course. Such a course offers 12 meetings on issues such as basic labor rights; how to read a wage slip; safety at work; special rights of women at work; pension laws; on-the-job relations with co-workers and the manager; solidarity versus individualism at work; the Histadrut's strengths and weaknesses; the role of a trade union and what is WAC. Participants in these courses become the link between the workers and the offices of WAC.

WAC's efforts among women in agriculture open the way toward a broader trade union. As they and thousands of others gain experience, they will look for protection and will come to WAC. In Israel and the Arab localities, there has never been a tradition of unionizing *from below*. The Histadrut drew its influence and status from its connections to the state. It never had to unionize a workplace. In the Arab localities, the Histadrut was historically identified with the ruling Labor Party, which until 1966 imposed martial law on them.

LOBBYING DECISION MAKERS, PUBLIC CAMPAIGNS, AND NETWORKING

WAC has taken a critical stance toward the economic and social policies of successive Israeli governments, which have adopted an unfettered neoliberal agenda. Since 1993, farmers have been granted permits to import 29,000 agricultural workers from Thailand, constituting half the hired workforce in this branch. Some 15,000 of the jobs could have gone instead to Arab women, enabling them to lift their families out of poverty. As long as the Thai workers remain the main labor force, WAC workers remain temporary workers, a mere reserve. This adds difficulties to WAC's efforts to find stable jobs.

The problem is the gap between the government's declared policy and its actions. The official program of Ehud Olmert's government (April

2006 to April 2009) asserted the necessity of increasing the participation of Palestinian women in the workforce. Yet not a month had gone by when his new Agriculture Minister announced his intention to import 4,000 more agricultural workers from Thailand, claiming a lack of local workers. In the budget proposal for 2009, and in the emergency plans for the coming economic recession, no mention was made of reducing the import of foreign labor.

WAC continually seeks points where it can work together with government bodies, exerting influence and advancing WAC's priorities. WAC participates on a regular basis in meetings of the Knesset Committees on Labor and Welfare, on Migrant Workers and on Women's Issues. WAC has developed a line of cooperation with the Employment Authority. WAC also has established a working relationship with the professional staff in the Ministry of Agriculture; they coordinate with WAC field organizers in the effort to locate farmers who need workers.

WAC has established its standing with the Bank of Israel, the Prime Minister's Office, and the National Economic Council. These groups have invited WAC several times to present its positions concerning the situation of Arab workers, unemployment, and policies of job creation. At the decision-making level in government, there is general agreement on the need to end importation of foreign labor. At the close of 2007, a committee under the deputy governor of the Bank of Israel Zvi Eckstein issued a policy paper, stating the need to reduce the quota of migrant workers in agriculture to 5,000 within 6 years (Eckstein, 2008).

This consensus position does not come close to implementation, however, in part because of the powerful farmers' lobby based in the kibbutz and private farmers movements, and in part because of lobbying by the personnel agencies, which exploit the migrants for enormous sums. This interest group relies heavily on foreign workers, whose cheap labor constitutes a form of governmental subsidy to Israeli farmers. The farmers' lobby claims that the local workers do not want to work. WAC has disproved this claim with its agricultural laborers and with a database of jobseekers. WAC's systematic activity at the grass-roots level serves as evidence for the potential that exists in this field.

In October 2007 the government launched a plan to allocate 5 million shekels (€900,000) to encourage local workers in agriculture. WAC was invited to present its position at meetings in the Prime Minister's office and in the Finance, Industry and Agriculture ministries. WAC argued that the money was insufficient and that the plan was inadequate. WAC agreed to help with its implementation, however, if and when the Knesset approved it. Yet so far the plan has not been implemented, because the Ministries of Agriculture and Finance each claims that the other should do the funding (Natan, 2007b).

Together with other organizations, WAC has succeeded in pressuring the Ministry of Industry to announce that the employment of migrant workers, as of June 2008, is to take place through the International Organization for Migration (IOM)[4] and not through profit-driven companies. If workers do not come to the country "bonded by debt," they will be free to struggle for their rights. In that case, local women will be able to compete with them on a more equal footing. However, because of the strength of the farmers' lobby, the implementation of the announcement faces many obstacles; it is reported that foreign workers have not experienced any benefits so far.

In order to reach Israeli public opinion, WAC organizes public events with the participation of it female workers and supporters. They march for jobs, reach the media, and empower themselves by fighting for their cause. They broaden their horizons by meeting new supporters in Jewish cities. In organizing these events, WAC cooperates with other organizations, creating networks with labor organizations, women's organizations, academic figures, and social activists. For example, the most important events in 2006 were a march in Tel Aviv on International Women's Day (Horodi, 2006); a public outdoor event in Tel Aviv on May 1; the Conference on Employment in Agriculture, which invited Israeli and Arab academics and activists to discuss employment issues; and the Art Sale Exhibition "Bread and Roses" by a large number of Jewish and Arab artists, whose income is an additional source of support for the gender activities of WAC. In April 2007, WAC hosted an international delegation to investigate agricultural labor relations in Israel. With the help of Video48, WAC recorded the delegation's experience in a documentary called: *Who Will Pick the Avocados?* (Ben-Efrat, 2007). Together with Kav LaOved (Workers' Hotline), WAC recently presented an appeal to British trade unions and social groups to put pressure on local retailers to check exporters' implementation of workers' social rights in their supply chains (Jackson & Adiv, 2008). In January 2011, WAC organized a forum that brought together native women from Galilee, Negev, and Triangle (Wadi Ara region), as well as migrant workers, to discuss women's employment conditions and paths to women's empowerment (Ben Efrat, 2011).

CONCLUSIONS AND RECOMMENDATIONS

WAC believes that the recruitment of Palestinian women to the organized workforce and their participation in independent grassroots union activity are essential not only for them as women, but also because it empowers the working class and the Palestinians in Israel as a whole. The connection between women, the working class, and unions is the key to the struggle against poverty and for social and economic rights. Educational and cultural activities that empower working women increase their self-confidence, broaden their horizons, and enrich their cultural experience. The combination of empowerment through work, unionizing, and gender activities can convince Palestinian men—especially working-class men—to support Palestinian women.

The struggle to gain decent jobs for Palestinian women in Israel becomes much more urgent with the threat of international recession and economic crisis. The various forms of abusive employment, including the heavy use of personnel agencies and exploitable migrant labor, were at first directed against Palestinian women. Now they have become a social disease threatening the majority of working people, Arab and Jew, male and female. WAC believes that governments should take responsibility for the employment and the welfare of their citizens. If the Israeli government does not change its neoliberal economic policies and its discrimination against Palestinians, there will be an explosion.

Women form the weakest link in a conservative and undeveloped society. At the same time, they can become a force of social change, once they integrate into the labor market, become aware of their rights, and become involved in unionist and social activities. Palestinian and Israeli NGOs have submitted recommendations to advance the situation of Palestinian women. One such list was presented to the Committee on the Elimination of All Forms of Discrimination Against Women. These recommendations are comprehensive and wide-ranging, placing a special emphasis on rectifying Israel's discriminatory practices toward its Palestinian population, and demanding government investment in infrastructure, industrialization, and education. WAC does not wish to repeat these, and prefers to add further recommendations that, in its view, are vital for Palestinian working women, especially in agriculture:

- Stop the policy of importing migrant workers, in order to open job opportunities for Palestinian women.

- Stop all human trafficking that goes on without the control of the IOM and other international agencies.

- Impose a quota on farmers, mandating the percentage of their workers who must be local.

- Stop the activities of personnel firms and subcontractors. Employers should employ their workers directly.

- Organize and unionize Palestinian women in agriculture and in all other branches that employ nonunionized workers.

- Encourage the participation of Palestinian women in the workforce by opening attractive job opportunities and by providing professional training.

- Raise media awareness concerning the plight of Palestinian women workers.

- Strengthen workers' movements throughout the world by enhancing national and international cooperation among trade unions, labor organizations, women's organizations, and academics.

NOTES

1. There is a growing literature on these issues. In addition to the sources cited in this chapter, see also Krauss (2002); Swirski, Swirski, and Konor-Atias (2003); and Swirski, Swirski, Konor-Atias, and Yecheskel (2001).

2. The Worker's Advice Center at http://www.wac-maan.org.il.

3. Some Israelis choose to marry in a civil court in Cyprus, thereby avoiding a religious marriage.

4. UN Office of the High Commissioner for Human Rights, Fact sheet No. 24. Retrieved May 2009 http://www.unhchr.ch/html/menu6/2/fs24.htm.

REFERENCES

Adiv, A. (2005). WAC: Reclaiming jobs in agriculture. *Challenge*, 90.

Adiv, A. (2006). The breaking of organized labor in Israel. *Challenge*, 98.

Ben-Efrat, R. (2007). Thailand and the Israeli labor market. *Challenge*, 103.

Ben Efrat, R. (2010). *"Black Labor"—Granting voice and color to the unseen worker*. Workers Advice Center (WAC/MAAN). http://www.wac-maan.org.il/en/print/article.

Boulus, S. (2003). *The integration of Arab women in the labor market in Israel: Impediments and suggestions for improvement*. Tel Aviv, Israel: The Association for Civil Rights in Israel.

Boxbaum, Y. (2008). *Female workers in an unstable labor market*. Haifa: Mahut Center.

Eckstein, Z. (2008, May). *A report for policy making on the issue of non-Israeli workers*. Submitted to the Knesset Committee on Foreign Workers, Kiryat Ben-Gurion.

Fares, A. (1999). *The status of the Palestinian women in the labor market*. Tel Aviv, Israel: The Israeli Institute for Social and Economic Research.

Fichtelberg, O. (2004). *The participation of Palestinian women in the labor force in the past decade*. Qiryat Ben-Gurion: The Ministry of Labor & Social Affairs, the Authority for Personnel Planning.

Ghanem, H. (2005). *Opinions about the problems and rights of the Palestinian woman in Israel*. Nazareth, Israel: Women Against Violence.

Government of Israel. (1997, April). Report Submitted to the Committee on the Elimination of All Forms of Violence Against Women. CEDAW/C/ISR/1-2/. NY: United Nations.

Government of Israel. (2008). The Central Bureau of Statistics (September). Retrieved November 2009 http://www.cbs.gov.il/reader/.

Haidar, A. (2005a). *Arab society in Israel: Populations, society, economy*. The Van Leer Jerusalem Institute/The Institute of Israeli-Palestinian Studies/Hakibbutz Hameuchad Publishing House.

Haidar, A. (2005b, December). *The Sikkuy Report, Monitoring Civic Equality between Arab and Jewish Citizens of Israel, Two years after the Or Commission Recommendations*.Tel Aviv:

Hasan, M. (1999). The politics of honor: Patriarchy, the state, and murder of women in the name of family honor. *Sex Gender Politics*. Tel Aviv, Israel: Kibbutz Hameuchad Publishing House.

Hazan, R. (2007). Arab women and paid employment. In T. Tamir (Ed.), *Women in Israel 2006: Between theory and reality* (pp. 251–256).Ramat Gan, Israel: The Israel Women's Network.

Horodi, S. (2006). Demonstrating for jobs. *Challenge, 97*.

HRA-Arab Association of Human Rights. (2003). *Palestinian Arab women in Israel*. Nazareth, Israel: Author.

Jackson, V., & Adiv, A. (2008). Joint letter on migrant farm workers in Israel. *Worker's Advice Center* (June). Retrieved May 2009 http://www.wac-maan.org.il/en/article__45.

Krauss, A.N. (2002). *Women in the economy and labor force in Israel* (Compendium of Data and Information). Jerusalem, Israel: The Israel Women's Network. Retrieved May 2009 http://www.iwn.org.il/DataBookE.htm.

Lewin-Epstein, N., & Semyonov, M. (1993). *The Palestinian minority in the Israeli economy: Patterns of ethnic inequality*. Boulder, CO: Westview Press.

Mtanes, S. (2004a). *Poverty as policy: Report and comparative study: The average poverty level of Palestinian citizens in Israel during the past decade*. Haifa, Israel: Mada al-Carmel.

Mtanes, S. (2004b). *Unemployment and exclusion: The Palestinian minority in the Israeli labor markets*. Haifa, Israel: Mada al-Carmel.

Muhammad, A. E-S. (2004). *Palestinians in Israel: Socioeconomic survey*. Haifa, Israel: The Galilee Society & RIKAZ., Mada al-Carmel.

Nahmias, R. (2007, March 7). Interview with Amin Fares: "Mossawa Center Claims that Losses to Israeli Economy Due to the Lack of Integration of Arab Women in the Labor Market Reach 6.2 Billion NIS per Annum." Ynet. [on-line?]

Nasser, S. (2008). Conversation with farm worker Kamila Zeidan. *Challenge, 108*.

Nasser, S., & Assaf, A. (1996). Textile workers lose their jobs. *Al-Sabah*.

Natan, G. (2007a). *Employment of women in the Arab sector*. Tel Aviv, Israel: The Knesset Research and Information Center.

Natan, G. (2007b). *Report on "The Decision of the Government to Enlarge the Quota of Foreign Workers in Agriculture."* Tel Aviv, Israel: Knesset Committee on Foreign Workers.

Natan, G. (2008). *Background information on enlargement of the quota of Palestinian workers in Israel* (in Hebrew). Tel Aviv, Israel: The Knesset Research and Information Center.

Schwartz, M. (2007). Persimmons and empowerment. *Challenge, 102*.

Schwartz, M., & Agbarieh-Zahalka, A. (2008). Arab women in Israel, obstacles to emancipation. *Challenge, 108*.

Swirski, B. (2006). *Proposal for state budget for 2006 through the lens of gender*. Tel Aviv, Israel: Adva Center.

Swirski, B., Swirski, S., & Konor-Atias, E. (2003). *Two years of destructive economic policy: A gender view*. Tel Aviv, Israel: Adva Center.

Swirski, B., Swirski, S., Konor-Atias, E., & Yecheskel, Y. (2001). *Women in the labor market of the welfare state of Israel.* Tel-Aviv, Israel: Adva Center.

Tamir, T. (2007). *Women in Israel 2006: Between theory and reality* (in Hebrew). Ramat Gan, Israel: The Israel Women's Network.

Tayara, W. (2006). Not in anybody's pocket anymore! *Challenge 97,* 19.

Wartzberger, R. (2003, June). *Employment of workers in personnel companies.* Document submitted to the Committee for Advancing the Status of Women in the Knesset.

Workers Advice Center (WAC-MAAN). http://www.wac-maan.org.il.

Working Group on the Status of Palestinian Women in Israel. (1997, July). *The status of Palestinian women citizens of Israel.* Submitted to the United Nations Committee on the Elimination of Discrimination Against Women, Seventeenth Session.

Working Group on the Status of Palestinian Women in Israel. (2005, January). *Alternative pre-sessional report on Israel's implementation of CEDAW.*

FOUR

TUNISIA

Women's Economic Citizenship and Trade Union Participation

Hafidha Chékir and Khédija Arfaoui

The 1993 World Conference on Human Rights, which convened in Vienna, reasserted women's rights as an integral part of human rights, and of which they are an inseparable and inalienable entity. These rights are found in the International Bill of Human Rights that includes the 1948 Universal Declaration of Human Rights, the International Covenant on Civil and Political Rights (1966), the International Covenant on Economic, Social and Cultural Rights (1966), and the Convention on the Elimination of All Forms of Discrimination against Women (CEDAW; 1979).

In Tunisia, as in the other Arab nations, the various national and international instruments that govern the private and public spheres make for a number of differences. On the one hand, public spheres generally are defined by the application of international references and instruments based on the principle of gender equality and by social aspects of national legislations, which acknowledge the importance of men and women having the same rights. On the other hand, the private sphere is the favored realm for discriminatory legislation and behavior. However, ever since the Personal Status Code was promulgated on August 13, 1956, women have gained rights within the family sphere, most notably the right to freely, directly, and personally express their consent to wed, the right to a monogamous marriage, the right to a legal divorce, the right to adopt children, and in 1973, the right to an abortion. In 1998, women also gained the right to community property between spouses, which although optional, allows them to manage their property and choose joint tenancy for their immovable family property.[1]

Despite having gained so many rights, however, women remain discriminated against within the family sphere where fathers hold a strict monopoly on authority, thus continuing ancestral patriarchal traditions enabled by religion and which do not answer to the international instruments that aim for gender equality. Further proof of this is the stance taken by the Tunisian government when the CEDAW was ratified. The government expressed reservations regarding the dispositions toward women's rights within the family and private spheres, thus ridding the ratification of any new changes and the possibility of promoting women's rights. The next issue is figuring out whether discrimination, which is a dominant social behavior within the family sphere, is having repercussions in other spheres, most notably economic and social spheres, despite the adoption of nondiscriminatory international references and the government's supposed part in guaranteeing and ensuring that these rights are upheld. To do so, we attempt to define social and economic rights in the way they are acknowledged and upheld and we stress women's right to create and join trade unions as a fundamental right based on preserving their right to work.

This chapter focuses on women's role in the Tunisian economy, their involvement within trade unions, and the extent of their economic citizenship. As is seen here, despite women's increasing presence, and therefore "feminization" of sectors such as the textiles and clothing industry; despite the increased number of women who have joined trade unions; despite the state's gender equality policy and the state's gender equality policy and Tunisia's participation in the UN's World Conferences on Human Rights in general and on Women's Rights in particular (Vienna, 1993; Cairo, 1994; Beijing 1995), women are still underrepresented in unions, especially when it comes to leadership and decision-making positions. And because of the liberalization of the Tunisian economy, more and more women, especially those from the working class, face precarious employment.

The authors are associated with two women's rights organizations in Tunisia, l'Association Tunisienne des Femmes Démocrates (ATFD, also known as Femmes Démocrates) and l'Association des Femmes Tunisiennes pour le Recherche et Dévéloppement (AFTURD). One of us also has worked with the women's commission of the country's largest trade union, the Union Générale des Travailleurs Tunisiens (General Union of Tunisian Workers; UGTT). For this study, we have relied on our participant-observations, the relevant secondary sources, UGTT data, and reports written by scholar-activists within the women's and labor movements.[2]

WHAT ARE THE ECONOMIC AND
SOCIAL RIGHTS OF TUNISIAN WOMEN?

In Tunisia, women's right to work is now an accepted cultural fact, regardless of social backgrounds. In high schools and universities, girls do not doubt that they will have jobs afterward. The will to "earn a living" and achieve financial independence is one of their priority goals. As a result, the nation's professional spheres are overrun with women. Tunisian women work in all spheres of public and private life. Depending on their level of education, they have access to all work positions, even traditionally male jobs such as taxi drivers, pilots, and engineers.

Ever since achieving independence, Tunisia has ratified a number of conventions that focus on gender equality. These include International Labour Organization (ILO) conventions such as Convention 100 on the equal remuneration of the male and female workforce for labor of equal value (1951), Convention 111 against discrimination in the field of employment and occupation (1985), Convention 118 on equal treatment (social security) (1962), Convention 122 on employment policy (1964), and Convention 19 on equal treatment (work-related accidents).[3] They also include general international conventions that were adopted under the auspices of the UN and that have direct effects on women's rights.

Around the same time, Tunisia started adhering to three international conventions adopted by the UN General Assembly on women's political rights, married women's nationality, women's right to consent to marriage, the minimum age of marriage and registration of marriage.[4] Shortly before the third UN World Conference on Women—which took place in Nairobi, Kenya in 1985—CEDAW was ratified after having been signed in July 1980. Although ratification came with reservations, these fortunately did not affect the dispositions regarding women's work as defined by Articles 11, 12, and 14.[5] The same accounts for social legislations adopted after the Constitution came into force, each of which has established the principle of gender equality.[6] Acknowledging this principle means giving priority to the principles of equal treatment of men and women regarding recruitment, promotions, and staff positions as well as regarding career management and equal pay. However, the legislators deliberately provided loopholes; depending on the type of job position, exceptions to this principle are allowed, thus making way for all sorts of restrictions against women. The most blatant example of this is the creation of recruitment exams reserved for men with regard to certain jobs such as that of mailman.

Is having access to the world of work enabling and encouraging women to join trade unions? Do they think of the usefulness and importance of taking advantage of means of action to preserve the rights that they were granted when Tunisia declared its independence and when the Personal Status Code was promulgated? Does the UGTT, which, at the time of this writing, is the nation's sole labor confederation, come through as an ideal structure to demand not only the right to work but also the right to decent working conditions, complete with adequate pay and the possibility for upward mobility? What part do women play within the trade unions and what is the percentage of the Tunisian women's trade union participation?

The 1959 Tunisian Constitution granted women and men the right to work. Labor legislation recognized the right to work as well as specific rights concerning maternity and women's reproductive functions. In accordance with ILO provisions on maternity protection, there are bans on underground work and night work. The labor law allows pregnant women workers the possibility of leaving their jobs without having to pay contract termination fees even if they are under contract or nonstatutory workers. It protects women against contract terminations due to pregnancies or pregnancy-related illnesses, and grants them postnatal maternity leave and breastfeeding leave.[7] However, Tunisia did not ratify the ILO conventions on the matter (e.g., 3, 103, 183), which had extended maternity leave from 12 to 14 weeks with mandatory prenatal leave.

Obstacles prevent women from fully benefiting from these rights. The UGTT drafted a report on the textiles and clothing industry in Tunisia that exposed the loopholes in the Tunisian legal texts, especially concerning the "absence of a coherent legal system to manage the discharging of employees," which gives employers the freedom to resort to economic redundancy as a solution to problems (UGTT, 2005, p. 59). Understandably, the female workforce is particularly vulnerable to these loopholes in Tunisian law, as is demonstrated in this chapter.

As a rule, the legislation imbues women and not men with the responsibility of taking care of their children's upbringing and education. Thus far, the legislation has not been modified to acknowledge the social dimension of the reproductive functions, or replace maternity leaves with parental leaves so both parents may take leave, whether in turns or not, to care for their children and give them the necessary treatment and attention, on their own time or as their occupations allow. When it comes to taking care of infants or children with severe handicaps, the responsibility again falls to women; only in rare cases does it fall on the fathers when, in the absence of a wife, they cannot turn to their mother or a sister to help them. Thus, working mothers have been allowed to take a leave for up to 2 renewable years to raise one or more children under age 6 or with disabilities that require continuous care and treatment.[8] This also is the case for early retirement for mothers, which is exceptionally granted to the normal retirement of civil servants.

For early retirement to be approved, women must meet certain criteria such as the number of underage children in their care (three), the severity of a child's disability, their status as mothers and the number of years they have worked within the administration (15).[9]

From another standpoint, it is clear that the scope of women's rights is limited due to the absence of legal means to guarantee their effectiveness and protection. No legal text has implemented means or positive actions to guarantee and uphold women's right to work. No actions exist to set up a quota system of job positions to be handed to women at all administrative or decision-making levels, whether through job entrance exams or direct recruitment. No measures have been set up to sanction the discriminatory behavior of employers or heads of firms. Inevitably, this leads to discriminatory recruitment methods, wherein only men can be hired, due to criteria such as having completed military service, or by recruiting people who have no family obligations, which is to say women who have no children or are not married.

In fact, unemployment and socioeconomic difficulties are such that there is no effective protection for women in case of pregnancies or childbirth. This may explain the low percentage of married women who work, the postponement of the age of marriage, and the reduced number of children per family. Indeed, the Tunisian population's growth rate was at its lowest ever at 1.21% in 2004, whereas 10 years earlier it was at 2.35%. The Tunisian family structure is changing and now rarely includes more than four family members, and the Tunisian population is growing older.

Until 2004, no protection existed for women whose physical or moral integrity had been violated while working, despite the increase in sexual harassment at the workplace. Since 2004, as a result of a campaign against sexual harassment launched by the *Femmes Démocrates*, a new law has been adopted that sanctions sexual harassment in Tunisia's penal code.[10] The matter of sexual harassment, however, is still a taboo and women who have been victims of it do not always feel able to recount the assaults they have suffered. This is what the women unionists claim and according to them, the women who react this way do so because they do not want to have fingers pointed at them for matters that would "sully" them and do more harm than good. The ATFD also concluded that women who filed sexual harassment complaints to protect their dignity could end up being fired from their jobs. In that sense, the right to dignity would constitute an obstacle to their right to work. It is clear that any sexually related matter remains taboo for women. Furthermore, as was observed at a celebration at the UGTT's Tunis headquarters in March 2006 by a female unionist from the northwest of Tunisia, the application of the law differs in all regions of the country and is even disregarded by some local authorities.

The obstacles also stem from the government's political and socioeconomic choices. Educational advancement and full enjoyment of the right to an education are the first issues. Of the 1958 law on a national education system open to all children, only its free aspect remains, although it allowed education to be introduced in all urban and rural areas. Only in 1991, however, did the government introduce a law making education not only free, but mandatory as well.[11] An important measure was introduced, which benefited children because penal sanctions were delivered to parents who prevented their children, whether girls or boys, from going to school and furthering their education. In practice, however, the application of this measure is hindered by economic obstacles, such as the parents' lack of financial means, as well as by geographical obstacles, such as the long distance to the schools and the remoteness of some villages. In such cases, it is impossible to enforce the law, which means that children, including young girls, are not able to attend school when they live far away, especially in rural areas where parents are free to ignore the law.

Despite these limitations, the illiteracy rate for women and girls significantly dropped from 78.2% in 1966 to 36.1% in 1999 and to 31.1% in 2004–2005 (official statistics, cited in CREDIF, 2001b). Furthermore, according to national statistics, the percentage of female students today is 58.1%, which represents a significant change within the Tunisian society in comparison with the time of the nation's independence, as well as women's determination to achieve an advanced level of education. This is the result of having made education mandatory, which has reduced the impulse to keep girls at home or take them out of school at an early age.

Women's access to education has had a number of consequences. A legal age of marriage was set in 1956 when the Personal Status Code was promulgated, and in 1964, the government set it at 17 for women and 20 for men. Today, the average age at first marriage is far more advanced: 26 years for women and 31 years for men. Family size had dropped to 2 children since 1999 from 7.2 in 1966 (CREDIF, 2005, citing INS). This new outlook on marriage and the number of children mirrors the new priorities of women, which are threefold: get an education in order to reach a minimum level of education; obtain a job in order to provide for their basic needs and be autonomous; and get married and build a preferably nuclear-type family.

The distribution of the economically active population shows that the percentage of active women significantly increased between 1966 and 2002, rising from 6.1% to 25.3%, although they still only account for one-fourth of the overall active population. According to CREDIF (2002b), the rate is higher in urban areas (25.8%) than in rural areas (22.5%). The UGTT commissioned a study conducted by Dorra Mahfoudh-Draoui (1988), which broke down women's work into different categories, as seen in Table 4.1.

Table 4.1. Women's Presence in the Different Sectors and Within Unions

	Percentage of Salaried Women, 1984	Percentage of Female Unionists, 1983
Textiles, weaving, and confection industry	62	55
Public health	41	30
Banks and insurance companies	29	30
Education	29	23
Telecommunications	18.5	12
Agriculture	4.6	3.5

Source: Mahfoudh-Draoui (1988).

It is obvious that within the textiles and clothing industry, women are the majority. However, although in 2010 women represented 70% of all employees working in textiles, only one woman was a member of the National Federation of Textiles. In 1946, Cherifa Messaadi was the first and to date only woman ever elected to the executive board of the UGTT. (The Board of Higher Education and Scientific Research appointed its first woman member only in 1980.) In other words, the proportion of women in unions does not mirror the real number of women who work in the industry. As Mahfoudh-Draoui noted in her 1988 study, "The UGTT has a tradition of neglecting women" (p. 39), hence their lack of representation within leading structures. More than 20 years later, this had not changed.

Of the entire female workforce, divorced women make up 41.5%, widows 10.1%, single women 34.4%, and married women 18%. Single women who are heads of their households therefore make up 80% of the female workforce, whereas married women only account for about 20%. Where are women employed? A study of the distribution of women by job group shows that the majority of women are domestic helpers, which is to say 55.3%, whereas only 23.9% are salaried employees, 17.5% are self-employed, and 8.4% own their own companies (CREDIF, 2002a). However, it is important to note that women's presence at different levels and within different professions diminishes the higher the hierarchical level and the more important the task, whereas there are more women when it comes to menial or clerical jobs.

Thus, in the case of civil servants, for example, although women made up 21.6% of all government officials in the year 2000, their unequal distribution among the different government ranks means that they are underrepresented in certain decision-making positions. That year, there were no female state secretary generals and just 20 female director generals compared with 310 male directors, which is to say just a 6% female share at this level. Although male directors numbered 1,115, there were only 136 female directors, or just 11%. There were only 305 female assistant directors compared with 1,785 men in such positions, or a 14% female share. And just 20% of "heads of service" were women. All other female civil servants remained concentrated within clerical occupations (Saidi, 2001).

Salaried women in the professions are concentrated in the public sector, primarily in education and health care, and to a lesser degree in public administration. In 2010, women constituted 42% of tertiary-level educators, about half of all health workers, and 28% of members of parliament. According to the World Economic Forum's *Global Gender Gap Report 2010*, however, they were only 4% of those in ministerial positions and just 9% of all legislators, senior officials, and managers. Overall, 75% of all women work in agriculture, textiles, or in administrative, education or health care services. The remaining 25% is evenly distributed among social and cultural services; trade; and other fields such as agricultural processing, banking, insurance, transport and telecommunications; and the chemical, engineering, and power industries (CREDIF, 2002a).

Within the private sector, women mostly are grouped within the textiles and clothing branch, much of which consists of informal work. Women are mainly "textile workers" because the sector employs more than 30% of the active female workforce (CREDIF, 2001b, citing INS). The sector holds more than 2,000 firms, around 50% of which are foreign or foreign investment firms. Textiles and garments contribute to more than 45% of all exports and employ around 50% of the manufacturing industry, of which the majority are women (Ben Ali, 2005). For the past several years however, the number of laid-off women workers in the textiles and garments industry has been increasing. The women in this industry have to endure every single one of the sector's inherent difficulties, such as the consequences of outsourcing and the dismantling in January 2005 of the Multifibre Arrangement. This was followed by the closing-down of several textiles, clothing and leather firms, decreased production, and increased female unemployment (Gouia, 2001; Marouani, 2004).

In an effort to bypass the Tunisian Employment Code, especially with regard to dismissals, employers are no longer signing fixed-term contracts with their employees, which would allow job stability, better working conditions, and gradual upward mobility, and are instead taking on fixed-term outsourcing contracts or filling permanent positions by recruiting people through work experience placements that are paid less than the minimum guaranteed interprofessional wages, by using temporary management firms like *Intérim*. For some jobs (such as secretaries, cleaning staff, caretakers, and handlers), salaries generally are a little higher, although at the expense of social rights. Such workers often end up in precarious and unstable situations because of the job flexibility act. They suffer from poor working conditions because their basic social rights and their rights as women, especially regarding social security, are not upheld.

Theoretically, employment policies and social security legislation cover all women who work in the textiles industry. All employees are covered because social security is based on salary. It often is the case, however, even for those female interns, temporary workers and informal workers (cleaning ladies, domestic helps, rural workers) who do receive a salary, that their employers will not take out social coverage for them. Social studies show that most workers own health record booklets that allow men and women to benefit from social coverage, such as free health care in hospitals, as well as benefit from welfare (for the handicapped, the elderly, the poor) by contributing one dinar a day. Therefore, a form of social coverage does exist. However, a lack of training and information means that young women workers do not know whether or not they are covered by the Tunisian National Social Security Fund. The risk is that as informal and temporary jobs increase, social security coverage decreases.

Therefore, working conditions are not always entirely satisfactory and the rule is that jobs are precarious. In 1998, Mahfoudh-Draoui spoke of "extended work placements," because they were deemed "inconclusive" yet still renewed, although without overtime being paid due to "low productivity" or to compensate for a transit strike, a power cut or a blackout. Added to this are the frequent and unfair dismissals, which are made easier by the fact that work contracts often are not made in writing. This explains the high number workers who go on strike, occupy various locales and for their social rights, especially the right to proper working conditions and remuneration.

A good example is the case of the 275 women workers of Hotrifat, a textiles workshop in Moknine, about 180 kilometers from Tunis, who in January 2004, went on strike to protest their mass dismissal and occupy their place of work, the Hotrifat workshop. There had been no warning that the workshop would close its doors and the workers had always been careful of doing a good job in order to keep the workshop running, and earn a living. The director, a Dutch citizen, made the sudden decision with no thought or care for what would become of the 300 men and women workers who would be out on the streets. His personal material gain being his only care, he had for months been planning to open two new workshops in the neighboring town, Ksar Helal. The 275 women workers, therefore, went on strike to attract attention at local, national, and international levels, especially within unions, nongovernmental organizations (NGOs), political parties, public figures, and members of parliament. Their goal was to preserve their jobs and gain public support. Their claims were to receive their salary for the month of December 2003; to receive their production bonus for 2003; to be paid for their layoff during the month of January 2004: and to start negotiations between all involved in order to reopen the workshop.

The workers occupied the factory for over 1 month, during which time they slept on the ground, on pieces of cardboard, on wooden pallets, and on mattresses. Some brought their babies with them. Their distress was very real, as they had not been paid in 2 months. The authorities' proposals were not encouraging in the least: The workers were offered a mere 65 euros or U.S. $80 as "welfare," a 180 dinar bonus, and vague promises. In exchange for this, the strike was to end and the strikers were to go back home.[12] NGOs specializing in human rights and women's rights, such as the Tunisian League for the Defense of Human Rights and the ATFD answered the call and an important delegation, made up of people from various towns in Tunisia, such as Sfax, Sousse, Monastir, Tunis, Moknine and its neighboring towns, came to visit the strikers and show their support.

Also in January 2004, in the Mazallat workshop in the Sousse region, blind women workers who were earning 40 dinars per month, in direct violation of sectorial laws and conventions, went on strike to demand higher pay and defend their right to work. The negotiations led by the Regional Union of Sousse, the National Union for the Blind in Tunisia, and the Tunisian League for the Defense of Human Rights ended in the decision of the regional authorities to shut down the workshop, send all workers older than 50 years of age into immediate retirement, and fire those under age 50 with a bonus until the age of retirement.

Another example is Soupatex, a Belgian workshop that had relocated in Tunisia 30 years prior and that employed 350 workers. The workshop was one of the most flourishing but when management decided to cut the work time to 36 hours a week, salaries decreased as well. When the workers were not paid in 3 months, they went on strike. The women finally ended up being laid off from their job when the manager of the workshop disappeared!

In trying to remedy these risks and avoid ending up unemployed, women have been setting up micro firms within the informal economy, with the help of microcredits that are loaned to them by the Tunisian Solidarity Bank or NGOs such as ENDA. The firms often are developed as a means of survival for unemployed women to improve their family's living standard. The women's primary goal is less one of entrepreneurship than one of rapidly finding lucrative activities. Some possess a certain know-how and were able to set up sewing or confection shops, whereas others have opened up little neighborhood shops or have become itinerant traders and sell clothing and objects of all sorts (CREDIF, 2001a; ENDA, 1997). Small business development is part of the globalization agenda, but low-income women usually turn to this in the absence of stable paid employment and guaranteed social rights.

In other fields, women work outside of the law and in total ignorance of the legal texts in force and even of social customs and traditions. Such is the case of domestic employees, who, although protected by a law dating from July 1965 still work illegally or in direct violation of this law.[13] These women, of whom there are more than 50,000, are not recruited in any determined manner.[14] The duration of the job as well as the number of working hours are not predetermined and neither is their salary or any social coverage they may be enjoying.

Despite the fact that women's economic rights have a limited scope and are difficult to uphold, women still gravitate to the job market and have changed their priorities in line with their will to work in order to satisfy their basic needs and achieve autonomy no matter what part the government plays. Were women's social rights upheld and economic citizenship expanded, Tunisian women would flood the job market.

THE UGTT AND WOMEN WORKERS

According to the UGTT's policy, both active workers as well as retirees have the right to freely join. Its documents show that in September 2005, there were 517,000 members, 35% of whom were women (see, e.g., UGTT, 2005, 2006). Fully 38% of all members are under the age of 35, which means that the union is able to attract younger workers. Although Tunisian women's labor-force participation was increasing in the 1970s and 1980s, their numbers did not significantly change within the nation's trade unions, especially in leadership positions (CREDIF, 2002a, 2002b; Mahfoudh-Draoui, 1999). Women's first steps within trade unions would take place via teaching and the textiles and clothing industry.

An economic crisis like the one that hit the country at the end of the 1970s was probably necessary in order to help narrow the gap between the government and employers' and workers' organizations such as the UGTT, Tunisian Union for Industry, Commerce and Handicrafts (UTICA) and National Union of Agriculturists and help solve the issues linked with the numerous strikes around the country. The increase in salary that followed helped better the citizens' living standards. However, between 1986 and 1991, the minimum wage dropped 3% despite a 2% increase in average wages between 1992 and 1997 (Ennaceur, 2000). During this time of protest, the first female trade union was created at the International Women's Day celebration in March 1981 by a group of female scholars when female trade unionists decided to create a commission of women workers within the UGTT (Marzouki, 1993). The issue was once again brought to the fore a year later, in March 1982, during a meeting organized by women in higher education. The meeting's agenda was to the point because it was called "Women and Work." It exposed the different hardships endured by women within the world of work and brought attention to little-known problems that demonstrated the need to act fast. At this point, the creation of a women's commission within the UGTT was announced by Taïeb Baccouche.[15]

A few weeks later, a trade union committee on women's conditions was created. The members, of whom there were around 60, continued to convene until March 1983, although after that, unionists did not attend as often. The number of women who continued attending the meetings, among whom some were steadfastly against feminism, was low (CREDIF, 2002a). The commission is appointed for 4-year terms and aims to promote women workers protect their right to work and supervise and promote women's union work. However, the 13 members who were appointed to the executive board in 2002 were all men.

Education has played an important part not only in getting women to join unions but also with regard to the workers' young age because it also is within the youngest age groups that women are more likely to have joined unions. As the right to join unions is protected by the Constitution, a high number of young women workers have joined the UGTT, despite the distrust of their employers. The opposite is true when women gain more professional training and seniority, usually between the ages of 40 and 59 when only 18% are union members, as opposed to 30% of men in the same age group. Studies conducted by Dorra Mahfoudh-Draoui in 1988, 1999, and 2006 reached the same conclusion, which is that there are fewer women than men involved in unions, especially in leadership positions. Fear of being fired probably explains why the number of women who decide to join is not higher and why the right to join unions is recognized neither by national firms, nor by the foreign firms implanted in Tunisia. A glance at recent UGTT publications shows that unionism is still mainly men's territory. Indeed, women are rarely present in photos and, no surprise here, especially when representing leadership positions. There is a much larger number of women at lower levels.

The few studies on women and trade unions that exist provide interesting facts. (See Tables 4.1 to 4.5 for summary data.) Women union members are rarely illiterate. The women with the lowest salaries have noticeably increased their level of educational advancement and the number of unionized women is almost equal to that of men when their level of education is more advanced. Finally, women usually are more educated than men and it is these women who remain union members if they are still part of the job market (Mahfoudh-Draoui, 1991, 2006).

Women in the older age groups are less likely to be union members. What reason(s) is (are) there to explain women's absence within unions despite having successfully joined and "feminized" the world of work? Why is it more difficult for them to fill the positions they deserve within unions, in light of their position within the world of work? It seems that their youth is what first prevents them from being given union responsibilities. When they reach the age of 35, which is when studies show an increase in their departure from unions, it seems that women leave their jobs and/or unions in order to take care of their families. Past 35 indeed, women often choose to get married and focus on their children's education. The dearth of nurseries and day-care centers is an important factor, especially in rural zones; however, the weight of tradition and culture is also an important factor, according to which the role of educating children falls to mothers. Therefore, it seems that women join and leave the workforce earlier than men, who on the contrary, can go on to combine seniority with expertise and promotions (Mahfoudh-Draoui, 1999).

What is the impact of women's unionization? One may be that it encourages women workers' militancy, such as those described here. However, it has not been translated into roles for women in senior union positions. Table 4.2 shows the percentage of men and women who were on executive boards in 2001 in three unions. The male–female ratio for UTICA's executive board clearly shows the gap between men (88%) and women (a mere 12%). With respect to the Tunisian Union of Agriculture and Fishery, the gap is quite wide, as men represent 90.9% of the members, whereas women represent a mere 9.1%. A similar huge gender gap is evident with respect to men and women in higher-level positions at UGTT. The table shows that while the unions are attracting women, they remain traditionally male institutions, especially at senior and decision-making levels.

Table 4.2. Men and Women on Union Boards, 2001

	Members on UTICA's Executive Board, %[a]	Members in Higher-Level Positions at UGTT, %	Men and Women in Higher-Level Positions at UTAP, %[b]
Male	88	99	90.9
Female	12	1	9.1
Total	100	100	100

[a]Union Tunisienne des Industries, du Commerce et de l'Artisanat (UTICA), Chart: EVOFO NC6 "Distribution by gender of the members of UTICA's executive board" (2001).

[b]Union Tunisienne de l'Agriculture et de la Pêche (UTAP), Chart: EVOFONC4, "Distribution by gender of the members in high-level positions" (2001).

Table 4.3. Women and the UGTT Congress in 2002

Number of Male Delegates	Number of Female Delegates	Percentage of Female Delegates	Number of Female Candidates	Number of Women Appointed
457	27	5.9%	4	0

Source: UGTT, obtained by the authors.

UGTT information obtained by the authors shows that there has been a presence of women in the UGTT congresses. Out of the 27 female delegates (compared with 457 male delegates) at the 2002 UGTT Congress, only four were candidates, bravely attempting to enter a field that had thus far been only marginally explored by women. It is therefore unsurprising to observe that despite some women's efforts, no female delegate was appointed. In 2009, the situation was not significantly different; there was no growth in the presence of women in decision-making positions in labor unions.

Tables 4.3 and 4.4 show that the percentage of unionized women has remained low; this is especially the case within high-level positions, where there are no women. This could be so for a number of reasons: on the one hand, the men might not be ready to give up their decision-making positions and although they readily accept women's presence within unions, they are reluctant to give them additional responsibilities. On the other hand, female solidarity seems to be lacking and, according to a number of interviews, women are not able to come to an understanding and are not ready to be burdened with such important responsibilities. They are, however, aware of the secondary part they play and look forward to a change in their favor.

Table 4.4 Women in Decision Making Within the Unions' Intermediary and Higher-Level Structures (2002–2006)

Structures	Number of Men in High-Level Positions	Number of Women in High-Level Positions	Percentage of Women in High-Level Positions, %
Local federations and unions	39 (351)	19	5.4
Regional unions	24 (216)	2	0.9
Total	**567**	**21**	**3.7**
Executive board	13	0	0
Total	**580**	**21**	**3.6**

Source: UGTT, obtained by the authors.

Other data from 2005 to 2006 clearly show the low percentage of women within the UGTT's different sectors.[16] Table 4.5 shows that even within highly feminized sectors such as education, health care, and textiles in particular, women are reluctant to run for election. Thus, in the textiles sector, despite their overwhelming majority, only five women ran for election in 2005–2006 and the results (two out of the five were elected) seem to show that even women prefer voting for men, no doubt believing that men are more capable of defending their interests (see Table 4.6).

Another conclusion to be drawn by these data is that the presence of women within the trade union executive boards varies from one sector to another and is linked to their number within these sectors. The more workers of both genders there are within a sector, the more union members there are. According to Mahfoudh-Draoui, women's absence from wage labor has consequences upon their union work. Another reason for the low percentage of women within unions is the fact that women's union work is a relatively new concept, having only been launched in 1980 as stated earlier (Mahfoudh-Draoui, 1988).

WOMEN'S TRADE UNION INVOLVEMENT: THE 2006 SURVEY FINDINGS

The survey was commissioned by the *Collectif 95 Maghreb-Egalité*, a transnational network of women's rights advocates from Algeria, Morocco, and Tunisia. AFTURD and the *Femmes Démocrates* are the principal Tunisian women members of the Collectif, and the Tunisian side of the study—specifically, the analysis of women's roles in the UGTT—was supervised by AFTURD. It was conducted by Dorra Mahfoudh-Draoui, an early president of AFTURD and a sociologist who specializes in women's employment and work conditions.

In what way does women's involvement in trade union assemblies manifest itself? Not only are there few women present, but the women usually remain silent and many of them leave the meetings before the assemblies

Table 4.5 Women's Representation Within Intermediary Structures, 2002

Intermediary Structures	Female Candidates	Appointed Women
Local federations and unions	29	19
Regional unions	13	2
Total	42	21

Source: UGTT, obtained by the authors.

Table 4.6. Representation of Women Within Local Federations in Different Sectors With a High Number of Women (2005–2006)

Local Federations and Unions	Number of Candidates	Number of Appointed Women
Secondary education	2	1
Basic education	2	1
Supervision and counseling	6	4
Textiles	5	2
Health care	2	1
Professions and services	2	2
Post office	0	0
Social funds	2	1

Source: UGTT, obtained by the authors.

are over. How do they justify their behavior? The reasons they give for their absence/silence/early departures are numerous and are motivated by the same reasons for their family responsibilities: Making sure their children do their schoolwork and eat their meal; not knowing their rights; preconceptions that they are incapable of being efficient because of their lack of a militant background. Many women believe that men are better able to protect their interests due to their experience as militants and because women usually trust men.

Some women believe that the members who are present will or can speak for those who are absent, but their assumption is not always correct. Indeed, although male unionists may be accustomed to defending the union rights of employees, they, however, are not always capable of presenting the problems that directly relate to women. No matter what group they belong to, minorities (women, children, teachers, textiles, or leather workers) should be represented by a member of their own group. Unfortunately, and in the case of this study, although there are a large number of unionized female workers, few to none hold leadership positions.

How do women envision their roles within unions? Unionized women often claim that they are not at ease during union assemblies. The main reason for this unease is that they remain a minority to the male majority. They are aware that although they have been accepted within the UGTT, men are not ready to give up their positions to them. On some occasions, women are even booed, which is embarrassing, even humiliating, and discouraging to them. This awkward situation is a major factor in creating a hostile atmosphere to women and in which they remain a minority.

The 2006 survey of women union members in Tunisia is highly indicative of a situation that had hardly changed, despite an undeniable increase in the number of unionized women. The low involvement of women in contrast with that of men, is seen as the result of a lack of free time and interest, as well as of will and of knowledge of the union world (Mahfoudh-Draoui, 2006). Still, 61% of unionized women believe there should be as many women as there are men within the unions. Some 42% of all union members, however, believe there should be more men, whom they see as more capable and competent. According to 16% of the people who were polled, men also are deemed more available than women.

Are there any women who are in favor of a female majority? Unsurprisingly, according to the 2006 survey, only 4% hope for a female majority within the unions out of a belief that they are more capable than men and can better present the hardships they endure in the world of work (Mahfoudh-Draoui, 2006) There should be more women, especially within sectors where they are highly present such as textiles and health care. Thus, 55% of the women believe that women are more capable of presenting the problems they have as women workers. The issue of the need to change the UGTT's internal organization was raised by 40% of those polled (Mahfoudh-Draoui, 2006).

Of the 295 union members who were interviewed in 2006, 72% were men and 28% women. As stated previously, women's unionization is a relatively recent occurrence. This is apparent in the UGTT's very organization. The majority of the union members, which is to say 74%, have been members for less than 15 years, and one out of every three women has been a member for less than 5 years. Interestingly, despite the relatively low involvement of women, an overwhelming majority, 82% of the men, and 91% of the women are open to having a woman elected within the union (Mahfoudh-Draoui, 2006). Therefore, it is only a minority that is opposed to such an election, and speaks of women being weaker in this field, and of men being more capable. However, this seems to point to a latent mentality that explains why women are not present in the union's high-level positions, and that is that the world of trade unions is a man's world and while women have been let in, it is only as auxiliaries and not as persons in charge. This means, for example, that those who are open to electing women are, however, not willing to support and vote for them as members of the executive board. There is a reason why no woman sits on the executive board. At a local or regional level, voting for a woman is acceptable but that is where any support ends.

This begs the following question: How can women achieve greater visibility within the world of unions and more specifically, occupy high-level positions on the executive board? We believe that this is a necessary step toward the protection and expansion of women's social and economic rights.

CONCLUSIONS AND RECOMMENDATIONS

When compared with other Arab countries, the social rights of Tunisian women and their economic citizenship are more advanced. And yet, as we have seen, there are many deficits in terms of economic participation, work conditions, and economic decision making. In addition, the economic model pursued by the government of President Ben Ali had led to the deterioration of employment opportunities and social rights. This is a key factor behind the mass social protests that led to his downfall in early 2011.

The democratic transition that Tunisia began in early 2011 has its own challenges, but we believe that addressing the social rights and economic citizenship of women will help bring about a more robust democracy that serves all citizens and not just the elites. The fight against illiteracy needs to be sped up to allow women and young girls to aspire to better living standards, to know their rights, and to negotiate more effectively. Regional disparities in women's educational attainment, health care, poverty, employment, and household income should be narrowed. These disparities widen the gap between legal protection and the actual enjoyment of rights, and only serve to further inequalities between men and women (Tunisian Republic, 2004).

Measures are needed to alleviate employment instability and flexibility in order to guarantee job security and better protect unqualified women workers who, due to the precarious nature of their jobs are prevented from benefiting from professional training and occupational retraining toward their promotion within their place of work.

In order to promote women's status within the world of work, the concept of gender equality first needs to be recognized within families, which are a microcosm of society and where acceptance of the concept of equality is taking time. Indeed, despite the lasting changes brought about by the latest amendments, such as the 1993 amendment that repealed the clause that requires a wife to obey her spouse, the role of family head still falls to the father/husband and therefore prevents change from occurring within other parts of society, particularly regarding women's status within the unions.

There needs to be better recognition of women's reproductive functions as social functions that should be taken on simultaneously by both parents and by the institutions, and therefore prevent women from being forced to take on full responsibility for these functions. In fact, in 2006, a law was adopted to allow women to work part time and receive two-thirds of their salary. Under the guise of protecting women's right to work, this law will further discriminate against women at work, weaken their status, and prevent upward mobility as well as promotions to staff positions.

The government must ratify all international conventions regarding the specific rights of women, such as Convention C 183, 2000 on maternity protection, as well as modify employment legislation so women may benefit from pre- and postnatal maternity leave. More nurseries and day-care centers should accept a nominal fee, in order to avoid working mothers from having to suffer the consequences of having babies and putting them through school, and to reassure them of their children's safety when they are at work.

Measures should be taken to guarantee that women are able to effectively benefit from their rights, when being recruited, trained or promoted, by establishing a quota system on the number of women at all decision-making levels. With respect to the trade unions, it is crucial to make of parity an established fact in order to guarantee a more important and effective presence of women within the unions' high-level positions. A quota system also is recommended.

Women should be encouraged to massively join unions and lobby for the right to occupy decision-making positions in order to guarantee better female representation. To achieve this, a training program to develop women's union skills should be set up. Women's issues need to be addressed and various incentives created so that they are encouraged to become active union members (Mahfoudh-Draoui, 2006). Women should be persuaded that it is in their best interest to hold union responsibilities to improve their working conditions and promote their rights based on gender equality.

It should be noted that the partnership that has been established for the past few years between the UGTT and autonomous organizations such as AFTURD, the *Femmes Démocrates*, and human rights organizations such as Amnesty International and the Tunisian League for Human Rights has had a very positive impact, in that female union members have understood the importance of fighting for their rights as women. The UGTT and AFTURD have worked together on projects related to workplace sexual harassment, women's loss of work, and legal literacy, with funding from the European Union or the Tunisian government. The cooperation among civil society organizations also had a positive influence on government withdrawal of reservations to CEDAW. A common campaign to that effect took place in October 2005 at the headquarters of the *Femmes Démocrates*, followed by another in December 2006, to commemorate the Universal Declaration of Human Rights. Other meetings took place dealing with the CEDAW in the Arab world, in particular in Rabat, Morocco (June 2006); the outcome was the formation of an Arab regional network to help lift the reservations to CEDAW made by Arab states. In June 2009, another meeting took place in Amman, Jordan to consolidate this campaign. AFTURD and the *Femmes Démocrates* are determined to work toward the expansion of women's civil, political, and social/economic rights of citizenship; to that end, we continue collaborations with trade unions, human rights groups, and other networks in Tunisia, the Maghreb, and the wider Arab region.[17]

NOTES

1. Law No 98-919 of November 9, 1998, on community property between spouses. Law adopted by the Chamber of Deputies on October 20, 1998.

2. There is a large literature on these issues. In addition to the sources cited in the text, see the following: Ayachi (2006); Auvret (1983); Baffoun (1987); Chourabi (2005); Gaudier (1996); and Lochak (1988).

3. The laws mentioned above, respectively, were ratified as follows: Convention ratified by law 68-21 of July 20, 1969 (Official Journal of the Tunisian Republic, p. 743); Ratified by law 59-94 of August 20, 1959 (Official Journal of the Tunisian Republic, p. 886); Ratified by law 69-30 of July 2nd, 1964 (Official Journal of the Tunisian Republic, p. 816); Ratified by law 69-30 of July 2, 1964 (Official Journal of the Tunisian Republic, p. 816); Ratified by the French law of March 30, 1938, followed by Tunisia on June 12, 1959.

4. Each of these conventions was ratified by law 57-41 of November 21, 1967 (Official Journal of the Tunisian Republic, p. 1441).

5. Ratified by law 85-68 of July 12, 1985 (Official Journal of the Tunisian Republic, p. 919).

6. Adopted in 1959 by Civil Service Law, although only in 1993 by the workers' statute.

7. These provisions are found in Article 64, paragraph (a) of labor law, section on women workers in the private sector and Article 48 of Civil Service Law; Article 64, paragraph (b) of the labor law allows working women who are nursing mothers to take two 30-minute breastfeeding leaves daily, during hours and until the child is 12 months old.

8. With the obvious exception of the General Statutes on office staff and public establishments that have provided the possibility, since 1999, for one of the parents to choose to be available to educate one child or more, or to care for a child with a serious disability.

9. According to law No. 85 of March 5, 1985 on civil and military pensions and the survivors of the public sector (Official Journal of the Tunisian Republic) p. 359, as modified by law No. 88-71 of June 27, 1988 (Official Journal of the Tunisian Republic, p. 965).

10. Law No. 2004-73 of August 2, 2004, article 226 b was added to the Tunisia penal code to eliminate sexual harassment and define it, while article 226 c allows the presumed offender who has been cleared of charges to demand reparation for the prejudice cause on the grounds of calumnious denunciation.

11. Law No. 91-65 of June 29, 1991 on the educational system (Official Journal of the Tunisian Republic, p. 1308).

12. From the edition of Essabah (daily newspaper) of September 7, 2004 and RÉALITES (daily) of January 25, 2004.

13. Law No. 65-25 of July 1, 1965 on domestic employees (Official Journal of the Tunisian Republic, p. 826).

14. From the edition of Essabah (daily) of September 7, 2001 and RÉALITES (daily) of January 25, 2001.

15. Mr. Taïeb Baccouche was elected Secretary General of the UGTT at the 15th Congress (April 29–30, 1981), and remained in that post until 1988. In 1998 he was elected president of the Arab Institute for Human Rights.

16. These are photocopies of handwritten charts that were handed to us at UGTT headquarters, which cover 2002 to 2006.

17. In 2008, another amendment was made to Tunisia's Code of Personal Status, recognizing women's right to keep their house after a divorce when they have minor children in their custody (Chekir, 2009). This was another achievement of the women's movement toward women's social/economic rights.

REFERENCES

Ayachi, W. (2006, March). Les Femmes et le Travail Syndical: La Voie de L'Ouvrier. *Ben Arous Regional Branch Newsletter.*

Auvret, P. (1983). L'Égalité des Sexes dans la Fonction Publique. Revue du droit public et de la science politique: 1583.

Baffoun, A. (1987). L'Accès des Tunisiennes au Salariat: Caractéristiques et Incidences [Tunisian women's access to payment by salary]. In A. Michel, H. Agbessi-Dos Santos, & A. Fatoumata Diarra (Eds.), *Extrait de " 'Femmes et Multinationales"* (pp. 227–245). Paris: Karthala.

Ben Ali, A. (2005, April 8). Comment Sauver le Textile Maghrébin? *Réalités.* Retrieved May 2009 www.maghrebarabe.org/fr/Espace_information//presse/20050804.htm.

Center for Research, Documentation and Information on Women (CREDIF). (2001a). *Les Femmes Entrepreneurs en Tunisie, Paroles et Portraits.* Tunis: Author.

Center for Research, Documentation and Information on Women (CREDIF). (2001b). *L'Homme et la Femme en Tunisie à Travers les Chiffres.* Statistiques de l'INS. Tunis: Author.

Center for Research, Documentation and Information on Women (CREDIF). (2002a). *Femmes et Emploi en Tunisie.* Tunis: Author.

Center for Research, Documentation and Information on Women (CREDIF). (2002b). *Femmes et hommes en Tunisie en chiffres.* Tunis: Author.

Center for Research, Documentation and Information on Women (CREDIF). (2005). *La Femme Tunisienne Acteur de Développement Régional.* Tunis: Author.

Chekir, H. (2009). Les Femmes dans la Fonction Publique, le Principe de Non-Discrimination et l'approche Genre." In Mohamed Salah Ben Aissa (Ed.), *La Fonction Publique Aujourd'hui: Le Statut Général de laFfonction Publique 25 ans Après* (pp. 123–138). Centre de publications universitaires..

Chourabi, S. (2005). Soupatex: Licenciement Chômage. Retrieved November 2009 http://j-t-antimondialistes.blogspot.com.

ENDA. (1997). *La Débrouille au Féminin, Stratégies de la Débrouillardise des Femmes des Quartiers Défavorisés en Tunisie.* Tunis: Author

Ennaceur, M. (2000). *Les Syndicats et la Mondialisation: Le Cas de la Tunisie. Program des Institutions du Travail et du Développement.* Genève, Switzerland: Institut

International d'Etudes Sociales.Gaudier, M. (1996). *La Question des Femmes à L'OIT et son Évolution 1919–1994.* Program sur les Activités Éducatives et Intersectorielles.

Gouia, R. (2001, May). *Sous-traitance, mondialisation et travail des femmes.* Tunis.

Lochak, D. (1988). Réflexions sur la Notion de Discrimination. *Revue du Droit Social.*

Mahfoudh-Draoui, D. (1988, July-December). La Syndicalisation des Femmes en Tunisie. Les Femmes et la Modernité. *Peuples Méditerranéens,* pp. 44–45.

Mahfoudh-Draoui, D. (1999). *Les Femmes Tunisiennes entre le Travail et L'Engagement Syndical (Approche comparée par genre).* Tunis: UGTT, Département de L'Education et de la Formation Ouvrière.

Mahfoudh-Draoui, D. (2006). *L'Égalité entre les Femmes et les Hommes dans la Société Tunisienne. Famille, Travail, Syndicalisation.* Unpublished manuscript.

Marouani, M.A. (2004). *Effet de L'Accord D'Association avec L'Union Européenne et du Démantèlement de L'Accord Multifibres sur L'Emploi en Tunisie* (Working Papers). Paris, France: DIAL.

Marzouki, I. (1993). *Le Mouvement des Femmes en Tunisie au XXème Siècle.* Tunis: Cérès Productions.

Msalmi, A. (2005). *Les Ouvrières à Sousse se Mettent en Grève afin de Défendre Leur Droit au Travail et à une Vie Digne.* Sousse: Ligue Tunisienne des Droits de L'Homme, section de Sousse (Février).

Organisation Internationale du Travail (OIT). "Femmes, Emploi et Micro entreprises en Tunisie." Report prepared for URBACONSULT (Document de travail ISEP/02/F). cited where in text? date of publication?

Saidi, F. (2001). *Étude sur la Participation des Femmes dans la Vie Publique.* Tunis: CREDIF.

Tunisian Republic. (2004, March). *ICPD + 10: The Tunisian Report.*

Union Générale Tunisienne du Travail (UGTT). (2005). *Le Secteur Textile et Habillement en Tunisie et le Pari de la Réinsertion Professionnelle des Travailleurs. Opinions Syndicales.* Tunis: UGTT, Publications du Département des études et de la documentation.

Union Générale Tunisienne du Travail (UGTT). (2006). Représentation des Femmes dans les Fédérations et les Syndicats de Base dans certains secteurs à forte densité féminine: 2005–2006. Retrieved May 2009 www.maghrebarabe.org/fr/Espace_information//presse/20050804.htm.

FIVE

GENDERED ECONOMIC RIGHTS
AND TRADE UNIONISM

The Case of Argentina

Graciela Di Marco

This chapter examines the social rights of working women in the context of economic and labor relations, as well as the dynamics of social movements and the struggle to broaden women's rights in Argentina since the early 1990s. Three central trade unions coexisted during this period: the longstanding General Confederation of Workers (CGT), the Movement of Argentine Workers (MTA), and the Congress of Argentine Workers (CTA). I devote special attention to the emergence of CTA, both as a central trade union and as a social (and political) movement, and the role of women's mobilizations in CGT and CTA, in terms of the gains and failures related to gender rights and especially the right to work.

The analysis is carried out from a twofold perspective: In the first, organizations provide scenarios to construct and negotiate the meanings of gender; in fact, gender—not just actions attributed to women—is inscribed in them (Di Marco, 2006a, 2006b). Second, feminist policy should not be understood as a form of politics devised for the pursuit of the interests of women as such, but rather as the pursuit of feminist goals and aspirations within a wider context of articulated demands (Mouffe, 1992). Consequently, I start from the premise that there exist many forms of feminism instead of choosing *a priori* one suitable form of feminist policy as contrasted to that upheld by other social movements. If we stop to think how strategies and identities of actors involved in social movements result in their mutual implication, then the different ways in which women participate in movements that are articulated with other struggles—exclusively feminine or not—may lead the battle to lessen gender subordination (Alvarez, 1990. cited in Molyneux, 2000).[1]

The 1980s witnessed the beginning of the debate about women's citizenship in order to demand legal reforms and State-run programs. Various conferences held by the United Nations, notably the Fourth World Conference on Women (held in Beijing in 1995), regional conferences by the UN Economic Commission for Latin America and the Caribbean in 1994, and the instructions of international financial institutions, which in the 1990s began to establish requirements regarding gender equity in policies aimed at struggling against poverty—these drove nearly every country in the region to adopt stances in favor of women's integration into development policies (Molyneux, 2000). The growing presence of women in the institutions of the State as well as the design of gender agendas is the product of an intertwining between the activism carried out by women's movements through organizations, networks, and alliances, and the new agenda of the States in the region to yield to international pressure and show some leadership in issues related to citizens rights (Molyneux, 2000). This same process had an impact on trade unions.

Argentina's trade unions had to confront ruptures deriving from the different stances on neoliberal policies held by Presidents Carlos Menem and Fernando De la Rua. They also had to face loss of members owing to increasing unemployment and to member rejection of the leaders who agreed with labor flexibility and looked away while many factories were being closed down. New political actors emerged—the movement of unemployed workers, with their distinctive protest mode (roadblocks) and intense activity in the neighborhoods and the movement of recovered enterprises. Those were the years when the CTA became consolidated and articulated with that new world, redefining the neighborhood as a work space and giving equal treatment to workers, irrespective of categories such as employed, unemployed, or irregular. Along these lines, they offered in actual practice a definition of citizenship that did not depend on the labor status of men and women (Novick, 2001).

MOVEMENTS AND RIGHTS

Argentina's social movements reflect the efforts to rebuild new modes of organization focused on the demands for wider citizenship to be achieved by claims for fundamental rights like the right to work, to live free from violence, and the legalization of abortion (Di Marco, 2006a, 2006b). The activities carried out by women inside the movements intersect with the wider women's movement and with the feminist movement. Many women from these movements participate in the Women's National Encounters or the National Campaign for the Right to Abortion. In this type of collective action in the public sphere it is possible to generate the development of a social critical consciousness that permits the broadening of women's rights while also improving living conditions. But there are still two issues that remain unsolved: the lack of skilled jobs and training for women to overcome the traditional segmentation of the labor market, and rethinking the relations of power and authority in the family.

Depending on the sort of movement, women define themselves differently regarding their interests and rights, at the same time deploying different strategies: One phenomenon that could be observed was the advent of popular women's struggles, carried out by women picketers, female workers in recovered enterprises, mothers fighting against police repression, and struggling rural women. In recent years, the Women's National Encounters were attended by tens of thousands of women.[2] These developments suggest a new historical phase in women's movements, one that may contribute to the consolidation of popular feminism in Argentina, through an alliance among women coming from different social, urban, and rural sectors.

LABOR LEGISLATION IN ARGENTINA

Traditionally, labor laws in Argentina protected women in their role of mothers, as the dominant ideal was that the family should be supported by a breadwinning male. The male was regarded as the primary beneficiary of social rights insofar as women and children depended on him. Although Peronism valued the importance of the role played by women in the economic field, it maintained that their most important contribution consisted in running the home and raising their children. Social integration through salary policies articulated different protective measures and guaranteed services for workers and their families.

The following is a list of the rights protected by the Contract Labor Law (LTC) (20.744/1974) and the laws that modify it, ruling individual labor relations in the private sector (Pautassi, 2001; Pautassi, Faur, & Gherardi, 2004):

- Maternity protection (LTC, Cl. 177). Prevents dismissal between 7.5 months before or after delivery.

- Same proviso for dismissal 3 months before wedding or 6 months after wedding

- 90-day maternity leave, 45 before and 45 after delivery (LCT clauses 183 to 186). At least a 30-day leave after delivery is compulsory (the mother is forbidden to work during this period.)

- Establishes two 30-minute breaks per full shift for breastfeeding (LCT, Cl. 179).

- Two-day paternity leave (LCT Cl. 158). There is a half-sanction for a draft to extend paternity leave to 15 days and then to 1 month.

- Employers must provide child-care facilities suited to the number of female workers (LCT Cl. 179), but this clause has not been developed so far. Law 11.317 established a minimum of 50 female workers over age 18 years to make child-care facilities obligatory at workplaces. Another law established provision of nearby day-care facilities for female workers less than 18 years of age (20.582). Some collective labor agreements include this provision or economic compensation for noncompliance with the law.

- Sick leave and sick child-care leave (LCT Cl. 183). Only mothers are entitled to it. Some collective work agreements include fathers.

THE 1990S: WOMEN'S MOVEMENTS AND LABOR RIGHTS

The passing of significant laws for women's rights in Argentina and certain provisions related to sexuality, reproduction, family and marriage, and work was possible due to the various social actors demanding greater justice, equality, and respect for human rights. Women in movements uphold several rights: those related to equality at work and reproductive/sexual rights and to live free of violence. Women's participation in trade union movements through women's areas in them correlates with the spaces women have earned in various layers of the State. Women in trade unions acquired the right to participate more actively in the unions as well as to enjoy improved working conditions related to the overall gender agenda. Regarding labor relations, the following laws and decrees were enacted as from 1995:

- 1997: Decree To Receive Equal Treatment among public officials;

- 1998: Decree establishing the Equal Opportunity Plan for men and women alike in the field of labor.

- 1998: Discriminatory dismissal based on race, sex, or creed was introduced as an illegal figure in the Labor Reform Law.

- 1993: Sexual harassment at workplace was introduced in the norms regulating Central Public Administration; the Government of the

Autonomous City of Buenos Aires included this figure in 1994. The Province of Santa Fe introduced it in 2001 and the Province of Buenos Aires in 2005. In May 2006 the Senate sanctioned a draft law to include sexual harassment in the Criminal Code. If the House of Representatives passed the corresponding law, the national legislation would fill a legal void on this issue.

- 2002: approval of a norm that establishes a quota for women to access positions implying union representation (30%). In the same year, a law was passed establishing proportional participation of female delegates in collective negotiations of working conditions, depending on the number of female workers in each sector or activity. Regarding female participation in elective positions, the minimum 30% quota law establishes that the law is mandatory when the number of female workers amounts to or is higher than 30% of the total number of workers of both sexes. If the percentage of female workers is lower, the quota should be proportional to the number of women, and the election lists should include at least that percentage of women in places where they are likely to win a position (Faur & Gherardi, 2005).

- 2004: the CGT amended its statute to introduce the Female Trade Union Quota.

- 2008: the Congress passed the Law of Integral Protection on the Prevention, Punishment, and Eradication of Violence against Women.

Both in the private and in the public sector, labor norms establish equal opportunity to access work positions. Still, no norms indicating that it is obligatory to establish quotas for certain jobs and positions have been included (Faur & Gherardi, 2005).

THE NEW SOCIOPOLITICAL AND ECONOMIC MODEL

In the second half of the 1970s, the last and bloodiest military dictatorship began to outline a new economic model that marked a turning point regarding the industrialization model grounded on the import substitution that had ruled Argentina's economy for nearly four decades. The new economic configuration was based on a huge opening of the economy together with a low rate of exchange that favored imports and put the competitiveness of important economic sectors at a great disadvantage. This process was accompanied by an ever-increasing foreign debt that was to impose harsh restrictions on the democratic administrations that came to power as from 1983. Argentina's national industry reached the peak of its crisis in the 1990s, with the corresponding decline of trade union power, a significant decrease in membership, little capacity to exercise any influence on the political arena, and leaders whose main concern was how to acquire monopolistic control of the health insurance systems under their control, for these have traditionally been illegitimate yet frequent sources of trade union funding.

Privatization in the early 1990s and the trust generated by economic stability attracted foreign investment and helped boost production. Tariff reductions on imported goods reduced the competitiveness of local industry and, later on, cost-effectiveness was affected by increases in the cost of utilities, which grew faster than manufactures. After the Mexican crisis toward the end of 1994, several countries, including Argentina, experienced a loss of credit flows, followed by a rise in interest rates. This had a severe impact on investment, consumption, and levels of production, all of which dropped significantly. Thus, industry ended up by expelling labor.

Economic changes brought about precariousness, flexibility, and disappearance of thousands of jobs as well as unpaid overtime, irregular work, and loss of social and retirement benefits to those who had managed to keep their jobs. Deterioration became institutionalized in the 1990s through the reforms of labor laws (part-time contracts for a predetermined length of time) and the loss of rights regarding working conditions (longer hours, irregular work, lack of social and retirement benefits) in the case of those who were still employed. Workers agreed to the new working conditions under the pressure of the "exemplifying effect" provided by the unemployed seeking for jobs (Di Marco & Moro, 2004). According to Novick and Tomada (2001), data on irregular work are important because those working under such conditions were excluded from access to health and from social and other benefits related to wages and salaries. In 1975, irregular work amounted to 17%; in the early 1980s the figure rose to 18.7%, and in 1989 it went up to 27.2%, an increase of nearly 10%. In 2000, irregular work soared to 39% (Novick & Tomada, 2001). In 2006, according to the national census bureau, 44.2% of the population was engaged in irregular or informal work; this population was not eligible for benefits nor did they contribute a part of their income to retirement funds (INDEC, 2006).

In 1974, 10% of the population in the capital and in Greater Buenos Aires had 28.2% of the total income (there was no data for Argentina as a whole). Under the military dictatorship, the said percentage rose to 33.1%. In 1994, the richest 10% owned 35.5% of the total income. Toward the end of 2003, the richest 10% possessed 38.6% of the total income. In 2006, after a period of economic recovery, the income of the wealthiest 10% of the population was 31 times higher than that of the poorest 10%. As for unemployment, open unemployment reached 18% in 1995, while salaries and wages dropped by 5% (Beccaria, 2001). For the first quarter of 2006, some 11.4% of the workforce was unemployed. In 2009, the percentage was near the same amount.

The high unemployment rate, the predominance of precarious employment and the low wages and salaries are to be blamed for poverty in Argentina. In 2002, at the height of the crisis, 57.5% of the country's inhabitants had become poor, and 27.5% were paupers. According to figures of the second quarter of 2005, the poor were 33.8% of the population (13 million people). Indigence decreased to 12.2%, or 4 million people (Di Marco, 2005, 2006a, 2006b).[3] In 2006, the poor constituted 25% of the population. Eighty percent of female breadwinners in poor households work in the informal economy and are paid lower wages/salaries than men.

WOMEN IN THE LABOR MARKET

It is generally agreed that in the 1990s women entered the labor market in an attempt to make up for their husbands' dropping income and/or contribute to support their households in order to keep up the family levels of consumption (Pautassi, 2001; Wainerman, 2003). In 1990, the male rate of employment reached 48.5% and dropped to 46.1% in 1999, while among women the same indicators pointed to 25.6% in 1990 and 28.2% in 1999. During the whole of the decade, the female unemployment rate was higher than its male counterpart: In 1996, it was estimated to be 20% for women and 15% for men (Pautassi, 2001). A 2005 governmental report about women's labor situation highlighted several characteristics (Contartese & Maceira, 2005). Acceleration in the increase of female activity rates in the 1990s is best explained by women from low and medium income households entering the labor market, within the framework of a strategy aiming to alleviate the damage caused by male heads of household unemployment and/or precarious jobs. Despite the process that drove women from low and medium income households into the labor market, the female economic share was much higher and more stable among women with higher educational attainment. Although poorly educated women had only 58% of poorly educated men's employment, women with the highest educational levels had 88% economic participation compared with similarly educated men. Women without a high school diploma were 2.3 times more likely to be out of a job than those with higher education. The older and less educated the women, the more likely they are to be underemployed. Nonetheless, there was a tendency for highly educated young women to encounter difficulty in obtaining their first job. Important differentials in women's participation are observed depending on the number of minors in their care.

The report also noted that despite women's increasing presence in the labor market, the occupational structure still showed a marked gender-based vertical and horizontal segregation. Domestic service, teaching, and social and health services were confirmed as feminine activities, whereas women's presence was marginal in the building industry, transport, and storage. Regarding vertical segregation, fewer women than men were promoted to supervisory positions: only 27.4% of the employed who had personnel under them and 28.3% of those who hold executive positions were women. One in four women with a high school diploma or college degree had jobs for which they were over qualified.

About 40% of employed women work in the informal sector (domestic service or places employing up to five people); 60% of women employed in the private sector are irregular workers; and there are still gender gaps in salaries and average hour/salary ratios. The gaps tend to widen among the best educated, highest qualified members of the population, especially in the private sector. Implementation of the Household Heads Plan in 2002 made an impact on the female work rate. Some 67% of those who benefit from this program, which requires labor in exchange for the money received, are women. Thus, a large number of women who need to work hard at chores and caregiving in their own homes are obliged to join the labor market (Pautassi, 2001; Pautassi & Enriquez, 2004).

THE WORKERS' MOVEMENT IN THE 1990S

There were numerous social responses to the socioeconomic, political, and cultural model that was setting in. However, despite the fact that trade unions engineered numerous strikes between 1989 and 1995, several authors point to the gradual dismantling of the trade union-based protest mode, which gave way to a civic or rights approach (Schuster & Pereyra, 2001; Scribano & Schuster, 2001).

From 1983 to 1988, 75% of the protests were led by the trade unions, especially those related to industrial activity. Next in line were human rights issues. Mobilizations were composed of workers and trade unions that had been affected by industrial rationalization processes and of various middle-class sectors that had been injured by market reforms. Cities of the interior saw organized demonstrations where whole towns came out into the streets in defense of their interests.[4] The 1990s saw growing trade union protests involving State employees, teachers, and workers in companies at risk because of planned privatization (telephones, gas, and electricity). From 1995 to 2001, a wider range of protest was observed; much of it related to citizenship rights, such as claims for extended justice, equality of opportunity, employment, and complaints against police brutality. Protest actions taken by the unemployed and roadblocks also gathered momentum at this time (Di Marco, 2005, 2006a, 2006b). Following similar tactics, some enterprises were recovered by the workers in the sectors most deeply affected by either imports or the difficulties posed by exports: meat packaging houses, textile factories, tractors, trailers, metal working plants, and plastics.

In the midst of these protests, the CTA was established, as were the following: the Fighting Movement of Women Engaged in Rural Tasks; Rural Movement from Santiago del Estero; Coordinating Association against Institutional and Police Repression; the Grieving Mothers, and the the unemployed workers' movements. These movements established roadblocks, or "pickets," which finally led people to call these workers *piqueteros,* or picketers. In 2002, most picket organizations obtained subsidies for their members through the Unemployed Male and Female Breadwinners' Plan. The implementation of this program, one of the most studied cases in Argentina, shows paradoxical effects: It has contributed to the consolidation of unemployed workers' organizations as well as led many women out of their homes and into the public arena, for they must often perform some communal task in compensation for the subsidy they receive. Within the picket movement, about 65% of the people involved are women, especially dedicated to the management of community projects and who participate in the demonstrations and occupation of open spaces.

In the Workers' Recovered and Managed Companies (WRMC), male and female workers occupied factories and companies and started production, "without bosses" (as they say), on the face of the threat to the right to work implied by factory bankruptcies and closures. Men and women alike demanded genuine employment. After hard struggles, WRMC managed to retain their sources of employment, although the women did not ask for more skilled jobs or for training that would enable them to learn other trades and avoid labor segmentation. In this type of collective action in the public sphere, it is possible to generate development of a social critical consciousness that permits the broadening of women's rights while also improving living conditions.

Pay equality and activity rotation have benefited women, even though the functions they perform may be defined as gendered. On the other hand, equal pay and participation in decision making lead to higher levels of commitment with productive activity. Some women came to hold leadership positions, and not only where the majority of the workers were women, as in the textile industry. The glass ceiling was broken in two ways by women with no previous political or trade union leadership or militancy: They participated in collective decision making, and they led some of these decisions in the capacity of chairpersons, deputy chairpersons, or consultants to the cooperatives. They developed leadership and negotiation skills in the face of eviction threats, and this extended to their dealings with judges, law-yers, legislators, and government officials. Participation by female workers in the new cooperatives, together with their relations with social movements, political parties, academics, and legislators gave rise to an expansion of rights awareness and widened the scope of female workers' citizenship rights. They also began to take part in the Women's National Encounters, as did *piqueteras*, joining workshops where discussions were held about labor prob-lems, and others dealing with gender specific claims: legalization of abortion, distribution of contraceptives, and measures to fight violence against women (Di Marco, 2006a, 2006b; Di Marco & Moro, 2004; Di Marco, Palomino, Altamirano, Méndez, & de Palomno, 2003).

THE EMERGENCE OF THE CTA AND THE MTA

Novick and Tomada (2001) explain how Argentinean trade unionism arose and developed during times of full employment. But the Menem administra-tion of the 1990s brought about changes in the economy and labor market. Workers also changed, to the extent that many ceased to be workers. The changes turned them into holders of precarious jobs, subjected to short-term contracts, earning lower wages/salaries, and not always inserted into social security plans (Novick & Tomada, 2001). The world of workers (particularly in the case of the unemployed) shifted from the trade unions to the neigh-borhoods, whereas numerous social organizations flourished so as to protect the poor by means of relief plans that intended to alleviate the effects of the "adjustment" and *strengthen the civil society* by struggling against the poverty that had come about as a result of that very same structural adjustment.

Between 1946 and 1955, with Peronism in power, there appeared a model of economic growth accompanied by economic, social, and political integration of workers, who succeeded in obtaining legal enforcement for many of their labor demands of nearly 100 years (Basualdo, 2004). The Law of Professional Associations was passed in 1945, and workers' rights were included among other provisions in the new Constitution of 1949.

It is worth going over the organizational structure of CGT, Argentina's historical workers' confederation, in order to distinguish it from the one that emerged in opposition to the Menem administration. CGT's organiza-tion responds to the configuration of a trade union that has the exclusive representation for each branch of activity, in addition to a single, third-level confederation operating through district representatives or province located trade unions, national trade unions, or federations. Although CGT is a third-level agency, it is composed by first-level agencies, that is, trade unions. Workers do not join it individually. They do so at their respective trade unions, but they can only choose the organization that they wish to join.

In the early days of the Menem administration, the trade unions supporting the reforms decided on by the government split from those that opposed them. The latter group was led by a number of trade union leaders who disagreed with the CGT; they opposed the flexibility that they envisaged as one of the consequences of the new labor law. Among the dissidents there stood out service trade unions such as the Association of State Works (ATE), composed of state, national, provincial, and municipal workers all over the country, and the General Confederation of Argentine Workers for Education (CTERA), composed of teachers at different levels of the education system. In 1992, these two trade unions joined in the creation of the CTA. In 1997, the Congress was formally established as a workers' union that offered an alternative to those who did not agree with CGT. CTA's main objectives were to guarantee, practice, and defend the uttermost trade union autonomy from the State, employers, and political parties; to implement trade union democracy by promoting members' secret and direct vote at the time of choosing local, provincial, regional, and national leaders; and to reject sterile divisions and all sorts of sectarianism (Godio & Robles, 2001).

The year 1994 also witnessed the advent of an internal CGT sector that would fight for supremacy during the whole decade, until they succeeded in achieving it in 2005. In 1994, the powerful trade unions that gathered private and public automotive transport (truckers, pilots, etc.) created the Movement of Argentinean Workers (MTA), a group of trade unions with an enormous capacity to engineer high-impact protest because these groups controlled transport countrywide. In other words, they had the power to paralyze the economy both at province at nation levels. MTA was not planning a separation from CGT, but rather the creation of an internal "current" with the aim of leading the General Secretariat. They achieved their goal in 2004, under a *troika*, and 1 year later, they succeeded in gaining control of the Central.

CONGRESS OF ARGENTINE WORKERS

CTA claims to be a new employed and unemployed Workers' Central, founded on three essential notions: direct membership, participative democracy, and political autonomy. This Central does not depend on economic groups, governments, or political parties.

Direct membership made it possible for people to join CTA either individually or through whatever trade unions, associations, or federations that are, in turn, members of this organization. This opened the door to non-unionized workers and to various associations, as is discussed later. Women constitute more than 52% of the total (Chejter & Laudano, 2001). CTA is composed of more than 240 organizations and its Internet site claims to have more than 1 million members, all part of small and medium union groups, social organizations created in poor neighborhoods, tenants, squatters living in condemned buildings, the Argentine Association of Prostitutes (AMMAR) and groups of unemployed people, besides CTERA and ATE.[5] CTA is consulted by the Ministry of Labor and takes part in several negotiation bodies together with CGT. One example of this is the role it plays at the Council of Basic Salary, where it is on equal standing with CGT, although it still lacks legal status, for in the Argentine trade union model, the Act of Professional Associations grants these rights to the most representative body.

CTA's leaders demand legal status, and in 2005 they laid their claims at the International Labor Organization's (ILO) annual conference. The issue is that without these rights, CTA is not entitled to undertake collective negotiations or collect the trade union fees that employers deduct from members' salaries to be then transferred to the trade union or are destined to the administration of union health insurance. On the other hand, State workers of either sex may choose between joining ATE (a member of CTA) or the National Union of Civil Servants (UPCN; a member of CGT). CTA makes its presence felt in every arena where the country's situation is discussed; it does not restrict its participation to labor relations, a fact that underscores that, regardless of legal issues, CTA has become an extraordinarily important political interlocutor, even though it has faced legal challenges.

Summing up, CTA differs from CGT in that CTA proposes new forms of direct democracy: At the various levels (national, provincial, and local), its leaders are appointed by its members' direct vote. CTA is composed not only of such unions that are most seriously affected by adjustment policies, as is the case with State workers, but also by the unemployed and by women. These include women who work as prostitutes (AMMAR), besides retirees, pilots, journalists, metal workers (e.g., the Metal-working Workers' Union from Villa Constitución), workers of the film industry, and teachers at all educational levels, among others. CTA articulates different social movements through various federations, such as the Federation of Land, Housing, and Habitat, the Federation of National Health, Federation of slums and shanty towns in the Federal Capital; the Chaco's Indigenist Movement; the Movement of Squatters and Tenants; and Settlements and Church-based Community/Solano-Quilmes, Province of Buenos Aires. CTA depends on a solid intellectual support provided by academics and has its own Institute of Studies.

In brief, CTA constitutes a sociopolitical movement where inclusion is possible from a status of citizenship rather than from belonging in some category of the labor world (Dyszel, Pablo, & Gurrera, 2006; Novick, 2001). They have integrated into their political proposal class, gender, ethnic, and generation differences, as is shown by their heterogeneous membership. For example, AMMAR has been incorporated into CTA from this organization's own acknowledgment of their trade, since its members define themselves as sex workers. AMMAR's incorporation into CTA may be indicative of pluralism together with a tendency to avoid discrimination on the part of this institution. It is in this sense that some scholars regard the said inclusion as a sign of interest in gender equality on the part of CTA. The association of "sex workers," created in 1995 and incorporated into CTA, has long been denouncing police brutality, demanding that crimes committed against prostitutes be solved, and claiming for the prevention of sexually transmitted diseases and HIV. They have staged national encounters, and in 2005 these women opened a school of basic education for adults in the province of Cordoba.

Although it is remarkable that CTA has been the first to accept "sex workers," this does not close the debate on the characterization that AMMAR members offer concerning prostitution (i.e., whether the activity should be understood as work or as slavery). The differences in how they defined themselves and their practices brought about a split. During a national assembly held in 2002, one sector chose to name themselves *sex workers* and to include themselves within the working class, stating that the only way to put an end to exploitation consists in organizing those who are being exploited and providing them with the necessary tools so that they can choose their way freely.[6]

The women who parted ways abandoned CTA and created a nongovernmental organization called Ammar, Argentinean Women's Associations for Human Rights. These women privilege the gender perspective and their condition as subjects of rights. According to one member, "We acknowledge ourselves as unemployed women subjected to prostitution. This is something we wish to change, since it was not our own free choice" (Sánchez, 2006). They are engaged in political activities to achieve full enforcement of their rights, and their claims are supported by the Methodist Evangelical Church and the Government of the City of Buenos Aires. They receive staples just like other people living in poverty; training courses, insertion in HIV/AIDS prevention programs, and gynecological treatment and check-ups in public hospitals.

TRADE UNION QUOTAS AND THE REUNIFICATION OF THE CGT

In June 2004, the CGT changed its regulations in order to include the Trade Union Law of Female Quota, for a 30% female representation quota. The first direct consequence of the enforcement of this law resulted in a larger number of women appointed to the Executive Board (Vidal, 2004). By the time elections were to be held, the Executive Board had to arrange a smaller female quota (between 15% and 20%) because there were not enough women trade union delegates, particularly among the truckers' or bus drivers' unions.

The Trade Union Law of Female Quota is one of the most significant measures of positive discrimination. Orsatti (2004) writes of the tension existing between *the model of specific structures*, with female units or departments, and the *model of main structures*, or measures of affirmative action achieved through quotas in order to exercise a direct influence on the access to executive positions by setting aside a given number of seats on the Executive Board. He points out that in the International Confederation of Free Trade Unions the latest strategic agreements are clearly geared to reach legitimization of the latter model as part of an integral approach.[7]

Policies that impinge on gender equality are taken from the struggles held by female trade unionists and contradict the traditionally male leadership typical of these organizations. In a symmetrical pattern concerning what tends to be the norm in political parties and other organizations, leaders of traditional trade unions within the CGT are resistant to quotas. Moreover, generally speaking, there are no women in the most important political secretariats (those dealing with trade union policies and organization). It is furthermore thought that, in the case of traditional trade unions, women's secretariats operate as a place where favors are returned or as spaces occupied by women who uphold traditional gender notions.

In July 2004, after a long negotiation process, both CGTs reunified under a *troika* that would stay in office for 1 year. It was composed of an MTA leader, a Sanitation Works Union leader, and a woman leader as Health Workers' delegate. The unification intended to include a woman in the *troika* to show the importance of female leadership. Some analysts understand this move as a strategy to be included into the unification, since the dissenting CGT (MTA) leader exercised most of the political power. At the same time, whenever the female delegate's opinions were waived aside, it was easy to blame it on gender discrimination. In July 2005, the MTA leader became CGT's secretary general, with the consequent dissolution of the *troika* and the vanishing of the ephemeral protagonist role played by the female delegate.

WOMEN IN TRADE UNION ORGANIZATIONS

This section describes women's mobilizations and the emergence of new mechanisms for women's equality on the CGT, CTA, CTERA, and the ATE. In 1973, the CGT created a Women's Department. Some trade unions already had one, probably owing to the notion of the *Female Branch* so deeply rooted in Peronist culture, together with Eva Peron's heritage. 1984 saw the advent of the Trade Union Women's Panels and of the Trade Union

Women's National Movement. The former comprised the most progressive *justicialista* unions as well as independent sectors, and intended to fight discrimination against women, double shifts, and insufficient trade union representation. The latter claimed that women had already been integrated into the workforce and that equal opportunity had been achieved. In 1987, CGT created a Training and Advancement Department for Women, and in 1988 they organized the Training and Research Forum of Women in Trade Unions with the purpose of encouraging women's participation in trade union's decision-making bodies (Chejter & Laudano, 2001).

These factors gave rise to the foundation of the CGT Women's Institute in 1992, in the framework of the Unity and Normalizing Conference of the General Confederation of Workers of the Argentine Republic, included in the organic statutes of the workers' central organization. One of the most important trade unions in the Institute is the UPCN, as its Secretariat for Women, created in 1984, has a seat on the trade union's Executive Board.[8]

Since 1995 the Institute has been a member of the Mercosur Women's Forum, and in 1998 it joined the Tripartite Commission for Equal Treatment and Opportunity for Men and Women in the Field of Labor, an organization composed by IWO, CGT, CTA, the national government and the business chambers. At present, the Institute has become CGT's Gender Secretariat. The active participation of women in leading union positions at the confederation level within the CGT is very recent. Between 2004 and 2005 Susana Rueda was the first woman to be appointed co-secretary at the CGT's National Executive Board.

The UPCN is in some ways a pioneering trade union. Its Secretariat for Women, one of the first in the trade union field, was created in 1984, and in March 2001 it changed its name to the Secretariat of Equal Opportunity (Chejter & Laudano, 2001). Its priorities are "shared family responsibility, eradication of labor violence, integration of disabled workers, gender equality, equality to access jobs and to hold labor relations, equal training and professional advancement, equal pay for equal work, equal career opportunity and parity in decision making."[9] They also emphasize other achievements, such as the inclusion of Equal Treatment and Opportunity in the First Collective Work Agreement for the National Public Sector (1998). In 2005, the issue of labor violence was dealt with in the First Collective Work Agreement for the National Institute of Social Services to Retirees and in the Collective Agreements for the Legislature of the Autonomous City of Buenos Aires and Administration Nacional de la Seguridad Social. The female leadership attributes these achievements to the continued improvement of quality jobs for women.

CTA's Secretariat for Gender Equality and Opportunity was created following the statutory reform of 2000, which also included a minimum

20% female quota for executive positions at all levels (local, provincial, regional, and national). It is one of CTA's 16 Secretariats. Until 2000, women participated informally but were not officially recognized within the organizational structure (Chejter & Laudano, 2001). According to CTA's Website, the Secretariat aims to struggle "for full enforcement of Actual Equality of Opportunity and Treatment between Men and Women in the context of this institution, and proposes to foster and develop the gender perspective in our policies." The Secretariat's objectives consist in planning ways to fight all kinds of discrimination, particularly in gender issues; to develop policies tending to equate male and female workers' rights; to generate programs for the implementation of the points mentioned above; to design training courses for women, and to represent CTA in every space where male and female gender equality may be vindicated.

They insist that they are part of the women's movement as "pillars of resistance against ruthless neoliberal policies; [they find their identity] in the daily strategies that ensure survival; in the social, political, and communal organization" (CTA's Statute). They have demanded that

> household chores and tasks shared by men and women should be duly valued; [they have laid emphasis on] equal pay for equal work; rules for day care facilities, rejection of labor flexibility and its discriminatory effects on women; the struggle against poverty and unemployment; the defense of public education, family planning, distribution of contraceptives, legalization of abortion, the struggle against sexual harassment, free mass vaccination, prohibition of pre-employment discriminatory laboratory tests that exclude pregnant women from the labor market. (Chejter & Laudano, 2001, p. 9)

CTA's Gender Secretariat is a part of the Tripartite Commission of Equal Opportunities and Treatment as from its creation in 1998, together with CGT's Gender Secretariat and representatives of business unions. It is also a member of the Coordinating Agency of Trade Union Centrals for the Southern Cone, a body founded in Buenos Aires in 1986 for the coordination and articulation of trade union Centrals in Southern Cone countries. Information released about their activities reveals that they address a number of issues pertaining to women's social rights. One is collective negotiation as a tool to further gender equality, along with equality of employment opportunities. In their work on domestic and other forms of violence against women, they have joined the Monitoring Network included in the Province of Buenos Aires Family Violence Law (12.569). They also address the legalization of abortion, sometimes in open disagreement with male leaders, and in 2005, the Secretariat joined other women's organizations in launching the National Campaign for the Right to Legal, Safe, and Free Abortion. At the March 2006 CTA National Conference, they distributed materials and collected signatures for the *Campaign for the Decriminalization of Abortion*.

Although some might argue that abortion is not a trade union issue, disregard for this issue would mean ignoring that women define their rights from their own real-life experiences. As Vargas (2002) correctly says, the struggle for recognition of sexual and reproductive rights becomes a constituent part in the construction of women's citizenship.

CTERA—The Gender Secretariat at the Confederation of Education Workers of Argentina—is the biggest trade union organization of educators, encompassing education unions of every province. Some 45% of all Argentinean educators, totaling 300,000 individuals, are members of CTERA. As a large number of women in Argentina are in the teaching profession, 80% of the members are women. CTERA is a leading member of the American Confederation of Education and of Education International (EI), and it presides over IEAL, the American Regional Branch of EI.[10]

With an antecedent in the 1997 Commission of Working Women, the Secretariat of Gender and Equal Opportunity was created in 2001. The reformed statute established a minimum of 33% female or male candidates with a view to ensure a participation floor for both (Chejter & Laudano, 2001). CTERA's Executive Board is elected by the secret and direct vote cast by all members of the organizations it gathers. Women hold half of the leading and committee member positions in the Secretariats.

In 1987, the ATE had a Women's Department. In those days they busied themselves with commemoration ceremonies related to feminism (March 8, November 25, homage paid to Eva Perón) and also struggled for the Law of Shared Parental Authority, the Divorce Law, quotas in political parties' electoral lists, and day-care facilities (Chejter & Laudano, 2001). Already inserted in CTA, ATE women participated in the Fourth World Conference on Women, held in Beijing in September 1995. As can be read in an interview, they felt that in the dark years, when the country was undergoing an ever-worsening situation, "they were unable to succeed in being granted day care facilities and eight-hour shifts, and now there are young people who work for 12 hours or more without even going to the toilet. This drove them to work with unemployed women."[11]

GENDER DISCOURSES AND STRUCTURES IN TRADE UNIONS

Novick (2001) writes that after 50 years under a single Central, pluralism is an important phenomenon that appears when other Centrals are created, competing for workers' membership (by which she means CGT, MTA, and

CTA.) The question remains whether the said pluralism applies to women's rights. In both Centrals, male leaders hold an ambiguous relation with this issue. These rights are voiced, and both quotas and Equal Opportunity Secretariats are accepted but, with very few exceptions, the leading strategic positions in unions are still in men's hands.

As I have argued, the naturalization of gender relations exists both among the state officials and the leaders of social movements. It is possible to find more points of agreement between State officials (male and female) and movement leaders about redistributive rights than about the rights of women belonging to those very movements. This is a kind of alliance based on male domination that I have named *implicit conservative consensus*. In the co-existence of practices inside unions, as happened in unemployed workers' movements and in recovered enterprises, it is possible to observe the imbalance between the new social practices and the inertia of the old ones, reluctant to be discarded (Di Marco, 2005, 2006a, 2006b; Di Marco, Brener, Llobet, & Méndez, 2006).

The fight of trade union women for the rights of female workers can be defined through two interconnected objectives: They want to be listened to as representatives of women's demands, and to reach decision making positions in the trade union apparatus. Initiatives to improve women's rights also result in their media visibility, in women's movements, in the very trade union apparatus, and in international organizations. Two practices co-exist, depending on the structures where these women carry their activism: the *institutional practice* and the *movement-oriented practice*. Still, they should not be understood as two poles to be mechanically attributed to the dichotomy existing between the traditional CGT and the new CTA, or to a leadership model. Both types of practices can be found in both Centrals, and also in their differences when broaching the issues, for their approaches varies depending on context and situation (the struggle for space within the trade unions and the articulation with women's movements.) Despite the heterogeneity of its members, CTA is ruled by ATE and CTERA, the two unions related to services, and the trade union discourse overlaps with the movement and with gender discourse.

The path of *specific structures*—women's areas or departments (Orsatti, 2004)—does not necessarily give rise to the appearance of political-and-trade union actors capable to exert their influence when it comes to making decisions. In the view of those who subscribe to an institutionalist perspective, it is crucial that female workers should bring their claims and operations into the trade union arena, adopting the *main structures model*. Hence, the struggle is not restricted to a mere change of norms and to the opportunity to occupy an institutional space.

In some of the unions, ever since the 1980s and regardless of which Central they now belong to, women have been working to achieve articulations with women's movements while struggling for the rights they claimed. Historically, the pioneering union has been the UPCN. Regarding CTA's women, they worked in an informal environment after 1992, and were only granted recognition of a specific structure in 2000, when they were integrated into the 16 CTA secretariats and given a 20% quota to run for leading positions. This decision brought 400 women to leading posts, and 120 gender-equity secretariats were organized in Argentina.

Institutionalizing gender equality and women's rights in the unions requires at least three steps. The first step is to create specific spaces (women's areas, departments, and institutes, ultimately aiming at Gender and Equal Opportunity Secretariats) to deal with women's issues (or the specific structure model) resulting from the fact that it is vital for women involved in trade union activities and/or politics to occupy and profit from spaces where they can exert their influence on decision making. The second step consists in widening already existing spaces while promoting norms leading to mechanisms that will include more women in leadership/decision-making positions. The third step is an offshoot of the logic ruling the build-up of union power (the main structure model), where quotas are implemented and so is access to union leadership. This process requires female workers to be familiar with union norms, procedures, channels, and spaces so that they can take full advantage of them. Gender vindications are not seen as autonomous or contradictory issues, nor are they supposed to conflict with other union vindications or claims for rights, such as those that guarantee a life free of violence or the legalization of abortion.

How do women leaders within the trade unions articulate their views and status? In both Centrals, women leaders are divided in their view of their position within the unions. In one view, "are our male workmates are not always aware of the political and union role that women can play. Women are usually relegated to secondary tasks" (a national leader). In an opposing view:

> In CGT, we are really powerful. Let me tell you: we created CGT's Women's Institute, and we were the first to implement the union quota. . . . I myself am amazed; sometimes I can't believe how we came to learn about building up power . . . the only Trade Union with such a solid collective gender agreement in the Americas is ours . . . here it is about building up and trying . . . we managed to introduce women in the Women's Commission of the Central Coordinating Body of the Southern Cone; we managed to get

in, we put our foot down here at the CGT . . . we were not appointed . . . I learnt to use power and to say "Here I am! This is what I have decided, and what I have decided must be accepted by everybody else! That's the way it works!"[12]

Here, they lean on the strengths of women's movements, but that same leader acknowledges the need for support from their male counterparts: "You come to realize that women's power grows through women only. If you have support; without support I wouldn't have done much, wouldn't be here, wouldn't have been given this office, all of which was possible thanks to the Secretary General's [a male] support, and that is the truth." They are also aware of the gulf existing between experienced leaders in the struggle for rights and the rest of the female workers: "Women just don't gather courage to . . . and this is what happens in the enterprises."[13]

The only woman who became a leading figure at CGT may be considered a "token," to use the word coined by Kanter (1977) to name the few members of subordinate groups that reach positions of power. In the case of CGT's leadership it was clear that it was a means to appear as politically correct, boasting that women in such positions represented a "triumph for women." When consulted on how to improve wage disparities, the leader stated:

Mostly by giving women wider participation in the collective negotiations carried out in all trade union fields; giving them more space in spheres of power, health, education, justice, and security. Trade Union organizations play a crucial role in the compliance with the Law of Trade Union Female Quota and in the incorporation of women into areas of collective negotiation, for it is there where guidelines for salaries, access to education and promotion in the different activities are established. (BBC, 2005)

The first woman to occupy a leading position in CGT's Executive Board thinks that women's contribution to trade unionism has to do with the fact that their voice brings in what is good for the family.[14] This essentialist notion is connected with the idea that women, by virtue of their condition, will introduce an agenda in defense of the collective's rights.[15] These are her words:

Yes, I maintain that our contribution as women comes from a different place, and this is true of the way we look on things, our notions, the structure of our thought and the way we manage whatever job we are doing. When a woman discusses an idea or takes part in a debate, is always carrying an additional burden on her shoulders: the family. The family in whatever context (with offspring, a husband, parents, or grandparents). Such a burden—or complement, if you will—pertains to women only. (*La Nación*, 2005)

This approach takes into account the motherly role that defines the family "burden." It does not seem that women's responsibility in this respect calls to question—not even implicitly—the fact that men stand in a position where they shake off responsibility for the exercise of their paternal role. Thus traditional gender relations are reinforced.

Movement-oriented women show a wider, conceptually more "correct" gender pro-equity perspective, but with strong restrictions to penetrate trade union institutional spaces beyond women's areas. It would seem as if the very agenda of such areas shifted ambiguously from the movement's overall female vindications to female workers' priorities as such, serving the interests of the rules of the game as set by the trade union milieu.

TRADE UNIONS AND SOCIAL MOVEMENTS UNDER CONDITIONS OF LATE CAPITALISM

The social movements discussed thus far took traditional trade unionism by surprise, so to speak, and the same could be said about many trade union female leaders. When movements gathering unemployed workers and workers in recovered enterprises began to emerge, they were first met with responses that followed the traditional pattern of discourse typical of the working-class movement. A woman trade union leader coming from the feminist ranks has declared that "the other sectors, I mean, the sectors of the informal economy, have taken different ways; they have not chosen the structural path." For example, regarding female workers in a recovered enterprise (almost 90% of them women):

> There are legal mechanisms to file claims. Sometimes they are not used out of ignorance. On other occasions, they are not applied because no value is given to the processes of internal democracy and of legal measures. For example, these workers had a number of rights; they were entitled to start legal procedures. If they did not resort to them, let us suppose . . . that there is a two-year term to start them, there are union elections. This is also important because the comrades will perhaps say that the unions are in the hands of dinosaurs. They may well be right. And we cannot . . . but there is something that is related to participation, to constant presence, and . . . participation in trade union structures such as has happened

before is subject to changes, because there are elections every two years. Nothing prevented these comrades from joining an organization and struggling to win their union![16]

Another trade unionist said: "Whether their reasons be right or wrong, women generally do not trust the unions. They think that they have not been, or are not, the suitable structure to represent them."

On the other hand, CTA's movement-oriented approach succeeded in becoming a tool to achieve articulation between the union and male and female workers in recovered enterprises, as well as some picket movements. They are well aware of irregular employment and social economy. Among their members are precariously employed workers. Their structure includes a Department of Social Economy and another of Recovered Enterprises. CTA's women have participated in the picket movement and joined the vindication of a number of recovered enterprises, but they have not been energetic enough in their claims for quality employment, working conditions, and training segmentation. This is due to the fact that, in the face of flexibility and unemployment, together with the expansion of poverty, many trade union women did not feel they had the moral right to posit demands related to the quality of female employment.

At the March 2006 CTA conference, the main issue broached by the Gender and Equal Opportunity Secretariat was the right to abortion, but there are no records of initiatives regarding further steps in the struggle against discrimination and labor segmentation.

CONCLUSIONS

The main features of the urban labor market in Argentina since the mid-1990s were as follows:

- The gap between supply and demand in the field of employment widened considerably;

- women's participation increased;

- various modes of underuse of the workforce expanded;

- regarding employment, there was a modification in the relative participation of the various production sectors; and

- overall development of labor relations deteriorated (Pautassi, 2001).

As is the case with several spheres where women's rights are involved, the passing of the laws that acknowledge such rights has not permeated society's patriarchal structures and the corresponding areas. The Argentine juridical corpus for the protection and advancement of female workers improved to a certain extent during a decade whose salient characteristics in this respect were flexibility and precarious employment, both of which affected mostly subordinate groups like women. However, the contrast between the norms and the data about labor discrimination and segmentation presented in this chapter gives evidence of an abyss lying between norm and reality.

Trade union women furthered the institutionalization of gender issues and the quota law. At the same time, to a higher or a lesser degree, they joined women's movements in their claims for issues that are essential to women's lives, whether in labor or private situations. An example of this is the issue of sexual rights. UPCN women struggled for more than 15 years for a law against sexual harassment. Although it was subsequently adopted, this shows the slow pace these reforms are subject to, in spite of the fact that they open the debate of one of the most urgent issues to be solved worldwide: according to a 1996 ILO report, 16.6% of the women interviewed had been victims of this type of violence.[17]

Today it is necessary to intensify the search of strategies for women to have the same opportunities as men to access regular jobs, to be trained, and to work the same number of hours as their male counterparts. Equal pay and the free provision of child care are necessary resources for all citizens, male or female, but especially women, given that equal pay and the resolution of child care would permit them to decide their personal, family, and work life with greater freedom and dignity. In particular, the child-care problem, of crucial importance for women to enter and stay in the job market, remains an outstanding debt.

Novick (2001) states: "As regards labor relations, the Argentine case has experienced changes in every single dimension that composed the national system of such relations" (p. 25). As explained throughout this chapter, the endeavor to achieve protection and fulfillment of women's economic and social rights in 21st-century Argentina is based on the recognition of the changes and setbacks that have occurred and on the gaps between legislation and reality. The struggle for women's social rights—broadly defined to include all factors that facilitate women's economic participation and constitute economic citizenship—should be undertaken through the articulation of different political actors, including trade unions, social movements, and women's movements. The process of constitution of the demands for gender equality must take responsibility for the complexities of current labor relations, where people are found working in high-tech niches and where there are high percentages of irregular workers. In the case of women, the precariousness of their situation is a conglomerate of low wages/salaries, long working hours, insecure conditions, lack of training for future advancement, difficulties to take proper care of their children and/or share child care, and, more often than not, lack of recognition at home or at their workplace. The national budget does not acknowledge unpaid household chores either, ignoring recommendations issued by CEDAW's Committee, #17, Cl. 11 (Faur & Gherardi, 2005).

One case where women's rights are violated is that of the 900,000 women working in family households (domestic help). This category comprises 16% of female labor in Argentina, and is equal to the average in the rest of Latin America. Fully 95% is not recorded, and these workers are the tips of the iceberg as regards female irregular employment. The good news, however, is that the government finally passed a law in 2006 that offers tax deductions to encourage employers to regularize their situation. Additionally, nearly 100,000 women receive the Unemployed Household Heads subsidy. In exchange for this, they do tasks in some or other community service included in social movements or in local governments. These women need to seek strategies in order to solve their unequal standing. Many of them claim for a decent job, yearning for the salary-based society that has not yet been recovered.

There is no information available about what is being done to eradicate child labor, with the exception of CTERA, a confederation of teachers' unions. This is a vital point, since one aspect of child labor consists in the exploitation of girls, particularly as domestic help, although the worst form of exploitation is prostitution/trafficking in women. In 2000, a commission was established to work on the abolition of child labor; the commission depends on the Ministry of Work, Employment, and Creation of Human Resources (application of ILO's Agreement 138, ratified by Law 24.650).

Recovered enterprises teach a lesson to be taken into account for working modes applied in other companies, for the former is a good laboratory to see how certain approaches to work and workers' responsibility can be changed. However, gender relations at the workplace require clearer visibility, so that women workers in recovered enterprises are not subsumed under the central category of "workers." Apart from the romantic halo around some of the women that stood out in the struggle, sex segmentation of jobs remains, and women do not receive adequate training for the great technological changes that occur, and which in turn would allow women to aspire to a wider range of jobs and put their creativity and autonomy to good use (Di Marco & Moro, 2004).

It is to be noted that the new social situations and types of work are mentioned in the Tripartite Commission's Action Plan of 2000. The section on the informal economic sector acknowledges that most of the workers in it are women. Attention is also drawn to transnational enterprises and their effects on the labor market and to work modes that violate female workers' rights, including *maquilas* and outsourcing, telework, and work done at home. It also states that they will look into situations where migrant women's rights are violated (slave work, human trafficking, etc.) and speaks of fostering articulations among business chambers, public agencies, *social organizations and male and female micro-entrepreneurs*.[18]

Although it is necessary to ensure the largest possible number of workplaces for both men and women under situations that will neither discriminate nor segment the workforce, it is no less important that the jobs offered be quality posts respecting the dignity of male and female workers. Job quality is a complex notion that, besides including fair pay, comprises a number of objective factors that aid workers' economic and social well being as well as their integral health. The dignity *of* the job is as essential as the dignity *at* the workplace (Valenzuela, 2000). In many of these fields, women are still subject to specific discrimination in the labor market. Quality of work may be approached bearing in mind the following aspects: type, frequency, and regularity of income; number of working hours; reliance on job and income; job stability; position at workplace; social protection; child-care strategies; internal organization; decision making; work hazards; professional training; the social and work atmosphere (including work free of violence and harassment); work, social, and political consciousness (Di Marco & Moro, 2004; Valenzuela, 2000). Each of these aspects helps us to specify what is meant by "dignified work," and they are good analytical tools to evaluate men and women's jobs. They supplement statistical data by enriching it with substantive information taken from male and female workers' real world; in fact, they serve as a guide—one that may of course be enlarged and improved—to draw an agenda about women's economic rights.

NOTES

1. Molyneux (2003) discusses women's movements meaning all the different movements where women participate actively, including feminism.

2. Women's National Encounters are held once a year in a province chosen and run by an ad hoc committee of the participants. These yearly meetings started in 1986 at the initiative of a group of Argentine feminists who had taken part in the third UN world conference on women, which took place in Nairobi in 1985. The Encounters are attended by working-class and middle-class women, whether feminists or not. They are autonomous, pluralistic, massive, noninstitutionalized, and critical of the establishment (i.e., opposed to structural adjustment plans and neoliberal economic policy, the foreign debt, and corruption). This is a space for women to ponder, debate, discuss, and establish networks related to a wide range of issues/problems: contraception, abortion, health, education, living standards, and unemployment. Although 2,000 women were present at the 1986 Encounter, nearly 30,000 attended the 2006 Encounter in Mar del Plata.

3. Source: Encuesta Permanente de Hogares (EPH). In 28 urban centers. National Institute of Statistics and Census (INDEC) Argentine population: 36,260,130

inhabitants. Greater Buenos Aires: 8,684.437. Indigents are those who are poor and do not have enough incomes to buy the basic monthly food ($363) Poverty line: $791.

4. In 1993, the inhabitants of the capital city in the Province of Santiago del Estero held the Santiagazo. As a protest against fiscal adjustment increased, demonstrators set fire to the seat of the provincial government and tried to do the same with the buildings where the other powers of the State had their offices. They also attacked the private homes of legislators and politicians from the province.

5. CTA web page: www.cta.org.ar.

6. AMMAR web page—CTA

7. The First Continental Conference of CIOSL-ORIT Women: "Women building up the Trade Union movement in the Americas," Panama, September 27–29, 2004 also refers to this. A quota has been established in organizations of Argentina (CTA, CGTRA), Brazil (CGT and FS), Colombia (CUT), Ecuador (CEOSL), Peru (CUT and CGTP), Uruguay (PIT-CNT). Orsatti (2004).

8. Communication by the Argentine Republic submitted to the Follow-up Commission of Mercosur Social-and-Labor Declaration, drawn by the Tripartite Commission of Equal Treatment and Opportunity in the World's Labor Field, Argentina, July 2001. Retrieved May 2009 http://www.ispm.org.ar/documentos/parte_2.htm.

9. Karina Trivisonno UPCN's Secretariat for Equal Opportunity, Federal Capital Branch. Retrieved May 2009 http://www.upcndigital.org/articulo.php?accID=5574 19-05-2006.

10. Información institucional pagina de CTERA.

11. Interview with a female leader of ATE's former Women's Department by Chejter and Laudano (2001).

12. Author interview with a CGT and UPCN leader, 2002

13. Ibid.

14. In 2000, a woman joined CGT's National Executive as a third permanent Board Member

15. This approach could be understood as familiarization, an expression that refers to ideologies based on what are considered traditional family values and its extension to other social relations. See Barrett and McIntosh (1984).

16. From my interview with a trade union leader, 2004

17. The study was conducted in 36 countries. In a 1994 publication based on a survey of a sample of 302 female workers in the government area, the National Association of Public Officials reports that 47.4% (143) women declared they had been sexually harassed. DRAFT LAW (S-1793/05).

18. Tripartite Commission for Equal Opportunity Action Plan 2006 Towards Equal Inclusion in the Labor Market.

REFERENCES

Basualdo, E. (2004). Los Primeros Gobiernos Peronistas y La Consolidación del País Industrial: Éxitos y Fracasos. *La Pagina.*

BBC. (2005). Debemos Compartir el Poder. Interview March 15, 2005 with Susana Rueda. Retrieved November 2009 http://news.bbc.co.uk/hi/spanish/international/newsid_4556000/4556861.stm.

Beccaria, L. (2001). *Empleo e Integración Social*. Fondo de Cultura Económica. Buenos Aires. Retrieved November 2009 http://www.fce.com.ar/ar/libros/detalleslibro.asp?IDL=2746.

Chejter, S., & Laudano, C. (2001). Género En Los Movimientos Sociales En Argentina. CECYM—Centro de Encuentros Cultura y Mujer. Buenos Aires, Argentina. Retrieved November 2009 http://www.cecym.org.ar/pdfs/genero_en_los_movimientos_sociales.pdf.

Contartese, D., & Maceira, V. (2005). *An analysis of women's labor situation. Second quarter of 2005*. Retrieved May 2009 http://www.trabajo.gov.ar/left/biblioteca/files/estadisticas/05si.

Di Marco, G. (2005, September). *Social movements and gender rights n Argentina*. Paper presented at the workshop Feminist Perspectives on Rights-Based Development for the Institute of Development Studies, University of Sussex.

Di Marco, G. (2006a). Igualdad de Género y Movimientos Sociales en Argentina.In E. Maier and N. Lebon (Eds.), *De lo Privado a lo Público: 30 Años de Lucha Ciudadana de las Mujeres en América Latina* (pp. 249–270). México: Editora Plaza e Valdez.

Di Marco, G. (2006b). *Igualdad de Género, Movimientos Sociales y Estado en Argentina*. Congress of the Latin American Studies Association, San Juan, Puerto Rico.

Di Marco, G., Brener, A., Llobet, V., & Méndez, S. (2006). *Democratización, Ciudadanía y Derechos Humanos. Guía Teórico-Metodológica*. UNSAM—Secretaría de Derechos Humanos de la Nación, Buenos Aires, Argentina.

Di Marco, G.,& Moro, J. (2004). Experiencias de Economía Solidaria Frente a la Crisis Argentina: Estudio desde una Dimensión de Género. In M.E. Valenzuela (Ed.), *Políticas de Empleo para Superar la Pobreza* (pp. 111–160). Santiago, Chile: Editorial Andros.

Di Marco, G., Palomino, H., Altamirano, R., Méndez, S., & de Palomino, M.L. (Eds.). (2003). *Movimientos Sociales en la Argentina: Asambleas: La Politización de la Sociedad Civil*. Buenos Aires, Argentina: Universidad Nacional de General San Martín.

Dyszel, G.F., Pablo, J., & Gurrera, M.S. (2006, November). *El Sindicalismo de Movimiento Social. Algunas Reflexiones en Torno del Concepto*. Paper presented at Sociedad Argentina de Análisis Político,.

Equipo Latinoamericano de Justicia y Género. (2005). *Informe sobre Género y Derechos Humanos: Vigencia y Respeto de los Derechos de las Mujeres en Argentina*. Buenos Aires, Argentina: Biblos.

Faur, E., & Gherardi, N. (2005). El Derecho al Trabajo y la Ocupación de las Mujeres. In Equipo Latinoamericano de Justicia y Género. ELA, *Informe sobre Género y Derechos Humanos: Vigencia y Respeto de los Derechos de las Mujeres en Argentina*. Buenos Aires, Argentina: Biblos.

Godio, J., & Robles, A. (2001). Observatorio del Movimiento y Sindical Argentino. *Revista Pistas*, 3 (February).

Instituto Nacional de Estadística y Censos (INDEC). (2006). Buenos Aires: Author.

International Labor Organization. (2000). *Trabajo Decente para las Mujeres*. Montevideo, Uruguay: Organización Internacional del Trabajo (OIT). Retrieved

February 31, 2009 http://www.cinterfor.org.uy/public/spanish/region/ampro/cinterfor/temas/gender/doc/cinter/tra_dec.

Kanter, R.M. (1977). *Men and women of the corporation*. New York: Basic Books.

Molyneux, M. (2000). *Women's movements in international perspective: Latin American and beyond*. London: Palgrave Macmillan.

Mouffe, C. (1992). El retorno de lo Político. Comunidad, ciudadanía, pluralismo, democracia radical. Editorial *Paidos*; Buenos Aires—Argentina.

Novick, M. (2001). Nuevas Reglas del Juego en la Argentina, Competitividad y Actores Sindicales." In E. De la Garza Toledo (Ed.), *Los Sindicatos Frente a los Procesos de Transición Política*. Buenos Aires, Argentina: CLACSO.

Novick, M., & Tomada, C. (2001). Reforma Laboral y Crisis de la Identidad Sindical en Argentina in *HUMÁNITAS*. Caracas: Portal temático en Humanidades Cuadernos del Cendes.

Orsatti, A. (2004). Modelos de Participación Femenina en las Estructuras Sindicales. *Instituto del Mundo del Trabajo Revista Pistas, 13*.

Pautassi, L. (2001). Equidad de Género y Calidad en el Empleo: Las Trabajadoras y los Trabajadores en Salud en Argentina. In United Nations, *Pension Legislation and Gender Equity in Latin America*. Santiago, Chile: United Nations.

Pautassi, L., & Enríquez, C.R. (2004). *Taller de Discusión Informalidad y Género en Argentina: Vulnerabilidad Laboral, Instituciones Sociales y Género en Argentina*. Women in Informal Employment, Globalizing and Organizing (Wiego). Centro Interdisciplinario para el Estudio de Políticas Públicas (CIEPP). Buenos Aires. Centro Cultural de la Cooperación.

Pautassi, L., Faur, E., & Gherardi, N. (2004). *Legislación Laboral en Seis Países Latinoamericanos: Avances y Omisiones para una Mayor Equidad*. Chile: CEPAL.

Sánchez, S. (2006, May 5). Interview, *Página 12—LAS 12*.

Schuster, F., & Pereyra S. (2001). La Protesta Social en la Argentina Democrática: Balance y Perspectiva de una Forma de Acción Política In N. Giarracca (Ed.), *La Protesta Social en la Argentina: Transformaciones Económicas y Crisis Social en el Interior del País*. Buenos Aires, Argentina: Alianza Editorial.

Scribano, A., & Schuster, F. (2001). Protesta Social en la Argentina de 2001: Entre la Normalidad y la Ruptura. In *Observatorio Social de América Latina*, Consejo Latinoamericano de Ciencias Sociales (CLACSO), *2*(5). (September), Buenos Aires.

Valenzuela, M.E. (2000). La Calidad del Empleo, un Enfoque de Género. In M.E. Valenzuela & G. Reinecke (Eds.), *¿Más y Mejores Empleos para las Mujeres? Las Experiencias de los Países del MERCOSUR y Chile* (pp. 29–58). Santiago, Chile: International Labor Organization.

Vidal, J. (2004). La CGT les Abre un Espacio a Las Mujeres. *El País*. Retrieved November 2009 http://www.clarin.com/diario/2004/05/06/elpais/p-01802.htm.

Wainerman, C. (Ed.). (2003). *Familia, Trabajo y Género: Un Mundo de Relaciones*. Buenos Aires: UNICEF—Fondo de Cultura Económica.

WEBSITES

AMMAR web page—CTA:www.cta.org.ar
CTERA—Confederación de Trabajadores de la Educación de la Republica Argentina
CTA: www.cta.org.ar
Ministerio de Trabajo: www.trabajo.gov.ar/left/biblioteca/files/estadisticas/05
UPCN: www.upcndigital.org/articulo.php?accID=5574 19-05-2006

NEWSPAPERS

Página 12–Las 12: www.pagina12.com.ar.
Clarin: www.clarin.com.ar
La Nación: www.lanación.com.ar.

SIX

CAN A FOCUS ON SURVIVAL AND HEALTH AS SOCIAL/ECONOMIC RIGHTS HELP SOME OF THE WORLD'S MOST IMPERILED WOMEN IN A GLOBALIZED WORLD?

Cases From Ecuador, Ukraine, and Laos

Rae Lesser Blumberg and Andres Wilfrido Salazar-Paredes

What do you do if you're a poor young woman in a poor country and you've been offered a chance to make enough income to help your whole family overcome poverty—but at potential danger to your health or very life? This chapter examines three groups of young women who face just such a dilemma: Ecuadorians working in nontraditional agricultural exports (NTAEs, such as flowers and broccoli); Ukrainians economically desperate enough to risk going abroad for work that could turn out to be sex slavery, and Laotians working as bar hostesses ("b-girls") in bars sprouting up along the route of a refurbished road from China to Southeast Asia. The chapter links their situations to a broader definition of human rights on the one hand and globalization processes on the other. In today's global economy, can the human rights umbrella be stretched wide enough to protect the health and lives of imperiled women in have-not nations? What sort of government policy response can be achieved under these circumstances?

The basic argument is as follows. In all three cases, due to some trend or aspect of globalization, young women had an opportunity to earn unprecedented income. In all three cases, earning the income put their health and even survival at long-term risk. But at the same time, the income helped with their and their families' urgent needs—and it provided the women with the unique benefits of economic empowerment, benefits that, as discussed here, could transform their lives. Even if their governments tried policy/legal reform to help them, it so far hasn't been enough in a globalized world where poorer nations may have limited sway over their destinies.

So what can be done? To preview the conclusions and policy recommendations, this chapter argues that any viable policy solution must include two basic tenets:

1. Enhance and protect these women's economic empowerment, in order to maximize positive impact on the women, their families and their nations; and

2. Focus on the women's health and public safety, to raise the chance that a protective policy will be implemented.

Also, because their plight stems from globalization, reducing the women's risk while preserving their social and economic rights will require committed action at the global level as well (e.g., from the United Nations, the European Union [EU], international nongovernmental organizations [NGOs]/social advocacy groups, and the international trade union movement).

But is the women's dilemma something that falls under the purview of human rights? This chapter argues affirmatively. To begin with, the human rights perspective already has evolved greatly from its early, gender-blind focus on civil and political rights (Blumberg, 1998; Bunch, 1991; Carrillo, 1991, 1992; Tomasevski, 1993). Indeed, now gender equality itself is considered a human right—the third of eight Millennium Development Goals. Based on Blumberg's theories of gender stratification and gender and development (see later), we propose that earning and, more importantly, *controlling* income may be the fastest, surest route for women to move toward greater gender equality. In fact, for both theoretical and empirical reasons, in earlier work, women's economic empowerment has been likened to a "magic potion" for development (Blumberg, 2005).

What are the positive aspects of female economic power? Hypotheses from Blumberg's general theory of gender stratification (e.g., Blumberg, 1984, 1991, 2004a) and theory of gender and development (e.g., Blumberg, 1988, 1989a, 1989b, 1995, 2004b, 2006, 2009) posit that women's control of economic resources raises their: (a) self-confidence, helping them assert more

(b) "voice and vote" in household decisions, including economic issues, domestic well-being matters and fertility. Women's preferences on these decisions have implications far beyond the home (see below). Blumberg also posits that economic power leads to (c) more control of basic "life options" ranging from relative say in marriage choice to freedom of movement. These links can be seen as causal. And a growing body of evidence (summarized in Blumberg, 2006, 2009) provides empirical support. Also, evidence is growing for a key hypothesis of the gender and development theory (Blumberg, 1988): that income under female control provides a synergy effect for development because women tend to spend it on the nutrition, education, and health of sons *and* daughters, as well as economic aims. In turn, this increased human capital boosts national development. Because fertility is inversely linked to developing countries' income growth—and women who control income tend to curb their births—their empowerment further promotes national development.

Additionally, other research has found the level of women's economic power correlated with other important facets of national development. For example, recent data show that the higher the percent of women in a nation's labor force, the less its involvement in armed conflict both internationally (Caprioli, 2000, 2003) and intra-nationally (Caprioli, 2005; Melander, 2005). Negative links with corruption also have been found (Kaufmann, 1998; King & Mason 2001).

In sum, female economic power seems to be good news. But when we add globalization and health and safety issues, a more complex situation emerges—one that may greatly increase the price women pay for this empowerment and its boons for themselves and their families.

ECUADORIAN FLOWERS AND (BROCCOLI) FLORETS: WOMEN, WORK, AND THE CONSEQUENCES

We begin with NTAEs, which tend to be labor-intensive, high-value crops such as spices, flowers, and certain "healthy veggies" (e.g., broccoli and cauliflower). They have been promoted as a path toward export-oriented industrialization that, since around 1980, has been advocated as the best development strategy for the global South. Ecuador's experience with the NTAE path has proven to be often difficult, sometimes dangerous, generally profitable—and indisputably gendered.

A rapid appraisal research in August to September 1991 on Ecuador's new export sectors, (Blumberg, 1992), examined gender issues in the nascent but fast-growing export flowers and broccoli industries.[1] Findings showed that these two NTAEs already were proving transformative for several very different groups of women workers. Their stories are linked to (a) their geographic location, (b) the specific NTAE industry in which they worked, (c) whether their job was in cultivation or post-harvest processing for export, as well as their (d) education and (e) ethnicity. And although all earned above-average income for their local labor market, they were exposed to differing levels of harmful chemicals, ranging from exceedingly high to lower (but quite possibly still above the long-term danger threshold). The 1991 NTAE research was conducted in 20 firms in both the Andean highlands of Ecuador ("Sierra") and in the coastal lowlands ("Coast"). The 16 Sierra firms focused on flowers and vegetables, especially broccoli, and had labor forces ranging from 60% to 77% female (all data are from Blumberg, 1992, unless noted). Three Sierra labor forces were identified.

The first labor force consisted of mestizos working for the export flower plantations in both cultivation and post-harvest processing. The second consisted of mestizos who did post-harvest processing for export vegetables/fruits (predominantly broccoli). The third labor force consisted of very poor, indigenous cultivators who raised those crops (again, mainly broccoli). All three labor forces were situated in distinct geographic locations, had different levels of education, and were exposed to differing levels of danger from sometimes deadly pesticides.

The Labor Force in Flowers

In 1991, there were two main poles of growth for the flower industry: (a) just north of the country's main airport in Quito, centered around the towns of Checa and Quinche, and extending to Tabacundo and Malchinguí; and (b) to a much smaller extent, around the Southern Andes city of Cuenca. Although workers in both poles were largely mestizos (mixed Spanish-Indian, following Hispanic culture), they differed in average levels of education. Compared with the local average level of schooling, those working in the Cuenca pole seemed to have slightly above-average education. In comparison, those working in the near-Quito pole had declined in average educational level in the short period between the initial 1989 research (Paolisso & Blumberg, 1989) and the 1991 study. What had happened in the interim is that the flower industry near Quito had expanded so fast it began to have difficulty finding enough workers. By 1991, the Checa–Quinche flower firms had raised wages and scrapped the 1989 minimum of sixth grade and preference for ninth grade: Of the 15 workers interviewed, several recent hires had five grades or less, dropping the average to 7 years. The firms also began to provide almost-free or free, large, multicourse lunches to lure workers who previously commuted or moved to Quito. And they began to offer an increasing array of other benefits.

Conversely, in the Cuenca pole, jobs were scarce for women (especially around two of the three main flower firms, located fairly far from the city). Therefore, the firms could afford to insist on workers with above-average education for the area: complete primary school. The study found that this sixth-grade minimum was resulting in an interesting phenomenon: Local parents urging their younger daughters to stay in school so that they, too, eventually could be hired by the firms paying their older daughters what the parents considered very attractive wages (Blumberg, 2003). In comparison with the Checa–Quinche pole, the Cuenca-area firms paid less. But this area had lower living costs so, comparatively, the pay probably was just as above-average. However, unlike most Checa–Quinche firms, they did not enroll their workers in Social Security (which provides access to the government health system), and they provided few other benefits.

Still, the workers interviewed in both poles discussed their jobs in equally positive terms. Women in the Cuenca area seemed to feel almost as well off as those in the Checa–Quinche area because their firms offered females fairly steady employment (including lots of overtime at peak periods) at a locally desirable wage—a rarity in the region.

The Labor Force in Processing/Freezing Export Vegetables

These were surprisingly well-educated mestizos in the economically struggling area in and between the small Central Sierra cities of Riobamba and Latacunga. Here, job opportunities for young people proved very sparse. So the vegetable/fruit-processing firms (that exported mainly broccoli) could afford to be choosy: 70% to 100% of hires had baccalaureates, the top high school degree; more than 75% were women. These baccalaureates claimed not to feel defensive about their essentially manual work when talking with fellow graduates who had the "expected" jobs—bank tellers, office workers, clerks in better stores, and so on—their jobs paid more, they noted proudly, especially when overtime was factored in.

The Labor Force Growing the Export Vegetables

Among the cultivators who lived in the Central Sierra—a rural, indigenous, mostly female group exposed to major health risks—two subgroups were found: (a) those who cultivated broccoli seedlings for a major processing/export firm, and (b) those who cultivated the broccoli plants after the seedlings were delivered to the large dairy/cattle haciendas that grew them as a lucrative sideline, on contract with the export firm.

A five-person focus group of seedling cultivators consisted of four females and one male, a recent hire. All were indigenous, aged 16 to 18 and part of a 13-person team (12 women, 1 man). All had above-average education for co-ethnics in the area: sixth grade. They also made considerably more than other agricultural day laborers in the locality. They saw themselves as entitled to all the benefits the firm provided its post-harvest processing workers. But they didn't get them because the firm treated them as agricultural day laborers. And traditionally, such day laborers must provide their *own* tools and work clothing. The seedling cultivators, citing major health problems from the strong chemicals they were obliged to spray, long had clamored for protective clothing from the firm but only recently had received a few items. Still, they recognized that compared to most local agricultural laborers, they did quite well. This was poignantly illustrated during the course of the group meeting, when:

> A work-worn, toothless and raggedly dressed middle-aged indigenous woman trudged past and stopped to listen. She said she was a 39-year-old widow and made only about one-third as much as the seedling cultivators, working as a day laborer on a traditional hacienda—and that it wasn't enough to feed her children. (Blumberg, 1992, p. 28)

The broccoli cultivators employed by the haciendas/contract growers came from nearby poor indigenous villages. They were treated worse than the seedling workers. In group meetings at two of three haciendas, management listened in and claimed that everyone was enrolled in Social Security. The workers did not contradict their bosses out loud, although body language did it for them. Still, in all three haciendas, they earned about the same as the broccoli seedling cultivators. But their average education was lower and the age spread was much wider. It ranged from one girl of about 10 (she had never been to school and didn't know her age) to several fairly old people. All were considered agricultural day labor/occasional labor. So, in keeping with local custom, no protective equipment whatsoever was provided, even though broccoli cultivation on the haciendas was highly dependent on the use of strong pesticides.

HOW THE HEALTH-RISK PROBLEM WITH NTAES VARIED FOR THE THREE LABOR FORCES

The indigenous young broccoli seedling cultivators complained emphatically about the health risks. Most wore only t-shirts under their backpack sprayers and no gloves or masks; some were barefoot. They probably felt free to discuss their mostly unmet demands for protective gear because no supervisor was present. In contrast, none of the indigenous broccoli cultivators on the three contract grower haciendas even mentioned health risks at group meetings—in all of which foremen or other management representatives glowered within earshot. Overall, the other two (mestizo) groups were not as endangered as the indigenous broccoli cultivators. But even with protective equipment, all who handle export broccoli *or* flowers are sure to get toxic residues on unprotected skin and clothing; eventually, these can get into lungs, bloodstream, eyes, and so on. In flowers, cultivation and processing took place on the same plantation and post-harvest processers often had cultivation experience; they seemed more aware of the risks than broccoli processers who worked in modern plants far from the cultivators. Risk seemed to be inversely associated with size of firm among flower workers, in part because the larger firms already had begun to hire full-time medical doctors to monitor workers' health—and promote family planning practices. In summary, the women earned above-average wages for their localities and were exposed to varying levels of health risk from pesticides. Based on the theories mentioned above, three questions now arise:

1. Given that relative male–female economic power, measured as control of income/economic resources, is the most important (albeit not the sole) factor accounting for the level of male–female equality, to what extent did the women actually control their wages?

2. On what was income under their control spent?

3. To what extent did these women reap the theoretically posited benefits of economic empowerment?

With respect to the first question, the average level of control of their earnings was high, with some interesting variations (all data from Blumberg, 1992). Among young, single, childless people, only a small number of men claimed that their monetary contributions to the household were "nothing or almost nothing" or "only once in a while"; everyone else claimed they contributed more than that. At the other extreme, only a handful of very young women (almost all teenaged girls in their first job) claimed that they turned over all their earnings to their mothers. No one—man or woman—among the single workers living at home claimed that he or she turned over income to their fathers; it was invariably the mothers. The poorer the worker, the higher proportion of their earnings contributed (again, to the mother). Among married women, not a single one claimed that she turned over her earnings to her husband. Instead, many married women claimed that they pooled income (to an unspecified extent) with their husbands.

But many such women specifically noted that they themselves bought the food (i.e., they excluded household provisioning from income they pooled). From this, we conclude that the patterns resemble other studies in Latin America and elsewhere that have found that both men and most women who earned income controlled it in whole or large part (Vasquez, 2005).

Concerning the second question, on what income was spent, the answers also echo the Latin American and, indeed, worldwide, literature: Women with provider responsibilities tend to disproportionately spend their income on children's diet, education, and health, as compared with counterpart men or women without child responsibilities (Blumberg, 1988, presents the hypotheses). Another source of variation was whether workers lived in a rural area where they had space for small animals. Rural women with space claimed that they invested some of their money in livestock (chickens, guinea pigs, rabbits, pigs, a few sheep, and the occasional cow).

With respect to the third question, the hypotheses about the impact of income under female control once again found broad empirical support. The women in all the focus groups—especially those who had not worked for income before—generally agreed that they felt that their earnings and household contributions increased their self-confidence[2] and willingness to assert themselves; increased the respect they received from their own families; increased their "voice and vote" (voz y voto) in the household, including vis-à-vis three key types of decisions: (a) continuing to work for income, rather than stay home at a husband's request; (b) taking control of their own fertility, including use of female methods of contraception; and (c) postponing marriage, especially where income is high and jobs have very high levels of unpredictable, mandatory overtime in peak periods. Such overtime was greater for processing workers than for cultivation workers and more frequent for vegetable-processing workers than those processing flowers). So it is not difficult to see why many poor women would continue to put themselves at risk—especially if they were not aware of the level of danger or the chance of becoming sick some years in the future—in order to hold on to NTAE jobs they saw as so economically advantageous and transformative in comparison with their other alternatives.

What has happened since this 1991 research? The story of many changes of government from 1997 to 2006 is beyond the scope of this chapter. President Rafael Correa's present left-leaning government remains more popular than the last few but U.S. critics of some of his policies might cut the access of Ecuador's NTAEs to the U.S. market. The next section looks at the present status and likely future of export flowers and broccoli in the face of globalization; recent gender composition data, and government efforts to protect workers in general and women in particular.

GLOBALIZATION, THE FUTURE OF FLOWERS AND BROCCOLI IN ECUADOR, AND POSSIBLE GENDERED CONSEQUENCES FOR THEIR LABOR FORCES

Ecuador has risen to be the world's third-largest exporter of flowers after Holland and Colombia. Growth exploded during the 1990–1993 period, rising 154% (Noel, 1993), but flattened somewhat after 2000 when, among other problems, the dollar became Ecuador's currency, with particularly negative consequences for flowers. Exports recovered and grew at 11% a year from 2004 to 2008, to $565 million in 2008 (CORPEI, 2009a). The world economic crisis hit Ecuador in 2009: by September 30, jobs were down 16% (from 47,000 to 39,500), prices fell 15% to 30% and exports fell 7.7% (El Comercio, 2010). Ecuador faces severe competitive pressure despite climatic advantages (e.g., being on the equator means 12 hours of daylight year-round).

The nutshell view of the broccoli industry is of a unique niche: The Ecuadorian Sierra has some of the world's best climatic and altitude conditions for growing broccoli year-round; it produces a product with the most intensely green and densest florets. Export broccoli has enjoyed even faster growth than the flower industry since the early 1990s. Ecuador is now the principal broccoli producer and exporter in South America. And unlike flowers, with 64% of export earnings from the United States in 2008 (CORPEI, 2009a), approximately 58% of broccoli earnings came from the EU in 2006 versus only 28% from the United States and 14% elsewhere (CORPEI, 2009b).

Technologically, export flower cultivation and broccoli cultivation are in different eras. Flower growing is high-tech. But broccoli is grown by lower-tech methods and, most frequently, on large traditional haciendas where it is cultivated, as we have seen, by a low-cost indigenous day-labor force; it is treated as an income supplement to dairying/cattle activities (Araujo, 2006).

FLOWERS' GROWTH CURVE IN WORKERS VERSUS INCOME: A POSSIBLY FRAGILE FUTURE

Employment data show almost no growth in recent years: 36,855 people worked in flowers in 2002, 60% women and 40% men; the gender composition of the labor force remained constant from 2002 to 2005, when total employment inched up to 38,007 (Montenegro & Cadena, 2005); in 2009 it was 39,500 (El Comercio, 2010). Yet, the *industry* has grown—in a capital-intensive way. Still, the continuing high proportion of women (60%) is crucial because aside from flowers there are so few viable employment opportunities for rural women (Korovkin, 2005). Another relevant point:

Although Ecuadorian law permits workers to organize, this had occurred in only a tiny fraction of flower firms prior to Correa's election in late 2006.

Different authors see different dangers for the flower industry. Harari (2003) cites three problems: (a) international competition (mainly from Colombia, with a more mature, aggressive and subsidized flower industry); (b) "outsourcing" (see later discussion), and (c) "dollarization" (i.e., the impact of Ecuador's 2000 adoption of the U.S. dollar as its currency). A recurrent threat is that the free-trade agreement, the Andean Trade Promotion and Drug Eradication Act (ATPDEA), will expire. ATPDEA brings many products from Andean nations into the U.S. duty free, including flowers, fruits, and vegetables—thereby stoking the NTAE boom (Vasquez, 2005). It was renewed three times since 2001 but was set to expire December 31, 2009. On December 23, 2009, the U.S. Senate unanimously renewed it again for Colombia, Peru, and Ecuador, but not Bolivia (AFP, 2009). If some year, the treaty extension (or a bilateral replacement) is not passed, Ecuadorian NTAEs could face sudden disaster because, as noted, 64% of flower exports are to the U.S. market.

A partial solution would be to export more to the EU. But the biggest stumbling block is that Ecuadorian flower firms wanting to export to the EU have been required to adopt a Green Label program. According to Korovkin, a successful political campaign organized by European human rights groups and labor unions resulted in the German Association of Flower Importers and Distributors creating a certification program for flowers (Korovkin, 2005). One of the tenets Green Label program participants must adhere to is "health safeguards and a secure working environment" for its workers—but this requirement is sometimes finessed or otherwise evaded by some of the companies (Salazar, 2006a). And, in 2006, only 42 flower plantations (out of 525 exporters) were part of the program.

Adoption of a Green Label program *should* mean increased attention to worker health (Jumbo, 2006). But other data indicate that health hazards continue for workers in the flower industry: More than half of those tested had low cholinesterase levels, which causes long-term health problems (Harari, 2003). Many workers continue to lack awareness of risk, in part due to inadequate training (Salazar, 2006a). Consequently, sometimes workers don't use protective equipment (supplied by more than 85% of flower firms by 2002) because it interferes with freedom of movement and dexterity.

LEGAL AND POLICY RESPONSE: PROTECTING WORKER RIGHTS AND HEALTH, ESPECIALLY OF WOMEN

Ecuador's position in the global economy is rather precarious, more in some industries than others. Globalization compels competitiveness and thus risks to worker well-being. The "outsourcing" controversy is a good example: In order to keep permanent labor costs down, many formal sector Ecuadorian firms resorted to hiring a "middleman" firm to supply them with just the right number of certain workers for just the right amount of time. Heeding the outcry that outsourcing exploited workers, Congress passed laws in 2002, 2003, and 2006 that, in theory, extended them basic labor rights (MTE, 2006), for example, receiving the minimum wage and being enrolled in Social Security (Salazar, 2006a). But outsourcing also kept workers from organizing because in order to form a union, there had to be 30 workers doing the same job. It is easy to see how a large firm that didn't want a union could keep the number of their own workers in each job category below 30, and hire the rest through an outsourcing firm (see also Vasquez, 2005). Then, in September 2008, 64% of citizens approved a new constitution that, in Mandate Eight, abolished outsourcing. But it seems that it never died. Instead, the outsourcing firms renamed themselves as providers of "complementary services" and "specialized technical services," which remained legal—and continued to provide the same sorts of labor (Lopez, 2009).

At least five government entities, from the Ministry of Labor to the Ministry of Public Health, are tasked with enforcement of labor and safety laws and regulations. Little actual enforcement occurs, although the Ministry of Public Health and the Social Security (government health) agency both, in theory, carry out yearly inspections (Salazar, 2006a). But these agencies lack the budget and, hence, the staff, vehicles, equipment, and so on, to carry out their oversight and enforcement functions. Similar problems confront the municipalities where the plantations are located. Many have passed decrees to prevent and control contamination by pesticides but lack enforcement abilities. And Ecuador's present economic situation dampens prospects for change.

Nevertheless, there is an evolving legal structure in Ecuador that regulates the agro-industrial sector so that chemicals are not misused (SESA n.d.). It is a combined effort of the Ministries of Agriculture, Environment, and Public Health; Social Security, and two private sector/civil society organizations (the Ecuadorian Service for Agro-Husbandry Health, and the Association for Crop Protection and National Health; Salazar, 2006a). One result of this effort is the publication of various manuals aimed at workers and intended to lower their health risks through improved safety procedures and protective clothing and equipment (APSCA n.d.-a, n.d.-c; Salazar, 2006a).

Sometimes, serious abuses come to light because of a media exposé or an international study that includes Ecuador. One example is an International Labor Organization (ILO) study of child labor in the flower industry (Castelnuovo, Castelnuovo, Oviedo, & Santacruz, 2000). Ecuador happened to be one of 19 countries where a rapid appraisal investigating child labor was carried out. The research revealed a high proportion of children working at least part time, sometimes as actual paid workers, sometimes as "helpers" who aided their employed parent to meet his or her weekly quota for some task. Most disturbing, both small boys and girls fumigated— and in one area, it seemed that the smallest children were more frequently used for this task. But the report itself recommended that no action be taken that might jeopardize the employment of the parents.

Women's Rights and Health

Labor laws pertaining to women's rights concentrate mainly on protecting women against gender discrimination and during pregnancy. The laws, however, have not been specific enough to cover the various health risks to which pregnant women are most prone. For instance, the general regulation concerning the use of pesticides does not deal with pregnant women's higher risks from contact with pesticides (Salazar, 2006a). But the 42 flower plantations involved in the Flower Label Program/Green Label are supposed to prohibit pregnant women from handling pesticides—though enforcement is unknown (FLP, 1998, 2003).

A problem with any kind of protective legislation that provides special considerations for women is that they make female labor more expensive. In a capitalist society, this may inhibit their being hired or retained. Paid maternity leave, subsidized or paid child-care centers, and similar benefits helped large proportions of women in the former socialist countries juggle work and home. But with the introduction of a market economy, such benefits raised the cost of female labor and led to women being disproportionately laid off. In summary, under capitalism, such protection may be a double-edged sword.

We end this discussion with some reflections on the Ecuadorian case, given its marginalized status with respect to globalization. In flowers, Ecuador remains at competitive disadvantage with Colombia and may lose tariff advantages. vis-à-vis the U.S. market if business groups' concerns about Correa's policies lead them to oppose renewal of the Andean Trade Promotion and Drug Eradication Act; at the same time, it might not be able to gain a bigger niche in the more demanding (and label-restricted) European market. For all their flower jobs' contradictory mix of economic benefits and health hazards, those who hold them rarely want to give them up. So it is significant that it may be precisely the flower jobs—and their female majority labor forces—that are most negatively impacted by these larger globalization-related issues. The world is a tough place out there if you're a small, poor country without some strong comparative advantage. . . . And it's an even tougher place if you're a disadvantaged woman working in a job that pays you more, but subjects you to more risks than most, and you work in an endangered industry in that country.

In contrast, Ecuador's export broccoli seems to have a comparative advantage over most competitor nations. Thanks to climatic conditions, there seems to be a little more "wiggle room" for broccoli contract growers than for the modern, capitalist flower firms to improve the lot of their workers without risking their position on the world market. But broccoli growers tend to be low-tech large haciendas with long traditions of servile labor: it was not until 1971 that the serf-like *huasipungo* system was abolished. Many traditions linger (e.g., not providing protective gear to workers). Will a "green campaign" launched in the EU (to which Ecuador sells more than half its broccoli) finally lead the mostly female, indigenous cultivators to get the safer treatment and gear enjoyed by the well-educated, mostly women mestizos who process the crop for export?

UKRAINIAN WOMEN AND EXPOSURE TO THE RISK FOR BEING TRAFFICKED INTO SEX SLAVERY

The Ukraine case mainly involves sex trafficking across international borders. By definition, it is a globalization issue. Based on Interpol's and other data, among criminal activities, the trade in women/forced prostitution/prostitution ranks behind only the arms and drug trades in level of profit (UNDP, 1999; U.S. Department of State, 2004). Some claim that sex slavery is the fastest growing of the three (e.g., Chon & Ellerman, 2006). Concerning profit, an estimated $9.5 billion is generated in annual revenue from all trafficking activities, with at least $4 billion attributed to the worldwide brothel industry (U.S. Department of State, 2004). Of the estimated 600,000 to 800,000 people trafficked across international borders each year, 70% are female and 50% are children. The majority of these victims are forced into the commercial sex trade (U.S. Department of State, 2004).

In Ukraine, trafficking has been characterized as generating high profits with low risk for traffickers (Pyschulina, 2002; Shelley, 1998). More recently, in Ukraine, traffickers earned between $8 and $12 billion annually from their crime (Pavlov, 2005). Most recently, the 2009 *Trafficking in Persons Report* states that Ukraine remains a source, transit and, to a lesser extent, destination country for trafficking (U.S. Department of State, 2009). With this background, we now turn to the situation in Ukraine as Blumberg's fieldwork found it in 2002.

First, let us consider that the main "push" factor that drives women into the risky business of seeking work abroad—thereby subjecting themselves to the risk for being trafficked[3] into sexual slavery—is economic.

Second, let us consider that of all the newly independent states that emerged in the wake of the fall of the Soviet Union, Ukraine, which became independent in 1991, suffered the greatest economic decline. Specifically, at its bottom in 1999, official gross domestic product (GDP) for Ukraine was only 35% of the level in 1989 (Schamper, 2002), and this constituted one of the most severe economic declines of any country in the 20th century (Dudwick, Srinivasan, & Braithwaite, 2002). Moreover, the economic free fall hit women disproportionately harder than men. National surveys conducted by the Ministry of Labor in 1994 and 1998 found that 80% of downsized employees were female (Dudwicket al., 2002). Statistics from the Cabinet of Ministers of Ukraine et al. (2000) found a large majority of women among the registered unemployed; that year, among people under the age of 28 years, the unemployment rate was 35.5% and women comprised about 75% of the jobless.

Another factor driving Ukrainian women to accept illegal work abroad, despite the risk that it might turn out to be a front for sex slavery, was that they had to pick up the slack when the economy's plunge drove many unemployed men into depression and alcoholism. Many women felt it was up to them to keep their desperate families afloat. Overall, Ukrainian women were considered among the most winsome, fair-skinned, and desperate of the potential supply for trafficking. This further raised the demand for them on the illicit sex slavery market

The period of the worst phase of the Ukrainian economic collapse corresponded to the Balkan wars and the subsequent arrival of international peacekeeper forces ranging from NATO to the United Nations. One unintended consequence of the wars in Bosnia and Kosovo was the rise in demand for sex workers to service these young men, and this, in turn, further exacerbated Ukrainian women's risk for being trafficked. Even without the Balkan wars, however, Ukrainian women continued in high demand. According to Pyschulina (2002), Ukraine is recognized as a country supplier of "human stock" not only to Yugoslavia, but also to Hungary, the Czech Republic, Italy, Cyprus, Greece, Turkey, Israel, the United States, and the United Arab Emirates. (The 2009 *Trafficking in Persons Report* adds Germany, Portugal, the United Kingdom, Lebanon, Benin, Tunisia, Bosnia and Herzegovina, Slovakia, Syria, Switzerland, Canada, and Belarus to the list of destinations.)

By summer 2002, during research on economic programs aimed at combating sex trafficking, the macroeconomic situation in Ukraine had stabilized somewhat (Blumberg & Shved, 2002). Official real GDP growth began to recover in 2000, when it grew for the first time since independence in 1991, rising 5.9%, followed by another 9% increase in 2001 (Schamper, 2002). But 2 years of macroeconomic GDP growth had little immediate impact on jobs for young women. At the individual level, we found that jobs remained almost unattainable in much of the country for the women at maximum risk. These were not women driven to look for work abroad because they lacked human capital qualifications for work at home. According to 2000 government data, women "make up 54% of a population of just under 50 million, and they constitute more than half the country's labor force" (Cabinet of Ministers of Ukraine et al., 2000). They also are better educated than their male counterparts. This is evident among the young women at greatest risk: In the 1999–2000 academic year, of the population aged 18 to 22 years, 53% of the women versus 46% of the men were enrolled in institutions of higher learning (Cabinet of Ministers of Ukraine et al., 2000).

Our research in Ukraine looked at the efficacy of programs designed to provide economic alternatives to going abroad. Our basic conclusion was that women who had taken the economic training programs and subsequently found jobs had no interest whatsoever in putting themselves at risk by accepting illegal work abroad. As the report noted, "Making a living seems to be the strongest 'preventive medicine' against falling victim to trafficking. In eight focus groups involving 39 women in three cities, not one woman who had a job or business mentioned the possibility of seeking employment abroad" (Blumberg & Shved, 2002, p. 14). Our research turned up many dramatic and heartbreaking vignettes of what happened to women who had taken those risks, and found themselves working not as waitresses or draftsmen or whatever the promised job had been, but as unwilling prostitutes, locked into brothels in, say, Bosnia, often, perhaps, servicing peacekeepers, with their passports and street clothes taken from them.

A trafficked woman, "Tanya," who was in one of our focus groups in the East, recounted how she was in imminent danger of being murdered for having testified against the brothel/bar owners who had enslaved her in Bosnia. Her story was that a German businessman married her girlfriend after a whirlwind courtship; he told her he'd be back to take her and a friend of her choice to Germany in 3 months and would get jobs for them. She invited Tanya, whose family was desperate for money. He returned for them but the wine at their "goodbye dinner" was drugged and the two women ended up locked in a Bosnian brothel. Several escape attempts later, Tanya finally reached UN headquarters in Sarajevo to denounce her captors and press charges. Three men were convicted but given short terms that were further reduced. All but one of the three already was out of prison when Tanya was interviewed. She said she had received death threats by phone from Bosnia, Moldova and, apparently, her home city of Donetsk. She said she believed she was being followed and was terrified for her life. She was convinced the police were in league with the traffickers and didn't believe they would protect her. We met with the American Embassy's lawyer and anti-trafficking officer, seeking to arrange some form of protection. We also worked with the Women for Women Center in Donetsk and the Ukraine office of the International Organization of Migration to get further information about the case and further protection for her if it proved necessary. We never found out what happened to Tanya.

At that time, Ukraine did not have a strong set of laws and policies aimed at curbing sex trafficking, as rights groups were demanding. Although the presence or absence of local wars that raise the demand for sex workers is beyond the policy reach of the Ukrainian government, and the fate of its economy depends on more than its own policies, it does have a direct role in creating laws and policies that enhance protections against sex trafficking for its citizens.

Ukraine's policy response has been somewhat problematic with respect to trafficking. Prior to the 2004 "Orange Revolution," the government took a number of steps (Salazar, 2006b). In 1998, the government added Article 124-1 to the Criminal Code, criminalizing trafficking in people. But the law was so vague it could not be used for successful arrests and prosecution. In 1999, it issued Decree 1768 for a comprehensive national Program for Prevention of Trafficking in Women and Children. The catch was that the government failed to fund the program. In 2001, the first post-Soviet-era Criminal Code was adopted, and Article 149 created the crime of trafficking in people—but it incorporated the vague, fatally flawed terms of Article 124-1 without clarifying or defining them. Around this time, traffickers shifted many of their "front businesses" from employment agencies to travel agencies (Pyschulina, 2002). Before, desperate women thought they were being hired for a job in another country; by 2002, travel agencies facilitated getting passports and visas for their "tourist" clients. Given tight restrictions on legal migration from developing countries to western Europe, women urgently trying to migrate for what they thought were lucrative albeit "off-the-books" jobs often had to deal with these trafficker-run agencies—only to find themselves trafficked instead. One loophole remained—women migrating to western Europe as "artists" or "dancers" still could do so legally. The catch was that many of these jobs turned out to be linked to the sex industry (Pyschulina, 2002).

Further clouding the government initiatives has been widespread and blatant corruption. For example, for several years prior to 2005, a gang of five traffickers "worked freely under the protection of corrupt police officers," illegally transporting girls aged 12 to 16 to Moscow, where they were sold for $1,000 each to a pimp (Pavlov, 2005). Nor was there a credible victim witness protection program, according to the U.S. Department of State (2005), resulting in few victims willing to cooperate in prosecutions. Even where (the few) prosecutions prove successful, two huge problems remain. First, victims are treated as prostitutes rather than people who suffered a serious crime; second, very few traffickers have been sentenced to time in prison.

President Viktor Yushchenko took power in the 2004 "Orange Revolution." In March 2005, the Ministry of Internal Affairs established a Trafficking in Persons Department, to which the U.S. Embassy gave large amounts of computers/equipment. The same month, the Ministry of Foreign Affairs established a center in Kyiv to coordinate assistance to Ukrainians abroad. The 2005 *Trafficking in Persons Report* viewed the new government as likely to respond more effectively to institutional weaknesses and corruption, which hindered the previous government's anti-trafficking efforts. It suggested expanding the legal definition of trafficking to conform to international standards, appropriating money to fund the anti-trafficking unit, creating a witness protection program and conducting sensitivity training to reduce victim blaming and breaching of victim confidentiality. Indeed, the new government seemed more willing to be proactive.

But economic and political problems continued as anti- and pro-Russian politicians vied for control of the state. All this curbed government efficacy. Accordingly, the 2009 *Trafficking in Persons Report* continues to give Ukraine Tier-2 Watch List status, indicating that the country does not fully comply with the minimum standards for the elimination of trafficking. Simply put, the risks to economically strapped young Ukrainian women indicate both government failures and the dark side of globalization. Such women are deprived of economic citizenship; in any ensuing precarious situations, they are denied the most basic human rights.

Two recent developments merit note. First, in the wake of the financial crisis, Ukraine increasingly is becoming a destination, as well as a source country, for sex trafficking. In 2005, the "Orange" government had dropped visa requirements for EU and U.S. citizens; now, 20 million people visit Ukraine each year and sex tourism—as well as child prostitution and pornography—have surged ("Summer of So-Called Love," 2009). Second, the January 17, 2010 election led to a runoff between Viktor Yanukovich, the pro-Russian candidate, and the top "Orange" vote-getter, Prime Minister Yulia Tymoshenko (Pan, 2010). The duration of the current economic crisis and the sex-trafficking policies of a new president remain unknowns at this time. But the mix of economic hardship and a reputation for beautiful women makes it likely that sex trafficking of vulnerable Ukrainian women will continue.

A BETTER WAY TO CURB SEX TRAFFICKING? COMBINING THREE TYPES OF NGOS AND THEIR PROGRAMS

As noted, our Ukraine study focused mainly on NGOs that provided training and business opportunities for women who might otherwise have been desperate enough to go abroad for "off-the-books" work. We found the NGOs to be doing a generally fine job despite scarce resources, and that the women who took their training and earned income as a result unanimously declared they would not even consider looking for work abroad. But we also found the following:

> At the [USAID-assisted] Women for Women Centers in Lviv and Donetsk, the free computer courses had waiting lists of about a thousand names. In both centers, women wait for months to get into a course that involves only 8 to 10 hours of instruction stretched over two to four weeks, where they may share a computer with one or two other classmates and are not given any additional time to practice. That they do so indicates how great women's need for economic alternatives to looking for work abroad continues to be. (Blumberg & Shved, 2002, pp. vii–viii)

Much of the efforts to combat sex trafficking have involved the legal/criminal justice system. We worked with two of the primary international NGOs operating in Ukraine that take such an approach. The U.S. Embassy also has emphasized a law-and-enforcement focus. But such efforts don't deal with reducing the supply side of the equation. We also were impressed by the approach of a local NGO in Odessa, Faith, Hope and Love. They didn't have the resources or expertise to provide something as capital-intensive as computer training, but did manage to run an anti-trafficking hotline that, in the first half of 2002, fielded 1,010 calls from women considering but worried about working abroad. They also gave psychological counseling and other social services to "returned women," especially those deported from Turkey. During the first half of 2002, the twice-weekly ships from Istanbul to Odessa carried 688 women deportees. The great majority had been trafficked against their will into forced prostitution. Faith, Hope and Love ran a small, four-bed shelter in a well-hidden, high-security house with resident social workers. This was for the worst cases of trafficked and prostituted women.

How can the synergies of the three types of programs—economic, legal/criminal justice, and social welfare for returned women—be harnessed and combined? Legal/criminal justice programs would benefit by linking up with economic opportunity training: If they ever develop a viable witness protection program (a high priority during this evaluation), these women will have to support themselves. Shelter/psychological counseling programs urgently need to hook up with both legal and livelihood programs. Many of their clients are precisely those who might testify if they had a good witness protection program. For that, as noted earlier, they would need a way to make a living. The economic opportunity programs could expand their reach—and their clout within the sex-trafficking field—by linking up with the first two types of programs. But they have the most sought after product:

Only they can make a difference in the supply side. And given global and local trends, Ukraine will continue to need good anti-trafficking programs.

LAOTIAN WOMEN IN THE PATH OF GLOBALIZATION: STDS AND THE ROAD FROM CHINA

Globalization has been a main factor driving the trend of more and more women earning income—a trend that accelerated in the last decades of the 20th century (Blumberg, 1995) and still continues. Globalization also led to a vast increase in the global transport network. On the plus side, this has led to unprecedented reductions in the cost of moving people and their products worldwide (Nolan & Lenski, 2009). On the negative side, this has played a large part in the spread of sexually transmitted diseases (STDs; including the HIV/AIDS pandemic) to even far-off backwaters of today's world economy. Roads and the junction points where they intersect have proven particularly important in the spread of STDs and HIV/AIDS. Worldwide, sex workers service those traversing the roads, from commercial drivers to casual travelers.

Transmission patterns—often involving roads and junctions—now result in higher female prevalence rates among younger age groups, especially in sub-Saharan Africa. There, 75% of all 15- to 24-year-olds living with HIV are female (Reaney, 2004, citing 2004 UNAIDs statistics) and cases increasingly are feminizing, with almost 61% overall now women (UNAIDS, 2007). The Lao People's Democratic Republic (PDR) has a much lighter—and newer—burden of STDs. But they have been soaring among those working on or in close proximity to a recently rebuilt road that suddenly connected some of the more remote regions of Laos to the good, the bad and the ugly of globalization. With respect to gender, it involves the same scenario encountered in the two previous cases—women seizing an opportunity for urgently needed income that was anticipated to be high enough to resolve sometimes desperate levels of poverty but proved to be accompanied by major risks to health and even survival. A few statistics set the scene. Laos has an estimated 2009 population of about 6.8 million, per the CIA (2009). According to UN statistics, it is still about 85% rural, cultivating mostly rice, and has the lowest population density in Asia (UN, 2006). It is usually thought of in terms of "off the beaten track," rather than in the midst of globalization. But globalization has brought STDs to Laos.

In summer 2001, Blumberg carried out research for CARE on how best to combat the rapid spread of STDs in two provinces of Laos: Oudomxai and Luang Prabang (Blumberg, 2001a). In 2001, Laos had little previous experience with STDs (they rated only a week in the medical school curriculum, according to the CARE doctors from the STD project). The precipitating cause of the surge in STDs was the fact that China had recently renovated the road it had constructed during the Vietnam War to bring materiel from China to North Vietnam. The road led from Yunnan Province to Laos' remote Oudomxai Province. After heading south for some miles, it turned abruptly east to pass through Luang Prabang Province. Luang Prabang City once had been the royal capital and retained its quaint beauty. The road from the capital, Vientiane, had recently been paved and brought in a small but increasing flow of tourists with hard currency. Similarly, the reason for refurbishing the "road from China" had to do with globalization, not war.

The major ethnic group in Laos, the Lao *Lum* (lowland Lao), comprise almost two-thirds of the population and are politically hegemonic. They also are one of the world's most gender-egalitarian people, where women traditionally have had the edge in property rights and economic power. Most women handle the household money regardless of who earns it and also are favored in the kinship system (Blumberg, 2002; GRID Center, 2000; Phengkhay, 1999; Schenk-Sandbergen, Rodenberg, & Phengkhay, 1997). The other two major ethnic groups are defined by the altitude at which they live—the mid-altitude Lao *Theung* (Khamu), and the highland-dwelling Lao *Sung* (Hmong). The Hmong are among the most patriarchal peoples in Southeast Asia and the Khamu are in between the Lao *Lum* and Hmong extremes (Ireson, 1996, 1999).

Traditionally, Lao *Lum* women are economically quite autonomous. Custom generally resulted in inheritance of the most valuable resource, irrigated rice land, passing from mother to daughters. Matrilocal residence traditionally has been preferred: The bridal couple goes to live with or near the bride's female kin. Youngest daughters were socialized from a young age that they would be the ones to take care of their parents until death, after which they would inherit an extra portion of rice land and the house as well. Since the household spirits also were believed to come with the house, they added some religious power to a youngest daughter's economic power base (Blumberg, 2001b). All in all, Lao *Lum* women are used to seeing themselves as quite independent and are known for their economic astuteness. Consequently, it is not surprising that some Lao *Lum* women decided to take advantage of the high-income, although somewhat socially stigmatized, opportunities for bar hostesses ("b-girls") in the beer bars multiplying in the wake of the economic boom brought by the newly reopened China road. Because she is felt to have control of her own body[4] and knew little about STDs, a Lao *Lum* woman may have seen nothing wrong in going out and sleeping with a customer who caught her fancy—thus increasing her income but not leading her to consider herself a sex worker. (Out-and-out prostitution is illegal in Laos as well as socially stigmatized.) Ironically, her self-definition as *not* a sex worker may preclude her from taking condoms on such a "date," even if they are readily available and free.

The contrast between the Lao *Lum* and the Hmong is stark. The Hmong are a patrilineal, patrilocal people who traditionally have practiced shifting cultivation (horticulture); they have been heavily involved in poppy growing and other upland crops, and also value cows. They are known as one of the world's "warrior complex" peoples (Blumberg, 1978) or, as Divale and Harris (1976) term them, a *male supremacist* group. Paternal authority over daughters is high. It can be speculated that a young Hmong woman b-girl in one of the new bars may have been more-or-less sold by her father, the likely main beneficiary of her earnings. If a customer wanted sex with her but didn't want to use a condom, it also could be speculated that she would be unlikely to insist, having been raised to accept subordination to men.

Reviewing the CARE project quantitative data, we found two interesting gender patterns: (a) women comprised 70.5% of the STD cases, 5,445 of 7,723 versus 2,278 men (29.5%); and (b) men were far less likely than women to be treated at hospitals. We then did rapid appraisals in various sites in both provinces, using key informant interviews, focus groups and observation (40 women, 66.7%, and 20 men, 33.3%). Here are three vignettes involving bar hostesses (All vignettes from Blumberg, 2001c, fieldnotes.)

The first setting was a beer bar near the wild and woolly border boomtown of Oudomxai in Oudomxai Province, about 5 miles from the Chinese border. There we tried to interview two young b-girls who appeared to be Hmong. The older of the two said she was 18 and didn't need to use condoms because, she insisted, she never went to bed with customers. She initially claimed to know little about condoms, given her abstinence. Eventually, she revealed that a b-girl in the same establishment had just gotten pregnant because she hadn't used a condom (i.e., thereby admitting that she knew that condoms were contraceptives). Aside from denying that she slept with customers, she passively complied with our requests. She aired out the large wooden building at our request (it smelled of old beer and old sex, which cast doubt on her denials about sleeping with customers). We talked with another b-girl, who looked about 15 years old. The *mama san* made small talk with us but the younger girl spoke only when spoken to directly. She, too, complied immediately with our small requests but otherwise barely spoke. We clearly weren't going to get any useful information concerning their knowledge about, and practices vis-à-vis protecting themselves from, STDs, so we left.

The second setting was a beer bar on a secondary road a few miles from the old royal capital of Luang Prabang, a beautiful town of spectacular *wats* (temples) and palaces, which was designated a UNESCO World Heritage site in 1995. We were greeted at the entrance to the main building, set up as a restaurant/bar, by a warm, friendly young woman. Her name was "Outhaki" and we accepted her invitation to move to the "cabins" on the hill. (The cabins were open-sided, made of bamboo with thatched roofs. Each contained a plank picnic table and benches, and had a gaily flowered curtain that could be drawn to partially shield the occupants. These cabins were just for drinking; if a b-girl chose to sleep with a customer, they had to go to a hotel.)

Outhaki was outgoing, and expert in making us buy far more beer then we wanted—and then some more. She radiated intelligent good sense and robust good health. Ethnically, she was Thai Dam, whose women have considerable economic autonomy and access to resources. Outhaki came to Luang Prabang city to earn money to help her very poor family. (She claimed to be 19 but was almost certainly older.) Eventually, she was hired as a b-girl. Initially, she didn't use condoms because she didn't consider herself a sex worker. But after her friend got sick she decided to protect herself. Now she accepts that she'll sleep with some of the customers (still at her choice, however) and uses condoms for *all* encounters. We never met the mama san, who was out for a night of drinking and massage with friends at a local steam bath. But her attitude was clear: atop every table in both restaurant and cabins was a circular napkin dispenser bearing the distinctive dark blue and off-gold logo of No. 1 Condoms. An NGO project supplied this condom brand to her free, so she gave them without charge to her bar hostesses.

Outhaki told us about her friend, "Boun," who had just contracted her second STD case. Outhaki said she had a foul-smelling discharge; she was trying to get her to go to the pharmacy but so far to no avail. Later, Boun appeared at our cabin. She was dazzling—a large-eyed, pale example of classic Lao *Lum* beauty. But she looked too delicate—fragile and wan. The best-looking physician (Dr. X) in our team tried to get her to open up. She said she was 18 and had worked there almost 4 years (she almost surely was older). She kept insisting that she never went with men. So Dr. X changed his style from everyday conversation/interview mode to romantic banter. Boun still insisted that this was more or less a first at the end of the evening when she whispered a price to Dr. X—if he would come back alone after we left. She told him it was only because he was "so handsome" that she'd spend the night with him. All evening long we kept telling her she was too beautiful to jeopardize her health and that she should take—and use—condoms each time she went out on a "date." We urged her to listen to Outhaki's advice. It turned out that Boun knew perfectly well that condoms protect against STDs, including HIV/AIDS, as well as pregnancy, but. . . . She projected the message that it was nice of us to tell her but she wasn't that kind of girl.

Boun felt she had the right to sleep with anyone she wanted—or not—but that this didn't make her a sex worker. So she didn't protect herself and twice had paid the price. We also interviewed some Lao *Lum* bus drivers and truck drivers who told us the male side of this story: They had to hide condoms so their wives wouldn't find out they sometimes slept around when they were on a run down the China road. Sometimes they hid them too well and ended up having unprotected sex. They didn't question their wives' rights to insist on monogamous sexual conduct—it was part of the same sense of personal autonomy and empowerment that Boun projected. But the result was the same: The social conventions of more conservative members of a relatively gender egalitarian group militated against their acknowledging that both men and women had the de facto right to play around—and should protect themselves in the process.

B-girls such as these are on the fringe of the sex industry. Peer counseling, which has proved so successful in Thailand in educating women who have intermittent paid sex, might be a very efficient and effective way to reach them (Morgan, personal communication, 2005). Women like Outhaki, relatively liberated but highly realistic, would make ideal peer counselors. With some resources and NGO support, such women could cut the health risks faced by these Laotian "imperiled women."

The globalized commerce that accompanied the refurbished road created new and locally lucrative opportunities for women. (Outhaki made it clear that she had made a huge difference in the lives of her family with the earnings she chose to send home.) Some of the women lured to b-girl work by economic need or hopes of economic empowerment were not prepared to deal with the resultant risk to health and survival. But with women like Outhaki, who could be trained and provided with a small monetary incentive to be a peer counselor, the growing numbers of b-girls would be less likely to become infected—and a danger to others as well. Are NGOs the only likely source of peer counselors who could help mitigate the gendered dangers brought by globalization's new opportunities? Would the government support such a program? To what extent has it been proactive on the issue of STDs?

A GLIMPSE OF GOVERNMENT INITIATIVES AND RECENT DEVELOPMENTS

During the field research, we came across the medical assistant in charge of the Luang Prabang laboratory that analyzes the tests for STDs. She revealed that she had participated in the Ministry of Health's 2000–2001 Behavioral Surveillance Survey, a rich data source we otherwise would not have learned about. It also showed us that the government was worried enough about STDs to spend scarce resources investigating them. The Ministry's Summary

Report (MOH, 2001) found that 100% of the bar girls used condoms at least some of the time, but only 72.7% of the bar girls used condoms during *every* act of sexual intercourse with clients in the past month (MOH, 2001). The medical assistant noted that a number of the b-girls turned out to have STD infections and study participants were given free treatment and condoms.

We were heartened to learn that the government was studying—and starting to deal with—the new scourge of STDs that was spreading in the parts of the country that were most exposed to globalization: border-crossing areas, the capital city (Vientiane), and along the road from China. At about the same time, the United Nations Development Program (UNDP) undertook a joint study with the Lao PDR's HIV/AIDS Trust and its National Committee for the Control of AIDS. It concerned the road system in five northern provinces (including Oudomxai and Luang Prabang) and its role in HIV vulnerability (Chamberlain, 2000). This participatory qualitative research also looked at the b-girls, calling them "service girls." It found that most of them were ethnic minorities with little awareness of HIV/AIDS—and that condom use was at the discretion of the man.

Another notable finding is that the b-girls are always free to choose whether or not to go with a customer; and have completed at least the 5th grade, and most had gone to lower secondary (Chamberlain, 2000). It can be speculated that part of the b-girls' above-average educational level may originate in the culturally valued emphasis on clever and slightly risqué conversational bantering: B-girls were expected to be adept in these skills so they could keep patrons interested long enough to keep spending money on beer. It also may represent mutual selection by mama sans and potential hostesses. Females with higher human capital presumably would opt for jobs with above-average earnings potential and, *ceteris paribus*, employers normally want the highest quality available labor force. In short, in Laos, too, we again see the combination of "cream of the crop" but economically stressed young women who often are pushed by poverty into well-paid, economically empowering employment—that turns out to have a high personal risk factor.

The fairly high education levels the Ministry of Health survey found among b-girls bodes well for government-sanctioned or -run educational programs about STDs and HIV/AIDS. Could this be combined with a "health and gender" approach and presented by peer counselors? A PDR government might not be receptive to linking STD education and prevention with a broad, and potentially political, human rights approach. But the Lao Women's Union (LWU) has been active in disseminating materials that teach women about their legal rights (e.g., to land). As a government-sponsored "mass organization," they are found in almost every village. At the national level, they have some political clout and contact with a wide array of international donor and NGOs. They already were active in STD efforts at the time of our 2001 research. Such programs should continue. Given China's rate of economic growth and plans to increase its land connections to Southeast Asia, continued globalization—with its promises and perils to women—seems to be a sure proposition. The link between the global transportation network and the spread of disease of all types, from STDs/HIV/AIDS to H1N1 flu, has become one of the most feared aspects of globalization. Recognition that no country is safe from pandemics already has led to rising global cooperation, even from some fairly closed societies that previously tried covering up public health problems (e.g., severe acute respiratory syndrome). Indeed, recognition of the ever more global nature of infectious disease may be the key to getting recalcitrant nations otherwise wary of a rights approach to accept enough of the human rights umbrella to protect the health and safety of their people.

Perhaps the best way to elicit the cooperation of such countries may be to (a) have it requested by an international entity seen as health—not rights—related; (b) have it deal with a problem acknowledged to be global in scope, and (c) make it clear to their governments that the health threat is already within their borders and spreading. Such an approach may initially ignore other serious problems faced by the "imperiled women" exposed to health risks in their relatively lucrative, globalization-related work. (Those problems may range from preventing workers from organizing to various negative aspects of their working conditions.) But it's an important start.

It would be even more important to make the state realize that the problem is gendered and that gender-disaggregated information is needed to monitor progress in combating it. The LWU is technically qualified to gather, analyze, and interpret the information on "imperiled women"—and men. The government might be more inclined to provide resources to the LWU for such a role if the international health entities were themselves backed by the international women's movement and its affiliated international social advocacy groups.

Once a public health approach has become institutionalized vis-à-vis the STDs most common along the growing road network, the LWU could work with neighboring countries (e.g., Thailand) that have created innovative techniques in their own battles against such diseases. This would be very timely: The Lao government is now promoting a new hotel-resort-casino complex along the Thai border ("Lao Tourism to Bring Profit, Vice," 2009) that could lead to a further upsurge in STDs.

EMPOWERED VERSUS IMPERILED:
SUMMARY, CONCLUSIONS, AND RECOMMENDATIONS

We have examined three cases of women, work, and social rights: NTAEs in Ecuador; sex trafficking in Ukraine, and the roads–gender–STD connection in Lao PDR. Globalization turned out to be even more consequential than expected. It affected all aspects of the story, including the need for women to earn income, and the new opportunities that carried promise of economic empowerment but also risks of danger and even death. Because of this global connection, we must go beyond nation-states for a broad-based solution. Poorer countries don't have the international clout to ameliorate problems that bring them economic disadvantage and hardship. Their own marginalized populations—such as the women discussed in this chapter—have even less influence acting alone. The chapter further argues that any viable policy solution must include two basic tenets: enhancing and protecting the women's economic empowerment, and enhancing and protecting the women's health and the public's safety.

To recap, research has shown that economically empowered women have greater gender equality, including household power, and use both their income and increased clout to increase their children's human capital—with positive effects for their nation's development. In the Ecuadorian cases where employers chose the best educated of a large, surplus labor force, there was preliminary evidence that parents were urging younger daughters to stay in school, so they could one day be hired for their older sister(s)' type of job. This further boosts human capital—and the economic power and life chances of the better educated younger women. Moreover, the fact that women in poor countries who control income *and* have more education tend to curb their fertility enhances their own options as well as their nation's GDP.

In summary, enhancing and protecting the economic empowerment of the Ecuadorian, Ukrainian, and Laotian women could result in more and more positive impact than denying them the economic opportunity in order to reduce the "imperilment" side of the continuum. This does *not* mean ignoring their health and safety needs. As noted, it may be easier to implement policies that expand women's social/economic rights when framed in worker's health/public safety terms.

Thus far, the campaign to introduce better health and safety practices in Ecuadorian flowers has been at least somewhat successful in mitigating women workers' risks while preserving their incomes. Significantly, there have been many social advocacy NGOs and trade unions involved: Even when not quickly victorious, they shone a strong light of (unappreciated) publicity on the flower firms and attracted the attention of European campaigners for worker rights and public safety. One result was the launching of the Green Label campaign; few firms have joined but the industry trade group trumpets the fact that such a movement now exists.

In Ukraine, in addition to being illegal and under the control of organized criminal mafias (some of whom may have corrupted public officials), sex trafficking is a crystal-clear danger to the health, safety, and even lives of the women involuntarily sold into sex slavery. This means that a health and safety rationale can be invoked, with or without a complementary legal/criminal justice and/or economic alternatives strategy. From a health and safety framing, it is a short leap to consider trafficking of Ukrainian women as a human rights issue.

In Laos, generally permissive sexual norms, a newly renovated road, and new bars mushrooming at or near the roadsides create an explosive combination that portends a rapid spread of sexually transmitted infections and a general public health and safety crisis. This is a problem even a human rights-leery government can feel justified in confronting: health and public safety are less threatening. Thus, in both Ukraine and Laos, one can expect more policy implementation from a health/safety than a "social and economic rights as human rights" approach.

Any viable policy must be both protective enough of women's economic empowerment to not inadvertently harm them in the name of protecting them from other dangers, *and* realistic enough to encourage implementation. The central question here can be phrased: Under what circumstances can the human rights umbrella be stretched to accommodate economic and health/safety rights of imperiled women workers?

From Ecuador, we learn that to realistically hope to improve worker health in NTAEs, we may have to water down "ideal-case" recommendations to take into account how competitive in the world economy are the firms and country involved. The export flower industry treated both its cultivation and post-harvest processing workers better than the export broccoli industry treated its "invisible" indigenous cultivation workers. But the flower industry was under far greater international competitive pressure. Any policy solutions aimed at further improving the health, safety and well-being of flower workers would have to be realistic so as not to interfere with the industry's competitiveness (you don't want to kill the goose that's laying golden eggs). This means cost–benefit analyses of proposed additional regulations. Only after establishing that new regulations are cost effective can you link the proposed reforms to workers' human rights.[5] Thus, a health and safety focus is a "foot in the door."

From Ukraine, we learn that it is much easier to put sex trafficking under the "human rights umbrella," with or without the added implementation inducement of a health and safety focus. There is widespread worldwide agreement that trafficking human beings for sex slavery is indefensible. Because it is illegal everywhere, those who do it are considered criminals, period. This means that trafficking is much easier to fit into a human rights framework because, on the one hand, we don't have to worry about causing economic harm to those deemed heartless criminals and, on the other hand, it goes along closely with two existing UN treaties: The Convention for the Elimination of All Forms of Discrimination Against Women, and anti-slavery. The supply of people at risk for being trafficked is closely linked to economic desperation, so even if human rights language is used, policy solutions *also* should be linked to economic initiatives that provide alternate livelihood options for high-risk groups.

Demand for trafficked women is exacerbated by (a) war—historically, soldiers and sex workers have been linked; (b) prosperity—men in more affluent countries can afford to indulge tastes for paid sex with exotic foreign sex workers, and (c) the intersection of sports and prosperity—men who come to world sporting events (e.g., the World Cup or the Olympics) provide a short-term but profitable market for paid sex. This means that UN efforts should combine human rights language with vigorous attempts to monitor that the foreign sex workers don't include those trafficked against their will. Government commitment is essential because the trafficking industry has the funds to corrupt and co-opt officials in many poorer countries. Where governments can't or won't make such commitments, thus allowing traffickers to operate with impunity, in concert with corrupt officials, a larger system is needed. Specifically, trafficking is a prime candidate for not only international human rights-oriented treaties but also an international certification system (such as the U.S. State Department's three-tier system, in which Ukraine still is on the second-tier watch list mainly because corruption has permitted trafficking to flourish).

From the Lao PDR we learn that it is possible to make progress on combating STDs and other contagious diseases spread by globalization even when a country does not get a gold star for its human rights commitments and practices. But even here, human rights language can be used concerning the right to treatment. If ethnic issues are sensitive, and many of the victims are ethnic minorities, the issue should be framed in terms of danger to the entire society. As a start, governments that view a human rights approach as too political and a possible threat to their hegemony can be approached by a "research and training" strategy. This means making such a government a partner in ongoing research; gaining its cooperation to treat research subjects who prove to be infected, and enlisting it in a public health-oriented approach to spread both information and access to cures. Very importantly, if there are other organizations within the society that are more receptive to human rights-based dialogue as well as women's issues, they can serve as the catalyst in bringing STDs at least partly under the human rights umbrella. In Laos, the LWU is well positioned to play this role. Policy efforts could be coordinated with them and initiatives put under their supervision where beneficial. For something like STDs, the most effective programs are those that (a) don't further marginalize and stigmatize the target group, and

(b) include peer counselors (who have had considerable success with women on the fringes of the sex industry in Thailand).

In summary, it should not be hard to promote an expansion of women's rights to the issues of worker health and safety within the larger social/economic realm. If it is done in a participatory manner that also protects the livelihoods of the women, and in a realistic manner that doesn't injure the global competitive position of the private sector firms the women work for—or put unfunded economic burdens on poor governments in poor countries—such initiatives should be acceptable to all parties. Nonetheless, "stretching the human rights umbrella to include some of the world's most imperiled women" will be an incremental process. It can go faster with sex trafficking and, if handled sensitively, STDs, than with protecting women working in the most cut-throat-competitive sectors of the global economy. But a judicious application of the two tenets—enhancing women's economic empowerment for maximum impact, and promoting the health and safety argument for greater likelihood of implementation—should yield results in the cases discussed here. Even greater success is likely where UN, women's social advocacy, trade unions and other international groups join forces.

NOTES

1. I have worked almost three dozen times in Ecuador from 1989 to 2002. I have also worked in Laos three times and once in Ukraine (all over the country). All told, I have done development-related work in more than 40 countries worldwide, mostly using my own version of rapid appraisal (Blumberg, 2002). I have studied gender issues as a primary or secondary focus in almost all these places.

2. The increase in self-confidence stemming from their own income also was reported in the other studies of Ecuadorian female flower workers reviewed here (e.g., Korovkin, 2005; Vasquez, 2005).

3. Trafficking here refers to the cross-border exploitation of vulnerable individuals in some form of coerced labor from which they have no easy escape. Although female sexual bondage is empirically the largest component of trafficking in people, the labor can range from domestic service to farming, involving all ages and both genders.

4. According to informants from the Lao Women's Union (and as I learned in previous fieldwork in Laos), young Lao *Lum* are expected to sleep with each other before marriage, and it's viewed as perfectly normal as long as they're not too young, because the preferred age of marriage is not until 18 or so for women and 22 for men.

5. Remedies for reducing risks to women and children in export flowers ranged from a timid first recommendation by an ILO study of child labor that said not to propose anything that could endanger their parents' jobs (thus doing more harm than good) to sweeping calls for expensive new benefits that might have destroyed the competitiveness of the industry.

REFERENCES

AFP. (2009). *El Congreso de EEUU extiende por un año las preferencias arancelarias andinas.Yahoo Noticias*, December 23, 2009. Retrieved January 17, 2010 http://espanol.news.yahoo.com/s/afp/091223/negocios/eeuu_comercio_latam_politica.

Asociación de la Industria de Protección de Cultivos y Salud Animal (APCSA). (n.d.-a). *Factores que Inciden en la Eficiencia de los Productos Fitosanitarios. Curso de Capacitación Sobre el Uso Racional de Plaguicidas, Productos Biológicos y Nutrientes de las Plantas.* Programa Nacional de Capacitación Para el Uso y Manejo Seguro de Productos Fitosanitarios. Retrieved June 2006 http://www.sica.gov.ec/agro/insumos/APLICACION.pdf.

Asociación de la Industria de Protección de Cultivos y Salud Animal (APCSA). (n.d.-b). *Manejo Integrado de Plagas. Curso de Capacitación Sobre el Uso Racional de Plaguicidas, Productos Biológicos y Nutrientes de las Plantas.* Programa Nacional de Capacitación Para el Uso y Manejo Seguro de Productos Fitosanitarios. Retrieved June 2006 http://www.sica.gov.ec/agro/insumos/MIP.pdf.

Asociación de la Industria de Protección de Cultivos y Salud Animal (APCSA). (n.d.-c). *Precauciones de Seguridad en la Aplicación de Plaguicidas o Fitosanitarios. Curso de Capacitación Sobre el Uso Racional de Plaguicidas, Productos Biológicos y Nutrientes de las Plantas.* Programa Nacional de Capacitación Para el Uso y Manejo Seguro de Productos Fitosanitarios. Retrieved June 2006 http://www.sica.gov.ec/agro/insumos/PRECAUCION.pdf.

Blumberg, R.L. (1978). *Stratification: Socioeconomic and sexual inequality.* Dubuque, IA: William C. Brown.

Blumberg, R.L. (1984). A general theory of gender stratification. *Sociological Theory, 2,* 23–101.

Blumberg, R.L. (1988). Income under female vs. male control. *Journal of Family Issues, 9,* 51–84.

Blumberg, R.L. (1989a). *Making the case for the gender variable: Women and the wealth & well-being of nations.* Washington, DC: Agency for International Development (PN-ABC-454).

Blumberg, R.L. (1989b). Toward a feminist theory of development. In R.A. Wallace (Ed.), *Feminism and sociological theory* (pp. 161–199). Newbury Park, CA: Sage.

Blumberg, R.L. (1991). Introduction: The "triple overlap" of gender stratification, economy and the family. In R.L. Blumberg (Ed.), *Gender, family, and economy: The triple overlap* (pp. 7–32). Newbury Park, CA & London: Sage.

Blumberg, R.L. (1992). *Gender and Ecuador's new export sectors.* Washington, DC: GENESYS and USAID/Office of Women in Development.

Blumberg, R.L. (1995). Engendering wealth and well-being an era of economic transformation. In R.L. Blumberg, C.A. Rakowski, I. Tinker, & M. Monteon (Eds.), *Engendering wealth and well-being: Empowerment for global change* (pp. 1–14). Boulder, CO: Westview.

Blumberg, R.L. (1998). Gender equality is a human right. *INSTRAW News 28,* 7–20.

Blumberg, R.L. (2001b, August). *The impact of the CARE STEM Project: Results of rapid appraisal in Oudomxai and Luang Prabang provinces and quantitative analysis of M&E indicators.* Report for CARE International, Vientiane and Luang Prabang, Lao PDR.

Blumberg, R.L. (2001a, January). *Adventures along the gender frontier: Encounters with gender equality in Ecuador and Thailand and glimpses in Guinea-Bissau and China.* Paper presented at the International Conference on Gender and Equity Issues: Humanistic Considerations for the 21st Century, January and published in the conference Proceedings. Bangkok, Thailand: Srinakharinwirot University Press.

Blumberg, R.L. (2001c). *In the land of a million elephants and No. 1 condoms.* Excerpts from my fieldnotes for rapid appraisal research on gender stratification in Laos.

Blumberg, R.L. (2002, August). *A "natural experiment" for gender stratification theory? The Lao of Northeast Thailand and Laos.* Paper presented at the meetings of the American Sociological Association, Chicago.

Blumberg, R.L. (2003, October). *Patrilocality, farming systems and the gender gap in rural education in Africa and Asia.* Keynote speech presented at the Fourth International Forum on Education, China Education Association for International Exchange (CEAIE) and Ministry of Education, Beijing.

Blumberg, R.L. (2004b). Extending Lenski's schema to hold up both halves of the sky—A theory-guided way of conceptualizing agrarian societies that illuminates a puzzle about gender stratification. *Sociological Theory, 22*(2), 78–291.

Blumberg, R.L. (2004a). Climbing the pyramids of power: Alternative routes to women's empowerment and activism. In P.H. Smith, J.L. Troutner, & C. Hunefeldt (Eds.), *Promises of empowerment: Women in Asia and Latin America* (pp. 60–87). Lanham, MD: Rowman & Littlefield.

Blumberg, R.L. (2005, August and October). *Women's economic empowerment as the "Magic potion" of development?* Paper presented at the annual meetings of the American Sociological Association, Philadelphia, and UNESCO, Paris.

Blumberg, R.L. (2006). *How mother's economic activities and empowerment affect early childhood care and education (ECCE) for boys and girls.* Paris: UNESCO.

Blumberg, R.L. (2009, February). *The consequences of women's economic empowerment vs. disempowerment: From the "Magic potion" for development to the "Four Horsemen of the Apocalypse"?* Paper presented at the UNESCO Women's Studies and Gender Research Networking Conference, Bangkok.

Blumberg, R.L.,& Shved, O. (2002). *Curbing sex slavery abroad by helping women earn a living in Ukraine: Assessment of the economic empowerment aspects of the anti-trafficking project, USAID/Kiev.* Washington, DC: WID Tech/USAID-Office of Women in Development.

Bunch, C. (1991). Women's rights as human rights: Toward a re-vision of human rights. In C. Bunch & R. Carrillo (Eds.), *Gender violence: A development and human rights issue.* Highland Park, NJ: Center for Women's Global Leadership/Plowshare Press.

Cabinet of Ministers of Ukraine, State Committee of Statistics of Ukraine, UNDP Promoting Gender Equality Project. (2000). *Gender statistics for monitoring the progress in the area of equality between women and men.* Kiev, Ukraine: UNDP.

Caprioli, M. (2000). Gendered conflict. *Journal of Peace Research, 37*(1), 51–68.

Caprioli, M. (2003). Gender equality and state aggression: The impact of domestic gender equality on state first use of force. *International Interactions, 29*(3), 195–214.

Caprioli, M. (2005). Primed for violence: The role of gender inequality in predicting internal conflict. *International Studies Quarterly, 49*, 161–178.

Carrillo, R. (1991). Violence against women: An obstacle to development. In C. Bunch & R. Carrillo (Eds.), *Gender violence: A development and human rights issue*. Highland Park, NJ: Center for Women's Global Leadership/ Plowshare Press.

Carrillo, R. (1992). *Battered dreams: Violence against women as an obstacle to development*. New York: United Nations Fund for Women (UNIFEM).

Castelnuovo, C., Castelnuovo, A., Oviedo, J., & Santacruz, X. (2000). *Ecuador, Trabajo Infantil en la Floricultura: Una Evaluación Rápida*. Programa Internacional para la Erradicación del Trabajo Infantil. Organización Internacional del Trabajo. Retrieved June 2006 http://www.ilo.org/public/spanish/standards/ ipec/simpoc/ecuador/ra/flowers.pdf.

CIA. (2009). *CIA World Factbook, Lao PDR*. Washington, DC: Central Intelligence Agency. Retrieved January 12, 2010 http://www.cia.gov/cia/publications/ factbook/index.html.

CORPEI. (2009a). *Perfil del sector florícola*. Quito, Ecuador: CORPEI. Retrieved January 16, 2010http://www.ecuadorexporta.org/archivos/documentos/per-fil_de_flores_2009.pdf

CORPEI. (2009b). *Perfil del Brócoli*. Quito, Ecuador: CORPEI. Retrieved January 12, 2010 http://www.ecuadorexporta.org/contenido.ks?contenidoId=273&co ntenidoId=273.

Chamberlain, J.R. (2000). *HIV vulnerability and population mobility in the northern provinces of the Lao People's Democratic Republic*. Vientiane, Lao PDR: UNDP-Vientiane/UNOPS; The HIV/AIDS Trust, Lao PDR; The National Committee for the Control of AIDS.

Chon, C., & Ellerman, D. (2006, June 10). Soccer with a side of slavery. *The Washington Post*, p. A19.

Divale, W.T., & Harris, M. (1976). Population, warfare, and the male supremacist complex. *American Anthropologist, 78*, 521–538.

Dudwick, N., Srinivasan, R., & Braithwaite, J. (2002). *Ukraine gender review*. Washington, DC: The World Bank, Social Development Unit—Europe and Central Asia Region.

El Comercio. (2010). *La reducción del desempleo no convence*. Guayaquil, Ecuador: Redacción. Retrieved January 17, 2010 http://ww1.elcomercio.com/noticiaEC. asp?id_noticia=327965&id_seccion=6.

Flower Label Program (FLP). (1998). *International Code of Conduct for the Production of Cut-Flowers*. Retrieved June 2006 http://www.fairflowers.de/fileadmin/flp.de/ Redaktion Dokumente/ICC_eng_050719.pdf.

Flower Label Program (FLP). (2003). *Articles of Association*. Retrieved June 2006 http://www.fairflowers.de/ uploads/media/statutes_FLP_01.pdf.

Gender Resource Information & Development (GRID) Center. (2000). *Marriage and family in the Lao PDR*. Vientiane, Lao PDR: Lao Women's Union/GRID Center in Cooperation with the National Statistical Center.

Harari, R. (2003). Fuerza de Trabajo y Floricultura: Empleo, Ambiente y Salud de los Trabajadores. *Ecuador Debate, 59*, 45–62.

Ireson, C.J. (1996). *Field, forest and family: Women's work and power in rural Laos*. Boulder, CO: Westview Press.

Ireson, C.J. (1999). Gender and changing property rights in Laos. In I. Tinker & G. Summerfield (Eds.), *Women's rights to house and land: China, Laos, Vietnam* (pp. 145–152). Boulder, CO: Lynne Rienner.

Jumbo, B. (2006). *El Comercio.* Retrieved June 2006 http://www.fairflowers.de/fileadmin/flp.de/Redaktion/ Dokumente/Presse_Berichte/ElComercio_Avril2006.pdf.

Kaufmann, D. (1998). Challenges in the next stage of anti-corruption. In *Perspectives on combating corruption.* Washington, DC: Transparency International and World Bank.

King, E.M., & Mason, A.D. (2001). *Engendering development: Through gender equality in rights, resources and voice* (A World Bank Policy Research Report). Washington, DC & New York: The World Bank and Oxford University Press.

Korovkin, T. (2005). *Exportaciones Agrícolas No–Tradicionales y la Pobreza Rural en Ecuador.* Retrieved June 2006 http://www.alasru.org/enceq/Korovkin.pdf.

Lao Tourism to Bring Profit, Vice. (2009, August 1). *Bangkok Post,* p. 13.

Lopez, A.K. (2009). *La tercerización nunca fue eliminada. Vistazo,* Oct. 22, 2009. Retrieved January 14, 2010 http://www.vistazo.com/impresa/entrevista/imprimir.php?Vistazo.com&id=2994.

Melander, E. (2005). Gender equality and intrastate armed conflict. *International Studies Quarterly,* 49, 695–714.

Ministerio del Trabajo y Empleo (MTE). (2006). *Legislación Laboral.* Ecuador: Author. Retrieved June 2006 http://www.mintrab.gov.ec/MinisterioDeTrabajo//Documentos/54.doc.

Ministry of Health (MOH). (2001). *Summary report.* Vientiane, Lao PDR: Behavioral Surveillance Survey (of STDs); MOH National Committee for the Control of AIDS; Family Health International; Lao PDR Office, Population Technical Assistance Team.

Montenegro, L., & Cadena, G. (2005). *Ecuador: Crecimiento de Mano de Obra Directa, Número de Trabajadores Sector Floricultor.* Retrieved June 2006 http://www.sica.gov.ec/agronegocios/productos%20para%20invertir/flores/manodeobra.htm.

Noel, N.A. (1993). *Gender and the flower industry in Ecuador.* Unpublished doctoral thesis, University of Windsor, Ontario, Canada.

Nolan, P., & Lenski, G. (2009). *Human societies.* Boulder, CO: Paradigm Press.

Pan, P.P. (2010, January 18). Ukraine election heading to runoff. *The Washington Post,* p. A12.

Paolisso, M., & Blumberg, R.L. (1989). *Non-traditional agricultural exports: Labor, gender and socio-economic considerations.* Washington, DC/Quito: International Center for Research on Women-USAID/Ecuador.

Pavlov, V. (2005). Human trafficking remains among top crimes affecting Ukraine *The Ukranian Weekly.* Retrieved June 3, 2006 http://www.ukrweekly.com/Archive/2005/ 350511.shtml.

Phengkhay, C. (1999). *Women and land allocation in Lao PDR.* Unpublished master's thesis, Asian Institute of Technology, School of Environment, Resources and Development, Bangkok, Thailand,.

Pyshchulina, O. (2002). *Human trafficking in ukraine and perspective of its prevention.* Kiev, Ukraine: Association of Humanitarian Initiative. Retrieved June 3,

2006 http://www.belgium.iom.int/StopConference/relevantdocs/030%20Pyschu-lina.%20Human%20Trafficking%20in%20Ukraine%20and%20prevention.pdf.

Reaney, P. (2004, November 24). HIV/AIDS afflicts more and younger women, U.N. report says. *USA Today*, p. 10A.

Salazar, A. (2006a). *Ecuador's NTAEs and worker safety: Literature review and bibliography.* Unpublished manuscript, University of Virginia, Charlottesville.

Salazar, A. (2006b). *Ukrainian policies, laws and regulations relevant for sex trafficking: Literature review and bibliography.* Unpublished manuscript, University of Virginia, Charlottesville.

Schamper, J. (2002). *Macro-economic analysis—Ukraine.* Kiev, Ukraine: USAID.

Schenk-Sandbergen, L., Rodenberg, H., & Phengkhay, C. (1997). *Land, gender and social issues in Lao PDR.* Vientiene, Lao PDR: AusAID.

Servicio Ecuatoriano de Seguridad Agropecuaria (SESA). (n.d.). *Marco Legal que Regula el Registro y Control de Plaguicidas de Uso Agrícola. Curso de Capacitación Sobre el Uso Racional de Plaguicidas, Productos Biológicos y Nutrientes de las Plantas.* Programa Nacional de Capacitación Para el Uso y Manejo Seguro de Productos Fitosanitarios. Retrieved June 4, 2006 http://www.sica.gov.ec/agro/insumos/SESA.pdf.

Servicio de Inteligencia de Mercados (SIM). (2005). *Estudio de Caso: Brócoli Ecuatoriano.* Columbia: Ministerio de Agricultura y Desarrollo Rural. Retrieved June 4, 2006 http://www.agronet.gov.co/www/docs_agronet/200642717741_ESTUDIODECASObrocoli.pdf

Shelley, L. (1998). Organized crime and corruption in Ukraine: Impediments to the development of a free market economy. *Demokratizatsiya*, 6(4), 648–663.

Summer of So-Called Love: Ukrainian Feminists Confront a Growing Sex Tourism Industry. (2009). *Ms. 19*(2), 30–31.

Tomasevski, K. (1993). *Women and human rights.* London & New Jersey: Zed Books.

UNAIDS. (2007). *2007 AIDS epidemic update.* New York: Author.

United Nations Development Program (UNDP). (1999). *Gender analysis of Ukrainian society.* Kiev, Ukraine: Author.

U.S. Department of State. (2004). *Trafficking in persons report 2004.* Washington, DC: Office to Monitor and Combat Trafficking in Persons.

U.S. Department of State. (2005). *Trafficking in persons report 2005.* Washington, DC: Office to Monitor and Combat Trafficking in Persons.

U.S. Department of State. (2009). *Trafficking in persons report 2009.* Washington, DC: Office to Monitor and Combat Trafficking in Persons.

Vasquez, M.E. (2005). *The illusion of getting a job: Women's work on flower plantations (a case from Ecuador).* Unpublished master's thesis, University of Florida, Gainesville.

PART II

REPORTS FROM THE FIELD

Trade Union and Multilateral Perspectives

SEVEN

THE ILO, GENDER EQUALITY,
AND TRADE UNIONS

Shauna Olney[1]

This chapter provides a general overview of the intersection between wom-
en's social and economic rights, international labor standards, and trade
unions. A significant point of intersection between these is found in the
interrelationship between the structures and instruments of the International
Labor Organization (ILO). We first examine the structure of the ILO, and
the role of women therein, then the key gender-equality conventions, and
finally the role of trade unions with respect to the equality conventions.

THE ILO, TRIPARTISM, AND WOMEN

The oldest agency of the United Nations family, the ILO arose out of the
Treaty of Versailles in 1919, as part of the League of Nations. It was founded on tripartism, promoting cooperation between employers, workers, and
governments in the pursuit of social justice. Governments, employer, and
worker organizations have an equal voice at the highest decision-making
levels. This tripartite structure is a feature making it unique in the UN
system. As seen in Fig. 7.1, worker and employer organizations also have
an important link to the secretariat of the organization (the International
Labour Office), through the Bureau for Workers' Activities and the Bureau
for Employers' Activities.

There are 183 member states of the ILO, 28 of which are represented
on the governing body, the executive body of the office, which meets three
times a year. There also are 14 worker representatives, and 14 employer representatives. At present, four of the regular worker members of the governing

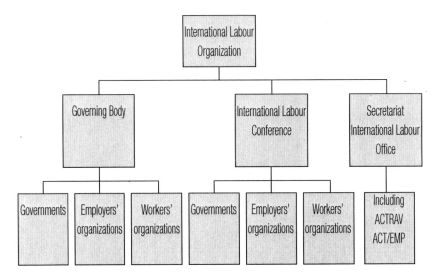

Figure 7.1. Structure of the International Labour Organization.

body (28.6%), and two of the employer members (14.3%) are women. The governing body has a key role in addressing a wide range of issues, including regarding program and policy orientations and budget allocations, and determining which subjects will be considered for discussion or standard-setting at the International Labour Conference (ILC).

At the level of the ILC, which takes place annually and hosts approximately 4,000 participants, among other things, international labor conventions and recommendations are adopted, and cases relating to the application of conventions are discussed and conclusions reached. The ILO Constitution provides that "When questions specially affecting women are to be considered by the Conference, one at least of the advisers should be a woman."[2] At the first ILC in 1919, 22 women attended, all as advisers: 13 for governments, 1 for employers and 8 for workers.[3] In terms of the gender composition of more recent delegations, including delegates, substitute delegates, and advisors, there was an increase between 2000 and 2006 in the number of government and employer female participants—from 26% to 30.5% for governments, and from 15% to 19.7% for employers. In the same period, the participation of women from workers' organizations decreased (from 19.5% to 17.2%).[4] However, from 2006 to 2009, there was an increase in the overall participation of women from all the groups—33.2% for governments, 22.7% for employer representatives, and 24.1% for worker representatives, with a total of 28.5% (see Fig. 7.2).[5]

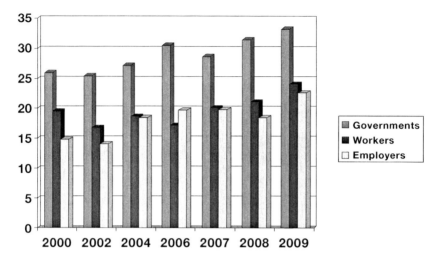

Figure 7.2. Women Delegates at the International Labour Conference (%).

An examination of the women who attended the ILC as full delegates shows lower numbers. As seen in Fig. 7.3, the percentage of female government delegates fluctuated from 2000 to 2006 (16.7% in 2000, 18.6 in 2002, 16.5 in 2004, and 18.8 in 2006). Among the employer ranks, the percentage of women as full delegates increased between 2000 and 2006—from 8% to 12.7%. The workers' group had a high of 15% women in 2004, declining to 10.1% in 2006. However, between 2006 and 2009, there was a steady increase in the number of women delegates from all the groups—reaching 25.9% for governments, 18.8% for employer representatives, and 14.1% for worker representatives in 2009.

In 2009, the tripartite ILC adopted Conclusions on Gender Equality at the Heart of Decent Work, which called on the ILO to take measures to improve the representation of women at all levels, including in the governing body and the ILC.[6]

THE ILO AND EQUALITY

Equality is at the core of the ILO's decent work agenda. The Declaration of Philadelphia, of 1944, which is part of the ILO Constitution, affirms that "all human beings, irrespective of race, creed or sex, have the right to pursue both their material well-being and their spiritual development in conditions of freedom and dignity, of economic security and equal opportunity." The 1998 ILO Declaration on Fundamental Principles and Rights at Work recalls

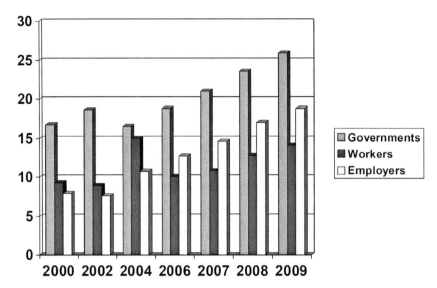

Figure 7.3. Women Delegates at the International Labour Conference, 2000–2009 (%).

that all member states have an obligation to respect, promote, and realize the principles concerning fundamental rights, whether or not they have ratified the relevant conventions. These fundamental rights include the elimination of discrimination in respect of employment and occupation.[7] In 2008, the ILO constituents adopted the ILO Declaration on Social Justice for a Fair Globalization, highlighting the importance of an ILO global and integrated strategy for decent work, with equality and nondiscrimination being cross-cutting issues.[8] The importance of respect for fundamental principles and rights at work, including nondiscrimination, was recently highlighted in the context of the international financial and economic crisis, with the adoption by the ILC of a Global Jobs Pact.[9] Since 2000, the ILO has had a series of action plans on gender equality and mainstreaming. The most recent, the ILO Action Plan for Gender Equality 2010–15, has among its aims to facilitate effective and gender-responsive delivery of the Decent Work Agenda.[10]

KEY GENDER-EQUALITY CONVENTIONS

International labor standards addressing women and equality have been high on the ILO's agenda since 1919. In the first years, ILO standards directed specifically at women had been aimed at providing protection through restriction, prohibition, or special measures. The first ILC in 1919 adopted six conventions, including one providing for maternity protection (No. 3) and one prohibiting night work for women (No. 4). In the ILC in 1937, a resolution was sponsored to re-examine the status of women, on the grounds that "much protective legislation would be unnecessary if women enjoyed equal civil and political rights with men."[11] In the 1950s, the first instruments explicitly promoting equality were adopted.

With respect to discrimination in the world of work, the ILO has the most comprehensive, dedicated instrument on the subject, namely the Discrimination (Employment and Occupation) Convention, 1958 (No. 111). This convention is among the most widely ratified, with 169 countries having taken on the obligation to declare and pursue a national policy to promote equality of opportunity and treatment in respect of employment and occupation, with a view to eliminating discrimination. The convention prohibits any distinction, exclusion, or preference based on specific grounds, that has the effect of nullifying or impairing equality of opportunity or treatment in employment or occupation. The enumerated grounds are race, color, sex, religion, political opinion, national extraction, and social origin.[12] Discrimination often involves cumulative disadvantage, with a person being discriminated against on more than one ground, which can be the situation for many women. The convention also recognizes that the manifestations of discrimination can change over time, or that existing forms become recognized. It thus provides for a member state to determine, after consultation with worker and employer representatives, and with other appropriate bodies, other grounds to be covered under the convention.[13]

Another fundamental convention is the Equal Remuneration Convention, 1951 (No. 100), which represents the first international instrument on this issue. Adopted more than 50 years ago, it was a very forward-looking instrument at the time providing not merely for equal pay for equal work, but for equal remuneration (a concept broader than pay) for work of equal value, allowing a comparison of different jobs. Such a breadth of comparison is essential owing to occupational segregation, with women and men often being concentrated in different jobs. The convention allows for the means of application to evolve, and such evolution has been ongoing. Both Conventions 100 and 111 have been widely ratified, indicating a general consensus on the importance of and a commitment to the principles enumerated in those conventions.[14] Additionally, given the importance of ensuring maternity protection and addressing the need to reconcile work and family responsibilities if there is to be true equality of opportunities between women and men, two other conventions have been acknowledged as being key gender-equality conventions: the Workers with Family Responsibilities Convention, 1981 (No. 156), and the Maternity Protection Convention, 2000 (No. 183). The universal ratification of Conventions 100 and 111 was called for in the 2009 ILO Conclusions concerning gender equality at the heart of decent work, as well as the promotion of improved ratification rates and analysis of the obstacles to ratification of, among others, Conventions 156 and 183.[15]

TRADE UNIONS AND EQUALITY CONVENTIONS

Trade unions are given both a procedural and substantive role with respect to the equality conventions. There is a role for them set out in the ILO Constitution, as well as in the conventions themselves. Pursuant to Article 22 of the ILO Constitution, trade unions and employers' organizations have a role in the regular reporting process. The government must report at regular intervals on the measures it has taken to give effect to the conventions it has ratified. A copy of this report is to be sent to the representative workers' and employers' organizations,[16] which can forward their own observations on the application of the convention. The government's report, along with any observations of the trade unions or employers' organizations, are examined by the independent Committee of Experts on the Application of Conventions and Recommendations. Trade unions are often in a privileged position to provide the Committee of Experts with information on the implementation in practice of many conventions, since their members and potential members often are directly affected by their implementation or the lack thereof. Some of the observations made by the Committee of Experts are then examined during the ILC, by the tripartite Committee on the Application of Standards. In this forum, worker and employer representatives have a voice in determining which countries will be called on regarding which conventions, as well as taking part in the substance of the discussion and in the adoption of conclusions. In recent years, of the 26 observations that are examined by the Committee on the Application of Standards each year, a number have been on the Equal Remuneration Convention, 1951 (No. 100) and the Discrimination (Employment and Occupation) Convention, 1958 (No. 111).[17]

As per Article 24, the Constitution provides not only a regular reporting mechanism where conventions are ratified, but also a representation procedure. Trade unions have a role in bringing, as well as addressing, allegations of violations of the relevant gender-equality conventions. The representation can be lodged by a trade union, among others, and owing to the structure of the organization, if the representation is found to be admissible, it will be examined by a tripartite committee appointed by the governing body. Therefore, worker and employer representatives, as well as government representatives, can be called on to address allegations of violations of the equality conventions, and issue conclusions and recommendations.

The Discrimination (Employment and Occupation) Convention, 1958 (No. 111) and the Equal Remuneration Convention, 1951 (No. 100) also provide a substantive role for trade unions, as well as employer organizations. As noted previously, under Convention 111, the grounds of discrimination can be extended beyond the seven enumerated grounds. This is to be done in consultation with representative worker and employer organizations.[18] Trade unions can play an important role in raising awareness with respect to new manifestations of discrimination, or old manifestations that have not yet been acknowledged at the national level, and promoting their coverage under Convention 111.

Convention 111 also gives trade unions a proactive role in promoting equality in employment. It states that member states are to seek the cooperation of employer and worker organizations, and other appropriate bodies, in promoting the acceptance and observance of the national equality policy.[19] The convention allows for special measures of protection and assistance, including affirmative action, again after consultation with representative employers' and workers' organizations.[20]

The Equal Remuneration Convention also specifically recognizes the key role of trade unions, along with employers' organizations, in promoting the principle of the convention. It provides that each member state is to cooperate with employer and worker organizations for the purpose of giving effect to the provisions of the convention.[21] Both Conventions 100 and 111 view collective bargaining as an important vehicle in promoting the rights contained therein.[22]

CONCLUSION

Trade unions have a privileged place in the structure of the ILO, which also is recognized in the conventions themselves. Therefore, they play a key role in the ILO in promoting gender equality at work, as they can help shape the organization's agenda, policies and priorities, they have considerable procedural rights, and at the national level, the relevant international instruments give trade unions an active role in promoting equality in employment. As gender-equality issues affect women and men every day, and are not theoretical musings, and because the workplace is a privileged entry point for addressing discrimination in society, trade unions must be key actors in this area. The ILO provides trade unions with at least some ways to take on this catalytic role, and there is considerable potential for them to continue to take a proactive approach to maximize this opportunity.

NOTES

1. Coordinator, International Labour Standards Department, Equality, Migrant Workers and Indigenous and Tribal Peoples Team. Responsibility for opinions expressed

in signed articles rests solely with the author and publication does not constitute an endorsement by the ILO

2. Article 3(2).

3. See Women's Empowerment: 90 Years of ILO Action!, Gender Equality at the Heart of Decent Work Campaign, ILO, Geneva, 2009, http://www.ilo.org/gender http://www.ilo.org/wcmsp5/groups/public/---dgreports/---gender/documents/publication/wcms_105088.pdf. This brochure contains a concise history of the role of women in the ILO.

4. See Gender Balance in the International Labour Conference: Background statistics on the representation of women and men in the ILC, 2000–2006, Bureau for Gender Equality, ILO.

5. See Gender Balance in the International Labour Conference: Background statistics on the representation of women and men in the ILC, 2003–2009, Bureau for Gender Equality, ILO.

6. See Conclusions of the Committee on Gender Equality, Provisional Record No. 13, International Labour Conference, 98th Session, 2009, ILO, Geneva, Paragraph 55(c).

7. ILO Declaration on Fundamental Principles and Rights at Work and its Follow-up, 1998, Article 2(d).

8. ILO Declaration on Social Justice for a Fair Globalization, 2008, Part I(B).

9. Recovering from the crisis: A Global Jobs Pact, 2009, paras 7 and 14.

10. ILO Action Plan for Gender Equality 2010–15, ILO, Geneva, 2010.

11. See Women's Empowerment: 90 Years of ILO Action!, Gender Equality at the Heart of Decent Work Campaign, ILO, Geneva, 2009.

12. The Discrimination (Employment and Occupation) Convention, 1958 (No. 111), Article 1(1)(a).

13. Convention No. 111, Article 1(1)(b).

14. As of September 2010, Convention No. 100 had been ratified by 168 member States, and Convention No. 111 by 169.

15. As of September 2010, Convention No. 156 had been ratified by 40 member States, and Convention No. 183 by 18.

16. Article 23 of the ILO Constitution. If the country has ratified the Tripartite Consultation (International Labour Standards) Convention, 1976 (No. 144), employers' and workers' organizations are to be consulted by the Government before each report on ratified Conventions is finalized and forwarded for review by the Committee of Experts.

17. The Committee on the Application of Standards discussed the following individual cases in recent years: 2008: C. 111, Czech Republic, Dominican Republic, Islamic Republic of Iran; 2009: C.100, Mauritania; C.111, Islamic Republic of Iran, Republic of Korea, Kuwait; 2010: C. 100, India; C. 111, Czech Republic, Islamic Republic of Iran, Russian Federation

18. Article 1(1)(b).

19. Article 3(a).

20. Article 5(2).

21. Article 4.

22. Convention No. 100, Article 2(2)(c); Recommendation No. 111, paragraph 2. See also S. Olney et al, Gender equality: A guide to collective bargaining, ILO Geneva, 2002.

EIGHT

WOMEN'S RIGHTS AND LEADERSHIP

A Central Trade Union Agenda

Jo Morris

This chapter reflects on the changing gender-power relationships in the trade union movement, with particular reference to the United Kingdom. I argue that, along with practically every other regional, national, and international institution, much remains to be done to establish parity between women and men in leadership positions at all levels of trade unions—but that trade unions are making more progress than often credited. Despite a deficit of women in leadership positions, the trade union movement has a long history in terms of representing women's rights at work, underlining that solidarity between workers is an important hallmark of progressive trade unionism and delivers new rights for women at work.

Before reviewing the change strategies adopted by British unions over the past three decades, I provide a historical context to the formative role that British trade unions have played in promoting women's rights at work since the 1870s, influenced by a tradition of class solidarity. I then describe some of the ways that the demand for instrumental change in gender-power sharing in union hierarchies has been augmented by changes in organizing priorities and policy development, marking an important development and sophistication in the gender-equality work of trade unions. This chapter is largely based on examples and brief case studies, and is augmented by reference to three key documents in cataloguing the changes that have taken place in trade unions since the late 1970s—the (statutory) TUC Equality

Audits reports of 2003 and 2005, and the report of the Guide to Trade Union Good Practices of the European Project on Parity between Women and Men in Trade Union Organizations, 2003.[1]

THE MATCH WORKERS' STRIKE FUND REGISTER 1888

A famous early struggle of young London women workers illustrates the way in which socialists and early feminists worked within the trade union movement, co-opting the support of the London Trades Council, a bastion of male skilled labor interests. The famous strike of the east London Match Girls in 1888 was an early advance in a woman's right to organize and join a trade union, as well as solidarity of skilled male workers being extended to their exploited sisters. The following section is taken from a study on the "New Unionism" available on the TUC Website.

> On an early July afternoon in 1888 a crowd of 200, mainly teen-aged girls, arrived outside a newspaper office in Bouverie Street, off Fleet Street in the City of London. They had left their work at the Bryant and May match factory at Bow in the East End in protest when three of their colleagues had been fired. Management had accused them of telling lies about their working conditions to a radical journalist, Annie Besant. They had come to her for help. In June Besant had heard at a meeting of socialists in Hampstead that Bryant and May, had announced monster profits with dividends of 22 per cent contrasted with paying wages of between 4 and 8 Shillings [20–40p] a week.
>
> From the crowd of 200 women at the door, Besant brought a small group into her office where they set up an organizing commit-tee. Besant had been pessimistic about the organization of unskilled women factory workers and shortly before the strike had criticized the Women's Trade Union League in *The Link* for espousing unworkable ideas. Bryant and May tried to break the strike by threatening to move the factory to Norway or to import blacklegs from Glasgow.
>
> Besant took a group of 50 workers to Parliament. The women catalogued their grievances before a group of MPs, and, afterwards, "outside the House they linked "arms and marched three abreast along the Embankment. . . ." The socialist paper *Justice* reported that, "A very imposing sight it was too, to see the contrast between these poor 'white slaves' and their opulent sisters."
>
> *The Campaign.* Besant's propagandist style was bold and effective and she had a fine eye for the importance of organiza-tion. . . . The strike committee called for support from the London

Trades Council. This body, formed in 1860, represented the skilled tradesmen of the capital. It had always behaved exclusively, reject-ing contact with the poor and unskilled and cultivating respect-ability. But they responded positively, donating £20 to the strike fund and offering to act as mediators between the strikers and the employer. . . .

Yet the element that the middle class and especially the employers could not comprehend was the degree to which these workers could help themselves. They were usually depicted as feckless or tragic victims of their own inadequacies tossed around by market forces. . . . Match workers' open struggles went back at least to 1871, when the government had imposed a match tax, which threatened jobs. Match workers, and the communities from which they came, surged out of the East End in a vast march on Parliament, which ended with a brutal battle with the police in Trafalgar Square and the Embankment.

The Match Workers stayed out for three weeks. The London Trades Council, at the Strike Committee's invitation, arranged a meeting with the employers. At that meeting, Bryant and May conceded almost all the women's demands. It was agreed that all fines and most deductions would be abolished, . . . and that there would be no victimization and the firm would recognize a union formed by the women.

On 27 July 1888, the inaugural meeting of the Union of Women Match Makers was held. Clementina Black, from the Women's Trade Union League, gave advice on rules, subscriptions and elections. Annie Besant was elected the first secretary. With money left over from the strike fund, plus some money raised from a benefit at the Princess Theatre, enough money was raised to enable the union to acquire permanent premises. By October, 666 members had been enrolled . . . [T]he Matchmakers Union [was] open to men and women, and the following year sent its first delegate to the Trade Union Congress (TUC). Although the Matchmakers' Union continued to exist only until 1903, the action taken in 1888 had both immediate and long-term reverberations in the trade union movement.

It is easy to see how those women provided the inspiration. They were young. They were loud. They were confident. They charged about the area holding meetings and parades. They forced the Bryant and May bosses to climb down. And they won! The "Match Girls" have had an astonishing power to speak to us over the last century. The meeting at the factory gate that June, of the socialist activism and the group of angry young working class women, was a key moment in the birth of a vast social movement, which would be celebrated, in labor and socialist history as the New Unionism. . . .

But the strike is not just of historic interest. It is an absolutely critical example of how after decades of low struggle and disappointment a militant movement can revive. Its genesis could come from the most unpredictable and apparently unpromising source. Call centre personnel? Supermarket till staff? Well, not in 1888! It was 12 to 15 year old kids in the match industry![2]

Later examples of union solidarity, where women's struggles were supported by their male trade union representatives and workmates are recorded in the TUC oral history equal pay project *Recording Women's Voices* films—in particular the way that the seminal equal pay and grading strikes at the Ford Motor Company, with its largely male production line, of the sewing machinists (all women) in 1968 and 1984 that were supported by male union members and the Convenor of the Transport and General Workers Union. The 1968 strike led more or less directly to the passing of the 1970 Equal Pay Act in the United Kingdom. In subsequent years, it has been trades unions that have supported financially and organizationally the large-scale equal pay for work of equal value claims of women workers led to payouts worth millions of pounds for the women taking equal-pay cases.[3] More importantly, their successes led to large-scale institutional pay and grading reviews that benefited whole classes of undervalued women in the public sector through collectively agreed reforms (such as The National Health Service Agenda for Change).

Class solidarity frequently does override gender and race divisions in trade union struggles. For example, in the British Airways Gate Gourmet strike, which brought the airline to a standstill globally, baggage handlers and other male, White manual workers came out in support of the mainly female Asian food preparation workers at Gate Gourmet. This solidarity of class interest and the unique role of trade unions in their collective bargaining role, within the workplace and across whole sectors of employment, are features that mark unions out from special interest nongovernmental organizations (NGOs). What is noteworthy is the extent to which unions and NGOs interests have coalesced over recent years and the way that their mutual effectiveness is improved through joint campaigns—for example, the 2004–2005 Play Fair at the Olympics global campaign on the working conditions of (largely female) sports goods production workers included international and national NGOs and global unions working together in a campaign with a unique international reach (see case studies).

INSTRUMENTAL CHANGE IN TRADE UNION LEADERSHIP

Although progress has been made since the 1970s, as with so many organizations much remains to be achieved in the profile of women in leadership positions in the trade union movement. I outline some approaches of the British Trades Union Congress, the national confederation of British trade unions with 68 affiliates and around 6.5 million members. The work of the TUC mirrors similar types of initiatives taken by union confederations throughout Europe and other parts of the international trade union movement.

For nearly a century, the TUC has held a Women's Conference, with the power to pass conference decisions with recommendations to the TUC governing body, the General Council. The TUC Women's Committee, an elected body with an advisory role to the TUC General Council, runs the conference. For three decades there have been rules in place on the election of the TUC General Council, which have ensured that the General Council includes significant representation of women through their inclusion in union delegations and through the election of four women in the "smaller union" section. Similar rights to representation now also exist for Black, disabled, and gay members, reflecting a TUC commitment to representation from all equality committees. The vast majority of affiliated unions have in place mechanisms to ensure the representation of women—from women's structures, quotas, and reserved seats, to the requirement that election to committees is on a proportional basis to the gender make up of the membership the committee serves (e.g., public sector Unison). In 2001, the TUC made its most recent rule change in this area, obliging affiliated unions to amend their rulebooks to commit themselves to actively promote equality (as opposed to being nondiscriminatory) and to participate in a biennial TUC Equality Audit so that progress toward equality in representation and organization could be measured. This is an important public instrument, which applies to all areas of equality, introduced in the wake of the definition of institutional racism following the inquiry on the police handling of the racist murder of teenager Stephen Lawrence.

The TUC Statistical Review of Women in the Trade Union movement gives a detailed analysis of the position of women in trade unions in 2004, included in a later section in this chapter. The review shows that women are playing a larger part at lower-level representational roles, with some improvement at the higher levels of trade union decision making.

UNION MEMBERSHIP AND LEADERSHIP AMONG WOMEN

In this section we survey women's roles in unions, beginning with an overview of their labor-force participation and employment patterns in general.[4]

In 2003, women accounted for 44% of those in employment, with no change since 1998 (although there has been a growth since 1990, when women were 42.5% of those in employment). Significant numbers of women work part time, and again this proportion has not changed since 1998. There has been a small increase in the number of men working part time to 9%, up from 8%. The proportion of women of working age (16–59 years) in employment is now 70%, a small growth since 1998 when 68% of women were in employment. The rate of economic activity for women (which includes those in employment and those looking for work) has grown from 72% in 1998 to 73% in 2003. The employment rate for men of working age (16–64 years) is 80%, an increase from 78% in 1998. But the rate of economic activity for men has remained at 84%.

Women in the U.K. labor force are highly concentrated in particular occupations, with almost one-fourth of all women working in administrative and secretarial jobs. Table 8.1 shows the proportion of women and men in each occupational grouping and highlights the low numbers of women who work in skilled trades and as process, plant, and machine operatives. The columns in Table 8.1 that give figures for women as a proportion of all in employment for each occupation also show that the concentration of women in certain occupations has changed little in recent years, and, if anything, has become more pronounced with higher proportions of women in administrative and secretarial work and fewer in skilled trades. There has been a slight worsening of the position for women in management occupations and in associate professional and technical occupations.

In 2002, for the first time, the proportion of women who were trade unionists was the same as the proportion of men at 29%. This reflects a trend where union density (the proportion of employees who are members of trade unions) has been declining at a slower rate among women than men. In 1991, 42% of all male employees were trade union members, compared with 32% of female employees. The decrease in union density for women to 29% in 2003 was smaller than that for men (also 29%). Figures from the autumn 2003 Labour Force Survey showed that women working full time were more likely to be in a trade union than full-time men: Union density for full-time women was 34% compared with 31% for full-time men. The same also was true for part-time women, 23% of whom were in a union compared with 12% of part-time male employees.

The majority of U.K. union members are in trade unions affiliated to the TUC and the unions provide membership figures to the TUC each year. Between 1998 and 2003, the number of affiliated unions dropped from 76 to 71, and the total membership fell from 6.75 million to 6.69 million. Over the years, women's membership share increased from 38% to 41% in 2001 and 2002 but declined to 39% in 2003. Table 8.2 gives an overview

Table 8.1. Women and Men by Occupation

	Percentage of Women in Each Occupation		Percentage of Men in Each Occupation		Women as a Proportion of All in Employment, %	
	1998	2002	1998	2002	1998	2002
Managers and senior officials	12	10	19	18	32	31
Professional occupations	9	11	11	12	40	40
Associate professional and technical occupations	11	14	9	14	50	45
Administrative and secretarial occupations	25	23	7	5	74	78
Skilled trades occupations	2	2	20	20	9	8
Personal service occupations	16	13	6	2	67	85
Sales and customer service occupations	11	12	5	4	63	68
Process, plant, and machine operatives	4	3	14	13	19	15

Source: Modified from Trades Union Congress 2005 TUC Equality Audit 2005, p. 43, Available at http://www.tuc.org.uk/extras/auditfinal.pdf

Table 8.2. Membership of 10 Largest U.K. Unions, 2003

	Description	Female, %
UNISON	Public services, including local government, health and energy	72
AMICUS	Manufacturing, technical, and professional staff (formed from merger of AEEU and MSF in 2001)	NA
T&G	General union, including transport, agriculture, manufacturing	20
GMB	General union, including food, textiles, retail and public services	40
USDAW	Shop workers and retail distribution	59
PCS	Government employees and IT and service companies	60
CWU	Post and telecommunications	21
NUT	Teachers	76
NASUWT	Teachers	69
GPMU	Printing and papermaking	17

Source: Modified from Trades Union Congress 2005 *TUC Equality Audit 2005*, p. 45. Available at http://www.tuc.org.uk/extras/auditfinal.pdf

of the 10 largest unions, who they organize, and proportions of women in membership.

How are women represented in the unions' decision-making bodies? Information and data in this section come from biennial surveys of women's position in unions carried out by *Labour Research* magazine—published by the Labour Research Department—and are significant indicators of women's participation in decision-making structures within trade unions. Apart from the information on general secretaries, which covers all TUC-affiliated unions, and on workplace representatives, the data refer to the 10 largest U.K. unions, representing more than three-fourths of the membership of TUC-affiliated unions.

Women have usually only become leaders of the smallest TUC-affiliated trade unions, although in recent years, two of the larger U.K. unions have elected a woman to lead them: the ATL teaching union and the Association of University teachers. It has been years since a woman was elected general secretary of any of the United Kingdom's largest unions; Brenda Dean was leader of the SOGAT print workers union until 1991. As seen in Table 8.3, the proportion of women general secretaries increased from 8% in 1998 to 17% in 2004.

The number of women represented on the union's main decision-making body, the national executive committee (NEC), has been an important issue for those campaigning for equality. Representation has in some cases been improved by the introduction of reserved seats—for example, this accounts for the improvement seen in the T&G union, as Table 8.4 shows. The first column for each year shows the percentage of women in membership to see how close each union is to proportionality. The female-dominated unions are those with the largest proportion of women on the NECs: UNISON (public services), USDAW (retail), and NUT (teachers).

The number of women representing their unions at the union movement's most important motion-based conference—the annual meeting of the TUC—is another indicator of how far women are involved in union decision-making processes. Table 8.5 shows improvements in some of the

Table 8.3. Women General Secretaries

Year	Female, %	Total Number
1998	8	6 (of 73)
2000	9	7 (of 78)
2002	13	9 (of 69)
2004	17	12 (of 71)

Source: Modified from Trades Union Congress 2005 *TUC Equality Audit 2005*, p. 44, Available at http://www.tuc.org.uk/extras/auditfinal.pdf

Table 8.4. Women as Percent of National Executive Committee Members

Union	1997–1998		2002–2003		Percent Change in NEC 1998–2003
	Member	NEC	Member	NEC	
UNISON	78%	65%	72%	64%	−1%
AMICUS (AEEU)	6%	0%	NA	19%[a]	+19%
AMICUS (MSF)	31%	32%	NA	19%[a]	−13%
T&G	20%	13%	20%	33%	+20%
GMB	36%	41%	40%	36%	−5%
USDAW	59%	53%	59%	59%	+6%
CWU	19%	20%	21%	26%	+6%
PCS	NA[b]	NA	60%	37%	−7%[c]
NUT	75%	43%	76%	40%	−3%
GPMU	17%	22%	17%	22%	0%
NASUWT	NA	NA	69%	13%	+5%[d]

Source: Modified from Trades Union Congress 2005 TUC Equality Audit 2005, p. 45. Available at http://www.tuc.org.uk/extras/auditfinal.pdf

Source: Labour Research

NA, not available

[a]Figure for merged Amicus union (AEEU and MSF)

[b]Union created from merger in 1998

[c]Change 2000–2003

[d]Change 2003–2003

Table 8.5. Women as Percent of TUC Delegation

Union	1997–1998		2002–2003		Percent Change in TUC Delegation 1998–2003
	Member	TUC	Member	TUC	
UNISON	78%	61%	72%	61%	0%
AMICUS (AEEU)	6%	16%	NA	29%[a]	+13%
AMICUS (MSF)	31%	45%	NA	29%[a]	−16[a]
T&G	20%	25%	20%	29%	+4%
GMB	36%	33%	40%	36%	+3%
USDAW	59%	59%	59%	50%	−9%
CWU	19%	25%	21%	29%	+4%
PCS	NA[b]	NA	60%	40%	−8%[b]
NUT	75%	43%	76%	33%	−10%
GPMU	17%	15%	17%	15%	0%
NASUWT	NA	NA	69%	24%	+7%[c]

Source: Modified from Trades Union Congress 2005 *TUC Equality Audit* 2005, p. 46. Available at http://www.tuc.org.uk/extras/auditfinal.pdf

Source: Labour Research

[a]Figure for merged Amicus union (AEEU and MSF)

[b]Change 2000–2003

[c]Change 2003–2003

non-feminized unions, notably AMICUS-AEEU, but in other cases female representation has declined.

On the other hand, and as seen in Table 8.6, progress had been made in the representation of women as full-time officers. This is significant, as officers at this level are involved in collective bargaining in some unions. In all unions there has been an increase in the proportion of regional officers who are women (the CWU has no regional full-time officers). This too is an important change, as officers at this level may be involved in collective bargaining in some unions and sectors (see Table 8.7).

In 2001, the TUC agreed a historic change to its rules that committed all unions to promoting equality for all and eliminating discrimination as a condition of affiliation. At the same time, a process of carrying out equality audits—reviewing each union's work on promoting equality—was started, and the first report was presented to Congress in 2003. An audit is to be carried out every 2 years. In the equality audit, TUC affiliates were asked to complete a detailed questionnaire containing questions about the union's rules, structures, composition of its membership, collective bargaining priorities and activities, services and education, as well as its role as an employer. An evaluation of this audit process and the results it achieved is an example of good practice from the United Kingdom.

The TUC Equality Audit of 2003 asked unions whether they kept statistical records, broken down by gender, for the numbers of branch officials and workplace representatives (also known as shop stewards). Only 31% of the unions that responded to the TUC equality audit said that they had records of the number of women branch officials, and of these only eight were able to provide the actual figures. Table 8.8 (page 183) shows that women are not represented as branch officials in proportion to their membership in any of the unions listed. Only 28% of unions in the TUC equality audit said that they kept records of the number of women workplace representatives, or shop stewards, and of these only seven were able to provide the actual figures. Women's representation at this level was quite high in all but the rail service union.

Clearly, there have been gains in women's representation at leadership levels, but more needs to be done. Still, the instrumental/technical approach towards improving the position and status of women in trade unions must be underpinned by the strong organization of women workers in the formal and informal economies around issues such as pay equity and low pay, maternity protection, gender-based violence/sexual harassment, and the reconciliation of work and extended family life. In 1998, the TUC set up its Organizing Academy, which every year since then has trained a new cohort of young union organizers. Intake of trainees, highly competitive, has seen well over 50% women trainees accepted for the year-long training, and some

Table 8.6. Women as Percent of National Full-Time Officers

Union	1997–1998		2002–2003		Percent Change in National Full-Time Officers 1998–2003
	Member	National Full-Time Officers	Member	National Full-Time Officers	
UNISON	78%	65%	72%	64%	-1%
AMICUS (AEEU)	6%	0%	NA	19%[a]	+19%
AMICUS (MSF)	31%	32%	NA	19%[a]	-13%
T&G	20%	13%	20%	33%	+20%
GMB	36%	41%	40%	36%	-5%
USDAW	59%	53%	59%	59%	+6%
CWU	19%	20%	21%	26%	+6%
PCS	NA[b]	NA	60%	37%	-7%[c]
NUT	75%	43%	76%	40%	-3%
GPMU	17%	22%	17%	22%	0%
NASUWT	NA	NA	69%	13%	+5%[d]

Source: Modified from Trades Union Congress 2005 *TUC Equality Audit 2005*, p. 45. Available at http://www.tuc.org.uk/extras/auditfinal.pdf

Source: Labour Research

NA, not available

[a]Figure for merged Amicus union (AEEU and MSF)

[b]Union created from merger in 1998

[c]Change 2000–2003

[d]Change 2003–2003

Table 8.7. Women as Percent of Regional Full-Time Officers

Union	1997–1998		2002–2003		Percent Change in Regional Full-Time Officers 1998–2003
	Member	Regional Full-Time Officers	Member	Regional Full-Time Officers	
UNISON	78%	24%	72%	36%	+12%
AMICUS (AEEU)	6%	2%	NA	4%	+2%
AMICUS (MSF)	31%	16%	NA	NA	+4%[b]
T&G	20%	8%	20%	10%	+2%
GMB	36%	13%	40%	14%	+1%
USDAW	59%	24%	59%	31%	+7%
CWU	19%	NA	21%	NA	NA
PCS	NA	NA	60%	37%	+18%
NUT	75%	11%	76%	23%	+12%
GPMU	17%	5%	17%	10%	+5%
NASUWT	NA	NA	69%	38%	+2%[d]

Source: Modified from Trades Union Congress 2005 *TUC Equality Audit 2005*, p. 47, Available at http://www.tuc.org.uk/extras/auditfinal.pdf

Source: Labour Research

NA, not applicable or not available

[a]Estimate

[b]Change 1998–2002

[c]Change 2000–2002

[d]Change 2002–2003

Table 8.8. Women as Percent of Branch Officials and Workplace Representatives, 2003[a]

Union	Description	Women as Percent of Membership	Women as Percent of Branch Officials	Women as Percent of Shop Stewards
ACM	Managers in colleges	49%	37%	
ALGUS	Staff of the Alliance and Leicester bank	75%		57%
ASLEF	Rail drivers and supervisors	3%	1%	1%
GPMU	Printing and papermaking	17%	9%	
NASUWT	Teachers	69%	24%	55%
NATFHE	Further and higher education lecturers	49%	36%	
NGSU	Staff of the Nationwide Building Society	75%	44%	68%
UNIFI	Banking and finance	60%		53%
UNISON	Public services, including local government, health, and energy	72%	47%	49%
USDAW	Shop workers and retail distribution	60%	41%	53%

Source: TUC equality audit

[a]These figures may differ from those in Table 8.6 as they were provided at a different time of the year.

years exceeding 60% female intake. This reflects the importance attached to changing the methods and target of union organizing campaigns to keep up with important changes and feminization in labor market make-up—the decline of male manufacturing jobs and the increase of service-sector employment, where it is harder to recruit union members, is strongly female and often precarious work. There is an emphasis on "like recruits like" and young women organizers run recruitment campaigns in hard to organize workplaces.

FEMINIZING THE POLICY AGENDA

Extensive work within the TUC and affiliated unions since the 1970s to improve the profile of women in leadership roles has had some, but not enough, success. A more sophisticated analysis of the extent to which gender has been integrated into the trade union agenda must include an examination of collective bargaining issues and policy concerns. The 2005 TUC Equality Audit shows the range of issues with which unions are concerned in collectively bargaining and which has become significantly feminized over the past 20 years. This is influenced by the structures of the unions and TUC, with the appointment of women's officers and Equality Departments. Negotiations extend from equal pay and working/flexible hours to childcare provision, domestic violence, and women's health and safety at the workplace. Unions have perhaps shown more success in the "gender mainstreaming" of policy and negotiating issues than in the transfer of power in leadership positions.

In the following section, two examples are provided of the way in which the TUC has integrated a gender perspective in its international and global work. Both case studies are available for further examination on the TUC Website.

Understanding Gender Implications of Poverty Reduction Strategies and Decent Work

A current project between trade unions and gender and development academics and policy advisers has recently been awarded funding from the UK Economic and Social Research Council:

> Poverty eradication through international trade, economic growth and job creation is now at the heart of the international development agenda. Yet there is much evidence that the impact of trade and foreign investments in developing economies is contradictory in its effects and throws doubt on whether developing countries can simply work themselves out of poverty. There are clear links between the

growth in the feminization of work, low income and continuing poverty. The results of global corporations restructuring and reloca-tion strategies is systematic inequality and precarious work; not the "good jobs" identified by the OECD as the prerequisite for reducing poverty and building sustainable futures, or indeed the ILO's agenda for "Decent Work for All" in the formal or informal economies. New industrial employment is very often constructed as low paid, temporary and precarious work. It is usually set up outside of any regulatory framework of either labor rights or trade union organi-zation, and women are nearly always the preferred labor supply. Moreover, whatever the dilemmas around the conditions of industrial work may be, it is at least in the formal employment sector. The primary challenge is to find way of supporting the majority workforce who work, and will continue to work outside a protective regulator framework. . . . The new supply chains of the 'global' economy reach well into the informal economy, and in the manufacturing and new agricultural export sectors, are predominantly based on women's labor either in home based production, in small workshops or in dispersed and seasonal labor gangs. This construction of women as a cheap and peripheral labor supply reflects the fact that women are increasingly required to earn a money income in order to meet the basic needs of their families. But given that women's earnings in the informal as well as the formal sector tends to be lower than men's, the low returns and precariousness of women's work becomes a major factor in chronic household poverty.

Although there are now many actors concerned in some way with trying to advance employment in the new international economy, there is little agreement as to how to make work fairer or more sustainable. The vast majority of women do not enjoy the same rights as women in the North and if their work is to be sustainable their needs include equality in their access to educa-tion, training, health, credit and property as well as their rights as workers. Most women are beyond the reach of traditional forms of trade union organization. Now, in the context of challenging and difficult new trade and market relations, trade unions need to 'imagine' new ways of engaging with both the formal and informal employment sectors and on the broad range of issues that women workers in developing countries highlight.

The intention of the proposed seminar series is to enable the trade union movement, academics, policy makers and development practitioners to debate these issues and to engage in critical dialogue of international reach. . . . This is an example of the co-operation between feminist trade unionists and academic/policy advisers that helps produce a more integrated policy view of the continuum of poverty reduction to pro-poor growth and employment.

In a second example of feminizing the policy agenda, the Play Fair at the Olympics campaign in 2004 showed collaboration on issues around the impact of the global economy on women workers. What follows is the joint press release:

Sportswear Industry Violates the Olympics Spirit

Giant sportswear brands are violating the rights of millions of workers in order to get the latest sportswear into the shops in time for the Athens Olympics, according to anti-poverty campaigners and trade unions.

In a campaign—Play Fair at the Olympics, launched in the UK today—Oxfam, Trade Union Congress (TUC) and *Labour behind the Label* are calling on Puma and the British Olympic Association to clean up their act. The campaign report exposes the ruthless tactics employed by the global sportswear industry to produce the latest sportswear, cheaper and faster. In order to deliver, suppliers are forcing their employees to work longer and harder for less money, denying them the chance to work their way out of poverty.

Phan, a 22-year-old migrant worker who sews sportswear for Puma in a factory in Thailand said:

"We work until 2am or 3am during the peak season. We always have to work a double shift. Although we are exhausted, we have no choice. We cannot refuse overtime work, because our standard wages are so low. Sometimes we want to rest but out employer forces us to work . . . I would like to demand the improvement of working conditions. However we do not feel we can demand higher wages, welfare and legal status."

Brendan Barber, TUC General Secretary said: "The Olympic Games are supposed to be a showcase for fairness and human achievement. But the sportswear industry is violating that spirit by exploiting and abusing worker rights. We want the companies to talk to us so we can work together for fairness for workers in the industry." Jasmine Whitbread, International Director at Oxfam said: "The majority of workers in the sportswear industry are women. They are paying a heavy price for their jobs. Their health, the welfare of their children and their family life are suffering as a result of long hours, poor working conditions and low pay. If women workers are going to escape from poverty we need to change the way these companies do business and make trade fair."

Play Fair draws on the testimony of workers and factory managers in Bulgaria, Cambodia, Thailand, China, Indonesia and Turkey to reveal how companies such as Puma, Fila and Asics are undermining the very labor standards they claim to uphold:

- Companies' promises to behave responsibly are ignored by company buying teams who use cut-throat tactics to bring products to shop-shelves at cheaper prices, at a quicker rate and with more flexibility.

- Factory managers are failing to respect labor standards in the face of high-pressure demands from companies.

- Workers can be dismissed for trying to form or join a trade union and endure abusive and exploitative working conditions even though these rights are protected by law and despite the fact that sportswear companies have labor practices policies.

Play Fair argues that change is in the industry's own interest and demands that:

- Sportswear companies must make prices fairer, deadlines more appropriate and treat labor standards as important a criteria as cost, time and quality. Companies should work together with trade unions and NGOs to move toward an industry-wide agreement on respecting labor standards in global supply chains.

- The British Olympic Association must ensure that Olympics sponsors and licensees meet their responsibilities towards workers' rights in their supply chains by making this a provision in sponsorship and licensing agreements.

- The general public should put pressure on the sports wear companies and the International Olympics Committee (IOC) to respect workers rights in the sportswear industry—by emailing both the companies and the IOC at www.fairolympics.org

Labour behind the Label—a coalition of development agencies, consumer organizations, trade unions, human rights groups, home worker and women workers' organizations, fair traders and individual activists—aims to improve working conditions in the global garment industry. *Labour behind the Label* represents the Clean Clothes Campaign in the UK. (See www.labourbehindthelabel.org). Oxfam GB is a member of Oxfam International: a confederation of 12 organizations working together in more than 100 countries to find lasting solutions to poverty, suffering and injustice. See www.maketradefair.com and www.oxfam.org.uk.[5]

The TUC is Britain's voice at work. As of 2010, it represents 58 trade unions with 6.2 million members who are working people from all walks of life. The TUC is also part of the International Union Confederation, which represents 175 million working people in 151 countries through 305 national affiliates (including the TUC).[6] We campaign for fairness and decent standards at work, promoting partnership with employers and government to secure stable relations, growth and prosperity.

CONCLUSIONS

Trade unions have a distinctive and unique role and function. They are democratic organizations whose great strength comes from their representative structures, although this is a barrier for a quick-fix imposed change. Of course unions, like most other organizations do not have enough women in representative roles, but significant progress has been made over the last few decades through the democratic structure of trade unions. At the September 2010 TUC annual meeting, resolutions supported gender equality in the unions as well as the broader society, defended the welfare state, opposed cuts to public services, and called for inclusive education and active citizenship.[7] Meanwhile, union density among British women continues to grow at a rate faster than men's, and in nearly all occupation groups, according to a recent government document.[8] Feminists in trade unions do, and will, continue to work with their sisters in women's organizations, national and international organizations. But fundamental to effective trade union organization is the ability to ensure worker solidarity in our common struggle for justice and equality. In today's feminized and global world the trade union struggle has a new, female character and we count on the support of all trade union members in that struggle.

NOTES

1. See TUC Equality Audit 2003 and 2005, TUC, London www.tuc.org.uk; see also Guide to Trade Union Good Practices of the European Project on Parity between Women and Men in Trade Union Organizations: European Commission funded project with the UGT (Spain), DGB (Germany), FNV (Netherlands) and

TUC (UK) 2003.

   2. This text has been extracted from J. Charlton (1999), *It just went like tinder; the mass movement and New Unionism in Britain 1889: A Socialist History* (Redwords). Reproduced in the TUC website: http://www.unionhistory.info/matchworkers/matchworkers.php

   3. See Campaigning to Close the Gap—celebrating 30 years of the Equal Pay Act; TUC publications 2000 for details of equal pay and equal value cases

   4. These figures are all taken from the Labour Force Survey 2006 (a quarterly sample survey of private households undertaken by the National Statistics Office).

   5. See http://www.tuc.org.uk/equality/tuc-7711-f0.cfm.

   6. http://www.ituc-csi.org/about-us.html.

   7. http://www.tuc.org.uk/the_tuc/tuc-19501-f0.pdf.

   8. http://stats.bis.gov.uk/UKSA/tu/Press_Notice_Trade_Union_Membership_2009.pdf.

/

NINE

ACHIEVING EQUALITY THROUGH QUALITY

Public Services and the Role of Public-Sector Trade Unions

Nora Wintour

Public Services International (PSI) is the global federation of public service trade unions, with a membership in more than 150 countries and approximately 600 affiliated organizations. It has 20 million members; of whom it is estimated 65% are women. Members are from the State and local government, health and social services, the armed forces, emergency services, and police in those few countries where workers in these sectors have the right to form trade unions, and in the essential services, such as water and electricity and sanitation. PSI's membership reflects the highly segregated gender divisions in the labor market, with health sector up to 90% female membership and the utilities sector with up to 90% or more male membership. PSI works closely with its sister global union, Education International.

This chapter provides an overview of the analysis of PSI regarding the integral links between the provision of quality public services and the achievement of equality at work and in the social sphere. The focus of the chapter is on three issues. The first is how water privatization on the provision of services negatively impacts women both as users and as workers. In this connection, I discuss PSI's policies on quality public services and its work to promote new directions among the global financial institutions, which have done so much to undermine the role of the State in the delivery of essential services. Second, the chapter reviews the PSI campaign to promote pay equity as a practical example of how a global union federation can build capacity and action to address inequalities at work. Here the emphasis is on health and caregiving where women's work is viewed as an extension of women's caring role and has been traditionally undervalued; and the impact that the undervaluing of women's work has had on migration of health workers and the downward spiraling of the quality of health and care services as a consequence. Finally, the chapter reviews PSI's work to improve women's representation in decision-making structures and its recent historic decision to amend its Constitution to allow for gender parity on all its decision-making structures.

QUALITY PUBLIC SERVICES: AN EQUALITY ISSUE

PSI considers that gender equality is central to sustainable development, poverty eradication, and quality public services. Quality is defined as the interrelation between equality and social inclusion, user involvement and participation; new innovative ways of coordinating and delivering services, and quality work, including employment conditions, working practices, and professional development.

PSI advocates that deregulation, privatization, and trade liberalization have led to increases in inequalities between and within countries, between men and women, and between women of different races. Privatization is the process of creating a two-tiered system of for-profit services for those who can afford to pay and an underresourced public service delivery for the poor. Access based on the ability to pay transfers to women the responsibility for basic services, while reducing their opportunities for employment in the public sector. As PSI's women's committee has said "quality pubic services cannot be build on the backs of women."

From this perspective, much of PSI's work is devoted to campaigns to promote public services and to expose the failures of the policies of the international financial institutions and the private sector to deliver on commitments to provide services, such as water and health. PSI argues that there are no intrinsic advantages to be gained from private-sector operations in terms of efficiencies. In the case of water delivery, on the contrary, over the past two decades, there are well-documented examples of multinational companies withdrawing from concessions in major cities, in Bolivia, Argentina, and Tanzania, for failing to deliver improvements. In contrast, there are good examples of urban public water systems embracing an innovative reform agenda to expand service delivery and to provide an equitable and affordable service. PSI has supported the public partnership approach whereby public systems, which are performing well, share expertise on a not-for-profit basis with other public systems, which are underperforming.

In its March 2006 report, "Pipe Dreams," produced jointly with the World Development Movement, PSI chronicles the failures of the private sector to provide the necessary new investment or new connections to meet the United Nations Millennium Development Goal (MDG) of halving the proportion of people without sustainable access to drinking water and basic sanitation by 2015. In sub-Saharan Africa, East Asia, excluding China, and South Asia, it is estimated that 1 billion people will need to be connected, or a total of 270,000 connections per day to meet the MDG. In the past 10 years, the private sector has only delivered 900 new connections per day. Access to safe and affordable water is pre-eminently a human right and a gender issue as it is young children, predominantly girls and women, who are trapped into the time-consuming and exhausting task of fetching water, and it is women who must in the main bear the consequences of sickness and ill health brought about by poor-quality water and inadequate sanitation.[1]

Therefore, PSI is active on many fronts—at the UN Commission on Sustainable Development and as a member of the Kofi Annan Water Advisory Board, on the policy front seeking to argue against the prevailing neoliberal trends within the international financial institutions, and at national level through advocacy and coalition building. Women's committees of the PSI affiliates are participants in the many struggles for publicly owned water and are seeking to improve public management through building alliances with users' groups to argue for models of user participation in service delivery.

The following example of the work of women trade union leaders is instructive. Luz Mariana Rodriquez Rojas was dismissed from her job at the Lambayeque water and sanitation plant, in Peru, on September 8, 2005. She was the general secretary of the local trade union, SUTSELAM and president of the Regional Front to Defend Water and Life in Lambayeque. A well-known activist in the campaign to oppose water privatization and to improve the management of the company, Luz Mariana has held elected positions in the national federation of unions of water workers in Peru, FENTAP, which is an affiliate of PSI and in the General Confederation of Workers of Peru. She was dismissed with 1 week's notice on the grounds that she was not fulfilling her work obligations, although she was officially allowed leave of absence because of her trade union responsibilities. However, it is clear that the reasons behind her dismissal was linked to her work to clean up the management of the company.

FENTAP has been extremely active in mobilizing civil society to oppose water privatization, and with the support of the PSI was in contact with similar movements in other countries, such as Uruguay and Bolivia. A day of protest was organized on September 29, 2005. Throughout the country, the Front to Defend our Water and Our Lives organized protest marches and rallies, using the slogan "the defense of our water is the defense of our lives." The Front is a very successful coalition of community, peasant, and women's groups, together with the municipal water unions and politicians opposed to water privatization. In many towns, the health workers unions and nurses' associations also supported the protests because of the importance of clean water to health. Because of a PSI urgent action to call for her reinstatement and national pressure, Luz Mariana was reinstated. The campaign for publicly owned and managed water continued and PSI devoted International Women's Day in 2007 to campaign on the issue of the right to water.

PAY EQUITY AND QUALITY SERVICES

The PSI pay-equity campaign is an integral part of its work to promote social inclusion through quality public services campaign. PSI situates its pay-equity campaign within a rights framework and as fundamental to poverty alleviation strategies and socioeconomic development. Although equal pay is widely recognized as a fundamental human right, and is specifically mentioned in many international human rights instruments, including the Universal Declaration of Human Rights, Committee on the Elimination of All Forms of Discrimination Against Women, and notably the International Laor Organization Convention 100 on Equal Pay (1951), it is still clearly on the very back burner in terms of its relative importance in the overall sets of priorities relating to women's human rights in a global perspective.

No country in the world has achieved pay equity. Women in most developing countries can earn as little as between 50% and 80% of men's earnings. In the Nordic countries, the pay gap is much narrower (about 10%), but with the privatization of public services and the degradation in working conditions, the trend is for the gap to widen again.

Women's work in the public sector, particularly in the health and social services sector is undervalued and low paid. Some examples are helpful. At a hospital in the United Kingdom, a cleaner who washes floors for 39 hours per week earns less than a wall washer who works a 35-hour week. At a major hospital in the Philippines, an assistant midwife, who has 2 years of higher education and responsibility for assisting in the delivery room, on a shift basis, is placed well below the car park supervisor, who has no higher education and is responsible for looking after the cars of the hospital staff from 9 a.m. to 5 p.m. A local authority child-care assistant in the United States, who is responsible for looking after children under the age of 5, is paid 20% less than the "veterinary assistant," who is responsible for controlling vermin and pests on the premises.

In developing and transition economies, the dramatic rise in the number of health workers who are choosing to migrate abroad reflects the deterioration of their living standards over the past 20 years and the impact of globalization. Health employers in industrialized countries in turn have failed to invest in training and improvements in working conditions of their health personnel in the knowledge that they can rely on a pool of skilled and experienced migrant health workers. The impact on health services in developing countries is tangible and seriously handicaps the capacity of states to respond to the health needs of their citizens.

One of the major obstacles to progress on equal pay is that outside the industrialized countries, there is a lack of knowledge and understanding about the issue. It is too often equated with equal pay for equal work— unions, employers, and governments often are heard to say that equal pay is not a "problem in my country."

PSI, therefore, has focused on building trade union capacity, through training programs for women activists and union leaders, through workplace participatory surveys, and through advocacy outreach with human rights organizations and women's groups, as well as with community groups, beneficiaries of public services. PSI has lobbied for improvements in statistical measurements of the gender wage gap. It also has developed its own training manuals and materials on job evaluation free of gender bias, arguing that most of the systems currently in use are inherently biased against the recognition of women's skills and responsibilities. In some countries, with PSI encouragement, unions have been able to develop bipartite agreements to establish parity committees at their workplace, responsible for conducting equality reviews. Also, in some countries, public sector unions have been able to engage with government agencies to promote gender equality or with the national wage-fixing bodies, to build commitments to identify and address pay discrimination.

Equal pay can be a very powerful tool to mobilize women around quality public services. The recognition of a right denied is a force for change. Much of the work in developing countries has focused on the recognition of the right to equal pay and earnings and its implications for the division of power and responsibilities within the household unit. It also has positive implications for the health and education of the family as a whole and for the economy of the local community when women's earnings are increased

In terms of public service delivery, the introduction of equal pay awards can have a significant impact. It improves motivation and service delivery and if the public sector is good practice employer, with transparent wage-setting systems, it also can impact positively on employment in the private sector. The discussion on pay equity then becomes part of a wider agenda on the financing of public services as a whole. It has helped increase participation and broaden the audience in the debates on gender, national budgeting, the role of parliaments, and the imposition of conditionalities by international financial institutions.

50/50 CAMPAIGN

Since the 1980s, PSI has developed strong affirmative action policies designed to assist women members in articulating their own needs and concerns through women's committee structures. As an international organization, with a democratic and accountable system of governance, PSI has encouraged the formation of women committee structures, to act as advisory bodies to the main decision-making body at all levels of the organization, from national affiliates councils, subregional advisory committees, and regional and at world levels. The four regional and world women's committees have Statutory recognition, which brings with it a regular budget and resources. At its 1993 Congress, PSI made a commitment to reach 50% women on the decision-making bodies through a policy of encouragement combined with a program of capacity building and women's leadership training. It was also agreed that 50% of all PSI-sponsored activities, such as seminars, meetings, and conferences would be reserved for women. By 1997, however, it was clear that this was not sufficient. On most decision-making bodies, women made up only 20% to 30% and PSI's senior officers were all male. PSI could have maintained a position of general encouragement but it was decided to work toward a Constitutional provision for gender parity in 2002.

How did this happen? PSI had some major advantages. First, it had a group of extremely active, articulate, and determined women with relatively senior positions in their own unions who had the time, energy and clear objective of reaching gender parity. Second, PSI's own women's structures meant that these policies could be put forward step by step through the formal decision-making processes. Third, unions in some countries that had already adopted gender parity principles (e.g., Australia) could argue on the basis of best-practice experience. Fourth, a senior management, although male-dominated, was nonetheless convinced of the need for change and became active supporters of the proposed Constitutional change.

Thus in 2002, PSI amended its Constitution to allow for gender parity on all decision-making bodies and to elect co-chairs for all committees, one man and one woman. So overnight, from 22% women on the highest decision-making body, the Executive Board (EB), PSI reached 50% (see Fig. 9.1.).[2]

WHAT HAS REALLY CHANGED?

Women are there, they are visible, and many are vocal. The allocation of time on the agenda of meetings to equality issues has increased, not only for gender equality but also other equity issues, such as young workers, lesbian, gay, bisexual, and transgendered workers, and on issues such as racism

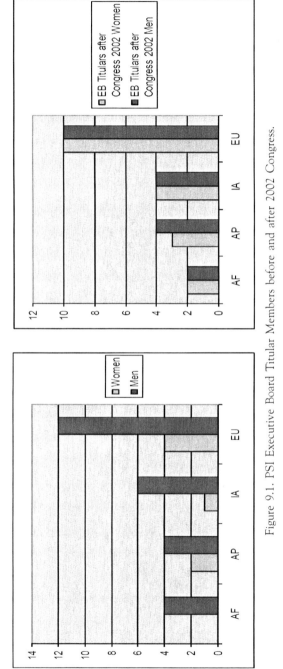

Figure 9.1. PSI Executive Board Titular Members before and after 2002 Congress.

and xenophobia, trafficking in women and children. Resource allocation for equality issues has increased in the regional budgets. It has become a political necessity for all male leaders to support publicly work to promote gender equality, although the practice may still be different. There is an increasing transparency in budgeting processes so women can track where the funds are going. There is recognition that all male podiums are no longer acceptable, and that participatory methods of conducting conferences and meetings are the right way forward. And as one woman commented to me, men have learned to use the word *gender* although they don't all necessarily know what it means.

Some patterns and trends are worrying. As can be seen in Fig. 9.2, PSI affiliates have yet to catch up to the changes adopted by the secretariat, and decision makers—presidents and general secretariat of affiliates—remain overwhelmingly male. On the other hand, there is gender parity in the education programs (see Fig. 9.3, page 200). Each subregion should elect its representatives on the basis of gender parity, but in many cases, the larger countries tend to elect the male representatives and the smaller countries elect the female representatives, thus weakening the power relations in the subregion for women. Another problem PSI has noticed is that women are not necessarily adequately briefed or informed. Women sometimes lack autonomy to make their own decisions or are otherwise controlled by their male leaders. Too often, real decisions are made by small groups, outside the formal decision-making structure.

As an international organization, PSI requires its women officers and leaders to attend meetings outside of working hours and to travel substantively. So in the end, no matter what affirmative action PSI takes, it is still dependent on changes in the household economy and division of labor to get more women to join unions, become active, and stand for office. PSI leaders are certain, however, that changes are inevitable in both gender relations and women's trade union leadership.

NOTES

1. http://www.psiru.org/reports/2006-03-W-investment.pdf.

2. The abbreviations AF, AP, IA, and EU refer to the regions of PSI affiliates: Africa, Asia-Pacific, Latin America, Europe.

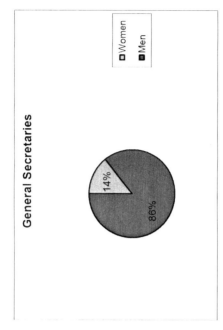

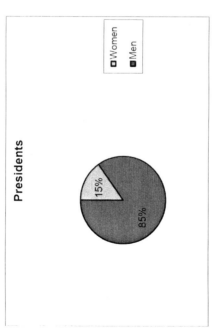

Figure 9.2. Presidents and General Secretaries of PSI Affiliates.

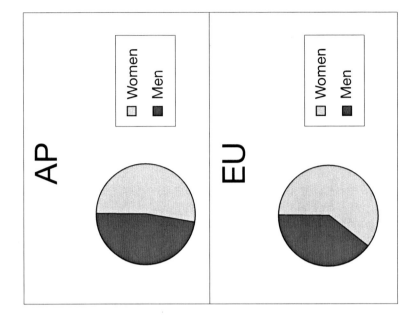

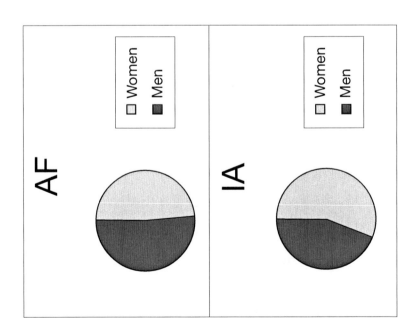

Figure 9.3. Participation in PSI Education Programs by Gender.

TEN

THE ROLE OF UNIONS IN THE PROMOTION OF GENDER EQUALITY IN FRANCE[1]

Pascale Coton

This chapter provides an overview of women's participation in French unions and in the labor market, from the perspective of a woman trade unionist. The focus is an analysis of union politics tied to the struggle for equal treatment between men and women and the improvements in work–family balance. How have they evolved? How do unions, and in particular the *Confederation francais des travailleurs chretiens* (CFTC), approach the issue of male–female equality and integration in union politics and the labor market? I also address the question of obstacles and enabling factors in women's union participation and their accession to positions of responsibility within firms as well as unions

The problem of the relationship between unionism and women is a vast and complex issue. As a reflection of society, unions recreate, reflect, and interrogate gender perspectives within their structures as well as outside of their structures. Here we pose some questions. How have women used the union machinery to assert and promote their rights? Is the involvement of women and their attainment of responsibility in union organizations currently enjoying renewed interest? What are the obstacles to the implementation of equality in the unions, and why do they remain in place? How have unions evolved, under the prompting of women in union organizations? Addressing these questions requires an examination of the evolution of the labor market, and the evolution of the position of women at family, professional, and social levels. Here we can only do so in summary fashion.

The situation of women in union organizations has very much evolved. The CFTC established itself in 1919 with the support of powerful women syndicalists. However, it remained largely a male institution, in both rank-and-file and leadership, in line with women's predominantly domestic roles. The rise in women's participation in the labor market and their access to civil and political rights allowed an increase in the number of women members parallel to a growing consideration of issues linked to male–female equality. Human dignity is one of the fundamental values of the CFTC and is written into the statutes, hence the importance that the CFTC attaches to the issues.

EVOLUTION OF THE PARTICIPATION OF WOMEN IN UNION ORGANIZATIONS

This section provides summary information on the evolution of women's participation in labor unions, linking such participation to the social context and drawing attention to the legal and policy changes that took place in each era. Here we highlight the most important dates and developments in women's union participation and activism, covering the period 1919 to 2006.

1919: Under the advisement and the impetus of female managers of power-ful confederations of unions, the decision was taken to create a Christian union confederation. At the time, of about 100,000 members, 45,000 were women. For more than 40 years, a key characteristic of Christian unionism was that within its ranks women should be represented and should be able to attain leading positions.

1938: The legal sanction of the husband's power and of the subordina-tion of the wife came to an end. Women were legally able to undertake professional activity and therefore to join a union. This is an era of great social advances, with the advent of paid holidays, but union organizations were still very masculine and unions barely took into consideration issues related to women's lives. The family remained anchored in the traditional sexual division of labor, with men having financial responsibility and women responsible for domestic duties, caregiving, and emotional work. For many segments of the society, attempts on the part of women to participate in the labor market, and therefore to emancipate themselves economically, were perceived as an attack on the role and authority of the man at the head of the family. Moreover, economically, it was possible to have only one income per household.

May 1968: This period of social upheaval marks the demise of the tra-ditional family model and the beginning of women's liberation. Women claimed their rights to be equal to men in the family and in the public domain. Their entrance in the labor market was not, however, accompanied by increased involvement in unions. According to the study of the European Confederation of Unions, this was explained by the existence of biases and hostile reactions to women's involvement, the presence of strict in-house regulations, the lack of confidence of women in their own abilities, the inconvenient nature of union meeting hours, the burden of family responsibilities, and the masculine and sometimes patriarchal character of the culture of unions. Parallel to this, women did not feel understood and saw the totality of their demands rejected by unions under false pretenses; men refused to take into consideration questions important to women.

Behind this generalized devalorization of women was the control of women's entry into the workforce and competition between the sexes. Historians have shown that the masculine opposition rested on the conviction that women belonged in the home or that women "by nature" were less competitive than men.

December 9, 1972: Wage equality between men and women was enacted into law. The recession of 1973 made the financial situation of families very difficult. Only one salary was no longer enough and women became integrated more and more into the labor market.

The 1980s: The involvement of women in union organizations increased considerably, and for several reasons. Unions experienced a demobilization of their members in the 1980s. Fewer in number, they were less powerful and became aware of the need to reorganize and reform their structures so as to attract new members. At the same time as this reassessment, women were beginning to enter the workforce in massive numbers but they did not join the unions in similar proportions. This may have been because union activity, although linked to professional activity, was distinguished in several aspects. Professional activity corresponds to a relatively definite duty, but there are no delimitations to union activity. Professional activity has the aim of producing well-defined goods and services, but union activity is imprecise and the nature and volume of tasks allowing its realization are indeterminate. The exercise of militant activity often leads to overinvestment and to numerous commitments. Although professional activity rests very often on a contractual basis, union activity rests essentially on personal choices and commitment. Union activity allows great freedom of action for its militants compared to professional activity but also a great deal of pressure. Finally, it is clear that a union career is less attractive than a professional career. All these distinctive features help explain the reluctance of women to join unions.

Nonetheless, in the 1980s, women became the best potential of recruitment and growth for the unions and the means to regain their faded power. It is in this way that the feminist movement—then impenetrable to the union movement—saw in it an opportunity to invest in the union movement so as to promote women's social rights and equality in the union. Unionism then went through an important first evolution because for the first time, it would consider problems of inequality between men and women in the labor market and in its own structure. Various strategies were subsequently put in place to take into account the specific problems of women. One was to create committees completely dedicated to women's issues. These active policies of promotion of the rights of women, however, amounted to sequestering women in a "women's section," which suggested that women were not capable of representing or defending the interests of the whole of society.

1992: The CFTC created the Committee of Women Workers, which committed itself to the advancement of women in the working world. In 2000, this committee became the Committee on Equality between Men and Women, widening its field of action to lead a fight against all forms of discrimination, be they tied to gender, age, origin, or skin color.

2006: The CTFC adopts a program for the promotion of professional and occupational equality for women and men. This reflects both the high level of women's labor force participation in France and the changing values and aspirations of working women. In addition to promoting such equality at the workplace, the CFTC also continued to educate its members on issues of discrimination.[2]

THE CURRENT LEGISLATIVE CONTEXT

Despite a very favorable legislative context at the national level, as well as at the level of the European Union (EU), inequalities persist even if advances can be highlighted, in particular in matters of integration of gender perspectives in overall union politics.

Numerous tools have been developed at the national level, as well as at the international level. At the national level as early as 1946, the preamble of the French Constitution recognized rights for women as equal to those of men. Since 1972 and the first law on wage equality between men and women, no fewer than four laws and a national agreement have been adopted to protect the equality of treatment between men and women in employment. The laws focus on specific subjects such as equality in wages or on more universal subjects such as professional equality or the fight against discrimination.

We can add to this legislative arsenal the inclusion of the theme of professional equality in the mandatory annual negotiation. The employer, therefore, has an obligation to furnish every year, to union organizations, a report on the comparative situation of men and women, which serves as a basis for negotiation on this topic. Many French institutions, such as the Haute Autorité de Lutte contre la Discrimination et pour l'Egalité, also have formed to fight against discrimination and to apply the legislatively recognized principles.

National legislation has been strongly determined by European legislation. In fact, since 1957, article 117 of the Treaty of Rome asserts the principle of equality of wages between male and female workers. Since this date, many directives have come to complement or modernize the European legislation regarding these themes.

Legislative and institutional tools are therefore numerous and complete but it must be noted that they are seldom or not at all applied. The facts are clear: Women for the most part have insecure contracts, part-time contracts, or contracts of a predetermined length; this constitutes some 82% of all women employed. They are still compensated on average 20% less than men and are largely employed in sectors that pay the least. A 2002 DARES study showed that when more than 70% of jobs in a professional network are held by women, salaries are not as high, work conditions deteriorate, and collective agreements are less protective. On the other hand, if the proportion of men in a professional network increases, salaries also will increase and work conditions will then be less restricting.

One of the principal roles of a union organization, therefore, is to be a major player in the development and implementation of standards. Social dialogue in companies, at the national level and at the European level, guarantees the application of these standards, the evaluation of their effectiveness, and the lifting of obstacles to the nonapplication of these standards. In this way, the unions are able to alert governments or employers of nonapplication of a standard or of the deterioration of a situation that needs to be remedied.

THE ROLE OF THE CFTC IN THE PROMOTION OF PROFESSIONAL EQUALITY

How is equality between men and women addressed in the CFTC? Here it is important to consider the three major stakes involved for the unions and for society as a whole.

1. *The Democratic Stake.* At the center of the struggle for equality

and justice is the defense and strengthening of democracy. This is translated into the application of and respect for the law, a willingness characterized by greater social justice and a daily fight against all forms of discrimination.

2. *An Economic Necessity.* Faced with competition, competitiveness, and the demographic reversals that companies face in France and abroad, women constitute a pool of skills that need to be rallied to respond to the needs of the modern economy.

3. *A Social Demand.* In our contemporary world, it is important that the different stages of life be valued fairly and carried out by both men and women. Equality is a matter of guaranteeing emancipation and shared responsibilities of men and women alike. Equality allows the woman to be more involved in her professional life and encourages men to participate more fully in family life.

The CFTC, for whom professional equality and the fight against discrimination has long been a major subject, deals with this issue both within the union and outside it. Internally, it promotes women to decision-making positions; externally, it promotes professional equality in the business sector. Internally, the CFTC has integrated professional equality in its overall politics. Equality between men and women occupies an important position in union deliberations. Especially important in this regard was the 2005 Congress in Bordeaux.

Equality of rights since the 2005 Bordeaux Congress, which endorsed equal rights and respect for diversity in the whole of society so that professional equality may become a reality between all men and all women, independently of their national or sociocultural origin. Today, in our increasingly intercultural environment, the fight to ensure diversity and non-discrimination is becoming a priority. Workers must be welcomed and supported to the height of the obstacles and hindrances that they now encounter in their personal life and/or in their work environment.

The fight against all forms of discrimination is thus considered by the CFTC in a comprehensive manner. In this regard, the CFTC developed and implemented an ambitious project called *Mixité, Egalité, et Qualité* [MEQ; gender integration, equality, and quality of life at work]. The aim of this project was to create a real dynamic bearing change and innovation with regard to social and professional promotion of women. It began with a tour of France that culminated in 2007 at the Défense district of Paris. The project objectives were threefold: rendering gender integration an enriching personal and professional reality; rendering equality between men and women an element of social cohesion; and rendering work–family balance an element of quality of life at work.

Gender Integration as an Enriching Personal and Professional Reality

Some professional networks remain inhospitable to gender integration. Reasons include the shortage of pools of male or female workers, the presumed nature of the work, the cost of integration, or sheer prejudice. The MEQ project allows the CFTC to meet women and men, whether salaried or not, as well as company managers and elected politicians to debate and offer propositions on gender integration, equality, quality of life at work. During these meetings, intense discussions have revealed truths about discrimination and exclusion.

Gender integration is part of the richness of diversity for firms as well as for unions. Exchanging cultures and differences in the workplace allows for better living at home and in society. Gender integration also means opening all schools, all professional networks to young women and young men so that they may have the opportunity to practice their job of choice. We can in this way act upon widening professional choices of young men and young women. This calls for interventions as early as primary schooling, making family and teachers aware of the importance of gender integration in the workplace. It also requires actions so that decision makers alter recruitment policies, showing that gender integration enhances productivity and is not a hindrance.

Equality Between Men and Women as an Element of Social Cohesion

Equality means that with equal work, there must be equal pay. Women, however, are on average still paid 20% less than men in the private sector and 12% less than men in the public sector. They are, from then on, doubly discriminated against because this under-payment is passed on to the level of pensions. This also means rejecting the current trend where mostly women hold part-time jobs, in general more tolerated than chosen, and insecure employment. At the same time, positions with responsibilities still remain widely unavailable to them. "Women, they are like oxygen, the higher you go, the less you find" was what one CFTC union official would often say.

In France, as in most of the rest of the EU, jobs with a largely female population are devalued and once these jobs are opened to men, salaries increase and agreements affording greater protection are able to be negotiated. Too often still, it is the woman who puts her career on hold to carry the responsibility of the household, including housework and care for children, parents, and grandparents. The time taken to care for children and elders must be acknowledged and valued when entering retirement. Here two remedies are suggested: one is compensation at retirement for women's double work load; another is change in gender relations so that men may participate more fully in family care work.

Taking into account the importance of professional equality in all national negotiations, company negotiations or branch negotiations is a way to achieve this equality. Promotion of women to positions involving responsibilities is another way, and that is the will of the CFTC.

Reconciliation of Professional and Family Life as an Element of Quality of Life at Work

Polls conducted in recent years by the CFTC and other entities reveal that 65% of parents believe they do not put aside enough time for their family, for their partner, or for themselves. One out of two parents believes that their job has a very important effect on the timing of having children and on the number of children they plan on having. Quality of life at work therefore is essential. Having a job is necessary but what is indispensable is being able to work in good conditions and having a job that will not infringe on the different life stages of the employee. Having safe and reliable transportation at all times so as to be able to go to work, having a workplace adapted to able-bodied or disabled workers, having lodging worthy to welcome a family, and at a reasonable distance from one's work—these are components that are as indispensable to improving quality of life as to carrying out professional duties.

This presentation of the MEQ project initiated by the CFTC is not exhaustive. The mobilization of the CFTC around this project has brought greater attention to certain situations such as the increase in the number of poor workers. Today, in France, some people can no longer live off their work with dignity. Another phenomenon is the situation of single-parent families. There is a multiplication of difficulties, in particular having a decent salary.

The tour of France that the CFTC undertook allowed women and men to speak on the three themes mentioned previously and to enrich union action. Therefore, the MEQ project was not there to create competition between men and women but rather to gather ideas and values.

For the CFTC, each person is unique and irreplaceable. Guided by the principle of human dignity and cognizant of the social construction of differences, the CFTC seeks to nurture the differences of each person and to "live better together." The CFTC wants to take it to the next level. The MEQ project should therefore have a follow-up project called "diversity, discrimination, exclusion," which will aim to fight against discrimination as a whole. The CFTC will once again go on the road in France to promote this project. As usual, it will collect the experiences of one and all and will draw from this propositions that will be presented to the whole of French political officials. The CFTC, as a union, is an important liaison between the expectations of workers and citizens and political officials.

As much on the national level as on the European level, France has at its disposal a solid legal arsenal to fight against discrimination. Despite this, discrimination in the field persists and it is for this reason that French unions are working together, including at the heart of the European Trade Union Confederation, to bring about a change in attitudes as well as policy. At the international level, it is wrong to believe that we are without resources. Without mentioning the agreements of the OIT (ILO), which are enforced with difficulty by certain states, international union activists have tools to promote dignity. The EU and France are in the lead in developing international framework agreements in which companies are committing to respect and to have their subcontractors respect the fundamental norms of the OIT.

Of course, these agreements are not yet very enforceable but they bear witness to a relatively new approach to real consideration of basic rights in companies the world over. This is what we would also call corporate social responsibility. Moreover, European and international union activists work to strengthen European works councils so as to open them up to representatives of non-EU countries, which will allow to improve ties and solidarity.

During these meetings in the field, the CFTC also always thinks of those who do not have the opportunity to express what they are going through. In France, today, a woman dies every 5 days from her husband or her partner beating her. In Afghanistan, some women will never be able to have a voice, to have the opportunity of showing us the expression in their eyes. And these are not the only intolerable situations. For French union activists, being shocked when faced with these realities is useless. How much better it is to do everything in our power to prevent these situations from happening and to help bring about real equality and justice.

NOTES

1. This chapter is translated from the French by Jessica Kanoski and Valentine M. Moghadam.

2. http://www.cftc.fr/ewb_pages/d/droits-salaries-5466.php.

PART III

WHERE NEXT FOR FEMINISM
AND THE LABOR MOVEMENT?

ELEVEN

TRADE UNIONS, COLLECTIVE AGENCY, AND THE STRUGGLE FOR WOMEN'S EQUALITY

Expanding the Political Empowerment Measure

Linda Briskin

In contrast to commonly used and internationally sanctioned measures of women's empowerment that focus on individual agency and representation, often in the parliamentary arena, this chapter argues for the importance of expanding empowerment measures to take account of *collective* agency. Undoubtedly, "making globalization work for women" will depend on collective organizing. This chapter contends that trade unions are uniquely situated as vehicles for collective agency, especially in the current global context. Unions seek to promote both social transformation and the institutional mainstreaming of equality, and can empower women to act collectively in their own interests.

This chapter considers trade unions as vehicles for changing workplace relations and conditions through collective bargaining; trade union commitments to equality as expressed in union policy and constitutions/rule books; trade union practice as democratic institutions; unions as equality resources at multiple levels and geographies, that is, at local, regional, national, and transnational levels; and trade unions as social movement vehicles. In such a collective agency paradigm, many indicators provide quantitative measures of trade union capacity as equality vehicles, these in addition to tracking numbers of women elected into union leadership positions. This chapter outlines both macro indictors such as union density, and institutional indicators such as programs to ensure equality representation; structures of representation such as women's committees and other constituency structures; and the constitutionalization of equality. These indicators offer a foundation for a new approach to measuring women's empowerment in reference to collective agency, and a frame for transnational campaigns for the rights of women workers.

INDIVIDUAL AND COLLECTIVE AGENCY

In many international policy documents and discussions of women's empowerment, the emphasis is on individual agency. For example, the UN Millennium Development Goal No. 3, the focus of which is to "promote gender equality and empower women," uses political representation as an indicator. Similarly, the Gender Empowerment Measure (GEM, in UN Human Development Reports), which has been used widely in advocating women's empowerment, highlights the extent to which women have influence in decision making, in politics, in professional life, and in organizations; its key measures are demographic distributions.[1] Even much of the literature on women in trade unions focuses on women's participation in leadership. An overemphasis on electoral strategies and demographic profiles offers a narrow view of the mechanisms for social, political, and organizational changes, and overestimates the impact of a few women in political parties, boardrooms, and unions. It also conveys a limited view of what constitutes "women's empowerment." Furthermore, as gender demographics improve, they can be used to suggest, mistakenly, that great strides toward equality have been made.

Undoubtedly, progressive leadership can play an important role in promoting equality and empowerment, and some research shows that women in political and union leadership positions can make a difference. For example, Walby (2002) reports that "In the case of the UK, female prospective parliamentary candidates for the 1992 election were more likely than male candidates to support women's rights in abortion, action against rape in marriage and domestic violence, and equal opportunities, as well as to adopt positions more typical of women in a range of other matters including nationalization/privatization, nuclear weapons and the death penalty" (p. 545).

Research also shows that it does matter who is represented at the bargaining table. Heery and Kelly's (1988) seminal study on full-time union officers (FTOs) in the United Kingdom concluded that "female representatives do seem to 'make a difference' to the conduct of trade union work.

The results suggest that women FTOs are more likely to make a priority of issues such as equal pay, child care, maternity leave and sexual harassment in collective bargaining" (p. 502). A decade later, in extensive studies of the process of collective bargaining across many European countries, Dickens (1998) concluded the following:

> the equality initiative would not have been taken; the good agreement would not have been reached, or progress on a particular issue made, had it not been for the involvement of women in the collective bargaining process. [The studies] also provide examples of . . . equality proposals being watered down or marginalized in male-dominated bodies. . . . The presence of women among negotiators can be positive for equality bargaining in terms of the issues brought to the negotiating table, the determination of bargaining priorities, and in the contribution of expertise and knowledge of women's concerns and working conditions. (pp. 34–35)

At the same time, when women as individuals are elected to positions of leadership, there is no guarantee, nor could there be, that they will represent women's interests, especially without organized constituencies to which they are accountable. In this regard, writing about women union negotiators, Dickens (1998) emphasizes the following:

> The presence of women among negotiators does not guarantee action to promote collective bargaining for equality. There is a distinction between "being there" and "making a difference." Female union negotiators, as well as male negotiators, will be acting on behalf of their normally mixed constituencies. There is nothing in the logic of liberal democracy to say that women elected from mixed constituencies should espouse the cause of women. The case studies indicate they are more likely to do this than are men, but the research also provides examples of women conforming to the traditional, male-centered agendas and priorities of bargaining. (p. 35)

Dickens' distinction between "being there" and "making a difference" highlights the limits of numerical strategies. The focus, then, on leadership demographics as a measure of women's empowerment can conflate presence and representation, and reflects a narrow view of vehicles for change. Furthermore, highlighting the success of a few women who attain leadership positions can make it appear that leadership is a personality trait rather than a social construction, and reinforce neoliberal individualism rather than social and economic transformation (Briskin, 2006c). Leadership demographics, then, are a limited measure of *collective* agency, and a narrow proxy for political empowerment. This chapter argues for the importance of expanding empowerment measures to take account of *collective* agency.

In her extensive literature review on women's empowerment and agency, Kabeer (1999) asks "How do changes in the rules of women's representation in parliament, for instance, translate into the greater political agency of women at the grassroots level?" She concludes that "While most of the measures of empowerment found in the literature . . . are defined at the level of the individual, analysis points to the structural roots of individual inequalities of power" (pp. 13, 10). Fukuda-Parr (2003), who has been involved in the UNDP's Human Development Reports, argues for the importance of moving beyond a focus on individual action and toward collective action:

> [C]ollective action, especially in the form of social movements, has been the essential motor behind progress in achieving major policy shifts necessary for human development, such as the recognition of gender equality, the need to protect the environment, or the promotion and protection of a comprehensive set of human rights. . . . The fact that progress in equal rights for women has come about largely through the efforts of women has highlighted the essential role of collective agency in human progress. (pp. 309, 314)

TRADE UNIONS AS VEHICLES FOR COLLECTIVE AGENCY

It is the view of this chapter that trade unions can empower women to act collectively in their own interests, and thus are key vehicles for advancing women's equality. Unions are uniquely situated to promote both social transformation and the institutional mainstreaming of equality, yet are undertheorized and often underrated as instruments to these ends. Despite the commitments of unions to equality policies and practices, and their multileveled structural and institutional resources, there is surprising inattention to the potential of unions in research and political discussions about global gender equality, human rights, and transnational feminism.

For example, in dialogue with the claim made by many feminists as well as the economist Amartya Sen that increasing women's freedom to work outside the home is crucial for increasing their freedom in domains such as the home, health care, education, reproductive control, and social and political life, Koggel raises questions about whether paid employment necessarily increases women's freedom and agency in all places and, specifically, under conditions of globalization. She calls for "an agency approach" that "takes women to be active agents who themselves promote and achieve social and political transformations that can then better the lives of both women and men." She suggests that "strategies that make use of the resources of national and international bodies to counteract disempowerment and exploitation experienced by women will be important" (Koggel, 2003, pp. 164, 166, 179). However, in detailing the problems faced by women, especially in the informal sector (such as lace makers in India) or the maquiladoras in Mexico, Koggel (as others) fails to consider union representation as a key strategy for increasing the agency of women waged workers. As a result, Koggel focuses on women as a collection of individuals rather than as a collective. She misses a vital link that would help ensure that women's participation in paid work enhances women's agency.

Like so many others, often writing in the development and human rights tradition, Kabeer (1999) recognizes the importance of "collective solidarity in the public arena" (p. 49). She argues that women's organizations and social movements have an important role to play:

> They are able to raise questions about forms of injustice that are taken for granted to such an extent as to appear natural, and to challenge forms of hierarchy that appear to be too deeply-entrenched to destabilize. They are also likely to be much closer to realities on the ground than official agencies of development. (p. 49)

Despite her reference to women's organizations and social movements, trade unions as vehicles for women's empowerment are never considered.

This pattern of absence continues in some recent and significant books. In *Remapping Gender in the New Global Order* (Cohen & Brodie, 2007), which includes a section on strategies and action for surviving and resisting neoliberalism, there is only one index reference to trade unions. In *Social Justice and Gender Equality: Rethinking Development Strategies and Macroeconomic Policies* (Berik, van der Meulen Rodgers, & Zammit, 2009), two chapters make reference to unions: the resistance to trade union organizing in the FTZ in Malaysia (Doraisami, 2009), and the fact that trade unions were declared illegal in Uruguay and collective bargaining discontinued (Espino & Azar, 2009). In Seguino's (2009) chapter "The Road to Gender Equality: Global Trends and the Way Forward," she does not raise the potential of trade unions and concludes with these questions:

> Which macroeconomic policies can alleviate constraints on gender equality in well-being? Can states actively intervene to create an environment where equality and economic growth are compatible?

How can capital be disciplined in such a way as to create the possibility for greater equality? . . . Can labor standards promote gender equality? (pp. 65–66)

It might be argued that the focus on labor standards rather than collective bargaining reflects concerns about the informal sector, and about the serious limits on collective bargaining rights in many parts of the world. As Blackett and Sheppard (2002) note:

The unequal access to collective bargaining reflects the extent to which dominant paradigms of collective bargaining fail readily to resonate with the plural structures of work, including but not exclusively in the informal economy, including, but not exclusively in the developing world. . . . [T]he picture of exclusion [is an] equality concern: those workers tend also to be members of groups that have traditionally faced disadvantage on the basis of race, gender, disability and other new and old prohibited grounds of discrimination. (pp. 1, 4)

They also note that "The difficulties of access to collective bargaining that have pervaded many parts of the developing world and that structurally disenfranchised groups in industrialized societies have faced are being extended in industrialized and newly industrialized economies to the mainstream 'core' of workers" (p. 13). Such a shift highlights the importance of rights to collective representation across both the North and South.

Despite these difficulties, initiatives around rights to representation among the most marginalized of workers are evident. For example, the Maquila Solidarity Network (MSN)—a labor and women's rights organization supports the efforts of workers in global supply chains to win improved wages and working conditions and a better quality of life. MSN collaborates "with local trade unions and labor rights NGOs [nongovernmental organizations] on focused campaigns supporting workers' right to organize and bargain collectively . . . and to be represented by independent unions."[2]

At a June 2002 meeting, the International Labour Organization (ILO) addressed strategies for addressing the standards for informal economy workers. Vosko (2007) notes that this meeting "afforded the opportunity for dialogue between representatives of official trade unions, feminist labor NGOs, and new unions of informal economy workers. It thereby offered a rare window into the tensions between the strategies new unions and feminist labor NGOs employ in representing informal economy workers and those typically adopted by recognized trade unions" (pp. 283–285). She concludes that the success of such collaborations will require unions to change: to recognize own account workers as workers; acknowledge and work with membership-based organizations of informal economy workers and new official unions of informal workers such as the Self-Employed Women's Association (SEWA),[3] as well as labor and feminist labor NGOs, and transnational feminist networks; and accept the importance of horizontal organizing "which may involve grouping together workers in different sectors, occupations, and employment relationships." Vosko points to the neglect of feminist labor NGOS not only by trade unions but also by feminist scholars:

> Distinctly feminist labor NGOs seek to expand the labor movement and to transform gender relations in this process. They are an important vehicle of collective organization, yet they are often dismissed by trade unions and neglected in the feminist scholarship on NGOs. They lie at the intersection between democratic membership-based trade unions, new unions, and labor NGOs. And they are a crucial site for advancing approaches to representation and organizing that embrace feminist practices of movement-building, involving the creation of solidarities that emerge from political movements (instead of being top-down) and that recognize (rather than elide) the diversity of work, workers' experiences, and workers' expressions of agency and their gendered character. (Vosko, 2007, pp. 278–279)

Just as Vosko rightly challenges the dismissal of feminist labor NGOs by the trade union movement, this chapter contests the parallel dismissal of the equality potential of unions and the persistent view of unions as unreconstructed patriarchal institutions. For example, Reyes (2007) argues: "Female workers historically have been neglected by worker organizations, especially by trade unions. Traditional trade unions are well known for their hierarchical and patriarchal structures from which female workers feel particularly alienated" (p. 229). Reyes sees this as the "context for the emergence of alternative organizations that advise and organize the workers to claim these rights through community grassroots work and transnational contacts." And yet, her account of the Red De Mujeres Sindicalistas de Mexico, or Network of Union Women of Mexico (RMSM) suggests a different narrative. The RMSM was created in 1997 with 52 members and a coordinating committee drawn from eight participating unions, which was made possible by solidaristic support from the Canadian Auto Workers Union (CAW). Reyes indicates that the collaboration with the Canadian unions was "based on the feminist workers' perspective building on the triple identities as worker, woman and unionist." She concludes:

Through its foreign network associates, this Mexican women's-cum-feminist organization has been able to legitimize and thus strengthen their demands in relation to their own "patriarchal" union leaderships. They have organized campaigns on labour–human rights, against labour violence and sexual harassment and cooperated with the Mexico City government in order to create special centres for women workers suffering from workplace related problems. [T]he RMSM has created spaces of its own in nearly all the trade unions belonging to the network. . . . [M]ost trade unions have accepted the legitimacy of equality programs and other female workers' demands within their general aims. (Reyes, 2007, pp. 236–237)

This account highlights the tension between the patriarchal and undemocratic realities of unions, and the agency of women workers and unionists who have organized, with some degrees of success, to challenge and transform them. Importantly, this trajectory is true both for the CAW, which has come to these solidaristic and feminist politics through the movement of union women inside that union, and for the RMSM whose interventions are reclaiming unions for women workers.

In another example, Elias (2007) points out:

The emphasis on trade union rights not only reiterates the privileging of formal forms of employment, but also fails to recognize the way in which trade unions themselves often reflect a pervasive male bias in terms of both rates of unionization and the upholding of gender discriminatory employment structures within the workplace. (p. 52)

Despite the thread of truth in this statement, such recognition should not be used to dismiss unions but rather to challenge their racist, sexist, hierarchical, and protectionist structures and policies. To dismiss unions erases the agency of women workers and unionists who have organized to transform them, and makes invisible the many parallel organizational and political initiatives taken by extra-union feminist labour organizations and movements of women inside unions.

Consider Swider's (2006) account of the Coalition of Domestic Workers Unions (CDWU) in Hong Kong in which she claims that the CDWU "successfully mixes characteristics of both a labor union and a transnational women's movement," what Swider (p. 111) calls "women's alternative economic organizations." Not unlike SEWA in India, the CDWU has been successful at "organizing the unorganizable." In addition to providing "English, leadership, and computer skills training to its members and education classes covering topics such as feminism, migration, and the global economy," it uses

> a host of strategies, including relying on networks and relationships with other organizations, many of which are transnational; providing services and assistance that are usually the purview of NGOs; pressuring governments through protests, campaigns, and invoking international treaties and standards; broadening their targets to include the state, the public, employers, and unorganized workers; and creating alternative economic and financial institutions such as alternative lending institutions, hiring halls, and employment services. (pp. 110, 118)

Undoubtedly, the CDWU is an exciting initiative that has had some significant successes.

What I find troubling, however, are some of the assumptions that frame Swider's discussion of the CDWU. In my view, she creates a false binary: "Women's alternative economic organizations are therefore distinctive structurally, ideologically, and strategically from both labor and feminist organizations" (p. 118). This approach makes invisible the organizing of women inside unions in ways and with goals that parallel many of the organizational strategies and ideological approaches she endorses. Swider goes on to declare of such "alternative" structures that "Although they are formally structured, they avoid the hierarchical and bureaucratic characteristics of unions and formalized feminist advocacy groups by putting their emphasis on process and democratic practices" (p. 118). Yet, the emphasis on process and democratic practice has been central to the concerns of the movement of union women in many countries, and alternatives to more bureaucratic union traditions have been modeled in union women's committees for decades (Briskin, 1999a, 2002). As this chapter documents, constituency organizing among women, people of color, workers with disabilities, sexual minorities, and aboriginal peoples, like the CDWU, has emphatically emphasized education and leadership training.

Swider argues that "Women's alternative economic organizations expand issues beyond the classical 'bread and butter' concerns of economic unionism or the gender-based claims of classic feminist movements" (p. 118). Setting aside the simplification of feminist movement strategies, the organizing of union women has reconstituted what are considered to be issues relevant to unions, expanded them well beyond the economic, recognized the permeable boundaries between the public and private issues, and set new and often successful bargaining agendas which attempt to gender all collective bargaining demands (Briskin, 2006a).

Finally, Swider claims that "these women's alternative economic organizations use multiple intersectional identities as a source of strength" and do not "demand the subordination of 'other' identities to an occupational or class solidarity" (pp. 118–119). Trade union women's organizing has challenged the generic worker and increasingly insisted not only on recognition of the significance of gender, but of other marginalized identities. Furthermore, in Canadian unions, an intersectional discourse is gaining prominence and unions are seeking to institutionalize ways to work across equity-seeking constituencies. Cross-constituency organizing in unions is helping to put intersectional politics and practice on union agendas, and challenging the essentialism sometimes associated with singular politics around gender (Briskin, 2008).

A foundational building block of this chapter is the often dramatic impact of the movement of union women, and other equality-seeking groups, on the practices, policies, and discourse of unions in many Western countries, and to some extent in unions of the South, as the Mexican example presented earlier suggests. It highlights unions as vehicles for women's collective agency, and women's agency as a source of union transformation. It assumes the significance and centrality of women's collective leadership in shaping and reshaping unions, and enhancing their potential as equality vehicles.

It is worth noting that the tendency to neglect the organizing of union women and their impact on unions also is evident in the burgeoning scholarship on union revitalization. In an exhaustive review, Kainer (2009) notes that union women's organizing has been "given scant consideration in debates on labour movement revitalization" and concludes that "most of the scholarship on union renewal starts with the premise that alternative forms of organizing are a recent response to labour movement decline" (p. 15).

CURRENT GLOBAL CONTEXT

Although women have worked in and against unions to further their workplace and equality agendas since the 19th century, changes in the current context are repositioning unions in the equality struggle. Three points are significant, all linked to globalizing forces and dramatic changes in labor markets: the decline in the standard employment relationship and deregulation of labor markets; the increase in global corporate economic rights; and the shifts in union densities and demographic profiles.

The Shift From the Standard Employment Relationship and the Deregulation of Labor Markets

As a result of economic and political restructuring, globalization, and regional integration through trade treaties, workers in many countries face deteriorating conditions of work, competitive wage bargaining across national boundaries, corporate and state attacks on worker and union rights, dismantling of social programs, decreases in the social wage, and a discursive shift to radical individualism. In the Canadian context, the deep restructuring of the labor market from the heavily unionized manufacturing sector toward private and difficult-to-organize services, and the transformation of work from relatively secure full-time employment to part-time, casual, temporary, and precarious employment has permanently altered the realities of work (see, e.g., Vosko, 2006). The rise in precarious work is often coincident with the deregulation of labor markets. Cohen (2009) outlines this deregulation in Canada, and undoubtedly there are parallels with many countries:

> This deregulation included more restrictive unemployment insurance at the federal level, a reduction in employment standards in most provinces, a very large reduction in the real minimum wage throughout the country, and a weakening of labor protections and their enforcement so that a more tentative type of employment could flourish. Both employers and the government were shedding their responsibility for social reproduction while in the process of creating a labor market that made full-time, full-year work an anomaly. The precarious nature of work increasingly demanded multiple income earners within families, and governments began to treat this as the norm within social policy: rather than ensuring that all workers received a living wage, the expectation developed that those workers with precarious employment would have the gap in their incomes filled by another family member. (p. 20)

Undoubtedly, precarious work is gendered, and deregulation has gender-specific impacts. A 1996 Organization for Economic Cooperation and Development (OECD) study concluded that "the incidence of low pay is directly related to the degree of labor market deregulation and that this incidence is particularly widespread among unskilled workers and other vulnerable groups, including women workers who are often segregated into low paying occupations and part-time employment" (reported in Strachan & Burgess, 2000, p. 374). Casualized work also is less easily subject to pay and employment equality legislation. Chicha (1999) refers to "implicit deregulation" to describe the growing difficulty applying these laws in the current context. She points out that these laws were structured to function in relation to a traditional labor market but the "relatively stable and precise boundaries that delimited the employer's identity, the status of workers, work schedules, job content, job skills and compensation methods are giving way to a workplace characterized by imprecise, continuously changing contours" (pp. 283–284). Not surprisingly, deregulation has facilitated decreased corporate commitments to equality initiatives. Wajcman (1998) argues:

Corporate restructuring is causing equality issues to move down rather than up the policy agenda. Trends in management and organizational practice are moving away from facilitating equality initiatives. . . . Fairness and equality in jobs are contingent upon a kind of certainty and stability that is being rapidly disrupted in many workplaces and completely eroded in others (p. 162)

Concomitantly, the state has been dismantling social programs, overtly diminishing its commitment to equality initiatives and decreasing the social wage, thereby intensifying pressure on collective bargaining to address such issues. The traditional role of unions in negotiating working conditions and pay has become increasingly important given changes in employment relations, and the coincident deregulation of labor markets. Where once Western states would more likely have provided framework protections for workers, increasingly the major collective vehicle to this end are trade unions.

Increase in Global Corporate Economic Rights

Unions also are being repositioned by the transnationalization of capital and the concomitant rise in corporate economic rights. As states relinquish their power to govern in key areas, and international bodies like the World Trade Organization support corporate economic rights and at the same time regulate nation-states (Cohen, 2007), trade unions have become one of the few institutional counterpoints that can challenge states, transnational corporations, and international bodies alike. In *Global Unions: Challenging Transnational Capital through Cross-Border Campaigns*, Bronfenbrenner (2007) documents campaigns to challenge the world's largest transnational firms through strategic analysis of the structure and flow of corporate power within each company (such as Exxon Mobil, Kraft, Starwood, Wal-Mart, etc.), and through cross-border campaigns to build global solidarity. These campaigns, proactive rather than defensive, offer hope in what is often a bleak landscape of corporate and neoliberal state power. Bronfenbrenner (2007) concludes: "Without question, a united global labor movement is the single greatest force for global social change and the single greatest hedge against the global race to the bottom. . . . Global unions are the future" (p. 225).

Shifts in Union Densities and Demographics

Not only has restructuring led to declining union densities, but also to significant shifts in the sectoral, age, and gender balance in union membership. For example, the European Industrial Relations Observatory reported in 2006 that "union membership levels are particularly low among young workers, while a greater proportion of union members currently consist of retired workers. Meanwhile, the proportion of female union members has now surpassed that of male union members in a number of EU [European Union] Member States."[4] In Canada, somewhat stable density numbers hide dramatic changes. In 2004, for the first time, the unionization rate for women was slightly higher than for men (Morissette, Schellenberg, & Johnson, 2005). In 2009, the rate was 33% for women and 30.4% for men. In the public sector where women are clustered, 75% of workers belong to unions compared with only 17.7% in the private sector ("Unionization," 2009). By 2002, women were half of the more than 4 million Canadian union members.

Although unions as vehicles for worker representation are undoubtedly weaker now than they have been, the feminization of union membership and union density in many Western countries are creating new opportunities to use unions as equality vehicles, both because an increased proportion of union members are women, and because union density among women is inching higher than that of men. For the United Kingdom, Colling and Dickens (2001) identify a paradox: The hostile environment for trade unions has "fostered a greater willingness to address the interests of women members, both current and potential. Unions, it could be said, 'discovered' the need to act effectively on behalf of women at a time when their ability to do so was particularly constrained" (p. 136).

TRADE UNIONS AS EQUALITY VEHICLES

Drawing on examples from Western countries, five themes emerge in regard to trade unions as vehicles for collective agency and equality:

1. trade unions as vehicles for changing workplace relations and conditions through collective bargaining;

2. trade union commitments to equality as expressed in union policy and constitutions/rule books;

3. trade union practice as democratic institutions;

4. unions as equality resources at multiple levels and geographies (i.e., at local, regional, national, and transnational levels); and

5. trade unions as social movement vehicles.

Unions undertake collective bargaining and external campaigns to transform the conditions of work and workplaces, and to promote social justice widely, and simultaneously engage in institutional transformations to reshape their internal workings around policies, practices, and culture. Not only do unions operate as equality vehicles through collective bargaining, but they also model institutional change. Where unions have often seen internal transformation as irrelevant to the project of workplace change, increasingly they understand the complex interrelationship between reshaping themselves organizationally and institutionally, on the one hand, and effectively defending the rights of their members, both as citizens and wage earners, on the other.

Trade Unions as Vehicles for Changing Workplace Relations and Conditions through Collective Bargaining

In a book such as this, the importance of collective bargaining to defending and improving the conditions of workers is assumed. So the question here is a different one: To what extent is collective bargaining an equality vehicle? Undoubtedly, collective bargaining itself has at times exacerbated inequalities, that is, discrimination has been embedded "within the bargains struck in collective negotiations" (Blackett & Sheppard, 2002, p. 2; see also Forrest, 2007). Yet at the same time, "Collective bargaining, resting on representative structures, provides a way of giving women a voice; an ability to define their own needs and concerns and to set their own priorities for action" (Dickens, 2000, p. 196). Indeed, despite some misgivings, Blackett and Sheppard conclude: "Collective bargaining, whose rationale is deeply rooted in notions of social justice, egalitarianism, democratic participation, and freedom, holds great potential to enhance equality" (p. 3).

Organizing by women unionists has forced unions to include an equality agenda in collective bargaining. In Canada, for example, a decades-long struggle on the part of the movement of Canadian union women has pressured unions to take up issues of child care, reproductive rights, sexual/racial harassment and violence against women, pay equity, and employment equity among others.[5] Initially, union hierarchies questioned the legitimacy of unions addressing such issues. With each victory, the boundaries of what constitutes a legitimate union issue shifted, the understanding of what is seen to be relevant to the workplace altered, and the support for social unionism increased.

In contrast to the focus of business unionism on wages, benefits, and job security, and in response to the organizing by the movement of union women, unions have moved toward what might be called *gendered social unionism*. Such an approach challenges the generic worker, which assumes a homogeneous and self-evident set of (class) interests among workers and union members. It recognizes the gender and equality implications in the entire range of traditional collective agreement provisions, what could be called gender/equality mainstreaming. It takes up a broad range of women's issues from violence against women to reproductive rights that embrace both the public and the private, and that recognize the links between the economic and social. Gendered social unionism, then, uniquely situates unions as policy and political vehicles in relation to both the workplace and the household.

And evidence suggests that such organizing has had a significant degree of success. Material from Canada, the United States, Australia, the United Kingdom, and the large-scale research project on Equal Opportunity and Collective Bargaining in the European Union demonstrates extensive gains in bargaining equality (Briskin, 2006a). These shifts demonstrate that collective bargaining is a flexible, responsive, and creative process, one that can offer much support for the equality project.

Trade Union Commitments to Equality in Union Policy and Constitutions/Rule Books

In 2007, the European Trade Union Confederation (ETUC), which represents 82 trade union organizations in 36 European countries, plus 12 industry-based federations, adopted a *Charter on Gender Mainstreaming in Trade Unions* that states the following:

> Gender equality is an essential element of democracy in the workplace and in society. The ETUC and its affiliates confirm their commitment to pursue gender equality as part of their broader agenda for social justice, social progress and sustainability in Europe, and therefore adopt a gender mainstreaming approach as an indispensable and integral element of all their actions and activities.[6]

A 2007 ETUC report (Sechi, 2007) documents which of these policy domains (collective bargaining, employment, wages, health and safety, working time, training, organizing) has been addressed by each of its affiliates.

In 2001, the Trades Union Congress (TUC) in the United Kingdom passed an historic motion to change its constitution. A commitment to equality is now a condition of TUC affiliation and each affiliate pledges to eliminate discrimination within its own structures and through all its activities, including its own employment practices. The text from the TUC constitution reads as follows: "It shall be a requirement of affiliation that an organization has a clear commitment to promote equality for all and to eliminate all forms of harassment, prejudice and unfair discrimination, both within its own structures and through all its activities, including its own employment practices."[7] The Equality Officer of UNISON, Gloria Mills, described this change as a "groundbreaking achievement": "This rule change provides the basis for bringing women's issues from the periphery to the heart of union culture" (TUC, 2005, p. 50).

Over the past 30 years, the Canadian union movement has produced extensive materials on equality-related issues, and the past decade has witnessed a remarkable development of union policy on racism, homophobia, sexism, and recently on transphobia and ableism (for Canada, see Eaton 2004; Hunt & Rayside 2007).[8] Preliminary research on equality-related language in 20 Canadian union constitutions reveals an increasing codification of equality in clauses on general equality, mandated equality-seeking committees, harassment procedures, leadership programs such as designated seats for members of equality-seeking groups, childcare support at union meetings, and staff support for equality-seeking initiatives. More than any other social institution, unions also have taken initiatives to transform their organizational practice and culture to ensure fairness and representation for equality-seeking members.

Despite the fact that these policies are not necessarily fully implemented in the daily life of unions, particularly at the local level, without a doubt, the passing of each policy has involved widespread education and mobilization. Union policies are adopted by memberships through democratic processes usually at union conventions; such processes often include prior education on the issues, and debate and discussion preceding a vote. In this regard, unions provide an interesting counterpoint to diversity policies at universities and corporations that often are exercises in public relations and implemented in a top–down process (Ahmed, 2007).

Trade Union Practice as Democratic Institutions

Inside unions, a dual strategy for democratization via initiatives around leadership and representation has emerged: on the one hand, the election of more women and members of other equality-seeking groups to union leadership positions to change demographic profiles; and on the other, constituency organizing to represent the interests of women and other equality-seeking groups.[9] These two separate but not unrelated projects recognize that presence in and of itself does not ensure voice.

Affirmative action (also known as positive action) programs have been a major, and now widespread, union initiative to address the demographic underrepresentation of women in top elected positions. In the 1990s, the International Confederation of Free Trade Unions (ICFTU) reported that trade union centrals in Austria, Belgium, Botswana, Burkina Faso, Colombia, Dominican Republic, Fiji, France, Great Britain, Guyana, Israel, Italy, Korea, Malaysia, New Zealand, and the Philippines all set aside special (sometimes called reserved) seats for women on their central leadership body (ICFTU, 1991; also 1994; see also Sechi on the ETUC, 2007; and TUC, 2007). In Britain's UNISON, Europe's largest public sector union, which was born in 1993 of an amalgamation of three unions, proportionality and fair representation are central to its constitution, and special representational measures exist for women, Black members, lesbian and gay members, and disabled members. In an important innovation, representative structures also provide seats for low-paid women (McBride, 2001).[10] The widespread institutionalization of affirmative action programs have put proportionality on the agendas of many unions; led to changes in union constitutions; and increased training and mentoring programs to support leadership by and of marginalized unionists. Anderson (2003) notes that "Many democracies have failed to correct chronic capability deprivations in substantial subsets of their populations. . . . [S]teps need to be taken to ensure that members of disadvantaged groups are heard. In a context of global gender inequality, this supports the call . . . to adopt policies to increase the representation of women in democratic offices, especially legislative bodies" (p. 252). The varied leadership programs adopted by unions may offer optimism in these efforts, and models to this end.

Over the past 30 years, constituency organizing inside unions, also called separate or self-organizing, has brought together members of equality-seeking groups—women, people of color, Aboriginal peoples, people with disabilities, and lesbian, gay, bisexual, and transgendered peoples—to increase their skills, self-confidence, and political power. It is expressed organizationally in both informal caucuses and formal committees (the latter sometimes mandated by union constitutions or rule books): Human Rights Committees, Rainbow Committees, Aboriginal Circles, Women's Committees and Pink Triangle Committees. Equality-seeking groups have organized in response to male and White domination; patriarchal, racist and homophobic union cultures; and hierarchical and undemocratic organizational practices in unions. Such self-organizing has politicized equality-seeking groups and produced them as vocal constituencies. Counterintuitively, separate organizing has not led to the ghettoization or marginalization of equality concerns; rather it has been a vehicle for mainstreaming equality concerns. For example, in Canada, through separate organizing, women have promoted women's leadership, challenged traditional leaderships to be more accountable, encouraged unions to be more democratic and participatory, and forced unions to take up women's concerns as union members and as workers—through policy initiatives and at the negotiating table (Briskin, 1999a; 2006b, 2006c; Hunt & Rayside, 2007).[11]

The various separate committees and caucuses that have played a critical if often unacknowledged role in transforming Canadian unions over the past three decades are now beginning to invent new political and organizational ways to work collectively and collaboratively across various marginalized constituencies—what I call *cross-constituency organizing*—which help to avoid intersectional disempowerment, on the one hand, and advance the union equality project, deepen democracy, and revitalize unions on the other hand.[12] In her study of the struggles of three clerical workers' unions (at Harvard, Columbia, and Yale universities), Kurtz (2002) concludes that "the unavoidable task . . . of each movement is to build internal coalitions" using "a multi-identity politics" (p. xviii). Cross-constituency organizing is a vehicle to develop institutional and political practices that take account of multiple, sometimes competing, identities (intersectionality), promote a culture of alliances, and enhance inclusive solidarity.

Despite the exponential interest in intersectionality, Verloo (2006) notes the relative absence of discussions about the political practice of intersectionality. Cross-constituency organizing inside unions offers a model of intersectional and coalitional practice for social movements, and other institutions committed to social justice, and also might help to address the "skepticism about the possibility and desirability of constructing trans-group practical identities" (Anderson, 2003, p. 255).

The evidence from unions suggest that increasing women's participation in elected leadership positions is not sufficient to en/gender democracy in the unions, empower women, or offer inclusive unionism to any marginalized group. In fact, the causal relationship may be the reverse. For demographic strategies to be successful, they may need to be deeply embedded in larger processes of democratizing organizational practices and union culture. In fact, if one considers impacts and outcomes rather than numbers, then it could be argued that constituency and cross-constituency organizing are democratic forms of leadership, which may be more effective than demographic representation as a vehicle for union transformation. In an interesting, if somewhat dated, study of public sector unions in Quebec, Nichols-Heppner (1984) concluded that establishing women's committees is a more effective strategy than seeking greater electoral representation, and that such committees "evoke more organizational responsiveness from unions" and are "the strongest determinant of the negotiation of collective agreement provisions favorable to women unionists" (p. 294). Although more comparative research is needed, evidence suggests that it is not the few in top leadership who promote systemic changes but rather mobilization by equality-seeking groups whose vision includes changing union practices, policies cultures, and structures (see Briskin, 1999a, 1999b). Certainly, in Canadian unions, calls for transformation in the gender order originally came, not from those in leadership, but from rank-and-file women organizing on the margins of unions.

This discussion of democracy in unions supports certain key claims in this chapter. First, democratizing initiatives inside unions around leadership, representation and intersectionality offer evidence of the potential of unions as equality vehicles; they also offer models for equality practice for other institutions especially given the widespread focus on leadership demographics as a measure of women's empowerment. Second, even inside unions, empowerment of women will depend on vehicles that enhance their *collective* agency. Although unions likely have taken more initiatives than any other institution to address the gaps in leadership demographics, it is constituency and cross-constituency organizing from which the most has been gained, and the most can be learned. Union initiatives around leadership, affirmative action, constituency, and cross-constituency organizing suggest that unions (despite their limits) might well be the most democratic of all institutions in liberal democracies, responsive to organized rank-and-file (grassroots) pressure in ways that perhaps no other institution has been. This highlights the paradox of unions; on the one hand, their resistance to change, and on the other, their potential as a vehicle for collective agency and equality.

Trade Unions as Equality Resources at Multiple Levels and Geographies

The union movement is unique in its structure, operating at multiple levels and geographies with explicit and often constitutionalized commitments to democratic practice and equality. Unions have resourced structures at local, regional, national, transnational, and global levels: "Labor has even a greater capacity than capital to be globally connected because it can connect with workers at every level" (Bronfenbrenner, 2007, p. 14). These multilayered structures enhance the democratic potential of unions, and their capacity as equality vehicles.

In any given country, most union members would participate at the local level, and the local–regional–national nexus is likely the most accessible and visible. However, at the transnational level, 11 different global union federations organized by sector and industry represent millions of workers in almost every country in the world, and each has an active women's committee. Additionally, the International Trade Union Confederation (ITUC), the umbrella organization to which the global unions belong, represents 168 million workers in 155 countries and territories and has 311 national affiliates; it too has an active equality program: "The ITUC's primary mission is the promotion and defence of workers' rights and interests, through international cooperation between trade unions, global campaigning and advocacy within the major global institutions. . . . Its main areas of activity include trade union and human rights, economy, society and the workplace, equality and non-discrimination, and international solidarity."[13]

Unions also are uniquely situated to promote the institutional main-streaming of equality. The ITUC works closely with the International Labour Organization (ILO) of the United Nations and the Trade Union Advisory Committee (TUAC) to the OECD. Building on the ILO's Decent Work agenda, the current ITUC campaign Decent Work, Decent Life for Women engages both the content of the gender-equality vision, and the means to implement it, and seeks to make change at multiple levels. It advocates for decent work for women and gender equality in labor policies and agree-ments, and simultaneously gender equality in trade union structures, policies, and activities, including an increase in women trade union members and women in elected positions. It highlights the issues of women in the infor-mal economy and export processing zones, domestic workers, and migrant workers as well as concerns about violence against women. The ITUC has taken these issues to the UN Commission on the Status of Women. At the 52nd Session of the Commission (February-March 2008), an ITUC-Public Service International (PSI)-Education International (EI) delegation of 40 women negotiated successfully for the inclusion of decent work in its Agreed Conclusions, an excellent example of the role the unions can play in mainstreaming equality concerns. As part of this campaign, the ITUC has developed *Achieving Gender Equality: A Trade Union Manual*, which not only includes material on organizing for equality, building the union, organizing the informal economy, gender relations in trade unions, role of women's committees, global campaigns for women, gender mainstreaming, right to work, but also a series of activities to support *local* initiatives in each of these areas. Its September 2008 report on the *Decent Work* campaign indicated that 82 national centers in 56 countries are participating in the campaign.[14]

Trade Unions as Social Movement Vehicles

Two recent Canadian surveys of union innovation help to articulate charac-teristics of what is called *social movement unionism* (SMU; Kumar & Murray, 2006):[15]

> Social movement unionism [is oriented] towards a broader defini-tion of collectivity, its emphasis on the worker as citizen as well as wage earner, its dedication to the transformation rather than the regulation of the market, its focus on both the workplace and society, the importance of political action, and its emphasis on the transformative character of conflict. . . . In practical terms, its emphasis is on the development of rank-and-file activism, workplace struggle as a form of membership education, and coalition-building

and community outreach as opposed to a narrower service-oriented unionism. (p. 82)

Certain strategic threads embedded in SMU help to illuminate both the potential and relevance of unions as equity vehicles. First, although the degree of institutionalization of unions suggests that unions are not themselves social movements, it is significant that sites of constituency organizing inside unions (such as women's committees) mirror social movement organizational practice in many ways: around participatory democracy and consensus decision making, the sharing of skills and knowledge, active leadership development, and broad visions for social change. Second, working actively in coalition with social movements and communities outside the unions, including cross-border cooperation and solidarity work is central to SMU, and has taken a variety of forms. For example, the 1990s witnessed the emergence of what is sometimes called *community unionism*. Focused on the unemployed and precariously employed, it includes community–union alliances to jointly unionize workers as well as organizations such as Workers' Centers that create broad solidarities among nonunionized workers and the working-class community through education, networking, and organizing (Cranford, Gellatly, Ladd, & Vosko, 2006; Fine, 2006).Certainly, coalition building "is regarded as one of the most innovative strategies for union revitalization" (Kumar & Schenk, 2006, p. 40; see also Clawson, 2003; Frege, Heery, & Turner, 2004; Kainer, 2009) and undoubtedly significant to enhancing the potential of unions as equality vehicles. In Canadian unions, coalition building as an equality strategy has a long history. Beginning in the 1970s, around issues such as pay equality, affirmative action, sexual harassment and violence against women, child care, and reproductive rights, union women have organized alliances and coalitions across unions and with social movements, contesting the isolationist tendencies within the union movement and legitimizing coalition building with groups outside the union movement.[16]

Such Canadian coalitions have organized a Quebec women's march against poverty in 1995, and a national march For Bread and Roses, For Jobs and Justice in 1996. The 2000 World March of Women endorsed by more than 200 countries and 2,200 organizations, was modeled on these events. Its goals were to eliminate poverty and violence in women's lives. Union women's organizing, then, has been instrumental in transforming the relationship of Canadian unions to other progressive movements, and initiating the trend toward social movement unionism that embraces a "wider definition of solidarity, i.e., that unions should defend all workers and not just their members . . . [and] seeks to promote the interests of the worker as citizen as well as wage earner" (Murray, 2005, p. 108).[17]

Innovative transnational initiatives, such as the *Pay Equity Now!* campaign launched in 2000 by the PSI, highlight cross-union, cross-border, and community–union coalition work in Europe, Africa, Asia, and Latin America:

> This campaign . . . culminated in national and global actions and campaigns which have had various impacts, including agenda setting for unions, employers and governments, raised public awareness through lobbying, and information campaigns about gender inequalities. Pay Equity Now! has also focused on how issues such as living minimum wages, poverty alleviation and the valuing of women's work through practical gender pay equity initiatives can be used as a tool for organizing and recruiting women. (Pillinger, 2005, p. 592)

The pay equity campaign is instructive on a number of levels. It demonstrates the importance of unions as equality resources at multiple levels and geographies; the policy and research concerns of unions; their focus on collective bargaining as a vehicle but also critical attention to low paid work; and their commitments to leadership training, constituency organizing and coalition work. Pillinger (2005) underscores that the "critical catalyst" for gender-equality initiatives has been women's activism, adding:

> Whilst the campaign has addressed economic resources and power relations within a context of globalization and economic restructuring, it has helped to promote new forms of global networking, learning and action. This has resulted in alliances between women's and other feminist and social movements, and links between activities in the public service unions to women's networks in the informal economy so that links are made between low value and low pay. (p. 595)

Undoubtedly, the current mainstreaming of social movement unionism not only enhances unions' potential as equality vehicles and resources, it also promotes the interests of both unionized and nonunionized workers, as citizens as well as wage earners.

QUANTITATIVE MEASURES AND INDICATORS

In the *collective* agency paradigm, many indicators provide quantitative measures of trade union capacity as equality vehicles, these in addition to tracking numbers of women elected into leadership positions. Not only are documentation and measurement important parts of developing, defending, and monitoring equality initiatives, they also are organizing and educational tools, and provide a reference point for transnational comparisons and campaigns. Such quantifiable measures also offer a challenge, an alternative or, at minimum, an additional framework to the widespread mapping of women's empowerment based on demographic leadership indicators, such as those found on the Websites of the UN, ILO, ITUC, the World Bank and the World Economic Forum.[18]

Macro Indicators

Three macro indicators are relevant: (a) access to unionization, the right to collective representation, and the right to bargain collectively as part of the broader freedom of association[19]; (b) union density in which unionization is conceived as one measure of or proxy for collective agency; and (c) union advantage data that unequivocally highlight benefits and protections for workers who are covered by a union. These may include better wages, benefits, job security, equity provisions, promotion opportunities, working conditions, and the like.[20] With respect to the latter, Jackson (2004) notes:

> Unionization is associated with formalized and equitable pay and promotion structures as well as layoff rules which tend to minimize some of the most overt forms of discrimination on the basis of gender and race, and many unions have consciously tried to promote pay and employment equality for their lower paid and women members through bargaining . . . [U]nionized workers are also most likely to benefit from legislated pay and employment equality laws than are non union workers because unions have the resources to make these laws effective. (p. 9)

Institutional Indicators

A wide variety of institutional indicators are relevant: equality demographics of membership, local and central leadership, union staff and committee membership, and in confederation and transnational union structures; programs to ensure equality representation such as affirmative action, designated seats, proportionality measures; structures of representation such as women's committees and other constituency structures; constitutionalization of equality (equality and mainstreaming clauses in union constitutions, rule books and charters); equality audits of collective agreements, including documenting collective bargaining gains in specified areas for women, and monitoring mechanisms for the implementation of equality provisions; and finally measures to ensure equality bargaining practices including desegregation of the collective bargaining committees to include women and members of other equality-seeking groups (Briskin, 2006a).

Many national unions, and union confederations have done excellent work documenting some of these measures. The example of data collection initiatives by the TUC in the United Kingdom provides a national model. In conjunction with the historic motion in 2001 to change its constitution to include a commitment to equality as a condition of affiliation with TUC, a comprehensive TUC equality auditing process on a biannual basis was established. Three audits have now been released, the last in 2009.[21] The periodic reports from the ETUC are likely the most comprehensive (ETUC, 1999, 2003; Sechi 2007). These reports document and track leadership demographics, mechanisms of mainstreaming including implementation and dissemination measures, existence of women's committees, and powers of women's committees (which include both integration and autonomy measures) among other issues.

CONCLUSION

Unions are key vehicles for women's collective agency, and have great potential as equality resources, given they are widespread, resourced, and institutionalized. This chapter challenges the tendency to ignore unions as instruments for women's equality and outlines those aspects of unions that may facilitate women's collective agency and enhance women's equality. It identifies the indicators that help to map trade unions as equality resources, and that offer new ways of measuring women's empowerment in reference to collective agency. It is hoped that this approach will shift discourse, both inside trade unions and in international policy discussions from individual to collective agency, and from leadership demographics to a wider range of equality measures, and in the case of transnational feminist networks and community-based women's organizations, toward a wider recognition of both the potential and the contribution of unions to women's empowerment.

At the same time, there is no doubt that the union record on equality is mixed. In many countries, unions have remained entrenched in old style bureaucratic, hierarchical, and patriarchal practices. However, movements of union women have demonstrated time and again the possibility of transforming unions. Although unions undoubtedly need to be pressed to reform and transform, at the same time, they need to be accepted as allies in the struggle for women's empowerment. In fact, it may not be too strong a statement to claim that making "globalization work for women" will depend on trade unions. Unions also have much to learn from the innovative and often nontraditional organizing of women's organizations.

The parallels in concerns and strategies suggest much ground for coalition work. In the current anti-union and anti-women context, building alliances across boundaries and borders—both national and institutional—will be critical.

NOTES

1. See UN Millennium Development Goals Homepage: http://www.un.org/millenniumgoals/gender.shtml.

2. See Maquila Solidarity Network 2007 Annual Report: http://en.maquila solidarity.org/sites/maquilasolidarity.org/files/MSN-AnnualReport-ENG-2007.pdf.

3. Fully 94% of working women in India are self-employed, eking out marginal livelihoods as small-scale vendors selling food, household goods, garments; home-based producers such as weavers, milk producers, handicraft producers; and laborers selling their services or labor including agricultural and construction workers, cooks, and cleaners. For these workers, conventional forms of trade unionism are not possible. Yet the Self-Employed Women's Association (SEWA) began in 1972 as a trade union of self-employed women, drawing on Gandhi's notion that a union should cover all aspects of workers' lives, both in the factory and at home. SEWA endorses trade unionism but it also organizes cooperatives as a vehicle to develop alternative economic systems through which workers control what they produce. SEWA's inspiring success demonstrates that even the most vulnerable of women workers can organize effectively, and reminds those of us from the North how much we can learn from women in the South. See http://www.sewa.org/.

4. See European Industrial Relations Observatory (EIRO), a monitoring instrument offering news and analysis on European industrial relations. http://www.eurofound.europa.eu/eiro/about_index.htm and http://www.eurofound.europa.eu/eiro/2006/03/articles/eu0603029i.htm.

5. "The Issues and Guidelines for Gender Equality Bargaining," Booklet 3 of the ILO's 2002 study Promoting Gender Equality: A Resource Kit for Unions from the International Labour Organization offers a very comprehensive list of issues for bargaining equality organized under five categories: ending discrimination and promoting equal opportunities, wages and benefits, family-friendly policies, hours of work, and health and safety. For each issue, there is an explanation, checklists for working with and thinking about the issue, text from relevant ILO documents, and examples from many countries. Available at http://www.workinfo.com/free/links/gender/cha_0.htm.

6. Found in the European Trade Union Confederation 2007 Charter on Gender Mainstreaming in Trade Unions adopted by the ETUC Congress in Seville, May 23, 2007, available at http://www.etuc.org/IMG/pdf_gender_mainstreaming_charter1_EN.pdf

7. Available at http://www.tuc.org.uk/congress/tuc-16855-f0.pdf.

8. A Bibliography of Union Equality Documents compiled by Linda Briskin includes reference to research reports, conference documents, policy statements, newsletters and educational material from Canadian unions since the 1970s. The material is organized alphabetically by union. See http://www.genderwork.ca/

unions_equity/Briskin_Unions_and_Equity_Bibliography_Nov_2005.pdf. Selected equity documents from the following Canadian unions are available online as part of the GenderWork Database: Canadian Auto Workers Union (CAW); Communications, Energy & Paperworkers Union of Canada (CEP); Canadian Union of Public Employees (CUPE); National Union of Public and General Employees (NUPGE); Ontario Public Service Employees Union (OPSEU); United Food and Commercial Workers Union of Canada (UFCW); and United Steelworkers of America (USWA).

9. This approach reflects Cockburn's (1996) distinction between sex proportional representation, and the representation of organized interests in which women "are elected or appointed not as individuals and not simply as members of a gender category but specifically to speak for the members of a disadvantaged social group: women" (p. 20).

10. Unison 2009 Rule Book: http://www.unison.org.uk/acrobat/17511.pdf.

11. There is also an extensive literature on separate or self-organizing in unions in the United Kingdom. See, for example, Colgan and Ledwith (1996), Healy and Kirton (2000), Humphrey (2000), and Parker (2006).

12. Without an intersectional practice, women of color might find themselves torn between participation in women's committees or committees for workers of color, and experience what Crenshaw (1991) calls "intersectional disempowerment." A recent study I did of cross-constituency organizing in three Canadian unions—CUPE, CUPW, and BCTF—illuminates some aspects of intersectional political practices, in particular, the institutionalization of intersectionality through constitutional, organizational, and representational intersectionality. It considers three cross-constituency models: what I call dual, parallel, and integrated structures and argues that cross-constituency organizing is a form of intersectionality in practice. Formalized cross-constituency organizing initiatives are relatively new in Canadian unions, emerging from a heightened awareness of diversity and a growing recognition of intersectionality, shifts in union demographics, and the necessity to address the proliferation of equality structures and committees (Briskin, 2008).

13. The Global Unions have a coordinated Website at http://www.global-unions.org/spip.php?rubrique12.

14. The 2008 Manual from the International Trade Union Confederation, "Achieving Gender Equality" is available at: http://www.ituc-csi.org/IMG/pdf/manuel_ENGOK.pdf. For more on the campaign for decent work for women, see http://www.ituc-csi.org/-decent-work-decent-life-for-women-.html?lang=en

15. The authors also note that some 66.6% of respondents indicated that their union had taken specific action to promote racial and gender equality.

16. In Briskin (1994), I argued that "In Canada, the political alliance of the last two decades between the movement of union women and the women's movement outside the unions provides a model for coalition building" (p. 103).

17. Union women's involvement in coalition building and international collaboration also has been described for the United Kingdom (Ledwith, 2006).

18. See for example, the 2005 World Economic Forum document on women's empowerment, http://www.weforum.org/pdf/Global_Competitiveness_Reports/Reports/gender_gap.pdf.

19. Here is the link to the ILO 1948 Freedom of Association and Protection of the Right to Organize Convention (C87): http://www.ilo.org/ilolex/cgi-lex/convde.pl?C087. Note that the United States has not ratified this ILO convention.

20. The Gender and Work Database includes an excellent statistical primer and demonstration on Canadian union advantage data. See http://www.genderwork.ca/cms/displayarticle.php?sid=44&aid=61&partid=1553.

21. The second TUC audit in 2005 includes breakdowns by gender of membership, local and central membership, trade union staff, workplace stewards, delegates to conventions, and committee membership, and also focuses on equality bargaining. Available at http://www.tuc.org.uk/equality/tuc-10487-f0.cfm. The third audit released in 2007 includes a comprehensive survey of union structures—rules, membership and recruitment, lay and full-time officials, and representation; unions as employers—equal opportunity policies, reviews of pay and conditions and staff profiles to ensure no unintentional discriminatory bias; union services and training—service and benefits to members, monitoring of employment tribunal discrimination cases, equality training of officers and lay reps; and campaigns, including successful initiatives. Available at http://www.tuc.org.uk/extras/2007equalityaudit.pdf. The 2009 audit http://www.tuc.org.uk/equality/tuc-16977-f0.pdf focuses on bargaining for equality.

REFERENCES

Ahmed, S. (2007). "You end up doing the document rather than doing the doing": Diversity, race equality and the politics of documentation. *Ethnic and Racial Studies*, 304, 590–609.

Anderson, E. (2003). Sen, ethics, and democracy. *Feminist Economics*, 92/3, 239–261.

Berik, G., van der Meulen Rodgers, Y., & Zammit, A. (Eds.). (2009). *Social justice and gender equality: Rethinking development strategies and macroeconomic policies*. New York: Routledge.

Blackett, A., & Sheppard, C. (2002). *The links between collective bargaining and equality* (Working Paper, ILO). Retrieved June 2010 http://www.ilo.org/wcmsp5/groups/public/---ed_norm/---declaration/documents/publication/wcms_decl_wp_12_en.pdf.

Briskin, L. (1994). Equity and economic restructuring in the Canadian labor movement. Special issue on "Women's Work and Political-Economic Change." *Economic and Industrial Democracy*, 151, 89–112.

Briskin, L. (1999a). Autonomy, diversity and integration: Union women's separate organizing in North America and western Europe in the context of restructuring and globalization. *Women's Studies International Forum*, 225, 543–555.

Briskin, L. (1999b). Unions and women's organizing in Canada and Sweden. In L. Briskin & M. Eliasson (Eds.), *Women's organizing and public policy in Canada and Sweden* (pp. 147–183). Montreal: McGill-Queen's University Press.

Briskin, L. (2002). The Equity Project in Canadian unions: Confronting the challenge of restructuring and globalization. Pp. 28–47 In F. Colgan & S. Ledwith (Eds.), *Gender, diversity and trade unions: International perspectives* (pp. 28–47). London: Routledge.

Briskin, L. (2006a). *Equity bargaining/bargaining equity*. Toronto: Centre for Research on Work and Society, York University. Retrieved June 2010 http://www.arts. yorku.ca/sosc/lbriskin/pdf/bargainingpaperFINAL3secure.pdf.

Briskin, L. (2006b). *Union leadership and equity representation*. For the Union Module of the Gender and Work Database. Retrieved June 2010 http://www.gender-work.ca/Briskin_Leadership_Paper_April_2006.pdf.

Briskin, L. (2006c). Victimization and agency: The social construction of union women's leadership. Special issue on Gender and Industrial Relations. *Industrial Relations Journal, 374*, 359–378.

Briskin, L. (2008). Cross-constituency organizing in Canadian unions. *British Journal of Industrial Relations, 46*(2), 221–387.

Bronfenbrenner, K. (Ed.). (2007). *Global unions: Challenging transnational capital through cross-border campaigns*. Ithaca, NY & London: ILR Press.

Chicha, M-T. (1999). The impact of labour market transformation on the effectiveness of laws promoting workplace gender equality.In R. Chaykowski & L. Powell, (Eds.), *Women and work* (pp. 283–304). Montreal: McGill-Queen's University Press.

Clawson, D. (2003). *The next upsurge: Labor and the new social movements*. Ithaca, NY: ILR Press.

Cockburn, C. (1996). Strategies for gender democracy: Strengthening the representation of trade union women in the European social dialogue. *European Journal of Women's Studies, 3*, 7–26.

Cohen, M.G. (2007). Collective economic rights and international trade agreements: The vacuum of post-national capital control. In M. Young, S. Boyd, G. Brodsky, & S. Day (Eds.), *Poverty rights, social citizenship, and legal activism* (pp. 183–200). Vancouver: UBC Press.

Cohen, M.G. (2009). Going too far? Feminist public policy in Canada. In M.G. Cohen & J. Pulkingham (Eds.), *Public policy for women in Canada: The state, income security, and labour market issues* (pp. 3–48). Toronto: University of Toronto Press.

Cohen, M.G., & Brodie, J. (Eds.). (2007). *Remapping gender in the new global order*. London: Routledge.

Colgan, F., & Ledwith, S. (1996). Sisters organising—Women and their trade unions. In S. Ledwith & F. Colgan (Eds.), *Women in organisations: Challenging gender politics* (pp. 32–48). Houndmills, UK: Macmillan.

Colling, T., & Dickens, L. (2001). Gender equality and trade unions: A new basis for mobilization? In M. Noon & E. Ojbonna (Eds.), *Equality, diversity and disadvantage in employment* (pp. 136–155). Basingstoke, England: Palgrave.

Cranford, C. J., Gellatly, M., Ladd, D., & Vosko, L.F. (2006). Community unionism and labour movement renewal: Organizing for fair employment. In P. Kumar and C. Schenk (Eds.), *Paths to union renewal: Canadian experiences* (pp. 237–251). Peterborough: Broadview Press.

Crenshaw, K. (1991). Mapping the margins: Intersectionality, identity politics, and the violence against women of colour. *Stanford Law Review, 43*(6), 1241–1299.

Dickens, L. (1998). Illuminating the process. In *Equal opportunities and collective bargaining in Europe*. Dublin: European Foundation for the Improvement of Living and Working Conditions. Retrieved June 2010 http://www.eurofound.eu.int/pubdocs/1998/56/en/1/ef9856en.pdf.

Dickens, L. (2000). Collective bargaining and the promotion of gender equality at work: Opportunities and challenges for trade unions. *Transfer: European Review of Labour and Research*, 6(2), 193–208.

Doraisami, A. (2009). The gender implications of macroeconomic policy and performance in Malaysia. In G. Berik, Y. van der Meulen Rodgers, & A. Zammit (Eds.), *Social justice and gender equality: Rethinking development strategies and macroeconomic policies* (pp. 187–212). New York: Routledge.

Eaton, J. (2004). Transitions at work: Industrial relations responses to the emerging rights of transgender workers. *Canadian Labour and Employment Journal, 11*, 113–141.

Elias, J. (2007). Women workers and labour standards: The problem of "human rights." *Review of International Studies, 33*, 45–57.

Espino, A., & Azar, P. (2009). Changes in economic policy regimes in Uruguay from a gender perspective, 1930–2000. In G. Berik, Y. van der Meulen Rodgers, & A. Zammit (Eds.), *Social justice and gender equality: Rethinking development strategies and macroeconomic policies* (pp. 127–153). New York: Routledge.

European Trade Union Confederation (ETUC). (1999). *The "second sex" of European trade unionism*. Bruxelles: Author.

European Trade Union Confederation (ETUC). (2003). *Women in trade unions: Making the difference*. Bruxelles: Author.

Fine, J. (2006). *Workers centres: Organizing communities at the edge of the dream*. Ithaca, NY: Cornell University Press.

Forrest, A. (2007). Bargaining against the past: Fair pay, union practice, and the gender pay gap. In G. Hunt & D. Rayside (Eds.), *Equity, diversity and Canadian labour* (pp. 49–74). Toronto: University of Toronto Press.

Frege, C., Heery, E., & Turner, L. (2004). The new solidarity? Trade union coalition-building in five countries. In J. Kelly & C. Frege (Eds.), *Varieties of unionism: Strategies for union revitalization in a globalizing economy* (pp. 137–158). Oxford: Oxford University Press.

Fukuda-Parr, S. (2003). The human development paradigm: Operationalizing Sen's ideas of capabilities. *Feminist Economics*, 9(2/3), 301–317.

Healy, G., & Kirton, G. (2000). Women, power and trade union government in the UK. *British Journal of Industrial Relations*, 38(3), 343–360.

Heery, E., & Kelly, J. (1988). Do female representatives make a difference? Women full time officials and trade union work. *Work, Employment and Society*, 2(4), 487–505.

Humphrey, J. (2000). Self-organization and trade union democracy. *The Sociological Review*, 48(2), 262–282.

Hunt, G., & Rayside, D. (Eds.). (2007). *Equity, diversity and Canadian labour*. Toronto: University of Toronto Press.

International Confederation of Free Trade Unions (ICFTU). (1991). *Equality: The continuing challenge-strategies for success.* Brussels: Author.

International Confederation of Free Trade Unions (ICFTU). (1994). *Implementation of the programme of action for the integration of women into trade union organisations.* Brussels: Author.

Jackson, A. (2004). *Gender inequality and precarious work: Exploring the impact of unions through the "gender and work database."* For the Union Module of the Gender and Work Database. Retrieved June 2010 http://www.genderwork.ca/conference/Jackson_edited_final.pdf.

Kabeer, N. (1999). *The conditions and consequences of choice: Reflections on the measurement of women's empowerment* (Paper 108). Geneva United Nations Research Institute for Social Development. Retrieved June 2010 http://www.unrisd.org/80256B3C005BCCF9/(httpAuxPages)/31EEF181BEC398A380256 B67005B720A/$file/dp108.pdf.

Kainer, J. (2009). Gendering union renewal: Women's contributions to labour movement revitalization. In J. Foley & P. Baker (Eds.), *Unions, equity, and the path to renewal* (pp. 15–38). Vancouver: UBC Press.

Koggel C.M. (2003). Globalization and women's paid work: Expanding freedom? *Feminist Economics, 9*(2/3), 163–183.

Kumar, P., & Murray, G. (2006). Innovation in Canadian unions: Patterns, causes and consequences. In P. Kumar & C. Schenk (Eds.), *Paths to union renewal: Canadian experiences* (pp. 79–102). Peterborough, Ontario: Broadview Press, Garamond and Canadian Centre for Policy Alternatives.

Kumar, P., & Schenk, C. (Eds.). (2006). *Paths to union renewal: Canadian experiences.* Peterborough, Ontario: Broadview, Garamond and Canadian Centre for Policy Alternatives.

Kurtz, S. (2002). *Workplace justice: Organizing multi-identity movements.* Minneapolis: Minnesota University Press.

Ledwith, S. (2006). The future as female? Gender, diversity and global labour solidarity. In C. Phelan (Ed.), *The future of organized labour: Global perspectives* (pp. 91–143). Oxford: Peter Lang.

McBride, A. (2001). *Gender democracy in trade unions.* UK: Ashgate.

Morissette, R., Schellenberg, G., & Johnson, A. (2005). Diverging trends in unionization. *Perspectives on Labour and Income, 6*(4), 5–12.

Murray, G. (2005). Unions: Membership, structures, actions, and challenges. In M. Gunderson, A. Ponack, & D.G. Taras (Eds.), *Union-management relations in Canada* (5th ed., pp. 79–111). Toronto: Pearson Addison Wesley.

Nichols-Heppner, B. (1984). *Women in public sector unions in Quebec: Organizing for equality.* Unpublished doctoral thesis, McGill University, Montreal.

Parker, J. (2006). Towards equality and renewal: Women's democracy in British unions. *Economic and Industrial Democracy, 27*(3), 425–462.

Pillinger, J. (2005). Pay equity now: Gender mainstreaming and gender pay equity in the public services. *International Feminist Journal of Politics, 7*(4), 591–599.

Reyes, E.D. (2007). Transnational class and gender networking between the north and the south: Overcoming diversity or reproducing dependencies? In M.G. Cohen & J. Brodie (Eds.), *Remapping gender in the new global order* (pp. 223–243). London: Routledge.

Sechi, C. (2007). *Women in trade unions in Europe: Bridging the gaps*. Bruxelles: European Trade Union Confederation.

Seguino, S. (2009). The road to gender equality: Global trends and the way forward. In G. Berik, Y. van der Meulen Rodgers, & A. Zammit (Eds.), *Social justice and gender equality: Rethinking development strategies and macroeconomic policies* (pp. 33–70). New York: Routledge.

Strachan, G., & Burgess, J. (2000). The incompatibility of decentralized bargaining and equal employment opportunity in Australia. *British Journal of Industrial Relations, 38*(3), 361–381.

Swider, S. (2006). Working women of the world unite? Labor organizing and transnational gender solidarity among domestic workers in Hong Kong. In M.M. Ferree & A.M. Tripp (Eds.), *Global feminism: Transnational women's activism, organizing and human rights* (pp. 110–140). New York: New York University Press.

Trades Union Congress (TUC). (2005). *TUC equality audit 2005*. London: Author. Retrieved June 2010 http://www.tuc.org.uk/extras/auditfinal.pdf.

Trades Union Congress (TUC). (2007). *TUC equality audit 2007: A statistical report on trade union action on equality*. London: Author. Retrieved June 2010 http://www.tuc.org.uk/extras/2007equalityaudit.pdf.

Trades Union Congress (TUC). (2009, August). Unionization. *Perspectives on Labour and Income* (monthly from Statistics Canada).

Verloo, M. (2006). Multiple inequalities, intersectionality and the European Union. *European Journal of Women's Studies, 13*(3), 211–228.

Vosko, L.F. (Ed.). (2006). *Precarious employment: Understanding labour market insecurity in Canada*. Montreal & Kingston: McGill-Queen's University Press.

Vosko, L.F. (2007). Representing informal economy workers: Emerging global strategies and their lessons for North American unions. In D.S. Cobble (Ed.), *The sex of class: Women transforming American labour* (pp. 272–292). Ithaca, NY: Cornell University Press.

Wajcman, J. (1998). *Managing like a man: Women and men in corporate management*. University Park: Pennsylvania State University Press.

Walby, S. (2002). Feminism in a global era. *Economy and Society, 31*(4), 533–557.

TWELVE

WOMEN'S LEADERSHIP IN THE
SOUTH AFRICAN LABOR MOVEMENT

Neva Seidman Makgetla

In 2006, women made up only one in four of the national leaders of major affiliates in the Congress of South African Trade Unions (COSATU). Moreover, of 21 affiliates, only 3 had women at the very top (one president and two general secretaries). The other women leaders were relegated to positions as deputy president or treasurer. Yet close to half of all union members in South Africa are women.

The weak showing of women in national leadership violated a number of COSATU resolutions, including a decision to impose quotas in 2000. Since its founding in 1985, COSATU has emphasized the need to promote women leaders as well as addressing discrimination against women in the workplace and in society as a whole. Despite considerable progress, however, the unions remained far from achieving their stated aims.

In this chapter, I analyze some of the factors behind the shortfall, using a combination of survey results and interviews with women leaders.

Ultimately, the relatively weak position of women in the South African labor movement in the mid-2000s was rooted in discrimination against women throughout society and in the workplace. The Constitution adopted at the transition to democracy in 1994 demanded gender equality, and from the late 1990s various laws banned gender discrimination in the workplace. Nonetheless, women were still less likely to be in skilled or managerial positions, more likely to spend hours a day on the household, and generally discouraged from leadership roles.

The subordinate position of women in society as a whole was reflected across the union movement. Women union members were less likely to participate in union elections or education programs. As a result, they could not provide a substantial power base for women leaders, who ended up dependent on structures dominated by men. Moreover, apart from one nurses' union, democratic elections tended to benefit male candidates, even where women dominated in membership.

COSATU's strategies for gender equality did not adequately address these difficulties. In particular, COSATU and its affiliates heavily relied on paid women officials, rather than elected leaders or shop stewards, to address women's issues. As a result, gender officers had little power within union structures. Most unions relied on relatively low-level administrators to coordinate gender activities, without a separate budget. Most affiliates did not ensure strong representation of women in key organizational positions, especially as organizers and educators. Since the late 1990s, gender structures and policies focused more on promoting women leaders at the regional and national levels than on integrating women's issues in the core union work of collective bargaining. Yet most women, like most men, joined unions because they wanted improved pay and better conditions at work. In these circumstances, the gender structures often focused narrowly on educational work and commemoration of women's issues. They did not mobilize caucuses of women members that could provide a power base in the unions. As a result, they could not attract much support from the few women in national leadership. Moreover, they often found it difficult to relate to men leaders, many of whom found it easier to express the ideals of equality than to fully live up to them.

In this chapter, I first briefly compare the extent of women's leadership with the targets set by COSATU. I then explore the position of women in the labor force and the unions. In the final section, I outline the structures and strategies COSATU developed in its efforts to address the problems faced by women workers.

THE PRESENCE OF WOMEN LEADERSHIP IN COSATU

The elected national leadership of unions in South Africa typically comprises a general secretary and a deputy general secretary—who actually manage the union—and a president, generally a shop steward who is expected to provide political direction. There also are one or two deputy presidents and a treasurer. COSATU itself, as a federation, has a similar structure for its national leadership.

In 2006, in COSATU's largest 14 affiliates, women held 27% of the national positions. Together, these 14 unions accounted for 90% of

COSATU's membership. COSATU itself had two women leaders, making up 40% of its national leadership. Representation in gender terms fell far short of COSATU's stated objectives. Still, it was better than the international labor movement, where women held an estimated 1% of positions in decision-making bodies in 1999, although they constituted 30% of membership (ICFTU, 1999). The 2006 figures reflected considerable progress over the previous 15 years. In the early 1990s, COSATU and its affiliates had virtually no women in national leadership. In 1998, women constituted 10% of affiliates' national leadership (Orr, 1999b).[1] COSATU itself elected its first female national leader in 1994.

The figures tend to overstate the influence of female leaders, however. As Table 12.1 shows, 85% of all women in the unions' national leadership in 2006 were in the comparatively powerless posts of deputy president or treasurer. The only exceptions were a female president and two female general secretaries, all of them in the health sector. Only one union—the Democratic Nursing Organisation of South Africa, which started as a professional association for nurses—had a majority of women across its top leadership. The other female general secretary was from the doctors' union, which had less than 10,000 members. In COSATU itself, the female leaders were a deputy president and the treasurer.

It is harder to find data for elected regional leadership and shop stewards. Generally, union regions elect a general secretary and a chair, plus a deputy chair and treasurer. A 1998 study found that women made up 18% of the regional leaders of COSATU's affiliates—almost twice as much as then prevailed among national leadership (Orr, 1999b). Women constituted close to 10% of regional secretaries, almost 20% of regional chairs, and 33% of treasurers.

In 2006, of eight COSATU provincial secretaries, none were women. The South African Democratic Teachers' Union (SADTU), and the metal workers' union, National Union of Metalworkers of South Africa (NUMSA), also had no regional secretaries, whereas the South African Municipal Workers' Union had at most one. In the South African Clothing and Textile Workers' Union women held most positions in the Western Cape but not in any of the unions' other four regions. The Finance Union had no women secretaries but did have some women regional organizers—none of whom were African, however. There were no recent figures on representivity among shop stewards. In 1992, one in three COSATU members was a woman, but only one in seven shop stewards (COSATU, 1997). In 2004, women comprised 17% of delegates to the NUMSA national congress, which is close to their share in the union's membership.

The poor representation of women in COSATU's leadership was particularly surprising in light of the quotas set by some affiliates and, since 2003,

Table 12.1. Women Leadership in Large COSATU Affiliates, 2005

Union	Women in National National Leadership, %	Women President, GS or Deputy GS, %	Women Membership, %	Total Membership
DENOSA: nurses	71	50	NA	65,000
NEHAWU: health and other public services	17	17	55	193,000
SACTWU: clothing and textiles	40	0	70	110,000
FAWU: food processing and agriculture	33	0	NA	100,000
POPCRU: correctional service and police	33	0	50	95,000
SACCAWU: retail and private services	33	0	60	108,000
SADTU: teachers	25	0	55	215,000
CEPPWAWU: chemical, paper, petrol	20	0	NA	59,000
NUM: mining and construction	20	0	5	262,000
SATAWU: transport and security	20	0	NA	82,000
CWU: communications	17	0	NA	29,000
SAMWU: municipal	17	0	40	114,000
SASBO: financial	17	0	NA	60,000
NUMSA: metal	0	0	20	217,000
Total COSATU	27	5	45[1]	1,758,000[a]

Source: Percentage women in national leadership calculated from information provided on affiliates on COSATU Website, downloaded May 2006 from www.cosatu.org.za and from individual affiliates' Websites. Information on share of women in membership calculated from NALEDI and COSATU. 2005. COSATU Survey. Information on membership from COSATU figures on affiliate fees for 2005, rounded to nearest 1,000.

[a]Refers to all COSATU affiliates, not just those listed here.

the Federation. In the mid-1990s, COSATU's September Commission proposed that half of all COSATU national leaders should be women, and that three should be elected in 1997. In fact, COSATU's 1997 Congress elected only two. In 2003, COSATU's Eighth National Congress resolved that "the quota system applicable to the Federation shall be set by the CEC [Central Executive Committee], and quota systems applicable to affiliates shall be set by affiliates. Quotas shall be based on the share of women in membership and the need to rapidly develop women leadership." In the event, neither the Federation nor the affiliates set quotas as they had agreed in this resolution.

The National Education, Health and Allied Workers' Union (NEHAWU), which was just over 50% women in 2005, adopted a 50% quota for women at all levels in the late 1990s. Yet in 2006, the union had one elected female national leader—admittedly the president—plus at most three regional secretaries. Women were better represented in its local structures. Oddly enough, in the teeth of this evidence, the union's Congress report in 2004 suggested that the quota was being met (NEHAWU, 2004). The teachers' union, SADTU, resolved in 2003 that three of its vice presidents should be women. It only managed to elect two women out of four vice presidents—one responsible for gender, and one for sport, art and culture.

In short, despite considerable progress over the previous decade, in the mid-2000s the leadership of COSATU and its affiliates remained unrepresentative in gender terms. Moreover, most female leaders held relatively weak positions. This situation flew in the face of COSATU's own resolutions, as well as the policies of some major affiliates. The rest of this chapter explores the factors behind this failure.

WOMEN'S POSITION IN THE ECONOMY[2]

Ultimately, women's position in the labor movement reflected their broader situation in society, and in particular their roles in the economy. These conditions were shaped in large part by the apartheid system, which was strongly gendered. In response, the democratic government emphasized the need to overcome gender oppression as part of the legacy of apartheid. Like the unions, it adopted policies aimed at liberating women; and as in the labor movement, many of these policies fell far short of their objectives. These broader social realities affected the unions' ability to promote female leaders. On the one hand, women continued to bear most of the burden of household labor, making it harder for them to participate in union activities. More broadly, the socialization of women continued to support subordination and compliance. On the other hand, the concentration of women in a few industries meant that some important unions had virtually no women union members, whereas women dominated in others.

Although apartheid was most notoriously associated with racial discrimination, it made special provisions for Black women, while providing a degree of equality and freedom for White women. The state essentially expected African women to stay home, preferably in the rural areas, and care for children and the elderly. For this reason, it made it more difficult for African women than for African men to obtain permits to stay in urban areas and to gain formal education, employment, or credit. In contrast, White female workers benefited from efforts to avoid promoting Black people and from the low wages for domestic labor that resulted from the apartheid system.

In response to the explicit discrimination embedded in apartheid, the liberation movement argued the need to fight simultaneously against racial, gender, and class oppression. After 1994, the ruling African National Congress (ANC) and the government took steps to combat discrimination against women. In particular, the ANC promoted women into elected positions at all levels, setting a quota of a third for national and provincial Parliament and, from 2005, half at local government level. As a result, from 1994 the South African Parliament was one of the most representative in the world in gender terms. The Constitution banned "unfair" discrimination based on gender, race, or sexuality. *Unfair discrimination* was defined essentially as discrimination that could not be justified in economic terms. Additionally, a number of laws, including the Employment Equity Act (1998) and the Broad-Based Black Economic Empowerment Act (2004) introduced measures designed to enhance women's economic position.

Despite these efforts, a decade after liberation most Black women remained in subordinate positions in the economy. Women were less likely than men to be economically active and more likely to be unemployed. If they had a formal job, the chances were that they worked in the private or public services or in light industry. Most women were in lower-level occupations that paid poorly (see Makgetla, 2004). And whether they had paying jobs or not, almost all spent hours a day taking care of their households and families. In September 2005, only 19% of women—and 13% of Black women—had a formal job, compared with 36% of men and 30% of African men. Less than 50% of women were economically active (i.e., either employed or actively seeking paid work), compared with 61% of men. In contrast, in comparable middle-income countries, on average close to 60% of women were economically active (UNDP, 2004).

Despite their relatively low participation rates, women—especially Black women—found it harder to get a job. At more than 25%, unemployment in South Africa overall was far higher than for comparable economies. The unemployment rate for Black women was even higher, at 37%, compared with 26% for African men. Moreover, a further 27% of Black women considered "economically active" actually wanted paid work but were too discouraged to look for it. The unemployment rate was 7% for White women and 4% for White men.

If an African woman found a job, she was likely to be employed in retail or domestic work. These industries accounted for just more than half of employment for African women, one-fourth for White women, and one-third for colored women. One in seven women worked in health or education, with about the same proportion of Black women, although not Whites, in light industry and agriculture. Wherever a woman was employed, she would almost certainly earn less than her male colleagues (see Table 12.2). Whatever their industry, Black women in particular were unlikely to get managerial positions. Even in the public service professions, where the majority of both women and men had degrees, women were less likely to be employed in supervisory positions.

Union density for women was only slightly lower than for men in most industries. In contrast, in many other countries women remain disproportionately unorganized (ICFTU, 1999). Generally, women union members earned more than non-members, and were more likely to have benefits and a permanent position. Still, they lagged slightly behind male unionists.

The sectoral and occupational allocation of women affected their role in the labor movement. First, paid domestic work was not organized at all, whereas union membership ran at only between 10% and 20% in agriculture

Table 12.2. Pay, Benefits, and Conditions for Women and Men Workers, 2005

	Women		Men	
	Members, %	Nonmembers, %	Members, %	Monmembers, %
Earning >R1,500/month	80	35	84	49
Permanent employee	95	62	95	59
Written contract[a]	89	57	90	61
Pension fund	89	31	90	37
Paid leave[1]	90	45	92	46
Medical aid	59	19	54	19
Working <45 hours/week	66	63	54	51

[a]The Basic Conditions of Employment Act required both a written contract and paid leave.

Source: Calculated from Statistics SA. 2006. Labor Force Survey September 2006. Pretoria. Database on CD-ROM.

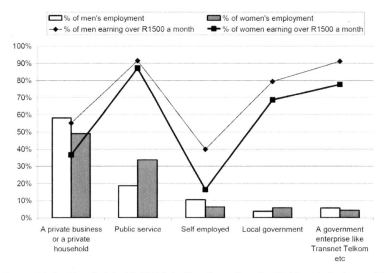

Source: Calculated from Statistics SA. 2006. Labor Force Survey September 2006. Pretoria. Database on CD-ROM.

Figure 12.1. Employment and Share Earning over R1500 a Month by Broad Sector and Gender, 2005.

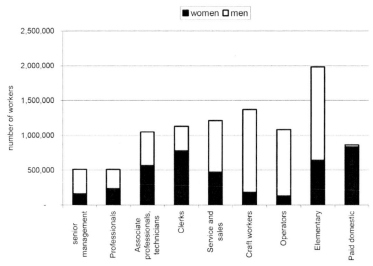

Source: Calculated from Statistics SA. 2006. Labor Force Survey September 2006. Pretoria. Database on CD-ROM.

Figure 12.2. Employment by Gender and Occupation, 2005.

and retail. Pay and conditions in these sectors, therefore, remained far below the norm for society as a whole. Second, union density reached close to 90% in the public service, including for nurses and teachers. Before 1994, the state had barred government employees from organizing unions. After the democratic state permitted public servants to organize, membership soared, especially after the introduction of an agency shop in 1998.[3] Nurses' and teachers' unions with mostly female members accounted for 27% of COSATU's total membership in 2006. In 2005, women constituted 37% of all union members (including unions not affiliated to COSATU), but only 28% outside of the public services.

Whether they had a paid job or not, most women in South Africa ended up with the primary responsibility for caring for the family and home. The 2000 time-use survey found that the average woman with paid work outside the home spent 3 hours a day on home labor, compared with 4 hours a day for women without a paid job (Budlender, Chobokoane, & Mpetsheni, 2001). On average, men spent half as much time as women on home work. Women with children aged under 18 years averaged around 1 hour a day on child care. Men spent just over 5 minutes a day. Many working-class households did not have running water on site or electricity for cooking, adding to the burden of home work.

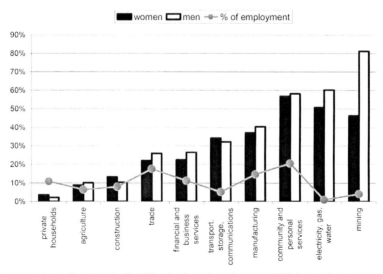

Source: Calculated from Statistics SA. 2006. Labor Force Survey September 2006. Pretoria. Database on CD-ROM.

Figure 12.3. Employment Density by Gender and Industry, 2005.

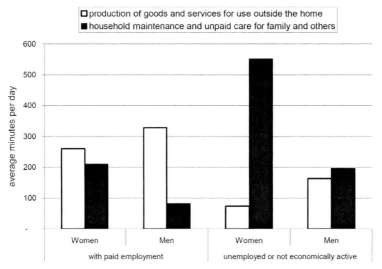

Figure 12.4. Time Spent on Home Work and Childcare by Gender and Employment Status, 2000.

In summary, the position of women in South Africa remained largely shaped by the legacies of apartheid, despite explicit efforts by the state and civil society to address the problem. Black women faced extraordinary levels of unemployment and if they had a job generally remained in subordinate positions and low-wage jobs. They were largely excluded from the traditional strongholds of South African unionism in heavy industry and the mines. Still, the dominance of women in health and education meant that women members constituted a growing share of the labor movement from 1994. But the burden of household and family labor made it difficult for them to participate in union activities.

WOMEN'S PARTICIPATION IN UNION ACTIVITIES

Strengthening female leadership of the labor movement was only possible if women increased their participation in union activities at all levels. Unfortunately, a 2005 survey found that female union members participated less than men in union meetings and educational programs.[4] As Figure 12.5 shows, women members were less likely than men to have taken part in shop steward elections, union meetings, or educational programs. This situation held true even in sectors where women formed the majority of union members, although the discrepancy tended to be higher in male-dominated unions. Women members also were less likely than men to feel they could influence their shop stewards. Moreover, if women non-members contacted a union, they were more likely to report that the union did not provide any help. The response rate was much worse in the public than the private sector, however, which in part explains women's poor experience (see Table 12.3).

The relatively low levels of active engagement by women in the union movement reflected a broader pattern. The 2005 survey found that female workers generally were less engaged in political and community organizations than men, although they were much more likely to engage in women's groups and school governing bodies. Union members as a group were more socially active than non-members, but male members were more active politically than female members (see Fig. 12.6). The survey asked members why the unions had relatively few female leaders. As might be expected, the responses of men and women differed substantially. Approximatley 25% blamed women's family responsibilities. Nearly 40% of women blamed discrimination or lack of support in union elections, compared with 30% of men (see Fig. 12.7). Young people emphasized family work more, whereas younger women and older men were more likely to blame discrimination.

Table 12.3. Perception of Influence Over Shop Stewards and Response to Efforts to Contact a Union by Gender, 2005

	Women, %	Men, %
Extent to which members feel they can influence the shop steward		
No influence	26	19
Some influence	30	42
A lot of influence	24	34
Don't know or no answer	20	5
Total	100	100
Response to nonmembers' efforts to contact the union		
No response	45	27
I met an official, but they did nothing	34	31
They provided help	10	24
Other	10	17
Total	100	100

Source: Calculated from COSATU/Naledi Workers' Survey. November/December 2005. Database on CD-ROM.

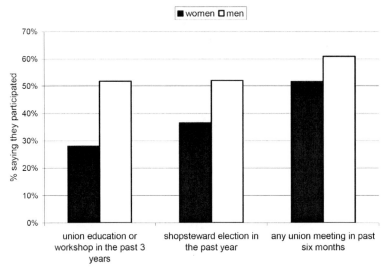

Source: Calculated from COSATU/Naledi Workers' Survey. November/December 2005. Database on CD-ROM.

Figure 12.5. Participation in Union Meetings, Elections, and Educational Programs by Gender, 2005.

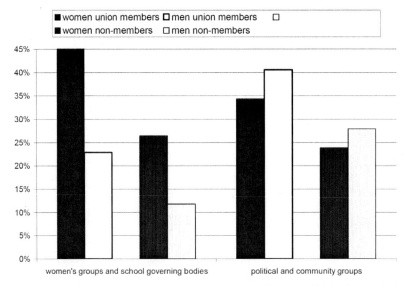

Source: Calculated from COSATU/Naledi Workers' Survey. November/December 2005. Database on CD-ROM.

Figure 12.6. Participation in Other Organizations by Gender and Race, 2005.

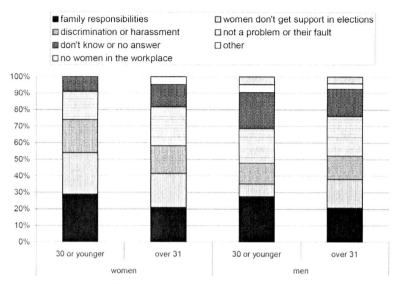

Source: Calculated from COSATU/Naledi Workers' Survey. November/December 2005. Database on CD-ROM.

Figure 12.7. Reasons Given for Low Levels of Women in Union Leadership by Gender and Age, 2005.

Overall, the picture was that women remained less active in union work, in part because of the failure of union structures to involve them consistently, and in part because of broader social factors that led to lower social engagement by women across the board. In particular, the heavy burden of household labor reduced the time women had for other activities. The lower level of participation by female members in the unions meant they did not provide a mobilized base to support female leaders at regional and national levels.

WHAT WOMEN MEMBERS WANT

In the event, most female union members did not see gender issues as their top priority. This might explain their failure to mobilize explicitly around female leaders. Both male and female union members told the COSATU survey that they joined the union mostly to improve their pay and working conditions. A fairly small study by the International Confederation of Federal Trade Unions (ICFTU) found similar results in most countries (ICFTU, 2000). In South Africa, women and men both saw improved pay as their main demand on employers. Women were far more likely than

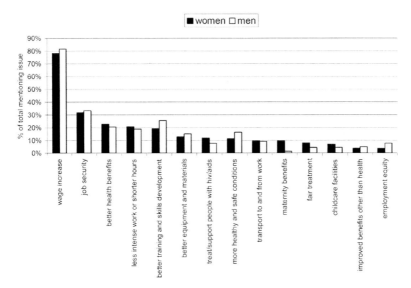

Source: Calculated from COSATU/Naledi Workers' Survey. November/December 2005. Database on CD-ROM.

Figure 12.8. What Workers Want from the Employer, 2005.

men to list maternity benefits (see Fig. 12.8). They also reported demands around child care and support for people with HIV/AIDS more than men. Still, for women as for men, these claims lagged far behind demands around pay and benefits. Neither men nor women saw gender discrimination or harassment as widespread in the workplace (see Fig. 12.9). This perception clashes with the economic outcomes discussed earlier. In contrast, 10% of African workers (although virtually no White ones) reported racist abuse at work, and 25% saw discrimination.

This finding aligns with experiences in other countries (see Forrest, 2001). The economic data demonstrate extensive gender discrimination in the workplace. But gender inequalities often penetrate the social fabric so deeply that women challenge only extreme instances. In these circumstances, union educational and consciousness-raising work becomes important in assisting women to challenge discrimination. As noted here, however, beginning in the late 1990s, COSATU's gender work began increasingly to emphasize equity in the labor movement rather than equity at work.

GENDER STRUCTURES AND STRATEGIES

For most of the past 20 years, COSATU and its affiliates have had some kind of structures for women, with a shift from women's committees to gender

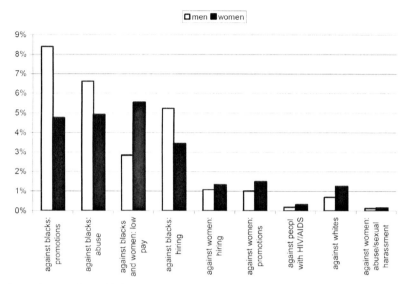

Source: Calculated from COSATU/Naledi Workers' Survey. November/December 2005. Database on CD-ROM.

Figure 12.9. Perceptions of Discrimination in the Workplace by Gender, 2005.

committees in the mid-1990s. These structures generally have functioned as part of union administrations, however, rather than a women's caucus. As a result, they have not provided a power base for women's struggles. They seem to have focused increasingly on campaigning for equality within the union movement rather than demands for women's equality in the workplace.

COSATU held its first women's congress in 1988. The congress called for women's structures at both the federation and the affiliate levels. A women's committee was established in COSATU's education department, which at that time also formed the main policy unit. Regional women's forums were set up 3 years later. In the mid-1990s, in a move that remains controversial, COSATU replaced women's committees with gender committees. Supporters argued that gender committees would do more to engage men in supporting women's emancipation. Opponents held that they would effectively dilute the ability of women to mobilize themselves and undermine the emphasis on addressing women's problems (Orr, 1999a; COSATU, 1999a). In most affiliates, gender committees were established in a hierarchy from local to national, in parallel with the unions' constitutional structures. COSATU itself set up gender structures at the national, provincial, and branch levels. Congress reports indicated, however, that the branch and even provincial structures often failed to meet for extended periods.

In any case, by the early 2000s the gender structures were perceived as largely ineffective. They were seen as focusing more on administrative issues and commemorating women's days than on promoting women within the union or ensuring the inclusion of women's issues in negotiations. One female leader said she stopped going because these meetings had become a "complainants' forum" (Interview with COSATU female leader in May 2006; see also Orr, 1999a). Fundamentally, the weakness of the gender structures reflected resistance from male leaders as well as the fact that most female members did not demand strong representation on gender issues. More specific factors emerged from interviews with gender activists and female union leaders.[5]

First, the gender structures were not part of the unions' constitutional structures. As a result, they were not constituted by elected representatives or led by an elected leader. Instead, they were drawn from activists and run by union officials. Moreover, they did not have decision-making powers. They had to refer their decisions to the national executive for confirmation. But in the national leadership, women were generally in a minority and gender issues almost invariably fell to the bottom of the agenda. The status of the gender committees placed elected female leaders in a contradictory position. They were effectively bound by the decisions of the national executive, even if that meant rejecting claims by the gender structure on behalf of female members. In any case, female leaders could not afford to push the demands of the gender structures to the point where they would alienate the rest of the union leadership. This situation led to a division between female leaders and the gender structures: The former felt the structures were ineffective, and the latter felt abandoned. Because gender structures were not constitutional, they did not have a dedicated budget. Instead, they had to piggyback their activities on educational and other work. The COSATU gender coordinator had a fairly large budget, equal to approximately 5% of the federation's total expenditure. It was, however, applied almost entirely to commemoration of women's days and meetings of the national gender structure.

Second, gender structures were generally driven by the only women in the union offices—that is, by lower-level administrators. The weak institutional basis of the gender committees, then, largely reflected the failure to promote women to higher-level employed positions, such as organizer or educator. COSATU itself had a full-time gender secretary, but all its provincial gender coordinators were administrators. The reliance on administrators had serious drawbacks. To start with, administrators were hired for their ability to run an office, not because of their political skills or understanding. Furthermore, their positions gave them very little political power within the organization. They generally did not form part of negotiations teams or other organizing work that lies at the heart of union activities. Most administrators were directly subordinate to the provincial secretary, with very little freedom of movement. Challenging that subordination when they acted as gender coordinators proved difficult. Additionally, gender coordination was added on to their other tasks. Often, the regional leadership saw it as coming second to administrative work—the coordinators' "real" job (Orr, 1999a).

Third, the gender structures faced persistent but usually underground resistance from many, perhaps most, male leaders. That resistance had two roots: underlying patriarchal attitudes, and the desire to protect male leaders' positions. The call for quotas, in particular, would necessarily displace some men. In COSATU, for instance, the gender coordinator argued that she could not finalize the decision on quotas from the 2003 congress because the national leadership refused to put it on the agenda for the CEC—the main constitutional decision-making structure between congresses. She said that gender issues generally were either excluded from the agenda or discussed only very superficially. This experience was echoed across the labor movement (Orr, 1999a).

Finally, the gender structures themselves were not placed to provide strong inputs on bargaining issues—the core work of the union and the main concern of most female members. In particular, they did not develop claims or campaigns around equity in the workplace. Instead, they tended to spend a lot of time on administrative matters (discussing minutes apparently became a major issue in many meetings). Beyond that, they focused on promoting female leaders and education and on the commemoration of women's days.

If the gender structures discussed bargaining issues, they tended to emphasize child care and maternity leave, rather than employment equity. In part, this reflected the broader weakness of COSATU and its affiliates on employment equity. Despite repeated resolutions, COSATU never managed to unleash a strong campaign for racial and gender equality in the workplace.

Beginning in the late 1990s, COSATU's gender resolutions emphasized almost exclusively internal relationships, with virtually no demands for workplace equality. In contrast, earlier gender resolutions had included detailed calls for equal pay for work of equal value and an end to discrimination in hiring and promotion. As noted earlier, however, female members generally turned to the unions primarily for help in improving pay and benefits. Unless the gender campaigns spoke to these issues, they risked remaining marginal in union work.

CONCLUSIONS

Unions cannot remove themselves from their society, and their gender politics and strategies generally reflect broader relations in the society. But

South Africa remained unusually contradictory on this subject. On the one hand, the political discourse was characterized by an explicit commitment to gender equality, overcoming the entrenched discrimination of the past. On the other, patriarchy was entrenched across the society and the economy, with most women subordinate in the home and at work. This contradiction emerged in COSATU's limited progress in improving the gender representivity of its leadership. Certainly, the labor movement made rapid and substantial progress especially after the transition to democracy in 1994. But the accomplishments remained far short of the unions' own targets.

Although COSATU's strategy on gender brought important gains in representation through the 1990s and early 2000s, by 2006 it seemed likely to stall. For one thing, most unions had some female national leaders, although almost all only as deputy presidents or treasurers. They could, then, argue that they had done enough in this regard. For another, the gender structures proved unable to provide a power base for female leaders and for women's demands. In these circumstances, more progress would require clear and enforceable quotas going beyond the second-level national positions. Even more important, it would require mobilization of a power base for female leaders, either through women's caucuses or by making the gender structures constitutional, with a very clear mandate.

COSATU's experience reflected some broader challenges for the labor movement in ensuring gender representivity at leadership level. In particular, most female members joined the union to ensure annual increases and protect them if they had a grievance. They did not particularly see the function of the union as addressing gender inequalities. Moreover, most did not see their low pay as a consequence of discrimination, despite the obvious subordination of women across the economy. Unions found it difficult to balance the need for a debate about gender with the overriding imperative of unity. Most leaders would see the establishment of women's caucuses or raising the status of gender structures to Constitutional level as divisive.

NOTES

1. In the 1980s, four unions had female general secretaries, but at that time the position was seen as purely administrative. As the general secretaries became more important in political and organizational work, men replaced them. (J. Barrett, personal communication, May 2006)

2. Unless otherwise noted, the data on employment in this section are calculated from Statistics South Africa 2005.

3. Under an agency shop, all employees must pay to support collective bargaining, whether they are union members or not. Not surprisingly, in these circumstances most affected workers prefer to join a union and get the full range of support and services.

4. The survey was conducted jointly by COSATU, the Center for the Advancement of Social Entrepreneurship, and the National Labour and Economic Development Institute of 3,000 workers, of whom one-third were union members and about one-fourth were in COSATU. A more detailed report can be downloaded from www.naledi.org.za

5. I am particularly grateful to Violet Seboni, the COSATU deputy president, and Mummy Japhta, the COSATU coordinator, for sharing their insights on these issues.

REFERENCES

Budlender, D., Chobokoane, N., & Mpetsheni, Y. (2001). A survey of time use: How South African men and women spend their time. Pretoria: Statistics South Africa.

Congress of South African Trade Unions (COSATU). (1995, December). Over the past 10 years, COSATU's character has changed." Shopsteward 4(6).

Congress of South African Trade Unions (COSATU). (1996a, June/July). Gender agenda: A turning point for working women. Shopsteward, 3.

Congress of South African Trade Unions (COSATU) (August/September). (1996b). Gender agenda: What's in a name? Shopsteward, 4(4)

Congress of South African Trade Unions (COSATU). (2003). COSATU gender policy. Retrieved June 2006 www.cosatu.org.za.

Congress of South African Trade Unions (COSATU). (2006). Congress and Central Committee Resolutions from 1997. Retrieved June 2006 www.cosatu.org.za.

Congress of South African Trade Unions (COSATU), & Naledi. (2005). COSATU workers' survey.

Forrest, A. (2001). Connecting women with unions: What are the issues? Erudit, 56(4), 647–675.

International Confederation of Federal Trade Unions (ICFTU). (1999). The role of trade unions in promoting gender equality: Report of the ILO-ICFTU survey. Retrieved June 2006 www.ilo.org.

International Confederation of Federal Trade Unions (ICFTU). (2000). Report on ICFTU pilot survey—ask a working woman. Retrieved June 2006 www.ilo.org.

Isaacs, S. (1995, December). No woman, no cry, Zabalaza. The Shopsteward, 4(6).

Makgetla, N. (2004). Women and work. www.genderstats.org.za. Database. ?

National Education, Health and Allied Workers' Union (NEHAWU). (n.d.) Gender strategy. Retrieved June 2006 www.nehawu.org.za.

NUM. (2006). Secretariat report to 2006 NUM Congress. Retrieved June 2006 www.naledi.org.za.

Orr, L. (1999a). Assessing gender structures in COSATU. Johannesburg: NALEDI.

Orr, L. (1999b). Women's leadership in COSATU. Johannesburg: NALEDI.

Statistics South Africa. (2006). Labor force survey September 2005. Pretoria. Database on CD-ROM.

THIRTEEN

WOMEN-ONLY UNIONS AND WOMEN UNION LEADERS IN JAPAN[1]

Kaye Broadbent

Union density in Japan has halved from a high of 35% in 1970 to 18.1% in 2008 (Kosei Rōdōshō, 2009). Reflecting concern over declining union membership, Japan's union movement developed the Union Identity (UI) movement in the 1970s. The union's four programs include "renewal of trade union symbols, total welfare policy, active participation in the firm's decision-making process, and organizing non-regular employees" (Fujimura, 1997, pp. 307–308). Three decades later, however, declining membership continues to be an issue for the UI (see Ito et al., 2007; Kuwahara, 2000; A. Suzuki, 2006). One of the key aims of the UI movement was the organization of nonregular workers, the majority of whom are women, but with the rate of unionization of nonregular workers[2] in 2006 estimated at 4.3% (Ito et al., 2007) it is clear this program has failed. Enterprise-based unions, the majority of Japan's unions—95.8% in 1997 (see Ito et al., 2007), exclude the growing number of nonregular workers from union membership, presenting a serious obstacle both in the development of solidarity between regular and nonregular workers and between workers in different enterprise unions.

The growth in and exclusion of nonregular workers from union membership led to the emergence of a "new" type of union (Kawanishi, 1992).[3] These new unions emerged from the late 1970s and organize workers on the basis of employment status, geographic location, or gender, specifically women-only unions. This has contributed to the limited cooperation between women union leaders and women-only unions in Japan. Cooperation also is hindered by the workers organized and the issues addressed. In the 1990s, a wave of women-only unions emerged in a number of countries, including Asian countries such as India, South Korea, and Japan (Broadbent, 2007; Broadbent & Ford, 2008; Broadbent & Moon, 2008). Women-only unions differ from mainstream unions as they focus on organizing workers who can't find representation within the mainstream union movement, including those in small and medium-sized workplaces, and nonregular workers. Women-only unions also address issues that mainstream unions can't or won't address, such as employment and wage discrimination and all forms of harassment. Future cooperation is not entirely beyond the realms of possibility however, with the formation in 2007 of the Action Centre for Working Women (ACW2). ACW2 membership is open to all women and although it runs workshops and seminars, as well as offering counseling and advice, it also aims to nurture and develop future union activists (I. Midori, personal communication, March 2009). Still in its early stages, ACW2 offers possibilities for attracting a broad range of women activists and workers, extending cooperation between women union leaders and women-only unions.

Research on Japan's new unions and the impact of women-only unions in English-language research is growing (see A. Suzuki, 2008) but still limited, so by way of a contribution, this chapter analyzes the formation and impact of Japan's largest women-only union—Josei Union Tokyo (hereafter Josei Union). In thinking about the emergence of women-only unions in Japan, I examine Briskin's (1999) categories of separate organizing and autonomous organizing and the conclusion that separate organizing or the creation of women's departments, caucuses, or committees within mixed unions rather than autonomous organizing or the creation of organizations within the "community" (Briskin, 1999) is the most viable strategy for women to fight back against current global economic and political changes. Using Briskin's categories, I examine Josei Union, Japan's largest women-only union as an example of an autonomous organization in Japan, to determine the applicability of Briskin's conclusion in the case of Japan.

The strategy of organizing women-only unions has disappeared in Anglo-European countries with the merger of Denmark's Women Workers Union, KAD, with a mixed general union in 2004 but has gained traction in some Asian countries (see Hill, 2008; Moon & Broadbent, 2008). Japan's first women-only union, Onna Kumiai Kansai, appeared in 1990 and by 2003, 12 women-only unions had formed in various regions of Japan. Josei Union appeared in 1995 and currently has a membership of 202 (personal interview with General Secretary, March 2009), a decline from a high of 250 in 2003 (Josei Union Tokyo, 2003c). As analyses of Japan's women-only unions are limited, and with very little literature available in either Japanese (see Kotani, 1999) or English (see Yuki, 2009), original fieldwork underpins the discussion for this chapter. My analysis draws on interviews conducted in 2003, 2004, and 2009 with paid organizers and members of Josei Union during the periods of fieldwork. In conducting fieldwork, I have attended bargaining sessions, court hearings, mediation sessions (in 2003 and 2004), monthly union meetings, and the 2009 annual general meeting. I also have translated from Japanese union documents, including surveys of members, and analyzed other Japanese-language materials.

The chapter is presented in five sections. The first section sets the scene by describing women in Japan's labor market. Next, I discuss the literature, including Briskin's analysis of women's organizing and the differences between women-only unions and predominantly women-dominated workers centers such as Domestic Workers United in the United States. The third section provides an overview of unions in Japan, women in unions in Japan, and early women-only unions. The focus of the fourth section is Josei Union as an organization, including discussions of its significance, its membership, and the issues it addresses. Finally, I examine the obstacles facing women-only unions in Japan and conclude that women-only unions are significant as they "fill a gap" created by mainstream unions through their exclusive focus on the economic conditions of regular (largely male) workers in large companies.

WOMEN IN THE LABOR MARKET

Between 1970 and 2006 the percentage of women workers in paid work increased from 33% to 41% of the paid workforce (Sōmuchō, 2007) and the age composition of women workers and the industries in which they are employed have changed. The peaks and troughs of women's workforce engagement over their life cycle are referred to in Japan as the M curve, reflecting the relationship between labor-force participation, on the one hand, and marital status and childbearing on the other. The major change over time in women's employment patterns is that the trough representing women's withdrawal from the labor market in their 30s on marriage or the birth of their first child has become shallower as more women combine marriage, children, and paid work (see Broadbent, 2008). Well before the recession of the 1990s, the myth of Japan's "lifetime" employment practices, including seniority-based wage increases for both women and men, had been well and truly exploded. Shinotsuka (1994) demonstrated that by age 30, women's pay rates trailed those of their male colleagues of the same age. In particular between the ages of 30 and 34 women's salaries peak, whereas men's wages continue to increase and peak between the ages of 50 and 54 years (Fujii, 2005). There also has been little improvement in the gender wage gap. In 2006, women workers only earned on average 64% of a male wage (Kosei Rōdōshō, 2006). When part-time workers are included, the majority of whom are women, the gap in earnings increases. Compared with the United States, United Kingdom, Australia, Germany, and Sweden, Japan's gender wage gap differs from 12% and 24% (Kosei Rōdōshō, 2006).

In many countries, service-sector industries have contributed to the expansion of employment opportunities for women and Japan has been no exception. The increase in women's employment in this sector has paralleled the growth of the sector in the economy since the mid-1960s. In 2006, 72% of women workers were employed in service industries compared with only 14.8% employed in manufacturing (Sōmuchō, 2007). Small businesses also provide an important source of employment with almost one-third of women employed in companies with less than 29 employees (Sōmuchō, 2007). Women also are overrepresented in the nonregular workforce. According to the 2007 Labour Force Survey, women comprised 57% of nonregular workers including part-time workers, casuals, labor hire/agency workers, and others such as seasonal and daily hire workers (Sōmuchō, 2007). In comparison with their male counterparts, working women in Japan face discriminatory employment practices including separate career paths, a significant wage gap, and the gendered construction of part-time work.[4]

SEPARATE OR AUTONOMOUS ORGANIZING? WOMEN-ONLY UNIONS IN JAPAN

Given the employment discrimination women face in the workforce and the reluctance of enterprise unions to address employment discrimination, workplace harassment, or sexism, women have adopted a range of strategies in an attempt to achieve equality and address these issues. How can we understand and evaluate the viability of these strategies? Briskin (1999) categorizes the strategies women have used to challenge workplace inequality as separate organizing and autonomous organizing. Drawing exclusively on research from Anglophone and European countries, Briskin defines separate organizing as "organizing inside of institutions, such as women's committees in unions" while "autonomous (or independent) organizing [is within] the 'community'" (p. 544). Briskin has defined autonomous organizing broadly to include all areas where women create women-only organizations, but for the purpose of this chapter, the term is used to refer to women-only unions. There is little further discussion of autonomous organizing, but Briskin differentiates between separatism and separate organizing. Briskin defines separatism as "a goal—and end in itself, and separate organizing as a strategy—a means to an end" (p. 545). Briskin argues that women workers can better achieve their goals through separate organizing within mixed unions and that the weakness of autonomous organizing is that "it is not institutionally located and may have very limited access to resources" (p. 544). Because Briskin's analysis was based on organizations and unions developed mainly in the Anglo-European context, separatism and autonomous organizing may have been synonymous; however this is not the case in Japan.

There have been separatist organizations in Japan. Japan's first women-only union Onna Kumiai Kansai (Women's Union Kansai) emerged from a group called Sexuality o Kangaeru Kai (Committee to Consider Sexuality) but which split off because Onna Kumiai Kansai recognized the necessity of cooperating with male union activists and unionists. Interviews with Josei Union organizers also indicated that the creation of a women-only union was a "means to an end" (personal interview with General Secretary, 2004), a strategy to organize women workers to address issues that enterprise unions don't, won't, or can't address. Josei Union's activities are predicated on creating a working life that benefits both women and men and its char-ter includes a commitment to "abolishing sex discrimination, equal pay for work of equal value and establishing work rights for women" (Josei Union, 2001, p. 1). The General Secretary (and one of the organizers) commented that when large numbers of women are organized (no specific figure given) then there would be no need for women-only unions (personal interview with General Secretary, 2004). In this way, Briskin's equation of autono-mous organizing and separatism differs from the motivation of Josei Union (and other women-only unions in Japan) and so for this reason I analyze women-only unions in Japan, not as a form of autonomous organizing, but as a strategy for organizing women workers. At the time of Briskin's analysis it was possible that social movements were only beginning to gain critical mass and so coalitions with the largest organized mass of workers was limited to the union movement. Social movements and worker networks in Japan such as the Anti-Poverty Network are still developing, but they are chal-lenging the mainstream union movement and provide an alternative voice for workers, the poor, the unemployed, and generally those marginalized in society (see Shinoda, 2009). Denmark's KAD and India's Self-Employed Women's Association (SEWA) demonstrate that women-only unions have had a positive impact on women's lives and working conditions (Hill, 2008; personal interview with KAD union official, 2003).[5]

Women-only unions in Japan also differ from the growing number of worker's centers in the United States, even when they are women-dominated like the Domestic Workers United (Fine, 2006). Fine characterized workers centers as "community-based mediating institutions that provide support to low-wage workers" (p. 2). Worker's centers provide services to empower their members and engage in a range of activities such as seeking to enforce basic labor and employment laws that they are unable to do so through collective bargaining (Fine, 2006).

THE STRUCTURE OF UNIONS AND WOMEN
AND UNIONS IN JAPAN

In the early 1990s, Japan's unions were organized by industry, factory, and workplace (Gordon, 1985; Price, 1997) and included unskilled workers. Japan's first unions, formed in the early 20th century, were illegal and remained so until the ratification of the Trade Union Law in 1947. Within the union movement, those unions affiliated with the illegal socialist and communist parties constantly suffered attacks in the form of police harassment, employer-fostered violence, and finally crackdowns due to the military buildup in support of the Fifteen Year War (1931–1945). These setbacks, combined with political factionalism within the union movement, negatively affected worker solidarity and women workers' attempts at union organization because during this time the majority of women union activists were organized within unions affiliated with the illegal communist and socialist parties. As the military buildup progressed, unions were forced to amalgamate into Sanpo (Sangyō Hōkoku Kai, Industrial Patriotic Association).

The devastation and poverty evident throughout Japan during the early postwar years solidified the demands of a surging union movement, led largely by industry-based unions and fostered by the U.S.-led Occupation Forces (1945–1952) as part of the move to "democratize" Japan. The industry-based union focus of the union movement was challenged in the late 1940s and early 1950s by increasing employer assertiveness, encouraged and supported by the Occupation forces and the Japanese cabinet (Kawanishi, 1992; Price, 1997). The resulting ascendance and dominance of enterprise-based unions from the 1950s has fostered the division of the working class on the basis of employment status and gender, stifling opportunities for resurgence in working-class mobilization.

In the 1970s, hostilities between private and public-sector union organizations deepened with the formation of Zenmin Rōkyō (Japan Private Sector Trade Union Council), an organization whose core member unions were drawn from large private-sector organizations. These large private sector-based unions intended from the outset to ideologically reorient Japan's union movement away from alliances with the socialist and communist parties to the conservative parties. It succeeded in 1987 with the formation of Rengō (Nihon Rōdō Kumiai Sōrengokai, Japanese Trade Union Confederation, Japan's largest national peak labor organization) and completed its goal in 1989 with the dissolution of the public-sector union organization, Sōhyō (General Council of Trade Unions of Japan). As the union movement was occupied with factional struggles, splits, and divisions between public- and private-sector unions, overcoming sexism in the union movement, and in society more generally, slipped down the list of priorities.

Court cases (see discussion of Sumitomo case later) have become for many women the primary means for dealing with employment discrimination in Japan (see Owaki, Nakano, & Hayashi, 1996). Japan's enterprise unions don't or can't address these issues that, combined with employer hostility, aggravate the employment discrimination working women face and that ultimately has a negative impact on the employment conditions of all workers.[6] The reluctance of enterprise-based unions to challenge management on these issues goes some way toward explaining why union membership continues to decline and why union density has dropped to less than one-fifth of the working population.

Women's low levels of representation on union committees and in some unions their lack of voting rights, exacerbates the difficulty for issues such as the gender wage gap and discriminatory employment conditions being included on union agendas. In 2000, women represented only 6.6% of Rengō's executive committee members (Rengō, International Division, 2002). This is best illustrated by low levels of representation of women on union executive committee members, which in 2004 was only 14.4% (Kosei Rōdōshō, 2005b). It is also acknowledged that increasing the number of women in union leadership positions will not necessarily create an atmosphere conducive for achieving equality (Briskin, 1999). Many of Japan's mixed, mainstream unions don't allocate all women executive members voting rights. Additionally, the decline in working-class mobilization and industrial action in Japan is indicated by the decline in the rate of strikes or disputes from 8,435 in 1975 to 662 in 2006 (Sōmuchō, 2009). If women unionists have not had any experience with working-class mobilization or industrial action this may have a negative effect on their confidence in conducting an industrial campaign over gendered employment conditions or sexual harassment and so further affect the potential of action on these issues.

Early Women-Only Unions

The situation in Japan contrasts with developments in Australia, England, the United States, Ireland, and Denmark where as early as the 1880s women workers organized, or were encouraged by management or male unionists to organize, women-only unions. Women formed their own unions to counteract and overcome the problem of largely male-dominated craft-based unions that excluded women (see Cobble, 1990), migrants, and other unskilled workers. Management and male unionists encouraged women to form their own unions as a way of preventing women's wages from depressing men's wages. Few of the early women-only unions survived with most either forced to dissolve or absorbed into existing male unions (Cliff, 1984; Jacoby, 1994; Nutter, 2000; Ryan, 1984). By the 1920s, they had almost disappeared as many unskilled workers, many women included, were organized into the emerging industrial unions, although women-only unions in the United States have a slightly longer history.[7]

Historically, women workers had been active in industrial issues even before the widespread development of the union movement. Since these early days, women have made valuable contributions to workplace struggles and have been significant actors in Japan's union movement (Mackie, 1997; Sievers, 1983; Y. Suzuki, 1989; Tsurumi, 1990; Turner, 1995). The growth in unionizing unskilled workers also brought women and their concerns into the mainstream union movements (Mackie, 2003; Tsurumi, 1990). Women workers faced resistance within the union movement (Mackie, 2003) especially when Yamakawa Kikue, one of Japan's leading socialist feminists, argued that the workers' movements needed to support "women's special demands" in order for women to overcome discrimination (Mackie, 1997). In the face of strong opposition from male unionists, she was proposing the creation of a Women's Department.

It was not until the 1950s that women workers created women-only unions in Japan, and in only a few cases. The formation of women-only unions predates the second wave of women-only unions formed in the United States, Canada, and India influenced by the political and social ferment of the 1960s and the appearance of groups demanding civil rights, and the women's and gay liberation movements. Unlike India's SEWA, those in Canada and the United States have since dissolved. Contrary to the examples just given, Japan's early women-only unions formed in feminized workplaces (textiles factories and a bank) and in two cases there were existing enterprise unions. The women workers' opposition to the existing union centered on excessive management control over workers' personal lives, on union leaders who were unresponsive to rank-and-file women workers' demands, largely because they were too close to management, and gender-discriminatory employment practices; issues that continue to have currency (Kawanishi, 1992; Price, 1997; Yakabe, personal communication, October 2003). The existence of women-only unions highlights the major issue facing Japan's union movement today, namely its increasing distance from the growing sectors of the workforce—women and the nonregular workforce.

Japan's early women-only unions were short-lived. The two early women-only unions both formed in silk mills in the mid- to late-1950s (see Broadbent, 2008, for more detail). In the landscape of union victories, their gains appear modest, but their legacy is that they fought back against management paternalism and management-friendly union leaders that in some cases succeeded in forcing both management and union officials to recognize and incorporate their demands (see Kawanishi, 1999; Price, 1997). The third women-only union formed in 1971 at the Nihon Shintaku Ginkō (a bank). This was a unionized workplace and once again women workers were faced with union leaders who enjoyed a close relationship with management. Their discontent surfaced after the union signed an agreement with management on promotion paths that ignored women workers' long years of employment (Kumazawa, 1994). The company did not directly discriminate on the basis of gender but by demanding women workers applying for promotion also have management experience it indirectly discriminated against women who were often denied access to positions where it was possible to gain any managerial experience (Kumazawa, 1994). It has been demonstrated that women workers have engaged in struggle and have successfully confronted management, enterprise unions and union officials by forming their own unions as alternatives to the existing enterprise union. Although women-only unions have been few in number, the example of Josei Union indicates a gender-specific organizing strategy can achieve successful outcomes. The following discussion analyzes the development and role of one women-only union that has organized workers beyond the boundaries of the enterprise and that remains independent from any national peak union organization.

JOSEI UNION: A UNION ORGANIZED "BY WOMEN, FOR WOMEN"[8]

Josei Union was formed in 1995 by two women organizers originally as a section within Japan's National General Workers Union (NGWU), a mixed union that organizes workers across enterprise, occupation, and employment status boundaries. Soon after its formation, Josei Union encountered resistance from male union officials who did not (or would not) understand issues faced by women workers. By 2002, ongoing harassment from male union officials over Josei Union's focus on "women's issues" convinced both women organizers of the need to form an independent women-only union. Josei Union is a general union, and like other general unions, organizes workers on any basis from diverse industries and occupations with a range of employment statuses. With very few workplace branches, the majority of its members join on an individual basis. The women involved in forming Josei Union adopted a women-only organizing strategy to overcome the resistance of the union leadership, not because they wanted to avoid activism with male workers (personal interview, Josei Union organizer, October 2003).

Josei Union's aims include expanding membership, supporting and improving the working conditions of union members, working toward the abolition of sex discrimination, working to gain women's industrial rights, equal pay for work of equal value, advancing the social status of women, and establishing networks with women's struggles internationally (interviews August 2003; Josei Union Tokyo, 2001). Josei Union remains independent from any peak national union organization but in the past has cooperated with Rengō's Gender Equity Department. Internationally, Josei Union has been involved in a sexual harassment claim against Mitsubishi in the US (Josei Union Tokyo, 1999) and participated in study groups and workshops organized by Korean women-only unions and U.S. unions. Josei Union is run by a committee that oversees the functioning of the union and is supported by several smaller committees responsible for the publication of materials, the organization of fundraising or solidarity activities, recruitment, and education/training.[9] The executive committee is elected by and from the membership at its annual general meeting. The union also holds monthly case meetings that are open to all members to inform them of the progress in bargaining or developments in the various cases the union and its members are involved in. Josei Union also participates in ACW2, which formed in January 2007 uniting women-only unions and nongovernmental organizations to lobby ministers and distribute information on women's working conditions (I. Midori, personal interview, March 2009).

The Significance for Josei Union of being a Union

The International Labour Organization (ILO) pronounced workers have three rights relating to the formation of unions. These include the right to form a union to defend their working conditions, the right to collective bargain with employers to improve working conditions, and the right to strike to protect and defend their working conditions. Japan is a signatory to these conventions and under the Trade Union Law in Japan, unions can register as a union with a minimum of two workers in the one workplace. This is a much more favorable situation for Japanese workers than for Australian workers where draconian legislation introduced in 2006 required a minimum of 50 workers in a workplace before a union can form. Once a union has registered, it can request that management bargain with it, and refusal by management to do so is a violation of the law. The possession of the right to bargain collectively with employers is a significant difference between women-only unions and workers centers or other nonprofit organizations that address labor and employment-related issues.[10] This right to collective bargain has given Josei Union more legal power than nongovernment or nonprofit labor organizations that are increasing in Japan. It is this legal power that has allowed Josei Union to pursue cases involving discrimination in employment conditions. As discussed later when considering obstacles to Josei Union's growth, the "right to collective bargain" is mitigated by the custom and practice that has developed, which marginalizes and discourages the formation of multiple unions in one workplace. This custom and practice has inhibited Josei Union's ability to unionize nonunionized workers who are excluded from membership in their workplace enterprise-based union.

Josei Union is small but its efficacy lies in its organization of nonregular workers and the issues it addresses. Josei Union has a current membership of 202, which is a decline of 48 members since 2004. Despite being small, Josei Union is important in Japan's union movement as it not only reaches out to regular workers with no union at their workplace and to nonregular workers, both of whom are neglected groups of workers in Japan, but it is able to collectively bargain on behalf of its members. In this way it is able to effect changes to the discriminatory employment conditions faced by women workers (see Briskin, this volume). Not only this but the existence of a union that is willing to struggle may have a transformative impact on the broader union movement (see Curtin, this volume). Sixty-eight percent of its members are employed as regular workers in nonunionized workplaces, 12% are employed part time, whereas the remaining 20% are a mixture of contract and labor hire/agency workers (Josei Union Tokyo, 2002a). With nonregular workers representing 32% of the union membership, Josei Union's unionization rate of nonregular workers is higher than the 4% national estimated unionization rate for nonregular workers. Women employed in the generic services industries (including financial and personal services such as care workers) rank highly, comprising 37% of the membership, while manufacturing workers represent 22%, which is consistent with women's employment in these industries. As a feminized occupation, clerical work is predictably well represented, comprising 48% of Josei Union's members, while specialist and technical staff represent 22% of the membership. Until 2006, Josei Union employed two full-time organizers who divided their time between appearing at specialized tribunals, dealing with phone inquiries, advising members and workplace affiliates, and negotiating with employers. In 2006, both organizers retired and two new organizers were voted in by the membership as replacements, one of whom worked part time. In February 2008, the part-time organizer resigned and there has been only one full-time organizer, a change that has significantly reduced the capacity of the union, and is one of the reasons attributed to the decline in membership (personal interview, General Secretary, March 2009). Recognizing the continued impact of this situation, ACW2 has started a series of courses designed to develop a layer of skilled union activists for the future.

Philosophically, Josei Union runs on the basis of "by women, for women" (Josei Union Workshop, 2002a), where women are encouraged to participate actively in the resolution of their issues, literally resolving the issue by themselves (*anata no mondai wa jibun de yatte moraimasu*). By encouraging women workers to retain responsibility they are encouraged to take charge of the elements of the grievance process, thereby gaining valuable knowledge and skills in employment conditions, employment and labor law, and grievance procedure remedies. This is resonating positively with members. In an anonymous survey conducted by the union, when asked "tell us what has been good about joining the union" responses included "I have gained the ability to bargain and to solve complicated problems," "I feel empowered," "I have learnt a lot," and "when facing employment problems I have learnt how to deal with them" (Josei Union, 2009b, p. 16). This also is in line with Josei Union's goal of fostering the "empowerment" of women (see also Kotani, 1999), as well as developing an engaged membership and also identifying a layer of future union activists. A more pragmatic outcome for the union however, is that this strategy allows it to use the limited time of its organizers and financial resources more effectively.

For the majority of Josei Union's members, unfair dismissal cases, for example, are generally resolved through securing a financial settlement. This is a positive outcome for the individual concerned, but the job market that has never been positive for middle-aged workers, women in particular, with the worsening economic crisis, is contracting further. Long-term prospects for regular employment are rapidly contracting, unemployment at 5.8%, and with nonregular workers being retrenched in increasing numbers, labor market prospects are tightening (for earlier indications see also Josei Union Tokyo, 2003a, 2003b).[11] Josei Union conducts collective bargaining, with negotiations generally conducted by the complainant(s) with a union organizer and in many instances with other women-only union members present (see also Kotani, 1999).[12] The union also reported that the proportion of collectively bargained outcomes in the February 2008-January 2009 year had increased to 40% followed by 23% settled by labor tribunals (Josei Union Tokyo, 2009a). As the majority of Josei Union's members join on an individual basis, there have still been a few instances where collective outcomes have been achieved from an individual case (see Josei Union, 2003a; interviews October 2003 and June 2004; Broadbent, 2008). Members reported that they gained more than just an outcome from the bargaining experience, also reporting in the aforementioned survey that "people I didn't know gave me a lot of support" and "I want the union to hurry and negotiate for me, this is not a yellow union (*goyō kumiai*)" (Josei Union, 2009b, p. 16), which means that the respondent considers the union to be independent of management.

Issues Dealt With and Josei Union's Strengths

To January 2009, of the 189 cases Josei Union dealt with the issues the union most commonly dealt with were sackings (34 cases), forced "retirement" (23 cases), and sexual harassment (22 cases; Josei Union Tokyo, 2009a). These figures are down from previous years and it is argued that this is because there is no one in the office regularly to take calls. This claim can be substantiated especially as anecdotal evidence suggests there has been no decline in these incidences, particularly in the current economic climate (personal interview, General Secretary Fujii, March 2009). If we look back to the February 2007–January 2008 figures when Josei Union employed two organizers, the issues didn't change but the union handled a higher volume of calls. The issues receiving the most calls were as follows: bullying (65 cases), sackings (56 cases), concerns about employment (44 cases), and sexual harassment (34 cases; Josei Union Tokyo, 2009a).

The 189 cases dealt with in the period from February 2008 to January 2009 can be broken down by employment status as follows: 48% of grievances were lodged by regular workers, the remainder were lodged by nonregular workers. Of the nonregular workers, contract workers represented 11% and part-time and labor hire workers followed with 10% each. These figures could be somewhat higher as the employment status of 11% of workers was unknown (Josei Union Tokyo, 2009a). Major issues for regular workers were sackings, forced retirement, and bullying. For nonregular workers the issues were sackings, bullying, and sexual harassment (Josei Union Tokyo, 2009a).

Since its formation in 1995, Josei Union has regularly dealt with cases of sexual violence and rape in the workplace. Until 2007, cases of (workplace) sexual harassment and rape were on the increase and it is highly probable that the absence of staff in the office has in part contributed to the decline in sexual harassment calls. Of the 22 cases dealt with in 2008–2009, 11 were from nonregular workers, eight were from regular workers and 3 didn't declare their employment status. The statistics indicate nonregular workers with more precarious employment reported a greater number of sexual harassment incidences, but it is clear sexual harassment is a major issue for all women workers. Although those consulting the union on workplace sexual harassment included those who had no avenue of consultation within the company, the majority of grievances were from women who said they had used the company's avenue to redress the issue but had felt they had been subjected to a second round of harassment. As a result they contacted Josei Union (Josei Union, 2009a). As one member commented "I feel relieved. . . . Friends, the legal system and the police disregarded me but union members were there for me and thanks to them I recovered" (Josei Union, 2009b, p. 16). In contrast to Josei Union, mainstream mixed unions in Japan rarely address the issues of rape, sexual harassment, or sexism in the workplace.

Increasingly, women workers facing sexism in terms of wages and employment conditions have had to prosecute employers through the court system because either the union refused to address the issue, or in some cases supported the company's policies. Examples include the Sumitomo Electric company wage discrimination case that continued for 10 years until in 2005 the Osaka High Court overturned an unfavorable District Court decision and recognized the company did discriminate against the women by refusing to promote them (The Group Leading a Major Victory over Sumitomo Metals Gender-based Wage Discrimination). Similar cases include the Akita Sogo Bank Case (1975), the Ishizaki Honten case (1996), the Hitachi case (2000), the Sumitomo Life Insurance Company (2002), and the Sumitomo Electric Company (2003), which have returned favorable outcomes for the plaintiffs (see the ILO Website; New Japan Women's Association Website). All companies with substantial enterprise-based unions. Josei Union and Onna Kumiai Kansai also have supported Yakabe Fumiko in her case against her company's wage and employment discrimination. In Ms. Yakabe's case, the enterprise union refused to support her, instead acting as a witness in defense of the company's policies (see Broadbent, 2008). Despite taking the case through two levels of courts, Ms Yakabe's employer went bankrupt. Her situation was resolved out of court prior to proceeding to the Supreme Court (personal correspondence, 2009).

Mainstream unions in Japan are increasingly isolated from the experiences of the majority of the working population as evidenced by the annual decline in their unionization rate. Josei Union's organization of nonregular workers, empowering workers and encouraging rank-and-file activism reaches out to and introduces an audience unfamiliar with unions and working-class politics. When surveyed for their reasons for remaining union members (and thus what they appreciate about the union), comments included "I want to learn about workers and worker's rights," "To connect with friends who are different from family or the company," "I want to learn to about labor issues and to negotiate," and "I continue to pay dues so the union can assist those who are bullied or are suffering at work" (Josei Union, 2009a, p. 17).

Mobilizing Women Workers

Josei Union is the largest of Japan's women-only unions, but with only a little more than 200 members there is a small pool from which to draw financial resources or activists, and with only one organizer, there are limited opportunities for recruiting new members. Josei Union faces issues of survival and growth, in the same way that limited financial resources and no organizational support have been identified as a constraint on the growth and continuity of autonomous women-only organizations in Anglo-European countries (Briskin, 1999). In this way, Briskin's analysis is supported by Josei Union's experience. Does this mean then that we just ignore Japan's women-only unions or encourage them instead to join mixed mainstream unions simply because this will increase their chances of achieving equality or overcoming sexism? Instead we need to look at alternative organizations that can provide the organizational support. The example of women-only unions in Korea is illustrative. The Korean Women's Trade Union (KWTU) formed in 1999 is affiliated with and supported organizationally and financially by the Korean Working Women's Association United (KWWAU), which ensures stability for the KWTU (see Moon & Broadbent, 2008). Japan's women-only unions have not had access to or received support from a major organization such as KWWAU, but the formation of ACW2 modeled on Korea's KWWAU is an attempt to address the issue of organizational support. ACW2 provides training for future activists including conducting collective bargaining.

Josei Union's involvement in surging social movement networks such as the Anti-Poverty Network provides exposure in a national arena that its size would generally prohibit. The creation of the "Agency Workers Village" in Tokyo's well-known central Hibiya Park over the end-of-year/new year holiday (2008–2009) gained widespread attention and focused on the agency workers who were evicted from their company dormitories when they were sacked just before the end-of-year/new year holiday (for further discussion see Shinoda, 2009). As the Anti-Poverty Network doesn't provide financial or organizational support, Josei Union still needs to resolve these issues.

Despite encouraging women workers' involvement in resolving their own grievances, demands on the union's organizer means there is little opportunity for recruiting new members or conducting recruitment campaigns. Instead, the union relies on media coverage and referrals from members past and present.

Josei Union's focus is not confined to advancing conditions for women alone. The union organizers and members interviewed argued their efforts were aimed at improving conditions for a greater number of workers, both women and male. Their beliefs are demonstrated by their participation in and support for actions for part-time workers, agency and temporary workers, as well as joint action on a wide range of campaigns, including increasing temporary workers' benefits. The union believes the issues of interest to women workers have been ignored/sidelined by the male-dominated enterprise-based union movement, but cooperation with Rengō's Gender Equity Department and involvement in broad campaigns supporting equal treatment for part-time workers and benefits for temporary workers ensures Josei Union's actions can contribute to broader working-class mobilization (personal interview, October 2003).

At the 2009 Anti-Poverty Network event, a symposium was held that included speakers from a range of nonprofit organizations, Josei Union

Tokyo (and ACW2) and Japan's three national union organizations: Rengō, Zenrōren (National Confederation of Trade Unions), Zenkoku Rōdō Kumiai Sorengo Kai, affiliated with Japan Communist Party) and Zenrōkyō (National Trade Union Council, Zenkoku Rōdō Kumiai Renraku Kyōgikai, unaffiliated). None of the speakers from the three major national union organizations suggested unions begin a concerted industrial campaign as a means of fighting back to regain declining wages and conditions. One speaker actually mentioned that they were leaving it to the workers social movement, indicating an acceptance by these union organizations that those unions which are large enough to challenge employers are unable or unwilling to take industrial action. Ito san from ACW2 (and former Josei Union Tokyo organizer) commented that unions affiliated with these national organizations possessed the "three rights" (the right to collective bargaining, freedom of association, and labor action) but didn't use them. She offered to run workshops to provide training for women leaders in their organizations![13]

Women-only unions in Japan, through their involvement with the expanding network of unions organized outside of the enterprise-based system and social movement groups, are commanding greater attention particularly as the economy continues to decline. In these circumstances, the mainstream union movement is being forced to debate ways to improve workers' lives with these unions and to acknowledge their growing power. Women-only unions address issues relevant to women workers such as sexism and sexual harassment, which often are overlooked by the mainstream union movement. With the impact of the global financial crisis particularly borne by nonregular workers, and whose numbers vastly outweigh those of unionized workers, this developing network of unions and social movement groups are becoming increasingly important. Women-only unions are significant as they introduce women workers who the mainstream union movement is unable or unwilling to organize to working-class politics.

Josei Union and other social movement unions are providing a challenge from outside the union movement forcing Rengō to create an Agency Workers Centre in late 2008 and open "work consultation" phone days for all workers but particularly agency workers in 2009. The impact of Josei Union's strategies and their involvement in social movements is challenging mainstream unions to rethink their attitudes and strategies toward workers it has previously overlooked.

OBSTACLES AND PROSPECTS

Josei Union is registered under and recognized by the Trade Union Law, but there are obstacles to its growth such as closed shop and union preference agreements. These agreements, which prevent more than one union in a workplace, limit their ability to organize workplace branches and restrict their access to potential nonunionized members. In 2004, 64% of workplaces were covered by a closed shop agreement, representing an increase of 6% since 1998 (Kosei Rōdōshō, 2005a), despite multiple unions in one work-place being legally recognized under the Trade Union Law (Araki, 2002).[14] Women-only unions, and other unions not organized on an enterprise basis, are prevented from organizing the growing nonregular workforce who, while organized in small numbers (see Broadbent, 2003), is generally excluded from the majority of enterprise-based unions. A survey of union officials indicated that between 33% and 40% of them nominated "contract reasons" for not organizing part-time and contract workers. The remainder indicated that it was their own reluctance that prevented them from organizing non-regular workers (Rengō-Osaka, 2001).

The combination of an increase in closed shop agreements and the growth in the number of nonregular workers—all but a small minority of whom are excluded from union membership—means that a growing propor-tion of Japan's workforce must seek out union membership individually from a nonenterprise-based union. On the surface this represents a potential pool of members for unions such as Josei Union, but the increase in closed shop agreements prevents other unions from organizing even the nonunionized workforce. The impact of closed shop agreements and the exclusive practices of enterprise-based unions denies nonregular workers collective organization within their workplace or forces them to conduct a covert campaign of union organizing to form a branch within their workplace.

At present, even without the hurdle presented by closed shop agree-ments, Josei Union does not have the organizers or the financial resources to hire more organizers to recruit and organize nonunion members in unionized workplaces. Josei Union's inability to expand its membership is affecting its ability to retain current members and recruit new members, increasing the risk for organizational instability and jeopardizing opportunities for gain-ing critical mass and intervention in the broader working-class movement. Josei Union is developing two options to resolve these issues. The first is to seek organizational support from ACW2, which is developing a network of working women's organizations or a broader range of women's organizations, similar to that supporting the Korean Women's Trade Union (Ee, 2005; Moon & Broadbent, 2008). The second is the establishment of connections with other new type unions and social movement groups. Given the cur-rent economic stagnation and worsening employment conditions this option has the potential to provide greater immediate opportunities. Drawing on the resources of working women's organizations would allow Josei Union to maintain its orientation to the working class, which could be compro-mised through support from a broader women's organization. For Josei Union establishing a coalition with new type unions, which are generally more democratic and activist-focused than enterprise-based unions, would create a larger support network and pool of resources for organizers and members. Josei Union's focus only on women need not necessarily be a barrier to the success of the coalition.

Milkman (1985) argues women-only unions in the 1970s were an important form of organizing in the U.S. context, as it "implicitly challenge[d] the established traditions of the labor movement while also working to expand the space of women within it" (p. 10). Similarly, an organizer of a women-only union in Chennai, India, Sujata Mody, sees women-only unions as fulfilling an important role for women workers because "trade unions see her [women workers] need to fight for her economic betterment, [but] they usually ignore her social responsibilities" (Mody, 2005, p. 13).

ACW2, chaired by the former Secretary-General of Josei Union Tokyo, aims to "support working women, ensure access to decent work and wages to all women, to eliminate discrimination and violence against women and to create a social structure where women are respected and encouraged" (ACW2 website).

Will Women-Only Unions and Women Union Leaders
Always Act Separately?

Numerically Japan's 12 women-only unions, including Josei Union, are small and have yet to gain critical mass. Their significance lies in the fact that they are legally recognized as a union and have the three rights of unions, organize nonregular workers and regular workers not organized by or unable to be organized by existing enterprise-based unions and the broader range of issues they focus on compared with enterprise-based unions. Low rates of unionization of workers in nonunionized workplaces or nonregular work-ers indicates a potentially huge membership that existing enterprise unions in Japan are unwilling to organize because of union leaders' resistance or inability to organize due to union leaders' resistance to challenge manage-ment imposed restrictions.

The creation of ACW2 provides future possibilities for women union activists to cooperate beyond the boundaries of enterprise unionism but this could be restricted to women active in unions that have a history of social justice or activism. As the union movement is presently constructed, union leaders and activists based in enterprise unions, which organize workers in large, private-sector organizations and who possess a stronger identification with both their organization and the needs of regular workers, who form the entire membership of most enterprise unions, may be less inclined to champion the concerns of nonregular workers employed in their organization or nonunionized workers employed for example by their subcontract organizations. If the proportion of the nonregular workforce continues to increase, it's possible this may act as the trigger for Japan's mainstream union movement to pay closer attention to nonregular and nonunionized workers, in which case the opportunities for collaboration and cooperation between women-only unions and women union activists and leaders in enterprise unions will increase.

Women-only unions could gain critical mass by continuing to unionize nonregular workers on an individual basis. They are prevented from organizing these workers and forming workplace branches because of agreements between management and enterprise unions to restrict the formation of other unions in the workplace. Identifying and organizing workers in nonunionized workplaces is, even if their access was not restricted, at present limited due to an unstable base. If the mainstream union movement is serious about union renewal, union leaders need to rethink the gains of closed shop agreements and take a more aggressive stance toward managements' reluctance to the organization of nonregular workers.

NOTES

1. In 2009 I spent 4 months conducting fieldwork in Tokyo. This research was supported by an Australian federal government Endeavour Award. My thanks also go to the organizers and members of Josei Union Tokyo for their assistance. Any errors of interpretation are mine.

2. There are two main categories of employees in Japan—regular (sei(ki) shain) and nonregular (hiseikishain). Regular can't be directly translated into English as full time as it also includes a distinction based on employment status. Part-time, subcontract, and labor hire (hakken) workers also can be employed for full-time hours equivalent to (or more than) a regular worker but are not considered "regular" workers despite having been "employed (i.e., annual renegotiation of their contract)" with the one company. I interviewed numerous union members (and nonunion members) who had been employed on 1-year contracts with the same company for more than 18 years, but weren't (and had never been) considered regular employees. Classification as a nonregular employee has a serious impact on the benefits an employee receives, including no employer contributions to employment insurance (unemployment benefits), severance pay, or retirement pay.

3. Kawanishi (1992) uses the term *new type unions* to refer to unions organized beyond the traditional industry, occupational, or enterprise basis. These include unions organized in geographical areas such as the Edogawa, a traditionally working-class area of Tokyo with a concentration of very small workplaces, community union, labor hire workers union, and women-only unions such as Josei Union Tokyo.

4. The government defines "part time" as working less than 35 hours per week, but many part-time workers, including women, work more than 35 hours per

week, receiving lower pay and benefits. For a discussion of the differences and the construction of part-time work in Japan see Broadbent (2003).

5. KAD amalgamated with a mixed mainstream union in late 2004. Personal correspondence with Professor Erling Rasmussen.

6. Examples include the organization established by and commemorating Ichikawa Fusae (leading feminist and politician and leading advocate of gender equality in Japan) where the chair of the foundation harassed women workers, in the department responsible for organizing seminars, for forming a union. The dispute lasted 10 years and the women workers were granted a favorable decision, only to have the foundation shut down their section for "earthquake-proofing repairs" to the building (interviews with members of the union 2004, 2009; participation in collective bargaining 2004).

7. Separate women-only waitress union locals existed until the 1970s (Cobble, 1991); women-only flight attendant unions have a long history (Cobble, 2004) and 9 to 5 still exists although its union branch is now part of the SEIU and no longer all women (Nussbaum, cited in Cobble, 2007).

8. Taken from a discussion of Josei Union (Josei Union, 2002a).

9. Josei Union runs a telephone counselling/advisory service, education and solidarity activities for activists, members and nonmembers, workshops and seminars, and fundraising activities such as the celebration of seasonal events. It also maintains a Website, and publishes a monthly newsletter to keep members informed of current issues, such as the impact of proposed legislative reforms on women and progress on current cases.

10. In Japan, centralized collective bargaining was introduced in the 1950s but not a central form; instead, enterprise bargaining was conducted, which then gave way to joint consultation at the shopfloor level (Kawanishi, 1992). Management also could refuse to negotiate (Price, 1997), resulting in future generations of union officials with little experience of bargaining. This inexperience raises questions about the frequency of collective bargaining, the bargaining strength of enterprise unions (Kumazawa, 1994), and the impact of enterprise bargaining on gender equity.

11. Unemployment of part-time workers is estimated at 4% and for temporary workers at 10% (Saito, 2009).

12. Although I participated as an observer in both collective bargaining and individual negotiation sessions with other Josei Union members, many of the other members actively participated in the negotiation. In the discussion afterward, members commented that they appreciated the solidarity and support received from everyone participating in their collective bargaining session.

13. Rengō established its own leadership training academy in 2001.

14. Data from 2004 indicates that only 11% of workplaces had more than one union, a decline of 3% since 1999 (Kosei Rōdōshō, 2005a). Membership in more than one union is not permitted in Japan (Araki, 2002).

REFERENCES

Action Centre for Working Women (ACW2). Statute. Retrieved July 2009 http://acw2.org/statute?lang=en.

Araki, T. (2002). *Labor and employment law in Japan*. Tokyo: The Japan Institute of Labor.

Briskin, L. (1999). Autonomy, diversity and integration: Union women's separate organising in North America and western Europe in the context of restructuring and globalization. *Women's Studies International Forum, 22*(5), 543–554.

Broadbent, K. (2003). *Women's employment in Japan: The experience of part-time workers*. London: RoutledgeCurzon.

Broadbent, K. (2007). Sisters organising in Japan and Korea: The development of women-only unions. *Industrial Relations Journal, 38*(3), 229–251.

Broadbent, K. (2008). Japan: Women workers and autonomous organizing. In K. Broadbent & M. Ford (Eds.), *Women and labour organizing in Asia: Diversity, autonomy and activism* (pp. 156–171). London: Routledge.

Broadbent, K., & Ford, M. (Eds.). (2008). *Women and labour organizing in Asia: Diversity, autonomy and activism*. London: Routledge.

Broadbent, K., & Moon, K-h. (2008). Korea: Women, labour activism and autonomous organizing. In K. Broadbent & M. Ford (Eds.), *Women and labour organizing in Asia: Diversity, autonomy and activism* (pp. 136–155). London: Routledge.

Cliff, T. (1984). *Class struggle and women's liberation 1640 to the present day*. London: Bookmarks.

Cobble, D.S. (1990). Rethinking troubled relations between women and unions: Craft unionism and female activism. *Feminist Studies, 16*(3), 519–548.

Cobble, D.S. (1991). *Dishing it out: Waitresses and their unions in the twentieth century*. Chicago: University of Illinois Press.

Cobble, D.S. (2004). *The other women's movement: Workplace justice and social rights in modern America*. Princeton, NJ: Princeton University Press.

Cobble, D.S. (2007). *The sex of class: Women transforming American labor*. Ithaca, NY: ILR Press, Cornell University.

Ee, J. (2005, June). *Women's labour unions in South Korea: Strategic separation or ghettoisation?* Paper presented at Women's Worlds 2005: Embracing the Earth East–West, North–South, Ewha Women's University, Seoul, Korea.

Fine, J. (2006). *Workers centers: Organizing communities at the edge of the dream*. Ithaca, NY: Cornell University Press.

Fujii, H. (2005). Women's labour in Japan. In S. Emiko, F. Harue, & M. Takashi (Eds.), *Sekai No Josei Rōdō* [Women's labour internationally] (pp. 39–75). Kyōto: Minerva Shōbo.

Fujimura, H. (1997). New unionism: Beyond enterprise unionism? In M. Sako & H. Sato (Eds.), *Japanese labour and management in transition: Diversity, flexibility and participation* (pp. 296–314). London: Routledge.

Gordon, A. (1985). *The evolution of labour relations in Japan*. Cambridge, MA: Harvard University Press.

Group Leading a Major Victory over Sumitomo Metals Industry Gender-based Wage Discrimination. Newsletter. Online. Retrieved May 19, 2006 http://www.k2.dion.ne.jp/~sumikins/en/en_about1.html.

Hill, E. (2008). India: The Self Employed Women's Association and autonomous organizing. In K. Broadbent & M. Ford (Eds.), *Women and labour organizing in Asia: Diversity, autonomy and activism* (pp. 115–135). London: Routledge.

International Labour Organization (ILO). *E.Quality@Work: An information base on Equal Employment Opportunities for Women and Men*. Online. Retrieved 19 May 2006 http://www.ilo.org/public/english/employment/gems/eeo/law/japan/dc.htm.

Ito, M., Yugami, K., Zhou, Y., Ota, S., Hirata, S., Otani, G., & Hiroaki, W. (2007). *Labor situation in Japan and analysis: Detailed exposition 2009/2010*. Tokyo: Japan Institute of Labor Policy and Training. Online publication. Retrieved April 2009 http://www.jil.go.jp/english/laborsituation/2009-2010.pdf.

Jacoby, R.M. (1994). *The British and American Women's Trade Union Leagues, 1890–1925*. New York: Carlson.

Josei Union Tokyo. (1999). *Onna ga Kaeru Rōdō Undo*. Tokyo: Author.

Josei Union Tokyo. (2001). *Josei Union Tokyo Charter*. Tokyo: Author.

Josei Union Tokyo. (2002a). *Josei to Union-Hitori demo, Hitori da kara Union*. Josei Union Tokyo Workshop. Tokyo: Author.

Josei Union Tokyo. (2003a, September 31). Fight! Tokyo: Author.

Josei Union Tokyo. (2003b, October 31). Fight! Tokyo: Author.

Josei Union Tokyo. (2003c). *Proposals for Ninth annual general meeting*. Tokyo: Author.

Josei Union Tokyo. (2009a, March). *Dai 15kai Teiki Taikai*. Tokyo: Author.

Josei Union Tokyo. (2009b, March). *Survey results*. Tokyo: Author.

Kawanishi, H. (1992). *Enterprise unionism in Japan*. London: Kegan Paul.

Kosei Rōdōshō. (2005a). *Heisei 15 nen Rōdō Kumiai Jittai Chōsa*. Online publication. Retieved May 2005 http://www.mhlw.go.jp/toukei/kouhyo/indexkr_11_9.htm.

Kosei Rōdōshō. (2005b). *Rōshi Kankei Sogō Chōsa*. Online publication. Retrieved August 2005 http://www.mhwl.go.jp.

Kosei Rōdōshō. (2006, June). *Heisei 17 nen Chingin Kōzo Kihon Tokei Chōsa*. Online publication. Retrieved February 2008 http://www.jil.go.jp/english/estatis/databook/documents/10-23.xls.

Kosei Rōdōshō. (2009). *Rōdō Kumiai Kiban Chōsa*. Online publication. Retrieved April 2009 http://www.jil.go.jp/english/estatis/eshuyo/200904/e0701.html.

Kotani, S. (1999, January). Josei no "atarashii" Rōdō Undo (Women's "new" labor movement). *Rōdō Shakaigaku Kenkyūkai (Journal of Labor Sociology)*, pp. 3–25.

Kumazawa, M. (1994). Joshi rōdōsha no Sengo. In S.J. Kenkyūkai (Ed), *Josei no Kurashi to Rōdō* (Vol. 6, pp. 275–305). Tokyo: Yoshikawa Hiromu Bunkan.

Kuwahara, Y. (2000). The future of the labour movement in Japan: Experiments and possibilities. In Changing patterns of employee and union participation: Toward new systems of industrial relations, (Vol. 3, pp. 74–84). International Industrial Relations Association 12th World Congress, Tokyo. Tokyo: IIRA.

Mackie, V. (1997). *Creating socialist women in Japan: Gender, labour and activism, 1900–1937*. Cambridge: Cambridge University Press.

Mackie, V. (2003). *Feminism in modern Japan*. Cambridge: Cambridge University Press.

Milkman, R. (1985). Women workers, feminism and the labor movement since the 1960s. In R. Milkman (Ed.), Women, work and protest: A century of US women's labor history (pp. 300–322). Boston: Routledge & Kegan Paul.

Mody, S. (2005). *Unionization of women workers in the context of globalisation: Case of Tamil Nadu, India. Women Workers' Initiative to Challenge Against Globalization*. KWWAU: Seoul.

Moon, K. & Broadbent, K. (2008). *Korea: Women, labour activism and autonomous organising*. Oxford: Routledge.

Nutter, K.B. (2000). *The necessity of organization: Mary Kenney O'Sullivan and trade unionism for women 1892–1912*. New York: Garland.

Owaki, M., Nakano, M.,& Hayashi, Y. (1996). *Hataraku Onnatachi no Saiban*. Tokyo: Gakuyo Shōbo.

Price, J. (1997). Japan works: Power and paradox in postwar industrial relations. Ithaca, NY: Cornell University Press.

Rengō, International Division. (2002). *We 2002–2003: This is Rengō*. Tokyo: Institute of Labor Education & Culture.

Rengō-Osaka. (2001). *Kigyōnai Jugyōin tō ni Kansuru Jittai Chōsa Hōkoku* (Report of survey of employees). Osaka: Rengō.

Ryan, E. (1984). *Two-thirds of a man: Women and arbitration in NSW 1902–08*. Sydney: Hale & Iremonger.

Saito, T. (2009). *How the rapid growth of non-regular employees will impact the next round of employment adjustment*. National Labor Institute. Retrieved July 2009 http://www.nli-research.co.jp/english/economics/2009/eco090325.pdf.

Shinoda, T. (2009, April 6). Which side are you on? Hakenmura and the working poor as a tipping point in Japanese labor politics. *The Asia Pacific Journal*, http://www.japanfocus.org/-Toru-Shinoda/3113.

Shinotsuka, E. (1994). Women workers in Japan: Past, present and future. In J. Gelb & M. Lief-Palley (Eds.), *Women of Japan and Korea: Continuity and change* (pp. 95–119). Philadelphia: Temple University Press.

Sievers, S. (1983). *Flowers in salt: The beginnings of feminist consciousness in modern Japan*. Stanford, CA: Stanford University Press.

Sōmuchō. (2007). *Labour force survey. Centre for the Advancement of Working Women*. Retrieved March 2009 www.miraikan.go.jp/toukei/002/statistics/data/pdf/p91.pdf)

Sōmuchō. (2009). *Nihon Tokei Nenkan* (Japan's Statistical Yearbook, Chapter 16—Labour and Wages). Retrieved April 2009 http://www.stat.go.jp/english/data/nenkan/1431-16.htm)

Suzuki, A. (2006). Nashonaru Sentaa no Soshiki Kakudai Seisaku no Rekishi (The history of National Centre's organising policies). In S. Akira & H. Seiichiro (Eds.), *Rōdō Kumiai no Soshiki Kakudai Senryaku* (pp. 37–65). Tokyo: Ochanomizu Shōbo.

Suzuki, A. (2008). Community unions in Japan: Similarities and differences of region-based labour movements between Japan and other industrialized countries. *Economic and Industrial Democracy, 29*(4), 492–520.

Suzuki, Y. (1989). *Jōko to Rōdō Sōgi*. Tokyo: Renga Shobo.

Tsurumi, E.P. (1990). *Factory girls*. Princeton, NJ: Princeton University Press.

Turner, C. (1995). *Japanese workers in protest*. Berkeley: University of California Press.

Yuki, M. (2009). The future of labor feminism in Germany and Japan. *The Journal of Kawamura Gakuen Woman's University, 20*(2), 187–196.

FOURTEEN

DEMANDING THEIR RIGHTS

LGBT Transnational Labor Activism[1]

Suzanne Franzway and Mary Margaret Fonow

Lesbian, gay, bisexual, and transgender (LGBT) individuals have become more visible in global workplaces, but campaigns for social and economic rights for LGBT workers receive little attention (Binnie, 2004; Cruz-Malavé & Manalansan, 2002). There is even less recognition of gay or queer activism in and around labor issues (Bronfenbrenner, 2007; Education International [EI], 2007; Wright, Colgan, Creegan, & McKearney, 2006). In this chapter, we discuss queer organizing within labor unions and explore how transnational labor movement networks are being mobilized for the social/economic rights of LGBT workers. We explore the goals, discourses, strategies, and tactics of queer labor organizing.

LGBT workers are adopting similar strategies to those used by women and other marginalized workers who are underrepresented in labor movements, including self-organizing in order to build political spaces within unions from which they can make claims for representation and participation (Colgan, Creegan, McKearney, & Wright, 2007; Parker, 2006). Like feminism, queer activism has the potential to revitalize the labor movement; but to do so, it needs to challenge the homophobia, transphobia, and sexual politics of organized labor and insist that unions live up to their democratic ideals. At the same time, queer activists take a route that is familiar to feminists and civil rights activists within labor who have had to leverage their alliances with other activists, advocacy groups, and grass-roots organizations outside the formal boundaries of unions in order to make their case for greater representation and equity (Githens & Aragon, 2009; Wright et al., 2006).

In the 1960s and early 1970s, for example, in the United States the Black caucus within the United Steelworkers of America used a dual strategy to advance its claims for equity within the organization. Union activists built extensive ties with local civil rights organizations and used the emerging body of civil rights laws, policies, and equity norms to augment the union's grievance mechanisms to press their legal claims for equity. The women's caucus used similar strategies and when the legal remedies based on race were inadequate to address gender discrimination they joined forces with the women's movement to lobby for new federal policies (Fonow, 2003).

Queer labor activists are borrowing strategies such as self-organizing within unions and forging external alliances with gay rights organizations, but also are creating new approaches and discourses that challenge unions to rethink how they mobilize their members for collective action. In the United States, queer labor activists from UNITE/HERE, a union representing more than 300,000 workers in hospitality, airports, laundry, food service, gaming, and textiles, videotaped for YouTube distribution a flash-mob action they staged in the hotel lobby of the Westin St. Frances Hotel in San Francisco to protest unfair labor practices and cutbacks in health care coverage. Activists were joined by the Liberation Brass Band to perform "Caught in a Bad Hotel" (a parody of Lady Gaga's "Bad Romance"), a song that proclaims "workers' rights are hot, don't get caught in a bad hotel" and calls for the public to boycott such bad hotels. This action is part of a larger campaign, "Sleep with the Right People," organized by the labor/gay alliance to steer people toward pro-union hotels and away from hotels in the United States and Canada that refuse to negotiate with workers or who outsource union jobs to nonunion workers.

In return for gay support for labor campaigns, unions expressed their solidarity with the gay activists in California by filing friends of the court briefs in the legal battle to reinstate gay marriage. They also have called for the boycott of the Manchester Grand Hyatt in San Diego because the owner Doug Manchester was a key financial backer of Proposition 8, which outlawed gay marriage in California. Although Proposition 8 was overturned by a federal judge in California on August 4, 2010, a protracted legal and political battle looms ahead as the judge's decision moves through the appeal process. This struggle will test the strength of the queer/labor alliance. Because the hotel industry is an industry that actively courts gay travelers and employs a large number of gay workers, it is especially vulnerable to boycotts organized by gay labor activists and their allies particularly in cities where there are large gay populations. LGBT activists who work in the industry are put in the unenviable position of calling for boycotts of their own worksites.

Boycotts, a mainstay in the repertoire of the labor movement, are given a cultural twist by LGBT activists who have tapped into the rich vein of popular culture to make their rights claims resonate with larger audiences. This attention to popular culture fits new research on the significance of cultural dynamics for social movement formation, mobilization, and success (Armstrong & Bernstein, 2008; Rupp & Taylor, 2003; Staggenborg & Lang, 2007; Taylor, Kimport, Van Dyke, & Andersen, 2009). Gay activists are effectively using cultural forms of politics not only to build internal solidarity and collective identification among activists and movement participants but also to affect broader political change. In this chapter, we draw on notions of discursive frames and mobilizing structures, sexual politics, and self-organizing, to help us understand transnational queer labor activism, and to argue for the value and necessity of queer organizing in the labor movement.

FRAMING MOBILIZING STRUCTURES

Collective action takes place through mobilizing structures—the networks of groups and organizations prepared to mobilize for action (Rucht, 1996). These structures, both formal and informal, serve as organizational mechanisms to collect and use the movement's resources. Although often designed for other purposes, they also serve as sites for collective action and identity formation. In order for unions to be viewed as mobilizing structures for achieving economic justice for existing and potential LGBT members, unions, and their networks have to be discursively framed as such. To identify and develop mobilizing structures effectively, activists must successfully frame them as useful and appropriate to the social-change tasks they will be used to facilitate. As Kelly (1998, cited in Heery & Conley, 2007) argues, framing is integral to the emergence of collective action by workers and that a key function of union activists is to form and diffuse interpretative frames that legitimate action against employers. In other words, strategic framing is central in shaping the available range of mobilizing structures.

A discursive frame "serves as an interpretive schema that simplifies and condenses the world out there by selecting, punctuating, and encoding objects, situations, events, experiences and sequences of actions within one's present or past environment" (Snow & Benford, 1992, p. 137). Heery and Conley (2007) observe that "framing can also occur within unions and be directed against union tradition and established leaders and interests as much as employers" (p. 13). Discursive frames are important because they

(a) help transform issues and problems into grievances about which individuals believe something can and should be done, and (b) help participants to see that unions can make a difference. "To be successful frames must seek congruence and complementarity between the interests, values, and beliefs of the potential movement participants and the activities, goals, and ideologies of social movements" (Fonow, 2003, p. 15). Finding this congruence will not be an easy task, however, because frames that resonate with queer folks may not resonate with "straight" folks.

Activists use discursive tools (such as conference resolutions, policy statements, newsletters, Websites, and educational programs), as well as institutionally sanctioned spaces (such as conventions, workshops, labor schools, committee structures) to create a network of resources that can be called into action to mobilize members and potential supporters at strategically important moments. Activists forge a collective sense of themselves as political actors through the day-to-day activities of building and sustaining these networks.

SEXUAL POLITICS AND LABOR MOVEMENTS

The political opportunities available in the labor movement cannot be realized without challenging the obstacles presented by the prevailing sexual politics. We are adopting and adapting the term *sexual politics* in order to bring the political back into the analysis of gender, which has lost much of its significance through becoming largely a descriptor to refer to women. Our notion of sexual politics builds on Kate Millett's (1969) concept, which broadened the definition of politics to include "power-structured relationships, arrangements whereby one group of persons is controlled by another" (p. 23). Millett made the radical claim (for its time), that the sexes, understood as a category in its own right (similar to races, castes and classes), should be seen as well-defined and coherent groups and thus subject to politics. In sexual politics, the political is intrinsic to whatever forms gender relations take.

More recent versions of sexual politics have tended to move away from Millett's understanding of the sexes, politics, and power, and toward a more direct emphasis on the sexual and sexualities. Perhaps most commonly, sexual politics has been deployed to claim a politics of sexual identities and difference (Seidman, 1997). Patricia Hill Collins (2004) defines "black sexual politics" as a set of ideas and social practices situated at the intersection of "gender, race and sexuality" that are faced by African Americans (p. 6). The political is central to struggles around sexual identities and Black sexual politics frames how men and women treat each other. Collins argues that Black sexual politics has largely silenced Black women and marginalized Black lesbian theorizing about sexuality. Judith Butler (2009) is equally focused on the politics of sexualities in contrast to the politics of gender relations. Butler moves sexual politics to the center of contemporary political life in a complex argument that links freedom and temporal progress. She points to political debates "which suggest that certain ideas concerning the progress of 'freedom' facilitate a political division between progressive sexual politics and the struggles against racism and religious discrimination" (p. 104). In this way, Butler distinguishes the sexual from the racial to argue that sexual politics are integral to the politics of race and to progressive politics broadly.

The value gained from reclaiming Millett's concept is found in its emphasis on power and the exercise of power over others. Sexual politics may be understood in contemporary terms as continually contested gender relationships, that is, as an ever-present relation of power, that produces resistance and dominance, social contracts and diverse pleasures. If sexual politics are understood as political and always contested, it follows that gender relations at any one time are characterized by the particular configurations of that contestation (Cobble, 2004; hooks, 2000). A renewed sexual politics incorporates the sexual and the political, an important move toward understanding the dominance of heteronormativity and the often hostile or repressive responses to queer activism.

Because sexual politics are dynamic and disputed, there are multiple possibilities in the configurations of gender relations. It is important to note that gender relations are not inevitably patriarchal (Connell, 1987), although this is the usual assumption in much feminist writing. Gender relations may be more or less patriarchal or egalitarian, and the shifts and changes may be more or less subtle. An important dimension of this understanding of sexual politics is that it throws light onto the continuing struggle that is intrinsic to the dominance of masculine heterosexuality and the resilience of men's power as men in much contemporary society, including in the labor movement. Sexual politics makes it possible to see that dominance and resilience are always being restated, reaffirmed, and reclaimed. It is through the contentions of sexual politics that perceptions of heterosexual men's concerns and practices are achieved as normative.

The politics of gender relations also are constituted by deeply ambivalent meanings of difference, including those of race, class, age, diversity, and so on. Political contestation in sexual politics produces multiple discursive meanings of gender and power, including the diversity and difference of contested power among women. Recognition of complexities and diversities of power among women also demands attention be given to the diversity of power among men and the dynamic of power across the field of sexual politics.

In analyzing the sexual politics of the labor movement, we aim to sidestep the way that gender has become coded to refer almost exclusively to women. We acknowledge that gender is an ever-present relation of power, and thus best conceived in terms of a sexual politics that engages and challenges power in all its diversity of positive and negative forms. This conceptualization of gender and sexual politics, in the contemporary climate, identifies the centrality and dominance of masculine, heteronormative sexualities/identities, and reframes the analysis away from an arithmetical "gender inclusivity" in which LGBT individuals disappear (Franzway, 2001). It is the dynamic and changing circumstances of sexual politics, in which gender relations contest and shape political opportunities and social identities that open up spaces for political action.

FRAMING THE SEXUAL POLITICS OF LGBT RIGHTS

The sexual politics of trade unions is clearly challenged by the interests and concerns of LGBT workers. Trade unions are dominated by masculine heterosexuality—hence the alarming rates of discrimination and prejudice in the workplace faced by lesbians, gay men, and transgender people. In the Australian study, The Pink Ceiling is Too Low, more than 50% of the respondents said they suffered from homophobic behavior or harassment, and 11% experienced verbal abuse, including threats of physical and sexual abuse (Irwin, 1999). Studies elsewhere also find that the careers of LGBT workers are affected by the culture of work organizations and policies (Wright et al., 2006). Where trade unions themselves have begun to collect data on the experiences of LGBT workers, they find that breaches of labor rights are common. For example every 3 years, EI conducts a survey on the status of gay and lesbian teachers in the education sector. The most recent survey conducted in 2007 found that there are regional and country variations in discrimination that are troubling. In Latin America, although there is no legal discrimination except in Nicaragua, the practice of bullying and harassment in schools is still a problem in most countries. In North America, there are big differences between the United States and Canada. Teachers unions in the United States bar discrimination in union contracts, but there are few government protections against discrimination. In Canada, such protections are found in both union contracts and in the country's laws (EI, 2007).

As the experiences, issues, and concerns of LGBT workers become increasingly visible, two points emerge: First, this category of workers is no more homogenous than any other, and second, progressive gains only can be made with persistent and focused political activism. On the issue of homogeneity, John Blandford (2003) argues that although sexual orientation has a significant influence on income, its submergence within the categories of married or nonmarried serves to distort analyses of causes, and therefore the framing of political campaigns to achieve pay equity. Likewise, American research on heterosexism in the workplace has found that studies on the impact of race and gender in the workplace that ignore sexual orientation tend to underestimate or misconstrue the effects of multiple identities on workers themselves, as well as on the value of antidiscrimination policies (Ragins, Cornwell, & Miller, 2003).

The argument for the necessity for political activism by and for LGBT workers recognizes that, overall, little attention has been paid to issues of sexuality in the politics or research literature of trade union movements, and still less has been paid to the hegemonic or homophobic dimensions of such movements. Such silence on issues of sexuality among union activists stands in strong contrast with the clear feminist view that the male heterosexual dominance of the labor movement can no longer be ignored or overlooked. Issues of the lack of representation by LGBT members in union leadership as well as workplace discrimination and sexual harassment must be addressed (Cunnison & Stageman, 1995; Ledwith, 2006). When LGBT issues do surface, there is a great deal of uncertainty and timidity among unionists about how to frame them effectively in the labor movement at both the local and the international levels.

QUEER ORGANIZING

Queer organizing is strongest in unions where other marginalized workers have carved out self-organizing spaces, where union feminism is active, and where there are large numbers of women (Bielski, 2005; Franzway, 2001; Hunt & Boris, 2007). Examples of women's self-organizing include women's conferences, caucuses, committees, forums, workshops, special educational programs, and Websites.[2] The rationale for creating separate or self-organizing spaces is predicated on the minority status of women in male-dominated unions and in their experiences of sexual harassment and sex discrimination on the job. These separate spaces can serve as staging areas for broader forms of organizational and movement participation. Mary Katzenstein (1998) makes the point: "For protest to occur inside institutions there must be protected spaces or habitats where activists can meet, share experiences, receive affirmation, and strategize for change" (p. 33). Such spaces may be clearly defined and defendable by activists, but their boundaries are not necessarily permanent or fixed. Women's self-organizing in unions provides them with the political space to construct union feminism. According to Curtin (1999), "separate spaces provide the opportunity for women to alter the discursive frameworks through which women's claims are constituted" (p. 33). LGBT union members have developed similar self-organizing internal support structures and policies despite resistance from some union officials and members. However, as Linda Briskin and Jennifer Curtin both make clear in this volume, it is important to recognize that these spaces serve as mobilizing structures and are not ends in themselves.

The seeds of queer self-organizing in unions had its beginnings in the 1960s and 1970s with the rise of public- and service-sector unions and the influx of women into the workforce. This occurred during a period of feminist resurgence that fueled the growth of union feminism (Cobble, 2004; Milkman, 2005). Growing numbers of women began to demand rights for themselves and as it became clear that the differences among women mattered, they subsequently expanded women's rights to encompass an ever larger set of diversity issues. As women feminized organized labor they brought more tolerant attitudes about sexual orientation with them. A survey of U.S. unions conducted by Bielski (2005) shows that white-collar public-sector unions with larger female membership have made the most progress on addressing discrimination against LGBT workers, whereas the less responsive unions were male-dominated, blue-collar unions. One anomaly that confounds the findings is the United Auto Workers, whose responsiveness to gay issues is attributed to its progressive history and to the willingness of individual activists to hold the union accountable to its own history on civil rights and women's rights.

Feminists spotlighted noneconomic concerns such as harassment and violence, and they legitimized the idea that traditional union culture was part of the problem (Briskin & McDermott, 1993; Colgan & Ledwith, 2002; Heery & Conley, 2007).

> Feminists not only raised labor's consciousness around discrimination, difference, and diversity, but pioneered the tactic of self-organizing into caucuses. Sexual minority activists were quick to model the idea of separate caucuses as a place to find support, formulated ideas, clarify demands, and strategize about how to confront conservative union leadership. (Hunt & Boris, 2007, p. 97)

LGBT labor activists reframed sexuality issues, such as the need for protection from homophobia in the workplace and for domestic partner benefits, as demanding political and unionized campaigns since the early 1970s. The first Australian Gay and Lesbian Trade Unionists Group, GayTUG, was formed in 1978. Twenty years later, GLAM, the Gay and Lesbian Australian Services Union Members was established to articulate its issues to the broad labor movement as well as within its union. In Canada, similar self-organizing by networks of lesbians and gay men established internal structures such as The National Pink Triangle Committee of the Canadian Union of Public Employees (CUPE) in 1991. In 1997, the Canadian Labor

Council organized its first national conference for gay and lesbian unionists, attended by about 300 people (Genge, 1998), and in 1999, the Canadian Auto Workers Union (CAW) added transgender issues to its bargaining agenda (Hunt & Haiven, 2006).

In the United States, LGBT rights were first publicly endorsed by a labor union in 1970, when the executive council of the American Federation of Teachers passed a resolution denouncing discrimination against teachers solely on the basis of homosexuality. In 1983, the American peak body, the American Federation of Labor-Congress of Industrial Organizations (AFL-CIO), formally condemned discrimination based on sexual orientation. Elsewhere, gay and lesbian unionists formed similar groups such as GLUE in Wellington, New Zealand which aimed to gain union recognition of the interests of lesbian and gay workers. By 2000, the New Zealand peak union body the Council of Trade Union had a network, the CTU Out@Work, established for lesbian, gay, takataapui, bisexual, intersex, transgender, and fa'afafine union members.[3]

A key aspect of queer organizing for social/economic rights in and around labor movements is that it often is built on discursive and material alliances with broader social movements. As McCreery and Krupat (1999) argue, "the challenge for lesbian, gay, bisexual, and transgendered movements to confront elitism and inequalities in their own ranks, is to acknowledge common cause with other social movements, and to wage their struggles at the intersections of class, race, and gender" (p. 5). Such alliances work to frame LGBT issues such as sex-based discrimination and domestic partner benefits as relevant to unions and workers. In 1981, for example, the Sisters of Perpetual Indulgence, a group of Australian LGBT community activists, organized a gay contingent to participate in the Australian May Day parade, the annual celebration of workers' rights (Towart, 2002). In recent decades, unions have participated in the Sydney Gay and Lesbian Mardi Gras march through the heart of the city, which attracts enormous crowds and live television coverage.[4] Such union involvement has incurred serious internal conflicts within some unions, meaning that the politics of winning resources and support is as significant as the actual event itself (Fortescue, 2000). Winning support within unions means challenging the prevailing heterosexist sexual politics, and building broad alliances with other social movements helps provide valuable material and discursive resources.

TRANSNATIONAL QUEER LABOR ACTIVISM

The emergence of an LGBT labor activism at the transnational level is the outcome of several decades of queer organizing within national unions in Canada, the United States, Australia, Brazil, South Africa, Great Britain,

Germany, and many other countries (Hunt, 1999; Krupat & McCreery, 2001). Additionally, there has been a proliferation of real and virtual political spaces where transnational activists from a variety of movements—gay, human rights, feminists, labor, and global justice—can meet to exchange information and strategies for change. These spaces include various UN forums, international labor conferences, the International Labour Organization (ILO), the World Social Forum (WSF), and the Gay Games/World Outgames. Such transnational networks have the capacity to be effective when they draw on trade union resources to create forums and spaces for lesbian, gay, and transgendered workers.

The ILO has responded to these campaigns by documenting and supporting social and economic rights for LGBT workers and trade union members. Referring to discrimination based on sexual orientation, a recent report noted that "homosexuality" is still illegal in some states and may lead to corporal punishment and imprisonment (ILO, 2007). The ILO went on to publish pamphlets of guidelines defining such discrimination together with suggestions to employers for actions to promote equality (ILO Helpdesk, 2009).

The Global Union Federations (GUFs) have become useful sites for transnational queer labor activism. These organizations are federated peak labor bodies, mostly headquartered in Europe, whose missions include building international support and solidarity for workers and their struggles for labor rights worldwide. The GUFs have expanded to every region of the world and have grown in size, scope, and political influence. Today there are 10 different GUFs representing millions of workers in almost every country in the world.[5]

The two GUFs that have been most receptive to LGBT activism have been female-dominated, feminist-influenced public-sector federations with well-developed equity programs and structures in place. The Public Services International (PSI), founded in 1907, is comprised of 650 affiliated trade unions in 150 countries representing 20 million public-sector workers in government, health and social care, municipal and community services, and public utilities. The EI is comprised of 348 affiliated organizations in 169 counties representing 30 million teachers and education workers from preschool through university.

Both PSI and EI have reframed their missions to encompass questions of equity, justice, and free access to public services and education. In these terms, they engage with international organizations concerned with labor standards, including the ILO and various UN suborganizations, employer organizations, and newer financial institutions like the World Trade Organization. When social/economic rights are violated, activists form broad alliances with the women's, environmental, and nongovernmental organizations (NGOs) to achieve results that would not be possible without a more equitable sexual politics.[6]

Gay activists from PSI and EI sponsored their first joint forum on sexual diversity at the 2004 WSF in Porto Alegre, Brazil. The forum developed a set of proposals for action on the rights for LGBT workers discursively framed as basic human rights. The resulting declaration recognized the diversity of the LGBT experience and argued that unions should take the lead in eliminating discrimination against these communities. It also noted that equal rights for LGBT workers would be strengthened if they were reframed as integral to campaigns for labor rights at national, regional, and international levels. Without the explicit recognition of LGBT rights in most international and national labor standards, discrimination and inequity based on sexual orientation and gender identity would persist at all levels of the world economy.[7] The PSI-EI Diversity Forum held at the WSF 2005 adopted an action plan that called for a multifaceted approach: establishing a sexual diversity network that would facilitate the sharing of resources and the coordination of national and international campaigns for LGBT labor and social rights; linking Web pages to provide a regular supply of news and updates about the work of the national networks; participating in the World Workers' Out Conferences; and holding a second joint international forum on sexual diversity prior to the PSI World Congress.

The second PSI-EI Sexual Diversity Forum was held in September 2007 in Vienna, drew more than 300 hundred participants, and addressed topics such as collective bargaining for LGBT equity issues, diversity and antidiscrimination training, bullying and workplace climate, alliance building, and protecting and expanding quality public services like free education for all. A joint PSI-EI sponsored forum Website has been established and serves as a useful discursive and political resource for labor and queer activists and is used to mobilize international solidarity campaigns—such as the one for a Polish educational official who lost his job for authorizing a teacher training guide on gay tolerance. The site contains research reports on the status of LGBT members, a training guide for incorporating LGBT issues into the work of the union, press releases, and links to the broader movement for LGBT rights.[8]

Likewise, the International Day against Homophobia and Transphobia held annually on May 17 and endorsed by PSI-EI serves a similar function as does the recent UN statement on Human Rights, Sexual Orientation and Gender Identity. As Fred van Leeuwen, EI general secretary has said, "The struggle to overcome discrimination based on sexual orientation and gender identity and to support vulnerable LGBT students and teachers requires capacity building and awareness-raising opportunities on these issues."[9] Thus, teachers require training in appropriate skills so they can address controversial issues, as well as the kind of collective support that peak bodies like EI and PSI and their union affiliates can provide. For example, the Pan-European Equality Seminar held by EI in November 2008 in Bratislava, Slovakia brought together 30 participants from 15 different countries and addressed a range of topics from personal stories of harassment to successful strategies for challenging LGBT discrimination.[10]

Queer labor activists also find political opportunities in global alliances at international gay rights conferences such as the international Out@Work conference that grew out of—and subsequently extended—global/local networks of gay, lesbian, and transgender workers. Conference declarations and action plans stress the political necessity of challenging global homophobic sexual politics that allows the continued appalling working conditions of those who "live in countries that still execute their homosexual citizens" (Workers Online, 2002). The World Outgames plays a similar role in its regular international events that incorporate a conference on human rights at which the rights of LGBT workers are addressed. In Melbourne, Australia in 2008 a related conference, the Asia Pacific Outgames, produced a declaration on human rights that endorsed "Respect for, and access to, social, cultural, political and economic rights" (Melbourne OutGames, 2008). The next international conference (now framed as a human rights conference) was held in Copenhagen in 2009. Links are evident for example in the role of Rebecca Sevilla, who is a co-founder of gay and lesbian organizations in Lima and LGBT equity expert for the PSI-EI Sexual Diversity Forum, and was the honorary co-chair of the Copenhagen games (World Outgames, 2009). Such transnational networks have the capacity to be effective when they draw on trade union resources to create forums and spaces for lesbian, gay, and transgender workers.

THE TURN TO HUMAN RIGHTS: THE YOGYAKARTA PRINCIPLES

As many of the chapters in this volume indicate, the UN has a well-developed architecture for advancing social/economic rights for women. Union feminists have been effective in leveraging the discourses and resources of the UN, particularly those of the ILO, to advocate for the social/economic rights of women. They have played an important part in the struggles to make the UN responsive to women and reactive participants at various UN and ILO conferences and forums in shaping many of the norms, conventions, and instruments dealing with women's international human rights (Hawkesworth, 2006; Moghadam, 2005). Union feminists are positioned strategically to take advantage of UN resources to challenge the sexual politics of the labor movement and to challenge workplace discrimination.

Because the UN does not have a well-developed infrastructure to deal with LGBT rights, labor activists and trade unionists have not been able to leverage the discourses, mechanisms, and networks of the UN to articulate a coherent human rights agenda for the LGBT workers in quite the same way that feminists have. Although it is not surprising that founding UN human rights documents do not contain references to sexual orientation or gender identity, it is still noticeable that more recent efforts dealing with explicit forms of race and gender-based discrimination fail to do so. Neither the Committee on the Elimination of Discrimination against Women nor the Committee on the Elimination of Racial Discrimination directly addresses LGBT issues (Miller, 2009). The UN Human Rights Council (HRC) has erratically applied the principles of non-discrimination to some select cases. European bodies do little better. The European Court of Human Rights in its Convention for the Protection of Human Rights and Fundamental Freedoms while endorsing nondiscrimination and human rights for everyone has failed to construct an autonomous provision about LGBT human rights, instead choosing to uncritically accept such rights as "other status" (Article 14), as specified in 1966, by the UN International Covenant on Civil and Political Rights (ICCPR). Which adds other status to the list: "race, colour, sex, language, religion, political or other opinion, national or social origin, property, birth." Even states that have sought to promote the human rights of people of diverse sexual orientations and gender identities in international fora such as the UN have faced resistance. For example, the report says "When Brazil presented a resolution at the former UN Commission on Human Rights in 2003 condemning human rights violations based on sexual orientation, States opposed to consideration of the resolution brought a 'no action' motion in an attempt to prevent the Commission from considering the issue" (O'Flaherty & Fisher 2008, p. 229).

The first rulings by the UN to extend human rights protections based on sexual orientation came from Australia but not until 1994 when, in *Toonen v Australia*, the UN HRC ruled that criminal prohibitions on gay male sexual activity violated the right to privacy contained in Article 17 of the ICCPR. The following year an Australia organization, the Coalition of Activist Lesbians, gained official accreditation as an NGO by the UN Economic and Social Council. A series of reports by various Special Rapporteurs followed on topics such as torture, executions, detention, and HIV/AIDS that incorporated attention to human rights violations in these areas against sexual minorities. In 2005, the UN High Commissioner for Refugees extended the definition of refugees fleeing for fear of persecution based on membership of a social group to lesbians and gay men (O'Flaherty & Fisher, 2008).[11]

Progress at the international level has been slow and inconsistent and there is no coherent body of rulings or human rights jurisprudence to guide the understanding of human rights for the LGBT population. It is against this backdrop of weak human rights instruments and LGBT activism that human rights experts came to Yogyakarta, Indonesia in November 2006 to discuss and develop binding legal standards to govern the application of human rights for LGBT people. The key focus was the gap between what people were experiencing on the ground and existing human rights law and addressed the question of how existing law dealt with the very real violations of LGBT human rights. The experts were guided by the words of a South African high court judge who wrote, "The rights must fit people, not the people the rights. This requires looking at rights and their violations from a person-centered rather than a formula-based position, and analysing them contextually rather than abstractly" (Long, 2008). The meeting produced the Yogyakarta Principles (YP) on the Application of International Human Rights Law in relation to Sexual Orientation and Gender identity, a set of 29 principles and 16 additional recommendations governing LGBT human rights to governments, intergovernmental organizations, civil society, and the UN.

Before LGBT individuals could be viewed as persons before the law they had to be recognized as persons—on their own terms. Principle 3 of the YP states "Everyone has the right to recognition everywhere as a person before the law. . . . Each person's self-defined sexual orientation and gender identity is integral to the personality and is one of the most basic aspects of self-determination, dignity and freedom."[12] Other principles grant privacy rights, the right to bodily integrity, equality rights, the right to free speech, and the right to freedom of association. The latter two are important because they secure the rights of LGBT populations to advocate for their rights and to participate in governance to protect those rights. They also are of particular concern to queer labor activism because they are an integral part of workers' rights to organize unions and to engage in collective bargaining. So too are the principles that outlaw employment discrimination on the basis of sexual orientation and gender identity (Long, 2008).

There are serious limits to what the YP can accomplish. They were drafted so that they must be adaptable to legal systems and have jurisprudential value. Hence, "the desire for consistency with the existing law resulted in the deliberate omission from the final text of a number of elements that had been considered during the drafting phase. For instance, there is not expression of a right to non-heterosexual marriage. Instead, Principle 24 on the right to found a family, paragraph (e) only speaks of a right to non-discriminatory treatment of same-sex marriage in those States which already recognize it." The YP have found their way into UN meetings, into universities and civil society organizations, and into the GUFs like EI and PSI, giving them more substantial discursive tools to argue for the social/economic rights of LGBT workers. PSI and EI Websites discuss the YP and provide a link to the full text of the document. Unions, civil society, and the governments of Brazil, Argentina, and Uruguay sponsored a UN forum in New York in 2010 to discussion and promote the principles.

Human rights discourse and advocacy networks are being challenged by LGBT rights activists to be more inclusive and although slow, some significant changes have occurred that make human rights fertile terrain for queer labor activists. For example, on June 17, 2011 the UN HRC passed the first ever resolution on sexual orientation and gender identity. The resolution introduced by South Africa, Brazil, and 39 other countries requests a study to document discriminatory laws and practices and acts of violence against individuals based on their sexual orientation and gender identity, in all regions of the world, and how international human rights law can be used to end violence and related human rights violations based on sexual orientation and gender identity. (PDF available at http://www.scribd.com/doc/58106434/UN-Resolution-on-Sexual-Orientation-and-Gender-Identity.) The study will be the foundation for a panel discussion during the 19th session of the HRC with the goal of developing appropriate follow-up measures. The resolution passed by a vote of 23 in favor, 19 against, and 3 abstentions. Activists have expanded our notion of human rights both in terms of what they cover and to whom they apply. Yet there is still much more work to be done. There are problems with definitions of sexuality and rights, conflicts between national law and global standards, competition within equity-seeking groups over interpretation and implementation of human rights, conflicts between individual rights and collective rights, and clashes between secular and moral rationales for who is entitled to rights, and developing approaches and conventions that can address individuals with multiple identity statuses before the law.[13]

CONCLUSION

The labor movement is formally structured to represent the economic and political interests of workers at local, national, and international levels, and thus represents a valuable transnational resource for feminist and LGBT activists. Networks and alliances between trade unions and LGBT activists are vital; but for collaborations to be effective the heteronormative sexual politics of labor movements must be challenged and workers interests be reframed to integrate the social/economic rights of LGBT workers. In this way, the New Zealand Council of Trade Unions was able to build an Out@Work network that has maintained close links with the wider LGBT community through other organizations and community events. Carol Beaumont, the New Zealand CTU secretary, saw that networks are important for contacting LGBT workers "as invisibility in a workplace setting is a particular difficulty and of course is why the fight for visibility is so important. The community link is of importance as a model to the rest of the union movement as we recognize the need to more strongly campaign in the community if we are serious about building union strength" (Beaumont, 2006, p. 2).

Complete consensus is unnecessary, but without such groupings, activists involved in queer organizing risk isolation and burnout. Although LGBT workers benefit from queer union organizing, the labor movement also gains in relevance, energy, and growth. However, the potential political opportunities arising from such alliances cannot be realized without first analyzing and challenging the obstacles of sexual politics within the structures of labor, as discussed in this chapter.

With their critique of heteronormative social relations, queer activists and union feminists have the potential to revitalize and expand the boundaries of the labor movement by pushing unions to consider new forms of organizing, new types of workers and workplaces, and different types of issues.[14] In turn, unions have the potential to provide queer activists and feminists with resources to participate in transnational politics that aims to win political justice and the social/economic rights of LGBT workers around the world.

NOTES

1. This chapter draws on our research for our book, Making Feminist Politics; Transnational Alliances between Women and Labor, 2010 from the University of Illinois Press. This a much revised version of ideas we originally developed in "Queer Activism, Feminism & the Transnational Labor Movement," S&F ONLINE, 7.3 Summer 2009 at http://www.barnard.edu/bcrw/. The papers developed for this special issue were drawn from the workshop, "Toward a Vision of Social & Economic Justice," held at the Barnard Canter for Research on Women in the fall of 2007. The final report of the workshop is part of the Barnard's New Feminist Solutions (Vol. 4) series can be found at http://www.barnard.edu/bcrw/newfeministsolutions/index.htm.

2. For the value of self-organizing see the special Industrial Relations Journal, 37(4), 2006.

3. Fa'afafine is a Samoan term that literally means to be like a woman, and Takataapui is a Maori term to describe intimate friends of the same sex.

4. For a critique of how these mega events have become commodified see Binnie (2004).

5. A Global Union Federation (GUF) is an international federation of national unions organized by industry, sector, or occupation. Unions are members of

the global union federation in their sector. For example, a steelworker in the United States would belong to the United Steelworkers of America and that union would in turn belong to the International Metalworkers Federation—the GUF representing workers in steel, auto, electronics, and precision instruments. GUFs are peak labor bodies because they pull together workers from different unions and different countries. To read more about GUFs see http://www.global-unions.org/.

6. See PSI Website http://www.world-psi.org/ and Website http://www.ei-ie.org/en/index.php.

7. See EI Website http://www.ei-ie.org/lgbt/en/.

8. See EI Website http://www.ei-ie.org/lgbt/en/.

9. http://www.ei-ie.org/lgbt/en/newsshow.php?id=775&theme=sexual&country=global.

10. http://www.ei-ie.org/lgbt/en/newsshow.php?id=880&theme=sexual&country=global.

11. See UNHCR Guidance Notes on Refugee Claims Related to Sexual Orientation and Gender Identity on United States Department of Justice Website at http://www.justice.gov/eoir/vll/benchbook/resources/UNHCR_Guidelines_Sexual_Orientation.pdf.

12. See Website http://www.yogyakartaprinciples.org/.

13. See Miller (2009) for an extensive discussion of the challenges of incorporating rights for LGBT populations into existing human rights jurisprudence. Miller participated in the process of creating the Yogyakarta Principles and this paper was commissioned by International Council on Human Rights Policy.

14. For an excellent discussion of the way women are transforming the labor movement, see Cobble (2007).

REFERENCES

Armstrong, E., & Bernstein, M. (2008). Culture, power, and institutions: A multi-institutional politics approach to social movements. *Sociological Theory, 26,* 74–99.

Beaumont, C. (2006). Stamping out homophobia all over the world. In *UK Trades Union Congress Conference—Stamping out homophobia.* London: UK Trades Union Congress.

Bielski, M.L. (2005). *Identity at work: U.S. labor union efforts to address sexual diversity through policy and practice.* New Brunswick, NJ: Rutgers University Press.

Binnie, J. (2004). *The globalization of sexuality.* London: Sage.

Blandford, J. (2003). The nexus of sexual orientation and gender in the determination of earnings. *Industrial and Labor Relations Review, 56,* 622–642.

Briskin, L., & McDermott, P. (1993). *Women challenging unions: Feminism, democracy and militancy.* Toronto: Toronto University Press.

Bronfenbrenner, K. (2007). *Global unions: Challenging transnational capital through cross-border campaigns.* Ithaca, NY: ILR Press.

Butler, J. (2009). *Frames of war. When is life grievable?* London: Verso.

Cobble, D.S. (2004). *The other women's movement: Workplace justice and social rights in modern America*. Princeton, NJ and Oxford: Princeton University Press.

Cobble, D.S. (2007). *The sex of class: Women transforming American labor*. Ithaca, NY: Cornell University Press.

Colgan, F., Creegan, C., McKearney, A., & Wright, T. (2007). Equality and diversity policies and practices at work: lesbian, gay and bisexual workers. *Equal Opportunities International, 26*, 590–609.

Colgan, F., & Ledwith, S. (2002). *Gender, diversity and trade unions: International perspectives*. London: Routledge.

Collins, P.H. (2004). *Black sexual politics: African Americans, gender and the new racism*. New York: Routledge.

Connell, R. (1987). *Gender and power: Society, the person and sexual politics*. Sydney: Allen & Unwin.

Cruz-Malavé, A., & Manalansan, M.F. (2002). *Queer globalization: Citizenship and the afterlife of colonialsim*. New York: New York University Press.

Cunnison, S., & Stageman, J. (1995). *Feminizing the unions: Challenging the culture of masculinity*. Aldershot: Avebury.

Curtin, J. (1999). *Women and trade unions: A comparative perspective*. Sydney: Ashgate.

Duggan, L. (2003). Crossing the line: The Brandon Teena case and the social psychology of working class resentment *New Labor Forum, 12*, 37–44.

Education International (EI). (2007). *The rights of lesbian and gay teachers and education personnel*. Triennial Report 2004–2007. Brussels, Belgium: Education International.

Fonow, M.M. (2003). *Union women: Forging feminism in the United Steelworkers of America*. Minneapolis: University of Minnesota Press.

Fortescue, R. (2000). Mardi Gras: The biggest labor festival of the year. *Hecate, 26*, 62–65.

Franzway, S. (2001). *Sexual politics and greedy institutions: union women, commitments and conflicts in public and in private*. Sydney: Pluto Press Australia.

Franzway, S., & Fonow, M.M. (2011). *Making feminist politics; transnational alliances between women and labor*. Champaign: University of Illinois Press.

Genge, S. (1998). Solidarity and pride. *Canadian Women's Studies, 18*, 97–99.

Githens, R.P., & Aragon, S.R. (2009). LGBT employee groups: Goals and organizational structures. *Advances in Developing Human Resources, 11*, 121–135.

Hawkesworth, M.E. (2006). *Globalization and feminist activism*. Lanham, MD: Rowman & Littlefield.

Heery, E., & Conley, H. (2007). Frame extension in a mature social movement: British trade unions and part-time work, 1967–2002. *Journal of Industrial Relations, 49*, 5–29.

hooks, b. (2000). *Feminist theory from margin to center*. Cambridge, MA: South End Press.

Human rights, sexual orientation and gender identity. (2011). Human Rights Council, 17th session. United Nations General Assembly. June 15, 2011.

Hunt, G. (1999). *Laboring for rights: Unions and sexual diversity across nations*. Philadelphia: Temple University Press.

Hunt, G., & Boris, M.B. (2007). The lesbian, gay, bisexual, and transgender challenge to American labor. In D.S. Cobble (Eds.), *The sex of class: Women transforming American labor* (pp. 81–98). Ithaca, NY: Cornell University Press.

Hunt, G., & Haiven, J. (2006). Building democracy for women and sexual minorities: Union embrace of diversity. *Relations Industrielles, 61*, 666–682.

International Labour Organization (ILO). (2007). *Equality at work: Tackling the challenges* (Report of the Director-General. Global Report under the follow-up to the ILO Declaration on Fundamental Principles and Rights at Work). Geneva: Author.

ILO Helpdesk. (2009). *Eliminating discrimination in the workplace*. Retrieved November 10, 2009 (www.ilo.org/wcmsp5/groups/public/---ed.../wcms_116342.pdf-).

Irwin, J. (1999). *"The pink ceiling is too low": Workplace experiences of lesbians, gay men and transgender people*. http://www.arts.usyd.edu.au/Arts/departs/social/jirwinpub. Retrieved March 7, 2011.

Katzenstein, M.F. (1998). *Faithful and fearless: Moving feminist protest inside the church and military*. Princeton, NJ: Princeton University Press.

Krupat, K., & McCreery, P. (2001). *Out at work: Building a gay-labor alliance*. Minneapolis: University of Minnesota Press.

Ledwith, S. (2006). The future as female? Gender, diversity and global labour solidarity. In C. Phelan (Ed.), *The future of organised labour* (pp. 91–134). Oxford: Peter Lang.

Long, S. (2007). Two Novembers: Movements, rights, and the Yogyakarta Principles. *Human Rights Watch*.

McCreery, P., & Krupat, K. (1999). Introduction. Out front: Lesbians, gays, and the struggle for workplace rights. *Social Text, 17*, 1–8.

Melbourne OutGames. (2008). *Melbourne Declaration of Human Rights*. Retrieved November 13, 2009 http://www.melbourneoutgames.org/.

Milkman, R. (2005). Labor unions. In G. Mink, M. Navarro, W. Mankiller, B. Smith, & G. Steinem (Eds.), *The reader's companion to U.S. women's history* (pp. 302–304). New York: Houghton Mifflin.

Millett, K. (1969). *Sexual politics*. New York: Avon Books.

Miller, A. M. (2009). *Sexuality and Human Rights*, International Council on Human Rights Policy. Versoix, Switzerland: International Council on Human Rights Policy.

Mogdaham, V.M. (2005). *Globalizing women: transnational feminist networks*. Baltimore: Johns Hopkins University Press.

O'Flaherty, M., & Fisher, J. (2008). Sexual orientation, gender identity and international human rights law: Contextualising the Yogyakarta Principles. *Human Rights Law Review, 8*, 207–248.

Parker, J. (2006). Towards equality and renewal: Women's groups, diversity and democracy in British unions. *Economic and Industrial Democracy, 27*, 425–462.

Public Service International (PSI). (2010). *About PSI*. http://www.world-psi.org/. Retrieved June 3, 2011.

Ragins, B.R., Cornwell, J.M., & Miller, J.S. (2003). Heterosexism in the workplace. *Group and Organization Management, 28*, 45–74.

Rucht, D. (1996). The impact of national contexts on social movement structures: A cross-movement and cross-national comparison. In D. McAdam, J.D. McCarthy, & M.N. Zald (Eds.), *Comparative perspectives on social movements: Political opportunities, mobilizing structures, and cultural framings* (pp. 185–204). Cambridge: Cambridge University Press.

Rupp, L.J., & Taylor, V. (2003). *Drag queens at the 801 Cabaret*. Chicago: University of Chicago Press.

Seidman, S. (1997). *Difference troubles: Queering social theory and sexual politics* Cambridge: Cambridge University Press.

Snow, D., & Benford, R. (1992). Master frames and cycles of protest. In A. Morris & C.M. Mueller (Eds.), *Frontiers in social movement theory* (pp. 133–154). New Haven, CT: Yale University Press.

Staggenborg, S., & Lang, A. (2007). Culture and ritual in the Montreal women's movement. *Social Movement Studies, 6*, 177–194.

Taylor, V., Kimport, K., Van Dyke, N., & Andersen, E.A. (2009). Culture and mobilization: Tactical repertoires, same-sex weddings, and the impact on gay activism. *American Sociological Review, 74*, 865–890.

Towart, N. (2002). Mardi Gras: The biggest labour festival? *Workers Online.*

United Nations. (1966). *International Covenant on Civil and Political Rights Article 14 and Article 17.* http://treaties.un.org/Pages/ViewDetails.aspx?src=TREATY&mtdsg_no=IV-4&chapter=4&lang=en. Retrieved July 3, 2011.

Workers Online. (2002). *Workers Out For Gay Games.* Retrieved August 15, 2007 http, //workers.labor.net.au/139/news83_gay.html.

World Outgames. (2009). *World Outgames conference.* Retrieved November 13, 2009 http://www.copenhagen2009.org/.

Wright, T., Colgan, F., Creegan, C., & McKearney, A. (2006). Lesbian, gay and bisexual workers: Equality, diversity and inclusion in the workplace. *Equal Opportunities International, 25*, 465–470.

FIFTEEN

NE'ER THE TWAIN SHALL MEET?

Reflections on the Future of Feminism and Unionism

Jennifer Curtin

The contributions to this volume reveal a multitude of pressures and possibilities for advancing gender equality in the labor market, as a result of, and despite, the advent of globalization. Trade unions and other social and political movements have (re)claimed the concept of social rights, an umbrella concept under which demands for full economic citizenship (read as decent work and equality in outcomes) can be advanced on behalf of women workers (among others).

In practice, all the chapters demonstrate the various ways that feminist activism (scholarly and grass-roots in form), transnationally and within states (developed and developing), has targeted labor movements and sought to engage the latter in what Moghadam (this volume) calls "difficult dialogues" around the gender-specific claims and "interests" of women workers. Moreover, it is evident that women remain an important resource for trade unions as potential members: The feminization of labor markets, formal and informal, once heralded as a new phenomenon (Jensen, Hagen, & Reddy, 1988) has become a permanent process, unlikely to disappear any time soon. Not surprisingly then, there has been a growth in the number of women workers joining trade unions cross-nationally, which has been replicated, albeit only partially, by an increase in women's representation within union hierarchies.

Moghadam's chapter suggests that it is feminist organizations that are most obvious in their activism around women's rights as workers, both social and economic—working with trade unions, but these organizations also act as the conscience of unionism, reminding and demanding the labor movement to recognize that it is no longer viable to view the "economic citizen" in terms of a male norm. In a sense, feminism is the conscience of unionism and, as a corollary of this, it often is the work of feminists within unions that leads to the substantive representation of women's claims and "interests"—activism that, although diverse in both approach and outcome, transcends the north–south divide.

There clearly are many success stories evident in this volume, but one underlying theme that cuts across all is the tension that remains between feminism and unionism despite both being movements aimed at the pursuit of universal social, economic, and political rights. In this chapter, I reflect further on this tension or divide.

Several manifestations of what might constitute the "divide" between feminism and unionism come to mind. The first and perhaps the most obvious is the complex and sometimes hostile historical relationship that has existed between feminism and unionism over the past century, reflective of the debates over the primacy of class oppression versus patriarchal oppression. On the one hand, trade unionists often have been suspicious of women's movements in their various guises, assuming they would dilute and fragment the class struggle and ultimately advance the cause of middle-class women at the expense of working-class women. On the other hand, feminists were not wrong to view trade unions as patriarchal institutions. There is ample literature that demonstrates the antipathy many trade unions exhibited toward the notion of women's permanent presence in the labor market, equal pay, women's representation, and with equal/different treatment of the sexes more generally. Remnants of this divide remain.

The second is the disciplinary divide that works to marginalize scholarship on labor movements and feminism. For example, within the discipline of political science (and international relations), trade unions as institutions seem to fall between the two analytical categories of state and civil society. Analyses of state tend to focus on the formal institutions of government and the political parties that make up those governments. Although labor movements have a connection with many labor and social democratic parties in government, they are not themselves considered to be "political" institutions. Rather, they are incorporated as "old" forms of interest groups and contrasted with the "new" groups associated with new social movements and "identity" politics (of which the women's movement is one). The renewed scholarly interest by political scientists in (global) civil society often has tended to overlook the capacity of trade unions in advanced Western democracies, to participate in advancing the claims and interests of citizens generally (and women in particular).

There are notable exceptions of course, including those scholars interested in explaining differences in comparative public policy whereby trade
union density and centralization were variables incorporated in models that
sought to explain cross-national variation in macro-economic policy and
welfare state outcomes (Boreham & Compston, 1992; Compston. 1994).[1]
However, in the main, the traditional view of what constituted "the political" (the ideas, institutions, and processes constituting the official political
process), meant trade unions tended to be classified as "industrial" or "economic" rather than inherently "political" institutions.

Additionally, this traditional perspective on politics meant that gender
inequality in the distribution of political power and the gendered nature of
the performance of politics in the public arena was left unchallenged until
feminist scholars and activists took up the cause. This feminist challenge
has incorporated two dimensions: The first, to increase women's presence
in the practice and imagining of formal politics and second, to redefine
and extend the concept of the "political" in order to better recognize and
value the often informal political participation by women in civil society
(Squires, 1999, p. 195).

Accepting this broader notion of the political reveals that women have
long been political actors. Much attention is given to the ways women have
been active in protest activity outside of the state through the women's liberation, peace, civil rights, and ecology movements. Women also have been
involved in groups that have targeted oppressive state structures and issues
that cut across national borders (Squires, 1999). By contrast, traditional
mainstream political institutions were viewed by some feminist theorists and
activists as inappropriate avenues for women's energies. They were deemed
male bastions of patriarchal power, and seeking change from within would
not advance a feminist project.

As a result, there is a third divide between feminism and unionism that
appears within feminist (political) thought. In discussions about advancing
gender equality, and in particular about how feminist activism in local and
global civil society might seek to transform the position of women in work
and society, women's activism within the trade union movement often is
forgotten. Although there is a small but significant body of scholarship that
focuses on feminist activism within labor movements (Briskin, 1993; Cobble,
2004; Colgan & Ledwith, 2002; Cook, Lorwin, & Daniels, 1992; Curtin,
1999; Fonow, 2003; Franzway, 2001; Kessler-Harris 2007; Munro, 1999, etc.),
in the main, the concentration on "first," "second," and "third" waves of
feminism has worked to eclipse the multiple forms of feminist activity that
have occurred over the past century, including labor feminism (Cobble,
2004). Thus, in a sense, this "oppositional" way of understanding what
constitutes the "political" for women has served to obscure the potentially

transformative politics of women's activism within trade unions. The work of this volume makes an important contribution in bringing to light the substantive nature of these transformations and what they might mean for labor movements in the future. In this chapter, I explore how we might bridge these divides by revisiting the way we think about the practice of labor movement feminism. First, I briefly review the way in which feminist strategies have been articulated in discussions of gender and political theory and explore the difficulties associated with categorizing strategies of inclusion as inherently nontransformative. Second, I revisit some of the practices of inclusion adopted by women union activists with a particular focus on the strategies of separate organizing and women's representation and reflect on how these might be interpreted as potentially transformative. I conclude by suggesting that the practice of labor movement feminism in both the recent and more distant past has much to offer the way we think about feminist politics, and about how feminism might continue to inform and challenge and unionism.

REFLECTIONS ON THE CATEGORIZATION OF FEMINIST STRATEGIES

There have been a number of different categorizations of feminist strategies in political theory. Here I examine briefly the analytical map developed by Squires (1999) but similar maps have been created by Ferguson (1993) and DiStefano (1990). Squires argues that the conceptualization of feminist political strategies within feminist (political) theory has tended to fall into three camps. The first includes those who argue for women's inclusion into mainstream politics; it creates problems with women's exclusion, focuses on achieving women's equality with men (gender neutrality) and is usually associated with liberal feminists. The second category refers to what have become labeled "radical" feminist strategies. It includes those who argue for recognition of women's difference (and therefore strategies of reversal), male advantage is problematic and the normative task to reconstruct politics in such a way that reveals the distinctive perspective and becomes more open to gender specificity. Third, there is the diversity approach, which (only partly) emerges in response to the oppositional position of equality differ-ence articulated by the liberal and radical strategies. It is primarily associated with post-structuralism and postmodernist feminism, and its proponents view the gendered world as the contentious issue; thus a strategy of displacement that would reveal the extent to which gendered identities are themselves products of discursive regimes (Squires, 1999).

Squires acknowledges that this process of categorization leads to the development of archetypes, and as such, in practice these three approaches are not mutually exclusive. However, she is clear in her argument that only the strategies of reversal and displacement have transformative potential. Indeed, at least theoretically, it is argued that the displacement principle is the most crucial component of any policy aimed at transforming gender inequalities (Verloo, 2005). By contrast, the strategy of inclusion is fundamentally integrationist, and as such might "further entrench the underlying premises of the patriarchal order, perpetuate its logic, and thereby prolong its dominance" (p. 346).[2]

Feminist strategies associated with including women in formal politics often have focused on women's representation. For example, it has been argued that women's interests, although not necessarily objective or fixed, still need to be represented by women. It is suggested that specific interests and needs that arise from women's experiences would not be adequately addressed in a politics dominated by men (Jonasdottir, 1988; Phillips, 1995). Phillips argues that challenges to ideas about an objective set of interests shared by all women, do not undermine, but strengthen, the case for increasing the number of women representatives. If women's interests are varied, fluid, or still in the process of formation, it is difficult to separate out what is to be represented from who is to do the representation. Representation in this situation is about the formulation of identities and interests as well as how they are represented. As a result, there is a stronger case for more women as representatives to help define areas of concern and construct appropriate policies (Phillips, 1991; cf. Saward, 2006). As such, women's inclusion in formal political institutions has the potential to be viewed as a strategy of displacement.

The male dominance of trade unions, often both at membership and at executive levels, has meant that it is men who have tended to dominate the definition of the interests taken up by trade unions. It is debatable as to whether male unionists can represent the interests of women workers without awareness or comprehension of what those interests are. In this sense, it could be argued that women are needed within leadership positions to provide awareness and to allow for women's interests to surface, thereby altering the discursive contexts through which women's interests are constituted. Many of the contributions to this volume reinforce this point—highlighting how, when women have control of the union agenda, whether in new or existing unions, the social rights of women at work and elsewhere are more likely to be addressed.

It is impossible for women in union hierarchies to represent the interests of all women. As Gatens (1996) argues, there are real limits to empathizing with, and gaining an understanding of, the specific and total context of the lives of those seeking representation. A practical solution, suggests Gatens, may be one where women are represented at all levels of legal, social, and political life. Including women from a range of occupations, industries, and identities as representatives within union hierarchies would at least ensure a voice for a broad range of working women's interests (although Briskin, this volume, is somewhat skeptical of placing too much weight on this prospect).

A second feminist strategy aimed at inclusion is that of separate organizing by women (Briskin, 1999). It can be interpreted as inclusive when the organizing occurs within a preexisting (political) organization (e.g., a trade union), or one of reversal if outside "formal" political institutions. Brown (1991) argues that a new feminist politics requires the cultivation of political spaces for posing and arguing about feminist political norms, for discussing the nature of the good for women and for developing a discourse on justice. She suggests such political spaces are scarcer and thinner today. And yet within the trade union movement cross-nationally, the creation of women's networks, committees, and councils, as well as women-only union education, has continued to increase since the 1970s. As authors in this volume reveal, such spaces provide women workers with the opportunity to develop their skills and ultimately allow for a variety of women's voices to be heard (see also Blaschke, 2003; Briskin, 1993; Cobble, 2007; Colgan & Ledwith, 2002; Cook, 1991; Fonow, 2003; Ledwith, 2006; Kirton & Healy, 2004; A. McBride, 2001).

Brown (1991) argues that although such spaces require elements of definition and protection, they cannot be "clean sharply bounded disembodied or permanent: They would be heterogeneous, roving, non-institutionalized and democratic to the point of exhaustion" (p. 80). Yet it does not necessarily follow that the institutionalization of separate spaces for women within trade unions has proved constraining for women unionists. Indeed, Brown's position seems to imply that it is the institution rather than the voices spoken within the institution that is important. Yet, if women's networks and committees within trade unions allow for continuing and varied discussions on what strategies should be pursued to improve the position of women workers, this is likely to be useful to the process of formulating and representing women's interests. Cook (1984) maintains that where women "have an organizational home within the unions—formal or informal, existing by union statute or custom, independent or dependent—they eventually seek ways to gain political skills, educate their male colleagues, and claim their representational rights" (p 19). It is impossible to claim that separate spaces either succeed or fail by virtue of being separate; rather the ability of women trade unionists to have their demands voiced, heard, and addressed is dependent on a complex set of contextual circumstances, including the governmental structure of the union confederation. Nevertheless, it is women's agency that has provided them with political space within trade unions;

women have agency within this space, which is an important strategy in the process of formulating and making claims.

Thus, although separate spaces for women may be institutionalized, or even marginalized by the trade union hierarchies at various points in time, institutionalization in itself should not be viewed as negative. Indeed, just as women's interests and claims are viewed as dynamic, so are the discursive contexts within which they are formulated: agendas change, those partici-pating change and such spaces may often be a window of opportunity for women to participate in agenda setting and to alter the discursive frame-works through which women's claims are constituted. As such, they have the capacity to provide women workers with the opportunity to organize themselves as a nonhegemonic counter public, whereby a space is provided for women to struggle about the agenda of gender equality in the labor market (cf. Fraser, 1989, 1997; see also Verloo, 2005).

Thinking about women's separate organizing and claims for represen-tation in this way suggests that although such strategies are based on the principle of inclusion they are not necessarily integrationist, but actually may have the potential to be construed as transformative. In pursuing this line of thought, the work of Jahan (1995, pp. 12–13) is insightful.[3] In her analysis of mainstreaming women in development Jahan uses an analytical framework that distinguishes between objectives of integration on the one hand and agenda setting on the other. Like Squires, Jahan takes integra-tion to refer to the goal of equality with men, whereby gender issues are taken up within existing (development) paradigms, offering little challenge to the prevailing system. As such, the overall (development) agenda is not transformed. By contrast, the agenda-setting approach implies "the trans-formation of the existing (development) agenda with a gender perspective" drawing from women's voices. This transformation requires the inclusion and participation of women as intimately involved in determining priorities. Women's participation at all levels of the agenda-setting process ultimately enables the reorientation of the dominant or preexisting paradigm. Thus, unlike Squires, Jahan's analytical frame allows one to view the activism of labor movement feminism as potentially transformative despite its guiding principle being one of inclusion. This is especially so given the strategy of separate organizing within the union movement provides women with space to generate, deliberate, and articulate their (nonhegemonic) interests, in order to then challenge the "traditional" industrial/political agenda of their trade unions. Moreover, as the chapters in this volume suggest, trans-formation can be interpreted as personal as well as "structural"—the work of unions and feminist activists in collaboration, can make a difference socially and materially to the lives of individual women (see also Parker, 2002; Rees, 1998).

REFLECTIONS ON LABOR-FEMINIST STRATEGIES

Women in the labor movement have a long history of seeking to have their interests as workers included on trade union agenda.[4] Initially, inclusion was prohibited, and so women were forced to organize separately. In a number of industrialized countries, women-only unions were established in several sectors, including the textile and clothing industries, and among waitresses, laundresses, and retail clerks (Balser, 1987; Boston, 1987; Dye, 1980; Kessler-Harris, 2007; T. McBride, 1985; Meyerowitz, 1985; Street, 1994). In Australia, the first women's union, the Victorian Tailoresses Union, was created in 1882 and, after 1890, more women's unions were established, some of which were restricted to a single occupation, whereas others spanned several occupational groups (Ryan & Prendergast, 1982). However, the arbitration system established in 1904 stifled the continued development of women's unions. Registered unions gained the sole right to represent employees in their particular industry or occupation and women usually lacked the precise coverage of a distinct occupational or industry group required by the courts. In New South Wales, domestic workers were excluded as an occupation eligible for registration, thus prohibiting union representation in this area of work where women dominated (Ryan & Prendergast, 1982).

In Austria, women who were excluded or ejected from membership in existing unions established their own, with the Association of Women Teachers and Governesses set up in 1870 and the Association of Women Postal Officials created in 1876. In 1901, the Union of Working Women was founded to represent women officials in banks, railways, insurance, and legal offices, as well as secretaries, typists, commercial employees, shop workers, seamstresses, and tobacco sellers (Anderson, 1992). Despite separate organizing by women's groups being seen as a bourgeois threat to working-class solidarity in Sweden, women in blue-collar occupations did initially organize themselves into women-only unions, which were ultimately absorbed by male-unions. In the white-collar sector, Swedish women had created national trade unions for nurses, schoolteachers, and women in the postal and telecommunications service and academic women. These women-only unions continued to exist until amalgamations began around 1955 (Qvist, 1985).

Apart from women-only unions, toward the end of the 19th century, reformist umbrella organizations were created whereby women activists sought to encourage trade unionism among women. In Britain, the Women's Protective and Provident League, the Women's Trade Union League (WTUL) and the Women's Trade Union Association were established (Boston, 1987; Lewenhak, 1977; Soldon, 1985) while the WTUL in the United States had branches across the country (Drake, 1920; Dye, 1980). These organizations resulted from alliances between working-class and middle-class women who saw themselves as both feminists and union-ists. The women in these organizations believed that women of all classes working together could organize women into trade unions and persuade the labor movement to include women in its ranks (Dye, 1980).

Although mobilization of women workers was encouraged through strike action and labor negotiations, other strategies focused on women's experiences. The WTUL in the United States emphasized the community as well as workplace, with visits to women's homes, providing places for young women to meet, and sponsoring afternoon teas and storytelling sessions (Hyman, 1985). In this way, advantage was taken of the already existing networks among women, as well as creating new ones in order to facilitate women's collective actions (Hyman, 1985). Such organizations also provided educational programs for women workers and special publications (Hyman, 1985; Lewenhak, 1977; T. McBride, 1985).

Over time, the relationship between women and the labor movement changed, with recognition by trade unions that the (permanent) presence of women in the labor market was inevitable. Women's unions gradually merged with general or male unions and the various women's trade union leagues were absorbed or disbanded and separate organization of women workers outside of the mainstream trade union movement became less common (for exceptions see Balser, 1987; Cobble, 1990, 1993; Milkman, 1985). However, as the chapters in this volume by Kaye Broadbent, Michal Schwartz, and Graciela DiMarco, among others make clear, union feminists are not afraid of pursuing a separatist organizing strategy on behalf of women.

Moreover, when women's unions were incorporated into male unions this did not necessarily quieten women unionists. In 1920, Barbara Drake argued that although mixed unions were the best option for women workers, their interests and point of view "tend to be if not actually overlooked, yet accounted as of secondary importance" (p. 213). To remedy this, she noted that the most commonly adopted devices put in place were the all-women's branch, the reservation of places for women on management committees and the women's advisory council (Drake, 1920). The role of the latter was to provide a real means of expression to women members, encourage women to be active in branch affairs, and promote their election through education and propaganda (Drake, 1920; Soldon, 1985). Although such strategies have not always been viewed as constructive by (male) unionists, contributors to this volume indicate that they remain a means to mobilize women workers and to increase the participation and representation of women within trade unions (see also, Briskin, 1999, 2006; Cobble, 2004; Fonow, 2003; Gabin, 1990; T. McBride, 1985; Soldon, 1985; Trebilcock, 1991).

In addition to the strategy of separate organizing, there has been an increased emphasis given to the explicit representation of women within trade union hierarchies, and a range of strategies implemented to facilitate this outcome. Women's conferences, committees, departments and officers, new approaches to union business, education for women workers, consciousness-raising through networks, the advocacy of such goals by international organizations, proportional representation, and reserved seats on executive bodies or other affirmative action policies (Briskin, 2006; Curtin, 1999; Ledwith, Colgan, Joyce, & Hayes, 2007).

Some of these strategies have received a mixed response from women trade unionists. In Sweden, the class tradition has complicated any discussion of special representation of women by women, with such strategies often viewed as (too) feminist and divisive to class solidarity (Curtin & Higgins, 1998). Similarly, in Austria, despite the existence of a reserved seat on the executive, the issue of quotas and affirmative action measures remains contested, with women unionists instead actively seeking to recruit more women as negotiators and shop stewards (see also, Blaschke, 2003).

By contrast, in Australia, union feminists have actively sought affirmative action strategies, and viewed them as necessary to increase women's representation (Caine & Pringle, 1995; Pocock, 1997; Shute, 1994). In 1991, the Australian Council of Trade Unions set a target of 50% women representation by the turn of the century and as a first step established three affirmative action places on its executive. This, combined with the election of two woman presidents and women leaders representing several women-dominated unions, has led to a substantial increase over the past two decades in the number of women present at executive level.

Women unionists in Sweden, Austria, and Australia have acknowledged that the presence of women in the upper echelons of trade unions does not guarantee the representation of all interests important to all women workers (Curtin, 1997, 1999). Nor has the strategy of gendered representation come with the assumption that there exists an overarching and fixed common interest between women workers. Rather, there is an explicit acceptance that women's class and gender interests are intersected by a multiplicity of other interests and identities. Nevertheless, having women in decision-making positions has been considered by women unionists as necessary in transforming internal trade union agenda and reconfiguring the gendered dimensions of labor market participation (Cobble, 2007; Ledwith et al., 2007).

LABOR-FEMINISM: BRIDGING THE INTEGRATIONIST-TRANSFORMATIVE DIVIDE

Labor-feminist strategies aimed at including women within the trade union movement are a century-old tradition. Part of the "appeal" of women's divisions was that they often were seen by trade unions as an acceptable means of incorporating and addressing the "woman question" without undermining the overriding cause of national or labor unity. Such divisions were seldom accorded any "official" institutional power, but this is not how women themselves read their role. There were (many) times when women's concerns were subordinated to those of class, but this was not a process in which women were necessarily passive (Broadbent, 2003, this volume). Elsewhere I have documented how, in many cases, women chose to prioritize the generic working-class political interest over the gender-specific, since it was thought that benefits would flow to both men and women with the arrival of socialism. Moreover, women's power resources were limited and establishing regulated wages and working conditions was difficult without the support of their male colleagues (Curtin, 1999).

The creation of separate spaces for the representation of women's interests has not been a fixed strategy. The disappearance and reappearance of gender-specific strategies by women unionists in Sweden and the creation of explicitly feminist women's spaces in Australian unions over the last three decades suggests that trade unions have been perceived by women unionists as remiss in addressing the interests of women workers (see also Franzway, 2000).

Although the structural positioning of women's representative spaces is relevant to the discursive integration of women's interests in industrial relations, the marginal status of such spaces does not necessarily equate with powerlessness. Nor does the fact that women's divisions are seldom accorded institutional power within the trade union hierarchy remove women's collective action as a possible strategy for empowerment. Indeed, conceiving of women's collective actions as without power precludes the identification of more local, partial and emerging acts of empowerment. At various times, women's sections in a number of countries have facilitated contact with women at the grass-roots level and have proven an important contact for women working in isolated or unorganized occupations. Women's committees and officers also have been critical in the gathering and dissemination of information, in politicizing women's claims and, along with women's conferences, have provided a space for women to discuss policies and formulate strategies that inform the agenda-setting process within trade unions. These strategies of inclusion are not necessarily integrationist. Although we are yet to see a total transformation of the inequalities experienced by women in the labor market, the intention of labor-feminists in advocating such strategies has been one more closely associated with the goal of transformation.

So what do these strategies contribute to a bridging of the multiple divides I identified in the introduction to this chapter? First, I would suggest that developments in both feminism and unionism (at the level of ideas and practice) have gone beyond debates about hierarchies of oppression (see also Ledwith, 2006). And both "movements" have had to deal with crises of "membership" and confidence in an era where globalism, individualism, and neoliberalism undermine the capacity for collective strategies. As such, it is almost common sense that the movements pool their ideas and resources to protect and promote the rights of (women) workers. Second, in revisiting what constitutes the political, scholars in political science need to be reminded of the importance of trade unions and their representative capacity as both political and industrial institutions. This is particularly important given the increasing professionalization of politics and the way in which trade unions continue to operate as training grounds for aspiring politicians (both women and men). Similarly, feminist scholars (in political science in particular) need to be reminded that trade unions are a vital part of civil society and a site of significant feminist activity that warrants attention. As such, as scholars interested in both unionism and feminism we need to remind those involved in the study of politics and feminism that the practice of labor feminism has important implications for the ways in which we conceive of feminist politics.

NOTES

1. However, trade union strength is not always used as a variable. Instead, strength of the left is operationalized by focusing on the left-wing governments. There are methodological reasons why both variables cannot be included, but it nevertheless serves to reinforce the notion the discipline of political science has tended to overlook trade unions (see, e.g., Castles, 2007; Norris, 1987).

2. Squires notes that the reversal-difference strategy may entrench gendered norms. She also elaborates on the difficulties with designing a normative project out of the diversity/displacement strategy.

3. The work of Verloo (2005) on conceptualizing gender mainstreaming as a displacement strategy with transformative potential helped inform my thinking for this part of the chapter.

4. I expand on the range of strategies and (contingent) solidarities used by women unionists in four countries in Curtin (1999).

REFERENCES

Anderson, H. (1992). *Utopian feminism: Women's movements in fin-de-siècle Vienna.* New Haven, CT: Yale University Press.

Balser, D. (1987). *Sisterhood and solidarity: Feminism and labor in modern times.* Boston: South End Press.

Blaschke, S. (2003, September). *Austrian trade unions: Towards mainstreaming gender.* Paper presented at IIRA, 13th World Congress, Berlin.

Boreham, P., & Compston, H. (1992). Labour movement organisation and political intervention. *European Journal of Political Research, 22*, 143–170.

Boston, S. (1987). *Women workers and the trade unions.* London: Lawrence & Wishart.

Briskin, L. (1993). Union women and separate organising. In L. Briskin & P. McDermott (Eds.), *Women challenging unions: Feminism, democracy and militancy* (pp. 89–108). Toronto: University of Toronto Press.

Briskin, L. (1999). Autonomy, diversity and integration: Union women's separate organizing in North America and western Europe in the context of restructuring and globalization *Women's Studies International Forum, 22*, 543–554.

Briskin, L. (2006). Victimisation and agency: The social construction of union women's leadership. *Industrial Relations Journal, 37*(4), 359–378.

Broadbent, K. (2003). *Women's employment in Japan. The experience of part-time workers.* London: Routledge/Curzon.

Brown, W. (1991). Feminist hesitations, postmodern exposures. *Differences: A Journal of Feminist Cultural Studies, 3*, 63–94.

Caine, B., & Pringle, R. (Eds.). (1995). *Transitions: New Australian feminisms.* St. Leonards, Australia: Allen & Unwin.

Castles, F.G. (Ed.). (2007). *The disappearing state? Retrenchment realities in an age of globalisation.* Cheltenham: Edward Elgar.

Cobble, D.S. (1990). Rethinking troubled relations between women and unions: Craft unionism and women activism. *Feminist Studies, 16*(3), 519–544.

Cobble, D.S. (1993). Introduction: Remaking the unions for the new majority. In D.S. Cobble (Ed.), *Women and unions: Forging a partnership* (pp. 1–18). Ithaca, NY: ILR Press.

Cobble, D.S. (2004). *The other women's movement.* Princeton, NJ: Princeton University Press.

Cobble, D.S. (Ed.). (2007). *The sex of class. Women transforming American labor.* Ithaca NY: Cornell University Press.

Colgan F., & Ledwith, S. (Ed.). (2002). *Gender, diversity and trade unions. International perspectives.* New York: Routledge.

Compston, H. (1994). Union participation in economic policy-making in Austria, Switzerland, The Netherlands, Belgium and Ireland, 1970–1992. *West European Politics, 17*, 123–145.

Cook, A. (1984). Introduction. In A. Cook, V. Lorwin, & A.K. Daniels (Eds.), *Women and trade unions in eleven industrialised countries* (pp. 3–33). Philadelphia: Temple University Press.

Cook, A. (1991). Women and minorities. In G. Strauss, D.G. Gallagher, & J. Fiorito (Eds.), *The state of the unions* (pp. 237–258). Madison, WI: Industrial Relations Research Association.

Cook, A., Lorwin, V., & Daniels, A.K. (1992). *The most difficult revolution.* Ithaca, NY: Cornell University Press.

Curtin, J. (1997). Engendering union democracy: Comparing Sweden and Australia. In M. Sverke (Ed.), *The future of unionism. International perspectives on emerging union structures* (pp. 195–210). Aldershot, UK: Ashgate.

Curtin, J. (1999). *Women and trade unions: A comparative perspective*. Aldershot, UK: Ashgate.

Curtin, J., & Higgins, W. (1998). Feminism and unionism in Sweden. *Politics and Society, 26*, 69–94.

Di Stefano, C. (1990). *Dilemmas of difference: Feminism, modernity, and postmodernism*. New York/London: Routledge.

Drake, B. (1920). *Women in trade unions*. London: Virago.

Dye, N.S. (1980). *As equals and as sisters: Feminism, the labor movement, and the Women's Trade Union League of New York*. Columbia: University of Missouri Press.

Ferguson, K. (1993). *The man question. Visions of subjectivity in feminist theory*. Berkeley: University of California Press.

Fonow, M.M. (2003). *Union women. Forging feminism in the United Steelworkers of America*. Minneapolis: University of Minnesota Press.

Franzway, S. (2000). Sisters and sisters? Labour movements and women's movements in (English) Canada and Australia. *Hecate, 26*(2), 31–45.

Franzway, S. (2001). *Sexual politics and greedy institutions*. Annandale: Pluto Press.

Fraser, N. (1989). *Unruly practices: Power, discourse and gender in contemporary social theory*. Oxford: Polity Press.

Fraser, N. (1997). *Justice interruptus: Ccritical reflections on the postsocialist condition*. New York: Routledge.

Gabin, N. (1990). *Feminism in the labor movement: Women and the United Auto Workers*. Ithaca, NY: Cornell University Press.

Gatens, M. (1996). *Imaginary bodies: Ethics, power and corporeality*. London: Routledge.

Hyman, C.A. (1985). Labor organizing and female institution-building: The Chicago Women's Trade Union League, 1904–24. In R. Milkman (Ed.), *Women, work and protest. A century of US women's labor history* (pp. 22–41). Boston: Routledge & Kegan Paul.

Jahan, R. (1995). *The elusive agenda*. London: Zed Books.

Jenson, J., Hagen, E., & Reddy, C. (Eds.). (1988). *Feminization of the labor force: Paradoxes and promises*. Cambridge: Polity Press.

Jonasdottir, A.G. (1988). On the concept of interest, women's interests, and the limitations of interest theory. In K.B. Jones & A.G. Jonasdottir (Eds.), *The political interests of gender* (pp. 33–65). London: Sage.

Kessler-Harris, A. (2007). *Gendering labor history*. Chicago: University of Illinois Press.

Kirton, G., & Healy, G. (2004). Shaping union and gender identities: A cast study of women-only trade union courses. *British Journal of Industrial Relations, 42*(2), 303–323.

Ledwith, S. (2006). Feminist praxis in a trade union gender project. *Industrial Relations Journal, 37*(4), 379–399.

Ledwith, S., Colgan, F., Joyce, P., & Hayes, M. (2007). The making of women trade union leaders. *Industrial Relations Journal, 21*(2), 112–125.

Lewenhak, S. (1977). *Women and trade unions: An outline history of women in the British Trade Union Movement*. London: Benn.

McBride, A. (2001). *Gender democracy in trade unions*. Aldershot: Ashgate.

McBride, T. (1985). French women and trade unionism: The first hundred years. In N.C. Soldon (Ed.), *The world of women's trade unionism* (pp. 35–56). Westport, CT: Greenwood Press.

Meyerowitz, R. (1985). Organizing the United Automobile Workers: Women workers at the Ternstedt General Motors Parts Plant. In R. Milkman (Ed.), *Women, work and protest. A century of US women's labor history* (pp. 235–258). Boston: Routledge & Kegan Paul.

Milkman, R. (1985). *Women, work, and protest: a century of US women's labor history.* New York & London: Routledge.

Munro, A. (1999). *Work and trade unions.* London: Mansell.

Norris, P. (1987). *Politics and sexual equality. The comparative position of women in Western democracies.* Boulder, CO: Rienner.

Parker, J. (2002). Women's groups in British Unions. *British Journal of Industrial Relations,* 40(1), 23–31.

Phillips, A. (1991). *Engendering democracy.* Cambridge: Polity Press.

Phillips, A. (1995). *The politics of presence.* Oxford: Clarendon Press.

Pocock, B. (Ed.). (1997). *Sex and politics in labour unions.* Sydney: Allen & Unwin.

Qvist, G.V. (1985). Women and the Swedish Federation of Labor, 1898–1973. In N.C. Soldon (Ed.), *The world of women's trade unionism* (pp. 153–163). Westport, CT: Greenwood Press.

Rees, T. L. (1998). *Mainstreaming equality in the European Union: Education, training and labour market policies.* London: Routledge.

Ryan, E., & Prendergast, H. (1982). Unions are for women too! In K. Cole (Ed.), *Power, conflict and control in Australian trade unions* (pp. 261–278). Melbourne: Pelican Books.

Saward, M. (2006). The representative claim. *Contemporary Political Theory,* 5(3), 297–318.

Shute, C. (1994). Unequal partners: Women, power and the trade union movement. In N. Grieve & A. Burns (Eds.), *Australian women: Contemporary feminist thought* (pp. 166–178). Melbourne: Oxford University Press.

Soldon, N.C. (1985). British women and trade unionism: Opportunities made and missed. In N.C. Soldon (Ed.), *The world of women's trade unionism* (pp. 11–34). Wesport, CT: Greenwood Press.

Squires, J. (1999). *Gender in political theory.* Cambridge: Polity Press.

Street, M. (1994), Working Women and Trade Unions in New Zealand 1889–1906. In P. Walsh (Ed.), *Trade Unions, Work and Society: The Centenary of the Arbitration System* (pp. 39–68). Dunmore Press, Palmerston North.

Trebilcock, A. (1991). Strategies for strengthening women's participation in trade union leadership. *International Labour Review,* 130(4), 407–426.

Verloo, M. (2005, Fall). Displacement and empowerment: Reflections on the concept and practice of the Council of Europe approach to gender mainstreaming and gender equality. *Social Politics,* pp. 344–365.

ABOUT THE CONTRIBUTORS

Khedija Arfaoui is retired from the Institut Supérieur des Langues de Tunis, Tunisia, and has been a longstanding activist of AFTURD, the Association of Tunisian Women for Research and Development. She is also a member of Amnesty International and ATFD, Tunisian Association of Democratic Women.

Rae Lesser Blumberg is the William R. Kenan, Jr., Professor of Sociology, University of Virginia. Her work revolves around her theories on gender equality/inequality (see, e.g., "A General Theory of Gender Stratification" (Sociological Theory, vol. 2 (1984), pp. 23–101) and gender and development. She is the author of over 100 books, monographs, articles and chapters and has collected data for her theories in over 40 countries in which she has worked in development.

Linda Briskin is professor in the Social Science department of the School of Women's Studies, York University, Toronto, Canada. She is the author of numerous publications on trade unions, union women, and socialist feminism, among them *Equity Bargaining/Bargaining Equity* (2006), and *Women's Organizing and Public Policy in Canada and Sweden* (co-edited with Mona Eliasson, 1999).

Kaye Broadbent is Senior Lecturer, Griffith Business School, Griffith University, Australia. She has conducted numerous studies on women and work, union organizing strategies and women's unions in Asia. She is co-author of *Women and Labour Organizing in Asia: Diversity, Autonomy and Activism* (2008).

Hafidha Chekir is a law professor in the Faculté de droit et des sciences politiques, Université de Tunis, and leading member of ATFD, the Tunisian Association of Democratic Women, AFTURD, Association of Tunisian Women for Research and Development, and the Tunisian League of Human Rights.

Pascale Coton has been long associated with the Confédération française des travailleurs chrétiens (CFTC), Paris; she is currently vice secretary-general in charge of promoting social protection and ending discriminations.

Jennifer Curtin is Senior Lecturer in Political Studies at the University of Auckland, New Zealand. She has published numerous articles on the representation of women in formal political institutions and policy making environments including parliament, the bureaucracy and trade unions. She is the author of *Women and Trade Unions: A Comparative Perspective (1999)* and co-author of *Rebels with a Cause: Independents in Australian Politic (2004)*.

Graciela Di Marco is Director of the Centro de Estudios sobre Democratización y Derechos Humanos–CEDEHU, Universidad Nacional de San Martín-UNSAM (Buenos Aires), Argentina. She is the author of many studies on social movements and on social policies in Argentina, and the co-editor, with Constanza Tabbush, of *Feminisms, Democratization and Radical Democracy* (UNSAMEDITA, University of San Martin Press, 2011).

Mary Margaret Fonow is Director of the School of Social Transformation and Professor of Women and Gender Studies at Arizona State University, US. She has written extensively on the topic of feminist methodology and is the author of *Union Women: Forging Feminism in the United Steelworkers of America* (2003) and co-author of *Making Feminist Politics: Transnational Alliances between Women and Labor* (2011).

Suzanne Franzway is Director of the Research Centre for Gender Studies and Professor of Sociology and Gender Studies at the University of South Australia. She is the author of *Sexual Politics and Greedy Institutions: Union Women, Commitments and Conflicts in Public and in Private* (2001) and co-author of *Staking a Claim: Feminism, Bureaucracy and the State* (1989) and *Making Feminist Politics: Transnational Alliances between Women and Labor* (2011).

Neva Seidman Makgetla is Deputy Director General at Economics Development Department—Johannesburg Area, South Africa and served previously as Co-ordinator, Fiscal, Monetary and Public Service Policy, Congress of South African Trade Unions (COSATU), Johannesburg.

Valentine M. Moghadam spent five years as Director of Women's Studies and Professor of Sociology at Purdue University; as of January 2012, she joins Northeastern University, Boston, as Director of the International Affairs Program and Professor of Sociology. She is the author of *Modernizing Women:*

Gender and Social Change in the Middle East (1993, 2003, third edition due 2013), *Globalization and Social Movements: Islamism, Feminism, and the Global Justice Movement* (2009, 2012), and other publications.

Jo Morris, formerly Senior Equality and Employment Rights Officer, Trades Union Congress in the UK, is now researcher and consultant on labour rights and gender to global unions and NGOs.

Andrés Wilfrido Salazar-Paredes, co-author with Rae Blumberg, currently owns and operates an import-export company in Ontario, Canada, that focuses on trading socially responsible products. He plans to return to graduate studies in sociology when he obtains Canadian residency.

Michal Schwartz is an Israeli peace and social justice activist associated with the Workers Advice Center (WAC-Maan), and Coordinator of women's work at Hanitzotz Publishing House, in Nazareth, Israel.

Shauna Olney is Coordinator, Equality Team, Standards and Fundamental Principles and Rights at Work Sector, International Labor Office (ILO), Geneva.

Nora Wintour was previously Deputy General Secretary, Public Services International Ferney-Voltaire, France, and is now the International Co-ordinator of World Class Cities for All campaign (WCCA).

INDEX